ETHICAL DECISIONS FOR SOCIAL WORK PRACTICE

EIGHTH EDITION

Ralph Dolgoff
University of Maryland, Baltimore

Frank M. Loewenberg
Bar-Ilan University

Donna Harrington
University of Maryland, Baltimore

THOMSON

BROOKS/COLE

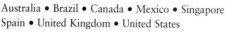
Australia • Brazil • Canada • Mexico • Singapore
Spain • United Kingdom • United States

THOMSON

BROOKS/COLE

Ethical Decisions for Social Work Practice, Eighth Edition
Ralph Dolgoff, Frank M. Loewenberg,
Donna Harrington

Development Editor: Tangelique Williams
Assistant Editor: Stephanie Rue
Technology Project Manager: Julie Aguilar
Marketing Manager: Meghan Pease
Marketing Assistant: Ting Jian Yap
Marketing Communications Manager:
  Shemika Britt
Project Manager, Editorial Production:
  Charlene M. Carpentier
Creative Director: Rob Hugel

Art Director: Caryl Gorska
Print Buyer: Linda Hsu
Permissions Editor: Roberta Broyer
Production Service: International Typesetting
  and Composition
Copy Editor: Lunaea Weatherstone
Cover Designer: Maria Ilardi
Compositor: International Typesetting
  and Composition

Library of Congress Control Number:
2007905724

ISBN-13: 978-0-495-50633-1
ISBN-10: 0-495-50633-8

Thomson Higher Education
10 Davis Drive
Belmont,
CA 94002-3098
USA

For more information about our products,
contact us at:
Thomson Learning Academic Resource
Center
1-800-423-0563
For permission to use material from this text
or product, submit a request online at
http://www.thomsonrights.com.
Any additional questions about permissions
can be submitted by e-mail to
thomsonrights@thomson.com.

CONTENTS

PREFACE

Every day social workers and other human service professionals are faced with stressful, even traumatic situations, such as child abuse, domestic violence, family tensions, the homeless, persons with chronic mental illness, and suicide. On occasion, social workers are faced with tragic deaths such as those that happened in Oklahoma City; at Columbine High School; at the Twin Towers, the Pentagon, and in Pennsylvania on 9/11; during Hurricane Katrina; and at Virginia Tech. These events shocked all Americans and others around the world. Everywhere the question was asked how such tragedies could occur. Almost immediately debates began about what more could have been or should have been done by all involved.

Many people—including social workers and other mental health professionals—were faced with questions. Did they miss warning signs that might have helped them prevent a tragedy or part of it? Even if they recognized potential danger signals, was there sufficient unambiguous information to predict violence? In some situations, there were suspicions about possible actions that might occur. However, what if no law is broken prior to violent acts? Should one act uncompromisingly to prevent uncertain but possible violent acts, despite any laws?

What is an acceptable balance between personal liberty and societal well-being? Where should respect for the self-determination of persons end? These are questions that have to be considered by social workers and will be considered in chapter 6. Our questions are not meant to fault any person but to point out how pervasive the requirement of ethical decision making is for social workers and other human service workers.

For this reason, more and more social work educators and the professional community are concerned with ethical conduct, as well as the preparation of students and professionals to recognize ethical dilemmas when they occur, to be prepared to assess these dilemmas, and to deal correctly with them. We believe that concern for ethical conduct should be included in every curriculum for professional education.

Those who teach in the area must keep in mind Thomas Aquinas's caution that when it comes to ethics "we cannot discuss what we ought to do unless we know what we can do" (*Commentary on De Anima*, I, 1.2). In other words, teaching the theory of ethical action is not worth much unless we also teach the skill of making ethical decisions. In this book, therefore, we will follow this dual focus. Some have said that virtue cannot be taught in a college classroom and that ethical dilemmas cannot be resolved by textbooks. However, we believe that the principles and techniques of ethical assessment and ethical decision making do have a place in a professional curriculum.

At the same time, we agree with those who have suggested that the concern of instructors should be less focused on presenting solutions to dilemmas than with efforts to encourage students to: (a) be alert to discovering and perceiving ethical issues; (b) be clearer about the values that affect their decision making; and (c) consider competing arguments, in examining both the strengths and limitations of their own positions, and in reaching thoughtfully reasoned conclusions. Our approach to ethical decision making is designed to assist social workers in reasoning carefully about ethical issues, to help them clarify their moral aspirations at the level demanded by the profession, and to achieve a more ethical stance in practice.

The exemplars presented and the exercises at the end of each chapter have been prepared to heighten students' sensitivity to the ethical aspects of social work practice, to aid them in developing a personal approach to such issues, and to help them consider the essential elements in ethical decision making in professional practice. Suggestions for additional readings also appear at the end of each chapter. In addition, we provide Internet sites so readers can look for additional information on many topics.

In our continuing effort to make this book more useful, this edition has been completely updated and includes the latest research. We have added to or augmented material on the following topics:

- Spirituality and religion
- War and the military
- Ethics of caring, virtue ethics
- Feminist ethics
- Case and cause advocacy and whistle blowing
- HIV and AIDS
- End-of-life decisions
- Accountability and evidence-based practice
- Compassion fatigue and secondary traumatic distress
- Ethics advocacy
- Ethical lapses of supervisees
- Expanded and updated suggested readings and Web resources

In addition to the many exemplars of ethical dilemmas provided throughout the book, one particular family situation is considered several times in the book from different perspectives. Additional information is provided each time we return to this exemplar. Finally, we have included a pretest for readers at the end of the first chapter.

We have retained the two ethical decision screens in this edition. We have received numerous comments that the screens have proved helpful in the rank-ordering of ethical principles and ethical obligations, thus helping social work practitioners identify priorities among competing ethical obligations. Our intent has been to suggest some principles and guidelines that can substantially help social workers making ethical practice decisions, and we have been gratified by the wide use of the screens. Although ethical and moral perfection remains an unattainable goal, social workers—like everyone else—must continue to strive toward that goal.

The exemplars in this book are taken from the real world, but none of them occurred in exactly the way described or to the people identified in each situation. No names or other identifying information came from social agency records or from social workers who worked with these people. Many new exemplars have been added to reflect newer areas of practice. Needless to say, the exemplars do not always typify good or desirable practice. They were chosen simply to illustrate ethical problems occurring in the real world of practice.

We thank our colleagues and students for helping us think through many of the issues involved in social work ethics. We also want to thank the peer reviewers for their very helpful feedback on this edition. They are Richard Boettcher, Ohio State University; Deanne Bonnar, Boston University; Ellen Burkemper, Saint Louis University; David Dupper, University of Tennessee; and Susan Manning, University of Denver.

Our thanks and appreciation to the Health Sciences and Human Services Library of the University of Maryland, Baltimore, and to the Milton S. Eisenhower Library of the Johns Hopkins University. Dr. Howard Altstein, Dr. Eva Sivan, Pat Hicks, Dr. Kathleen Walsh, and many students shared with us ethical dilemmas they encountered in practice situations.

We are pleased that our eighth edition is being published by Thomson Brooks/Cole. We appreciate the helpfulness of those at Thomson Brooks/Cole who have worked to bring this edition to fruition.

Finally, we thank our friends and spouses who have continued their everlasting patience with our not-so-minor foibles.

Ralph Dolgoff
Frank Loewenberg
Donna Harrington

INTRODUCTION TO ETHICAL DECISION MAKING

ETHICAL CHOICES IN THE HELPING PROFESSIONS

As a social worker, what is the ethical way to respond to the following situations?

- Your client tells you that he intends to commit a serious crime.
- A 26-year-old married woman wants a tubal ligation because she does not want to have any more children. She asks you not to tell her husband, and to help her find a physician who will perform this procedure.
- You believe that one of the residents of the detoxification center that you staff is potentially violent and may become a danger to other residents.
- A client who is HIV-positive tells you that he has unprotected sex with his wife because he does not want her to know of his condition.
- You discover that another social worker knows about a child abuse situation but has not reported the case to Child Protective Services.
- A board member who has helped your agency obtain a substantial grant that has made it possible to add services for adult alcoholics and members of their families now wants you to report that more clients have been served by this program than actually participated so that the agency can receive a larger grant next year.
- A surgeon at a pediatric hospital strongly recommends that a child should have surgery, but the child's parents refuse because of the possible risks. The physician asks you to convince the parents to agree to let him operate, regardless of the risks.

Most social workers are confronted every day with the necessity of making decisions that involve ethical issues or dilemmas. Sometimes a social worker may have an opportunity to think about all possible options, and perhaps to talk things over with a colleague or consult with an expert. More often, social workers—even student social workers—are alone when they must make difficult ethical choices. They cannot delay making a decision due to the immediacy of the problem that faces them. At best, they have a few hours or a few days to consider what should be done.

 ## THE COSTS OF AUTONOMY AND THE COSTS OF PATERNALISM

Basanti Madurai came happily to the United States from southern India five years ago after marrying a man who claimed to be an engineer, but was actually employed in a local gas station. She was only slightly familiar with English and unacquainted with American culture when she joined her husband in her in-laws' home. Her new family forbade her to make friends, and she was almost never allowed to leave their home as she was expected to stay home and take care of her two small children. When her husband discovered that she had brought less money to the marriage than he expected, he became verbally abusive. Gradually he also became physically abusive. Her in-laws were aware of his behavior but considered it acceptable and appropriate.

On her occasional walks in the neighborhood Basanti was always under the gaze of friends and family relatives. However, she managed to meet one young Indian woman at a local grocery. After a time, she began to trust her new friend and confided that she was practically a prisoner in her husband's home and was being beaten as well.

On her own initiative, this new friend spoke to Ellen Ashton, a social worker connected to a family service agency that provides a mutual support group for South Asian women. She encouraged Ellen to speak to Basanti. When she had an opportunity, Ellen struck up a conversation with Basanti in which she told her of her agency's support group. Basanti claimed that all was well at home and that she would not join a public group because she would not want to risk bringing shame on her family in India or her husband's family. She mentioned that she did want to try to make a better life for herself, her husband, and their children.

This situation poses a number of ethical dilemmas for Ellen Ashton. Can you identify some of these? Where will the social worker find help with the ethical aspects of this practice problem? How will she decide what course of action to follow? One should note that, in addition to Basanti and her husband, his parents and other family members, and the social worker, there are others involved, including neighbors and society, and even Basanti's family in India. For the moment, however, we will limit our focus to Basanti and Ellen, the social worker. In this book we consider only professional ethical dilemmas, and the social worker is confronted by a number of such dilemmas whose solutions should be congruent with ethical professional practice. We will briefly analyze several of these dilemmas.

Before we begin our analysis, please take a moment to write down what you think are the two or three most important dilemmas that the social worker must address. What, if anything, would you do based on the friend's report that Basanti is being abused by her husband? You will refer back to these thoughts as we progress through the book. In most practice situations, you will gain additional information each time you meet with a client, and your view of the situation may change as you learn more. We will use a similar approach in this book, returning to the Madurai family several more times, adding additional information each time and asking how the additional information changes the ethical issues involved.

The root ethical problem in this situation is that every social worker, including Ellen, fills two professional social work roles: (a) helper/enabler and (b) societal control agent. The conflict between these two roles triggers a number of ethical dilemmas. What is good for one participant is not necessarily what is best for another. A decision that is best for now may not be so for the long run. We also need to consider the degree of damage that can be permitted to occur before the social worker must intervene. We will now consider two areas of dilemmas from this situation: multiple-client systems and competing values.

Multiple-Client System The National Association of Social Workers (NASW) Code of Ethics requires that every social worker give priority to her[1] client's interests and to her client's self-determination. These principles are undoubtedly relevant in this situation. But who are this worker's clients? What are her responsibilities toward Basanti, her children, her husband, his and her parents, as well as toward the community and society? To whom does this practitioner owe first obligations?

 Competing Values Client self-determination, protection of human life, and enhancing the quality of life are three values to which all social workers are committed. As is so often the case, in this instance the social worker cannot follow these three principles simultaneously. If the social worker intervenes to protect Basanti's life without her agreement, she undermines her self-determination and perhaps her long-term quality of life. Yet, if she does not do anything, Basanti may suffer serious harm from her husband's continued physical and emotional abuse. There may be good reasons for giving priority to one rather than the other of these values. Nevertheless, the social worker must first recognize this conflict as a dilemma and then seek to resolve it.

In addition to the competing values identified above, this situation confronts the social worker with other value dilemmas. While she is committed to providing service to voluntary clients, she is not at all sure which professional values are relevant in this situation. She does not want to undermine Basanti's self-determination or her motivation to make a better life for herself. She also does not want to impose her own values on Basanti, her husband, and his parents. Should a social worker act upon the report of a neighbor, who may or may not have an accurate impression of the situation? Ellen clearly needs more information, but how can she obtain it if Basanti claims everything is all right and does not want to talk to her?

To summarize, in this situation, the social worker's ethics indicate that in her role as a helper/enabler, the first problem is to find a way to assess the level of risk. If she determines Basanti is at serious risk for physical abuse, she must consider how to

---

[1] Some social workers are men, many more are women. In recent years, many writers have used terminology such as *his or her* and *she or he*, or they have used the plural form such as *social workers believe.* However, these usages are clumsy and often tend to interfere with the clarity of the message. Because most social workers are women, we will refer to the social worker as *she* (except in exemplars where the social worker has been identified as a man) and to the recipient of the service as *he* (except where the recipient is a woman). We hope that male social workers and female recipients will bear with our usage.

intervene immediately. If she learns that the risk is not that great and immediate, she may seek ways to involve Basanti either in the group or in some other way. In this case, she must make certain Basanti is enabled to make her own thoughtful decisions, she must assist her to know and analyze alternatives, and she must facilitate access to helping systems that make these decisions possible. In terms of her role as social worker, Ellen must not intervene unless there is sufficient evidence of imminent danger.

There are many ways to prepare for this practice reality. First, it is important to recognize that every decision in social work practice includes ethical aspects. Next, social workers need knowledge and skill to clarify these aspects of practice in order to engage in effective ethical decision making. Knowledge and skill in this area (as in all other aspects of social work practice) must be developed and refined throughout a social worker's professional career.

This book has been written to help social workers, students as well as practitioners, become skilled in making ethical decisions. In preparation every social worker must consider the following questions:

- Who is my client?
- What obligations do I owe my client(s)?
- Do I have professional obligations to people other than my clients? What are my obligations to my own family, my agency, and my profession?
- What are my own personal values? Are these values compatible with the profession's values and with societal values?
- What are my ethical priorities when these value sets are not identical or when they are in conflict?
- What is the ethical way to respond when I have conflicting professional responsibilities to different people?

In this chapter, we introduce the complex and important topic of ethical decision making and define what we mean by ethical decision making. Social work students and practitioners have repeatedly asked for guides to help them grapple with ethical practice issues. In the past, these requests were answered only by the adoption of codes of ethics that were helpful in some ways, but left too many questions unanswered. Most social workers know instinctively that ethics are supremely important. The priority of ethics for social workers is underscored by the Purpose statement of the Code of Ethics that "professional ethics are at the core of social work" (NASW Code, 1999, p. 2) and are key for guiding practitioners' actions.

Ethical content and decision making are being taught in all phases of social work education, including continuing education following graduation from educational programs. In an age when scientists have cracked the genetic code, put men on the moon, transplanted hearts, transferred an embryo from the test tube to the womb, and cloned sheep, almost anything is possible from a technological point of view. The key question now is how to decide not what *can* be done, but what *should* be done. More and more social workers have come to recognize that they, too, face questions that go beyond the "techniques" of social work. This recognition has made the subject of professional ethics more visible in the professional social work curriculum. Since 1982, the Council on Social Work Education (CSWE) has required the inclusion of content about professional practice values and ethics throughout the curriculum. As of

2005, 31 state regulatory boards required continuing education credits in ethics for maintaining social work licenses, and additional boards were planning such requirements (Association of Social Work Boards, 2007).

ETHICS

What does the term **ethics** mean? The word comes from the Greek root *ethos,* which originally meant custom, usage, or habit. In contemporary usage it deals with the question of what actions are morally right and with how things ought to be. General ethics clarify the obligations that are owed by one person to another person. Some obligations, however, are based on the specific relations between two people (such as between a mother and her son), or they are based on a particular role voluntarily accepted by one of the parties. The latter are special obligations that apply only to those who have consented to accept that role position. Professional ethics are a codification of the special obligations that arise out of a person's voluntary choice to become a professional, such as a social worker. Professional ethics clarify the ethical aspects of professional practice. Professional social work ethics are intended to help social work practitioners recognize morally correct practice and learn how to decide and act *ethically in any professional situation.*

CONTEMPORARY INTEREST IN PROFESSIONAL ETHICS

Jane Addams (19th and early 20th century social worker) already was aware of the importance of ethical practice. In her wisdom, she understood that "action indeed is the sole medium of expression for ethics ... that the sphere of morals is the sphere of action, that speculation in regard to morality is but observation and must remain in the sphere of intellectual comment, that a situation does not really become moral until we are confronted with what shall be done in a concrete case, and are obliged to act upon our theory" (Addams, 1902, 2006). But many professional social workers still are not sure about the ethical aspects of practice. One of the paradoxes of our times is that the interest in professional ethics is high, even while the level of morality of society seems low. In the last century, more people were killed by violence than ever before. Hitler's genocide was not a one-time aberration, but has been duplicated (perhaps on a smaller scale) in Cambodia, Darfur, Rwanda, the Balkans, and elsewhere. At the same time, the Nuremberg Trials following World War II, the Civil Rights movement of the late 1950s and 1960s, and the many rapid advances in medical and computer technology have resulted in a greater awareness of human rights, including the rights of social work clients.

The current interest in social work ethics is, in part, related to this emphasis on human rights. It is also an expression of the maturation of the social work profession. The increasing attention on social work ethics may be partially the result of the rising concern of practitioners about the use of litigation by clients to resolve claims of ethical malfeasance and malpractice. Complaints and lawsuits against social workers insured by the NASW Insurance Trust increased over the last three decades but have recently leveled off. The number of suits appears now to be related to the increase or decrease in the number of social workers insured and the institution of tort (wrongful acts, damage or injury done willfully, negligently, or in circumstances of strict liability for which a civil suit can be brought) liability limitations by various states (Imbert, 2006; Houston-Vega, Nuehring, & Daguio, 1997).

Unethical conduct, corruption, and scandals in government as well as in industry have become commonplace. Almost daily, newspapers report unethical practices by corporate executives, legislators, scientific researchers, physicians, lawyers, accountants, and other professionals. The daily media headlines almost always involve ethical questions. In the past two decades, Americans have witnessed the impeachment of President Clinton; industrialists and accountants using ethically questionable and illegal accounting methods; insider trading scandals; Olympic Games corruptions; new dilemmas in medical research; the use of drugs in sports; and questionable political fund-raising methods. Ethical questions almost always are at the top of the public agenda. No wonder that courses in ethics are appearing everywhere—they are offered not only by universities but also by businesses, professional groups, and the military.

ETHICAL PROBLEMS IN SOCIAL WORK PRACTICE

Some have suggested that ethical problems occur only on very special occasions. They argue that in most practice situations a social worker requires only a high level of professional skill and insight because no ethical questions are involved. This is the approach to professional practice that was established by Sigmund Freud and that has been followed by generations of practitioners in all of the helping professions. The assumptions underlying this approach are supported by a number of philosophers who argue that most actions do not involve any moral question but are the result of a free choice among the various available alternatives. These alternatives are located in the "zone of moral indifference" (Fishkin, 1982) where from an ethical viewpoint it makes little difference which alternative is chosen. Other philosophers insist that there are ethical implications or ethical aspects to almost every professional decision. We follow the latter approach because we believe that professional social workers are not merely technicians who solve mechanical problems (such as providing services or supplying information), but they are also moral agents.

A closer examination of social work practice will reveal that almost all practice principles involve (or are based on) ethical principles. One of the sources for ethical problems in social work practice may be located in the multiplicity and contradiction of values that characterize contemporary society. While we often speak of ethical problems, it would be more correct to speak of the ethical dimensions or ethical aspects of social work practice problems. In the past, it was assumed that ethical issues arose out of, and were limited to, the dyadic relationship between social worker and client. Current ethical concerns also include those that arise out of the traditional worker–client relationship, which often involves others even if they never directly interact with the social worker, as well as the newer practice models, which purposefully include many participants in addition to client and worker. The breakdown of consensus concerning societal means and goals, the increasing scarcity of resources that are available for social welfare, and the use of new technologies not only have intensified traditional ethical dilemmas but also have given rise to what may well be a new generation of ethical issues in social work practice.

Ethical problems arise when there is a conflict about

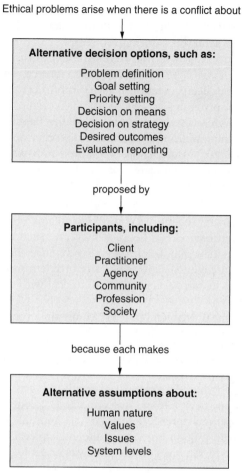

Alternative decision options, such as:

Problem definition
Goal setting
Priority setting
Decision on means
Decision on strategy
Desired outcomes
Evaluation reporting

proposed by

Participants, including:

Client
Practitioner
Agency
Community
Profession
Society

because each makes

Alternative assumptions about:

Human nature
Values
Issues
System levels

FIGURE 1.1 | ETHICAL PROBLEMS IN SOCIAL WORK PRACTICE

In this book, we will examine ethical problems and ethical dilemmas. Ethical problems raise the question: What is the right thing to do in a given practice situation? How can a social worker avoid unethical behaviors in that situation? Ethical dilemmas occur in situations in which the social worker must choose between two or more relevant, but contradictory ethical directives, or when every alternative results in an undesirable outcome for one or more persons. The seedbed for ethical problems in social work practice is portrayed in Figure 1.1. Any disagreement that different participants (e.g., relatives, professionals, landlords, employer, groups, and organizations) have with regard to alternate decision options or alternative assumptions will intensify the difficulties that social workers will encounter in ethical decision making. Examples of such difficulties occur in the following situations:

• A client wants a service that may affect another member of the family who does not want to receive that service: An adult daughter may want to place her aged father in a nursing home, but the father wants to remain in his own home.

- Conflicting values impinge on the decision facing the social worker: A young woman asks whether her fiancé (who is your client) is HIV-positive, while the client wants to keep this information secret.
- The community and the profession have different priorities: Everyone agrees that something must be done about domestic violence, but community leaders believe that better police protection is more important than providing prevention and treatment programs.
- The social agency prescribes a treatment modality based on one social work theory, although the practitioner knows that another approach is indicated for a particular client: The agency is committed to psychodynamic therapy, whereas research evidence indicates that in this situation cognitive-behavioral therapy is usually more effective.

Some social workers try to ignore the ethical problems and dilemmas that arise in these and similar situations, either because they are uncomfortable with making ethical decisions or because they think they already have the answer. Other social workers are aware of the ethical aspects of these problem situations but are uneasy because they think they do not yet have the skill to deal with ethical problems of this nature.

Two causes of ethical problems are (1) competing values and (2) competing loyalties. Social workers may benefit from paying special attention to these causes.

Competing Values An ethical dilemma may arise when a practitioner is faced with two or more competing values, such as justice and equality or confidentiality and protecting life. An example of conflicts regarding self-determination and protection from harm is found in Exemplar 1.1; conflicts regarding confidentiality are found in chapter 5 (Exemplars 5.1 and 5.2), justice and equality in chapter 8 (Exemplar 8.4), and protecting life in chapter 12 (Exemplar 12.6). Similarly, in a time of rapidly shrinking budgets and an emphasis on evidence-based practice, no practitioner can ignore considerations of efficiency and effectiveness, even though these constraints may do violence to what is thought to be best for a particular client. A worker may feel equally committed to two values, even when both cannot be actualized in a specific situation.

Competing Loyalties When competing or conflicting groups make claims for the social worker's loyalties, the worker may face an ethical dilemma. To whom does Ellen Ashton (Exemplar 1.1) owe loyalty? Basanti Madurai, society, herself, the friend who reported abuse, the agency? The social worker represents both the society and the potential client, with each having conflicting demands. There is little need to point to the more obvious examples of this cause of ethical problems. Even less blatant incidents, such as a request for giving preferential treatment to relatives and friends, can be problematic from an ethical point of view. Multiple loyalties are also a source of ethical quandaries when a social worker serves a multiple-client system, as is so frequent today. In these circumstances, identifying the person or unit that should receive priority becomes a crucial ethical issue.

Several exemplars from social work practice will now be examined. Consider how ethical issues arise in each exemplar. The ethical problems faced by the social worker who has been assigned to work with Blanca Gabelli in Exemplar 1.2 are similar to, yet different from, those faced by worker Ellen Ashton in Exemplar 1.1.

| **1.2** | Who Decides on Blanca Gabelli's Future? |

Blanca Gabelli, an 84-year-old retired physician, participates in a day treatment program and resides in an assisted living residence. Recently, she has become slightly more forgetful, falls more frequently, and has been somewhat less able to care for herself. She has also become increasingly irascible, and several staff members have complained about her demanding behavior. Your supervisor has asked you, her social worker, to arrange for her transfer to a nursing home because Blanca is a "pain," requires too much effort, and is upsetting staff members who have many other duties in the residential program.

Although you believe that Blanca is not yet in need of nursing home care, you contacted the only nursing home with a vacancy to arrange for her transfer.

Let us consider some of the ethical choices you, as the social worker, might make.

Goal Setting

Who should set the goals in this situation? If you comply with your supervisor's demand, you and your supervisor determine Blanca's future while also undermining her sense of autonomy. Do you and your supervisor have an ethical right to do so? What part should Blanca play in deciding her own living arrangements?

Role Conflict

A social worker is often an agency employee. What are the implications if you do not comply with your supervisor's demand? Does the social worker's role require that you always comply with the suggestions of your supervisor or that you always serve as Blanca's protector? Whose interests should receive priority consideration: your supervisor's, the agency's, yours, Blanca's, society's?

Value Dilemma

Your supervisor is demanding that you comply with the agency's decision. However, you and your supervisor have different assessments of Blanca's situation. Should you do what is best for the agency or what is best for the client? The agency wants to transfer Blanca and you think she should stay in the assisted living facility and in the day treatment program. To whom do you owe loyalty? In what ways do your professional and personal values clash? Should you tell Blanca what your supervisor said? How honest should you be and with whom?

Another set of ethical problems faces Sharon Gillette, the social worker in the following exemplar.

| Hurricane Katrina, the Gillette Family, and Choices

For days, all one heard was that Hurricane Katrina was on its way. Social worker Sharon Gillette's husband was in Seattle on business and unable to find a flight to return to New Orleans. She could not decide whether to try to leave or to stay because her house was on higher ground. People in New Orleans and throughout the region were struggling with preparations for the expected storm. Sharon's child care provider, Mrs. Carlyle, called to say she was frightened and would not come the next morning because she had found a ride out of town with her son and his family. With her husband still away, Sharon finally decided it would be best for her and her children to leave New Orleans and stay with family in Texas until the storm passed.

Sharon phoned her supervisor to let him know that she would be leaving New Orleans and would return as soon as possible after the storm passed. However, her supervisor informed her that she was being asked to report immediately to the Civil Emergency Center in the Louisiana Superdome to assist the many people—both able-bodied and those with physical and other challenges—who would be forced to stay in New Orleans because they did not have a way to evacuate. People were confused and anxious; many were trying to contact loved ones. What should Sharon do? Should she leave New Orleans for Texas as planned? Should she stay in New Orleans to help those in need? If she did stay in New Orleans, should she spend time trying to protect her home and children, or spend all her time helping those in the Superdome?

Competing Values Is it right for Sharon to evacuate with her family or should she stay in New Orleans to help those in need? What mother could go to work to help others while leaving her frightened and confused children at home, even though the news of a major disaster is being reported continuously on every radio and TV channel? On the other hand, what are her obligations as a professional social worker to the families being served at the Emergency Center? Obviously she cannot simultaneously evacuate with her children to another state and also remain in New Orleans working at the Emergency Center.

Ambiguity While we now know the outcome of Hurricane Katrina, Sharon would have had to make some decisions before the storm actually hit, without knowing what damage the hurricane would cause. She had to make choices without the benefit of the 20/20 hindsight we now have. Sharon would have been far less troubled by her decision if she had known that no harm would come to her children and/or if she had known for certain that her presence at the Emergency Center would make a critical difference in the lives of the victims of the hurricane.

What other ethical issues does this case pose? Where in the Code of Ethics can this social worker find help with the ethical aspects of emergency situations such as floods, hurricanes, outbreaks of violence, and war? How will the social worker decide what course of action to follow? The ethical dilemmas of this situation are relatively uncomplicated—as a social worker, Sharon has certain professional responsibilities toward her clients and her agency, especially in an emergency situation such as Hurricane Katrina, but she also has responsibilities to her family, which in this case includes very young, frightened, and potentially at-risk children. Which of these two obligations has priority?

CAN PROFESSIONAL ETHICS BE TAUGHT?

Teaching professional ethics was traditionally based on the assumption that knowledge about ethics would lead to the acquisition of attitudes and values, and that these, in turn, would produce the desired ethical behavior. This assumption needs to be tested. Is there any reason to think that studying ethics will motivate ethical behavior? Further empirical research is needed to discover whether and to what extent learning about ethics is helpful. Educators still do not know much more about value-and-ethics education than Socrates did 2,500 years ago when he told Meno that he did not know how values were acquired or whether they could be taught at all. These questions still require answers.

The widely accepted view is that attitudes determine behavior, but some leading attitude theorists teach the exact opposite—that is, they have proposed that behavior determines attitudes. Generally, it is held that our behavior is a direct consequence of our attitudes about the world, but the revisionist theorists suggest that a person tends to select beliefs and attitudes that are in consonance with or support his or her behavior. Following the traditional theory, it is widely believed that social workers' values influence their professional practice, such as the selection of treatment methods. The CSWE requirement for curriculum content related to values and ethics is also based on the assumption that a student who learns to value professional ethics will, as a practitioner, choose to behave in ethical ways.

It may be that there is something to both approaches; research suggests that both the attitude–behavior and behavior–attitude models are far too simplistic and unrealistic (Deutscher, Pestello, & Pestello, 1993). Under some conditions, their relationship is reciprocal and/or reversed so that at the same time attitudes influence behaviors and behaviors influence attitudes. However, more important is the fact that attitude is only one determinant of behavior; other causal factors include intentions, expectations of others, and beliefs about outcomes. Furthermore, situational constraints, vested interests, self-confidence, self-efficacy or perceived behavioral control, the ease or difficulty of performing a behavior, past experience and anticipated impediments and obstacles all affect the relationship between attitudes and behaviors (Ajzen, 2005; Manstead, 1996).

In the past the transmission of professional ethics was not problematic because they were transmitted by watching a master practitioner. This apprentice model was satisfactory for training professionals as long as the new practitioner faced the same type of problems as did the master teacher. Social work education, with its traditional emphasis on concurrent field instruction and educational supervision, suggests a partial continuation of the apprentice model. But this model may no longer be optimally effective in today's world of rapid changes. Innovative curriculum organizations and alternative teaching methods must be considered to supplement this traditional curriculum approach.

The impact of college and university courses on changes in values and ethics is not entirely clear. Feldman and Newcomb (1994), on the basis of an examination of more than 1,500 empirical studies conducted over four decades in undergraduate colleges and focused on general value systems in many different parts of the United States, reported some positive findings, though these differed for various types of colleges and curricula. One of their conclusions was that, with few exceptions, faculty members exerted an impact on values only "where the influence of student peers and of faculty complement and reinforce one another" (Feldman & Newcomb, 1994, p. 330). There are only a few empirical studies of value changes in professional social work education. These raise some questions about the efficacy of teaching values in academic courses.

While a number of studies report either negative outcomes or no significant changes (Brown, 1970; Cyrns, 1977; Hayes & Varley, 1965; Judah, 1979; Varley, 1963, 1968), others report some positive findings (Frans & Moran, 1993; Moran, 1989; Rice, 1994; Sharwell, 1974; Wodarski, Pippin, & Daniels, 1988). However, the usefulness of all of these studies is limited because they measured value changes as reflected by answers to a questionnaire and did not attempt to assess ethical behaviors in practice settings. More recently, a review of the empirical social work literature related to the professional socialization of social work students (Baretti, 2004) produced contradictory findings that raise critical questions. Value acquisition or adherence may not increase with the degree of socialization—in fact, a decrease may occur. Neither does prolonged and intense social work education necessarily change students' value orientations in the desired direction (Baretti, 2004).

Almost 50 years ago, Pumphrey (1959) noted that social work students viewed the teaching of social work values as something quite apart from (or even irrelevant to) practice. Many changes have occurred in the social work curriculum since Pumphrey undertook her study. During the interim, social work educational programs and the professional association as well as a number of authors have contributed to an expansion of interest in social work ethical decision making. In addition, ethical lapses in our society have also drawn attention to the ethical dilemmas that professionals encounter.

No academic course that is limited to thinking and talking about professional ethics will result in producing students who are more ethical practitioners. Thinking and talking must be supplemented by doing. Skill in using the decision making tools that we will present in this book, as well as the discussions and exercises, should help to improve the ability of students and practitioners to reason more effectively about ethical issues, improve the quality of ethical decision making, and result in more ethical professional behaviors in day-to-day practice.

Earlier we noted that ambiguity is an ever-present element in almost all social work situations. As daily life becomes more complicated, the level of ambiguity tends to proliferate. Because of this we try to avoid giving pat answers. Instead, we hope to convey the need for tolerance of ambiguity when it comes to professional ethics. In professional practice there is rarely, if ever, only one correct answer to an ethical dilemma. Our approach is to focus on ethical applications in practice situations rather than merely on the philosophical foundations of professional ethics. We agree with Hokenstad (1987) that instruction that is limited to ethics and values and does not at the same time concern itself with practice knowledge will not facilitate the development of ethical social work practice. The purpose of teaching professional ethics in a school of social work or in an in-service training program is not to develop philosophers or ethicists, but to train more effective and more ethical social work practitioners. The goal of such a program is to educate social workers who will be responsible for their own ethical professional conduct.

All social work educational programs are expected to provide specific knowledge about social work values and their implications, to help students develop an awareness of their personal values, to clarify conflicting values, and to analyze ethical dilemmas and the ways in which these affect practice, service, and clients. The following are reasonable objectives for a course in professional ethics. As a result of such a program students will be able to:

1. Become more aware of and more sensitive to ethical issues in professional practice
2. Identify and grapple with competing arguments by examining their limitations and strengths
3. Learn to recognize the ethical principles involved in their practice situations
4. Develop a greater understanding of the complexities of ethical decision making
5. Be able to reach thoughtfully reasoned conclusions and apply ethical principles to their professional activities
6. Be able to clarify moral aspirations and standards and evaluate ethical decisions made within the context of the profession

ABOUT THIS BOOK

In this book, we try to help students acquire skill in analyzing ethical quandaries, become aware of the ethical aspects of practice, and learn techniques and tools useful for making better ethical decisions. We will not present detailed prescriptions for solving specific ethical problems, nor will we offer a cookbook approach that indicates what to do in every practice situation. Instead, we will offer various models to help social work students and practitioners gain skill in analyzing and assessing the ethical dimensions of practice problems so that they can develop ethically appropriate professional behavior. We will suggest several analytic schemes that may help social workers resolve the ethical dilemmas they face in practice.

It is important to recognize that ethical practice is not only the obligation of each individual social worker, but it is also the responsibility of the employing organization and of the profession, as well as a societal phenomenon and responsibility. Although ethical conduct is intentional behavior for which each individual bears responsibility, the professional peer group and the agency setting can and must encourage professional behavior that is ethical. Professional peers and agencies can facilitate or impede, empower or undermine, the implementation of ethical behaviors. For too long, professional ethics have been the exclusive concern of the individual social worker. Ethics must become the concern of the social group—in this instance, the concern of each social agency—as well as of the total profession. The following chapters will provide context and tools for ethical decision making.

In chapter 2, we review the relation between values, general ethics, and professional ethics. Widespread concern about the relationship between law and ethics has led us to include a section on the relationship of ethical and legal behavior.

We will also examine the manifest and latent functions of professional ethics, as well as present a brief history of the evolution of professional ethics in the field of social work.

In chapters 3 and 4, we develop our decision-making framework. After briefly presenting several basic ethical theories and various approaches to ethical decision making in the helping professions, we will develop two decision-making screens, specifically designed to help in assessing the ethical alternatives that social workers face in their day-to-day practice.

The remaining chapters of this book are devoted to the presentation of a number of ethical problems and ethical dilemmas in professional practice. Eight of the chapters in this section cover a variety of practice problems. Each ethical problem and dilemma is important in its own right, but no claim is made that any one is more important than any other. For each dilemma, we have presented some relevant background information to help the reader examine the ethical dilemmas that arise out of the exemplars presented. The decision screens developed in chapter 4 should be applied in analyzing each of these ethical dilemmas.

In chapter 13, we again discuss the question of who is responsible for professional ethics. From what we have written in this chapter and from the development of our argument throughout the book, it will not come as a surprise that we place the responsibility for professional ethics not only on each social worker but also on the employing organization and on the organized professional group.

Exercises and suggestions for additional readings, as well as Web sites of interest, will appear at the end of every chapter. Additional exemplars and a glossary will be found in the appendices.

Ethical issues will continue to cause discomfort even after this book has been completed. This is because every decision a social worker makes entails ethical risks. Perhaps the most agonizing of these risks is the danger of making a choice that may hurt or damage a client or someone else. Nevertheless, fear of doing harm that leads to inaction can interfere with doing the right thing. We hope that the tools for ethical decision making that we will present, as well as the discussions and questions that will be raised, will alert social workers to their ethical responsibilities and help them become more skilled and more ethical practitioners.

PRETEST: HOW MUCH DO I KNOW ABOUT SOCIAL WORK ETHICS?

For each statement, circle true or false.

---

1. The Code of Ethics of the National Association of Social Workers was created by federal legislation.	True	False
2. An ethical dilemma is a question a client asks that you cannot answer.	True	False
3. The NASW Code of Ethics is directed mainly at organizations and groups of social workers, not individual practitioners.	True	False

4. Social workers must always decide between good and bad ethical choices. They seldom have to choose between two good or two bad ethical choices.   True   False

5. Social workers are expected to know and comply with the Code of Ethics of the National Association of Social Workers.   True   False

6. I know the mission of the social work profession and the profession's core values as identified in the NASW Code.   True   False

7. The Code includes ethical standards related to clients, colleagues, practice settings, individual professionals, the social work profession, and society.   True   False

8. The Code's ethical standards are written in such a way that they seldom conflict with each other. But, when conflicts occur, the Code also includes ways to deal with these problems.   True   False

9. If you are a person of good morals and are virtuous, you will not have any difficulty making ethical decisions and living up to the ethical standards of the social work profession.   True   False

10. The Code of Ethics applies only to professional, licensed social workers.   True   False

11. The Code of Ethics does not apply to social workers who are researchers, community organizers, social planners, and those who are employed in nonhuman service settings.   True   False

12. Ethical decision making is scientific and rational, and should be similar for all social workers facing similar situations and dilemmas.   True   False

13. If you are or become an excellent social work practitioner, it is unlikely you will experience any difficulty living up to the ethical standards expressed in the Code.   True   False

14. Cultural diversity is an important consideration in social work ethical decision making.   True   False

15. The personal values of a professional social worker play no part in ethical decision making.   True   False

EXERCISES

1. Why should social workers be ethical in their professional practices?

2. If you had to create a Code of Ethics for the social work profession based on your experiences and knowledge, what would you select as the three most important general principles?

3. If possible, ask a social worker to describe her most recent use of the profession's Code of Ethics. What was the dilemma? What was her decision? How did he or she decide what to do?

4. Put yourself in the Ellen Ashton situation (Exemplar 1.1).

   A. What ethical issues are involved in this exemplar?
   B. Without reference to the provisions of any code of ethics, what options are open to you?
   C. What do you think is the ethical thing to do?
   D. Do you think there is more than one ethical solution?

5. Study your local TV news and newspapers for one week. Identify the ethical issues that have implications for social workers.

6. In Exemplar 1, does the Civil Emergency Center have an ethical responsibility to provide child care services for volunteers or employees who are called in on an emergency basis to deal with a disaster such as Hurricane Katrina?
7. Visit one of the Web sites listed below and review the Code of Ethics or other material provided about ethics.

SUGGESTIONS FOR ADDITIONAL READINGS

A short list of readings we consider particularly helpful is found at the end of each chapter. Emphasis is given to the more recent literature rather than to the classics. The readings may amplify points that have been made, present other points of view, or raise additional questions. Reference to an article does not necessarily mean we agree with it, but in each instance, we have found that the author has made a thoughtful contribution to one or more of the subjects discussed in the chapter. The articles are mentioned only by author and year; the full citation can be found in the bibliography at the end of the book.

Goldstein (1987) presents a critical analysis of the moral aspects of social work practice. Aguilar, Williams and Aiken (2004) surveyed and compared the attitudes of social work practitioners and students to assess their attitudes toward appropriateness of sexual contact with clients, handling of colleagues who engage in sexual misconduct, and the extent of their educational preparation on sexual ethics. Manning (1997) argues for moral citizenship to guide ethical social work practice. Brill (2001) argues that a gap is growing between social work ethics and social work practice. Clifford and Burke (2005) advocate an antioppressive ethics in social work curricula.

WEB SITES OF INTEREST

The codes of ethics for most organizations can be found on the Web. Some codes of interest:

- National Association of Social Workers Code of Ethics: http://www.socialworkers.org/pubs/Code
- National Association of Black Social Workers Code of Ethics: htttp://nabsw.org/mserver/CodeofEthics.aspx?menuContext=720
- Clinical Social Work Federation: http://www.cswf.org/
- Canadian Association of Social Workers: http://www.casw-acts.ca
- Feminist Therapy Institute: http://www.feministtherapyinstitute.org/
- American Association for Marriage and Family Therapists: http://www.aamft.org/index.nm_asp
- The *Journal of Social Work Values and Ethics* (JSWV&E): http://www.socialworker.com/jswve

   This is a peer-reviewed, online journal that "examines the ethical and values issues that impact and are interwoven with social work practice, research and theory development. JSWV&E addresses ethical and value issues that encompass the full range of social problems and issues that social workers encounter. The journal provides the necessary historical perspectives on the development of social work values and ethics, as well as present articles providing value and ethical dilemmas stemming from state-of-the-art developments" (retrieved September 13, 2006, from: http://www.socialworker.com/jswve/).

VALUES AND
PROFESSIONAL ETHICS

The preamble to the NASW Code (1999), states that "the mission of the social work profession is rooted in a set of core values." This statement reflects the importance of values for social work. It is possible that few professions—perhaps with the exception of philosophy—concern themselves with values to the extent that social work does. Goldstein (1973) described social workers as "value laden individuals." For Vigilante (1974), social work values are "the fulcrum of practice." Frankl, a psychiatrist and creator of existential psychotherapy, also emphasized the centrality of values, not only for professional practitioners but for everyone. Life without values has no meaning, but only creates an "existential vacuum." For Frankl, the "will to meaning" is considerably more important than the "will to pleasure" (Guttmann, 1996).

VALUES

Social workers, like so many others, often fail to distinguish among such terms as **values, ethics,** and **morality** (or virtues). They use them rather loosely as if they all have the same meaning. Values, however, are not the same as virtues. Neither are values the same as ethics. One popular dictionary offers 17 definitions of *value*. Timms (1983) reviewed reports and publications from a number of social science fields and found no fewer than 180 different definitions for the term. A survey of the social work literature suggests that social work writers have used many of these definitions.

Maslow (1962) once observed that values are like a big container that holds all sorts of miscellaneous and vague things. Many philosophers have used the term *value* as if it meant the same as being interested and curious about something, but John Dewey used the term in a more precise way by noting that it must also include some element of appraisal or preference. Most social scientists have followed Dewey's definition, indicating that values are meant to serve as guides or criteria for selecting good and desirable behaviors. Kupperman (1999, p. 3) suggests that a value refers "to what is worth having or being" and that it "is preferable that it exist rather than not exist." Values enhance a life or the world and define "those conceptions of desirable states of affairs that are utilized in selective conduct as criteria for preference or choice or as justifications for proposed or actual behavior" (Williams, 1967, p. 23). Kluckhohn (1951) adds that "a value is not just a preference but it is a preference which is felt and/or considered to be justified" (p. 306). Most writers draw attention to the differences among societal values, group values, and individual values. Usually, values at these different levels are complementary or reciprocal, though at times they may be in conflict. Within any one society, most people, most of the time, agree about a core of societal values.

PROFESSIONAL VALUES

Social work practitioners take their basic professional values from societal values— that is, from the values held by the larger society in which they practice. These professional values are most often compatible with societal values, but there may be important differences in emphasis, priorities, or interpretation. It stands to reason, just as there is wide agreement about societal values, so there must be a wide consensus about basic professional values.

The central role that values play in social work has been recognized by many, as was noted in the beginning of this chapter, and professional values are considered as primary in practitioners' decision making and action. The Code of Ethics of the National Association of Social Workers (1999, pp. 5–6) summarizes the core values of the social work profession as follows:

1. Social workers elevate service to others above self-interest. (Service)
2. Social workers pursue social change, particularly with and on behalf of vulnerable and oppressed individuals and groups of people. (Social Justice)
3. Social workers treat each person in a caring and respectful fashion, mindful of in- dividual differences and cultural and ethnic diversity. (Dignity and Worth of the Person)
4. Social workers understand that relationships between and among people are an important vehicle for change. (Importance of Human Relationships)
5. Social workers are continually aware of the profession's mission, values, ethical principles, and ethical standards, and practice in a manner consistent with them. (Integrity)
6. Social workers continually strive to increase their professional knowledge and skills and to apply them in practice. (Competence)

There is a general consensus about social work values. For example, most professional social workers agree that client participation, self-determination, and confidentiality are among the basic social work values. However, disagreements are likely to occur when it comes to implementing these generalized professional values. Social workers may disagree about priorities, specific objectives, and the means necessary to put these generalized values into practice. Furthermore, little is known about how social workers' personal and professional values are used for practice decision making and whether the adherence to particular values differs by practice setting or field (Csikai, 1999; Pike, 1996). Thus the value "enhancing the dignity of life" may be used by one social worker to support a client's request for an abortion or assisted suicide, while her social work colleague may call on the same generalized value to support her professional decision to try to persuade the client to go through a full-term pregnancy or continue with palliative care. In fact, these examples illustrate how "nonprofessional" or "higher" values can affect practice decisions.

Bloom suggests that philosophic definitions of values do not really assist practitioners in the helping professions; according to him, the focus should be on "what values look like as expressed in action" (1975, p. 138). Professional values that do not provide guidance and direction are only of limited use. Nevertheless, they are important because ethical principles and rules can be derived from these values. When framed as a professional code of ethics, such rules and principles may provide social workers with the ethical criteria necessary for making difficult decisions. Note should be taken that ethical principles are always derived from values.

ETHICS

How to move from values to behavior is a problem that is not limited to professional practitioners. It is a more general problem that has become the focus of attention of ethicists. Ethics are generally defined as that branch of philosophy that concerns itself with human conduct and moral decision making. Ethics seek to discover the principles that guide people in deciding what is right and wrong. Another definition points to a key function of ethics: "Ethics is not primarily concerned with getting people to do what they believe to be right, but rather with helping them to decide what is right" (Jones, Sontag, Beckner, & Fogelin, 1977, p. 8).

Though the terms *values* and *ethics* are often used interchangeably, they are not identical. Ethics are deduced from values and must be in consonance with them. The difference between them is that values are concerned with what is *good* and *desirable*, while ethics deal with what is *right* and *correct*. A person's right to privacy, for example—a good and desirable thing—is an important value of American society. One of the social work ethical rules deduced from this value states, "Social workers should obtain clients' informed consent before audiotaping or videotaping clients or permitting observation of services to clients by a third party" (NASW, 1999, Section 1, 1.03f).[1] In the same manner, privacy is a desirable value, while informed consent and confidentiality are the ethical principles and the correct ways of practice that are derived from this value.

Even though values are meant to serve as guides for selecting desirable behavior, they do not always lead to these results because a person's behavior is not always consistent with his or her professed values. Social workers, like other professionals, at times practice in ways that are inconsistent with professional values or in ways that do not reflect societal values. For example, client participation in decision making is highly valued by social workers, yet some practitioners do not always make sufficient effort to involve their clients fully. One reason for the lack of congruence between values and behaviors may be that values are usually stated at a very high level of generality, while behaviors are very specific. Another reason for this incongruence may be the gap between professed (or public) and real (or personal) values of the person.

---

[1]Note: This reference is to the NASW Code of Ethics (1999). All such citations encountered subsequently in this work refer to the same source.

What additional factors do you believe contribute to the incongruence between values and behaviors?

There is broad agreement about the most generalized values, such as cooperation and success, but these are not sufficiently specific to help identify appropriate behavior patterns. The more specific a value, the more useful it will be as a behavioral guide. On the other hand, the more specific a value, the smaller the probability that it will gain wide acceptance. For example, everyone agrees that family life is a highly desired value—that is, everyone agrees as long as that value is not defined in more specific operational terms that may or may not reflect today's various types of families. This generalized value, however, does not help an adult son who has to make difficult decisions about how to care for his paralyzed, senile father without increasing the tensions that already exist between his present wife and his children from a previous marriage. Nor will the son's social worker find any specific ethical referents that may provide her with guidance in this situation.

MORALITY

George Bernard Shaw (1932) once wrote, "I don't believe in morality." His reference may have been to traditional values and rules of behavior promulgated by some external authority, yet it is hard to conceive of life in a society that is essentially amoral.

Morality consists of principles or rules of conduct that define standards for right behavior. One might hope that morality consists of a set of general rules that apply to everyone in a society. These rules are neither enacted nor revoked by a legislature but are accepted and changed by general consensus. They define the relationships among the members of a society. As Goldstein observed, "a moral sense . . . involves not only individual thoughts and actions but relationships with others" (1987, p. 181). Although in the United States there is a broad consensus about some issues, we are witnessing a growing diversity and multimoralities. There are deep divisions in American society about such issues as euthanasia and the right to commit suicide, human cloning, abortion, gay and lesbian marriage, and the responsibilities of individuals, families, and governments. On another level, values are clashing among immigrant, racial, generational, religious, sexual-orientation, and ethnic and cultural groups, among others. Social workers are increasingly confronted by a diversity of values and moralities; they practice in a society where there is less and less consensus about what is *the* proper moral stance.

The Educational Policy and Accreditation Standards (2004) of the Council on Social Work Education (CSWE) expect every social work education program to provide specific knowledge about social work values. This curriculum content is based on the previously cited core values identified in the Code of Ethics and their ethical implications. The educational goals of such content include assisting students to develop an awareness of their own values; developing, demonstrating, and promoting the values of the profession; and analyzing ethical dilemmas and the ways they affect practice, services, and clients.

The purpose of education that focuses on the core values of the profession is to help students understand and appreciate human diversity. This understanding and appreciation are the first steps to correct professional activity. Thus, knowledge and appreciation of race, color, gender, age, creed, ethnic or national origin, disability,

General Ethics: All persons shall be respected as equals.

Professional Ethics   All persons shall be respected as equals, but priority shall
                           be given to the interests of the client.

FIGURE 2.1 | THE ETHICS OF INTERPERSONAL RELATIONS

political orientation, and sexual orientation are important for professional purposes. Such groups represent a diversity of values and perspectives and, for many social workers, raise value dilemmas, both for themselves and for their clients.

PROFESSIONAL ETHICS

Professional ethics provide the guidance that enables a social worker to transform professional values into professional practice activities. Ethical principles do not describe professional practice, but provide screens for assessing practice options for their rightness or wrongness. Codes of professional ethics identify and describe the ethical behavior expected of professional practitioners.

Professional ethics are closely related to, but not identical to, general societal ethics. Just as social work values are derived from the values held by society but are not necessarily identical to those values, so professional ethics come from the same sources as societal ethics but may differ from them in important details. There may be differences in priorities, emphases, intensities, or applications. Illustrative of these crucial differences are the ethical principles governing the relationships among people. Both societal and professional ethics stress the principle of equality, but professional ethics give priority to the client's interests, ahead of the interests of all others. Figure 2.1 summarizes these differences.

For social workers, this professional ethics principle is expressed in the standard of the NASW Code of Ethics: "Social workers' primary responsibility is to promote the well-being of clients" (NASW, 1999, 1, 1.01). The implications of this professional ethical principle for social workers and their practice are many because every social worker is almost continually forced to choose (knowingly or not) between general ethics and professional ethics (see Figure 2.2). It is, of course, often easier to deduce and formulate an ethical principle in theory than it is to apply it in practice. The framers of the CSWE Educational Policy and Accreditation Standards recognized the importance of professional ethics for social work practice. They therefore mandated that the values and ethics that guide professional social workers in their practice should be infused throughout the curriculum (Council on Social Work Education, 2004).

FIGURE 2.2 | THE OVERLAP BETWEEN GENERAL AND PROFESSIONAL ETHICS

Some social workers can discuss professional ethics at length at staff meetings but fail to see how these principles affect their own practice. In Exemplar 2.1 the situation faced by one social worker will be analyzed; pay particular attention to the questions of professional ethics that this worker faces.

2.1	DIANA CAN'T GO OUT

Alexia Macedonia is a single parent, the mother of three children ranging in age from 7 to 16. Her oldest daughter, Diana, is a 16-year-old high school student. Until the beginning of this school year, she received good grades, but at midterm she was failing all courses. She seems to have lost all interest in school. For the past three weeks, she has not been in school at all.

Alexia is a clerical worker in the town's only industry. She goes to work early in the morning before her children leave for school and returns home late in the afternoon, hours after the children finish school. Alexia is a good home manager, but she has no friends.

Recently, Alexia turned to the local family service agency to ask for help. She told the social worker that she felt depressed because she did not know what to do with Diana. By talking with both Alexia and Diana, the social worker learned that Diana has to stay home every evening and every weekend because her mother does not want to be alone. Even though Diana wants to go out with her friends, her mother never allows her to do so.

Alexia's social worker faced a number of practical and ethical questions, including the following: Who is the client? Whose interests should the social worker make a priority? Is it Diana or her mother, who made the initial request for help? Or both? Is it ethical for the social worker to intervene with Diana even though she has not asked for help and (on being contacted by the worker) claims to have no need for help? What other ethical considerations are evident in this case? For example, a social worker's primary responsibility to promote the well-being of a client does not mean that the welfare of other people should be ignored or harmed in order to satisfy the client's needs. Nor does the social worker's primary responsibility to the client relieve the social worker of her responsibility to the larger society and to the needs or problems of others who are not clients.

No profession can establish for itself ethical rules that grossly violate the general ethical standards of the community. If a profession fails to take into consideration general societal ethics, it risks severe sanctions, including the possible revocation of part or all of its professional authority. Yet society recognizes that practice requirements make it impossible for professional practitioners to follow the identical ethical rules that people generally are expected to follow. Social workers, for example, may ask the kind of questions that in general conversation might be considered inappropriate or even an invasion of a person's privacy. However, before asking such questions, a social worker must be certain that this information is necessary and that she can keep it confidential.

Society often sets limits on what a social worker may do. These limits can add to the ethical problems that social workers face. In a number of foreign countries, particularly in some of the developing countries, social workers have been jailed because they chose to follow professional ethics and used a practice modality contrary to their government's expectations. Their fate highlights the fact that ethical problems in professional practice are real and at times can result in dire consequences. In a number of countries, including our own, some social workers have lost their jobs, have not received promotions, or have been shunned because they practiced in accord with professional ethical principles and in this way ran afoul of agency rules and expectations or certain societal values.

LAW AND ETHICS: THE PROBLEM OF UNETHICAL BUT LEGAL BEHAVIOR

Within the last two decades, Congress and all state legislatures have passed a large number of laws that affect social work practice. At the same time, the various state and federal courts, including the U.S. Supreme Court, have handed down a number of decisions that are of critical importance for social workers. "Good intentions" and "ignorance of the law" are no longer acceptable excuses for social workers who break the law. Lack of knowledge not only exposes practitioners to possible litigation for malpractice but may also contribute to unprofessional and unethical practices.

The purpose of this section is to help social work students and practitioners understand the interdependence of law and practice. We will also explore a number of key legal principles that are of vital importance for social workers. Less attention will be paid to specific legal questions because (a) in many instances the law differs in each of the 50 states, (b) law is constantly evolving, so if we were to discuss a specific law, there is a real possibility that it would be out of date even before this book is in the hands of the reader, and (c) we do not intend to make lawyers out of social workers.

CHARACTERISTICS OF LAW

The word *law* has been variously defined by different authorities. According to Albert (1986), laws are concerned with protecting people against excessive or unfair power—government as well as private power. Black (1972) emphasizes the social control aspect of law; for him, law defines the normative relations between a state and its citizens. Selznick (1961) considers justice to be at the very center of any adequate definition of law. Others note that law tells people what they can and cannot do. The law informs them what is likely to happen if they are caught doing something that is prohibited (Van Hoose & Kottler, 1985). Crucial characteristics of law are that it is enacted by legislatures, interpreted by courts, and enforced by the threat of punishment. Its observance is held to be obligatory.

Law changes continually. At any given time it tries to reflect current knowledge and mores. The adaptation and change of law to reflect contemporary culture is exemplified by the evolution of the laws on abortion. When the California Supreme Court, in *People v. Belous* (1969), reversed the lower court conviction of an obstetrician who had been found guilty of procuring an abortion, it discussed at length the history of the statute that classified procuring an abortion as a crime. It noted that when the statute was enacted in 1850, almost every abortion resulted in the woman's death because of the complete lack of modern antiseptic surgical techniques. The legislature in the mid-19th century, therefore, limited abortions to those rare cases in which the danger to the woman's life from continuing the pregnancy was greater than the danger of her dying from the abortion. The court noted that nowadays abortions during the first trimester are relatively safe—in fact, statistically safer than going through with the pregnancy. For this and other constitutional reasons, the court reversed the conviction under what it considered the antiquated abortion statute and thus, in effect, revised the law in line with contemporary knowledge and technology.

In societies where the broad moral consensus has eroded, laws may be more effective than "moral persuaders" because they are enforced by the police power of the state. Following the enactment of the Personal Responsibility and Work Opportunity Act (1996), several states began to challenge former court rulings related to the provision of public assistance. These challenges placed restrictions on benefits for new state residents who were treated differently from those who had resided in the state for some time. In 1999, the U.S. Supreme Court held in *Saenz v. Roe* that states could not treat long-term and new residents differently in relation to public assistance benefits.

No matter how it is defined, law is of direct and immediate concern to social workers. There are many different ways in which law affects social work practice. Laws authorize payment for specified services; laws direct that certain social services be provided for all who need them; laws authorize professional social workers to engage in some activities that other people are not allowed to perform, but they also limit social workers from other activities that can be performed only by practitioners of another profession. Laws require social workers to report certain information to designated government agencies. Because laws differ from state to state, we avoid mentioning specific ones. Our purpose is merely to indicate the importance of laws for all social workers, no matter whether they are agency-employed or in private practice.

All states require that cases of suspected child abuse and neglect be reported to a designated public child protective agency, no matter whether the social worker is employed by a public or voluntary agency or is in private practice. However, as is evident from the following research, some social workers may practice as if the law does not apply to them, using various rationalizations why they should not report. Two national studies of the incidence of child abuse and neglect and the reporting patterns of a broad representative sample of professionals who serve children found that many professionals failed to report substantial numbers of the children they saw who had observable signs of child abuse and neglect. Professionals failed to report to authorities 56% of apparently abused or neglected children, more than 85% of fatal or serious physical abuse cases (life-threatening or requiring professional treatment to prevent long-term impairment), as well as 72% of the sexual abuse cases. These data translate for the period studied into 2,000 children with observable physical injuries severe enough to require hospitalization that were not reported and more than 100,000 children with moderate physical injuries that went unreported. Over 30,000 apparently sexually abused children went unreported. Noteworthy is the fact that these nonreporting rates were discovered among relatively well-trained professionals, not among those less well-trained (Besharov & Laumann, 1996). In a study of child abuse and maltreatment reporting by 258 experienced mental health professionals, 51% of the social workers included failed to report at least one time during their careers (Weinstein, Levine, Kogan, et al., 2000), while another study found that

66% of social workers do not report all observed cases of suspected child maltreatment (Delaronde, King, Bendel, & Reece, 2000).

A study of mandated professional reporters found they identified many reasons for not reporting suspected child abuse and neglect, including: reports take too much time; fear of a lawsuit for reporting; discomfort with the family; child protective services overreacts to reports; the social worker felt she could help the child better herself; treatment was already accepted; reporting would disrupt treatment; lack of sufficient evidence that abuse has occurred; abuse or neglect not serious enough to report; the situation resolved itself; and the case was already reported (Zellman & Fair, 2002, 455–458). These findings are supported by a study of 101 mandated professional reporters in Georgia, almost 60% of whom were family therapists and social workers. Forty percent of the total group reported they break the law on occasion by not reporting; 60% reportedly were reluctant to report because from their perspectives child protective services may make the family situation worse because they are understaffed and inadequately trained (Strozier et al., 2005).

Zellman and Fair (2002) found that some respondents feared that reporting suspected maltreatment would result in a lawsuit, however, the Child Abuse Prevention and Treatment Act requires all states to enact mandatory child abuse and neglect-reporting laws that provide immunity from civil and criminal prosecution arising out of suspected child abuse reported in "good faith" (Smith, 2006). Weinstein et al. (2000) found senior mental health professionals experienced stresses when a report is to be made; as a result, 90% of these clinicians consulted at least one source about reporting. One explanatory theory offered for the reluctance and inconsistent reporting of suspected child abuse by mental health professionals is that, although they know the legal requirements, they have concerns about the impact of reporting on their treatment of clients. However, Weinstein et al. (2000) found that the mental health professionals' relationships with their patients were positive in almost 30% of the cases, 11% improved or improved after initial resistance, and there was no change in 32%. Seven percent experienced reporting as negative and continued their resistance, but only one in five (21%) terminated treatment.

DIFFERENCES BETWEEN LAW AND ETHICS

What are the similarities and differences between law and ethics? Law has an ethical dimension. Thus Albert insists that "it is altogether misleading to say ... that legal duties have nothing to do with moral duties" (1986, p. 9), but there are differences. While observance of the law is obligatory and enforced by threat of punishment, compliance with ethical principles is voluntary and reinforced only by a moral respect for values. Professional ethics, however, may also be enforced by professional sanctions; such sanctions may range from a simple censure to cancellation of permission to practice. A professional who is guilty of unethical or unprofessional behavior may be punished by a court of law and also may be disciplined for the same offense by his professional association.

Whereas ethics are often characterized by a sense of ambiguity and indeterminacy, law is said to be definitive. Yet the outcome of legal disputes is far from certain or predictable. Legal rules are pliable; whether a particular legal rule will apply often depends on the arguments presented by one side or the other.

Law is enacted by legislatures and can be changed by a subsequent enactment or by legal interpretations. Ethical rules, though they do change over time, are generally resistant to deliberate changes. Yet there is a close relationship between law and ethics because laws are often based on ethical principles. Thus, the legal principle of *privileged communication* is based on the *privacy* value and the ethical principle of *confidentiality* (see chapter 5 for a discussion of these principles).

CONFLICT BETWEEN LAW AND PROFESSIONAL ETHICS

Treating people wrongly does not become ethically right even when it is required or sanctioned by law. At times, a practitioner may follow the law and still be guilty of unethical professional behavior. In the past, a number of state legislatures enacted laws that mandated the involuntary sterilization of certain groups of felons and developmentally disabled persons. Can we say that a social worker who participated in these "lawful" programs practiced in an ethical manner? Many social workers claim that compliance with the law requiring the reporting and deportation of those who have entered this country illegally is contrary to professional ethics. Other social workers state that the application of the death penalty, even when authorized by law, is always unethical. Some suggest that there is a moral right, even a moral duty, to violate unjust laws (Pemberton, 1965). Social workers, for example, as advocates for civil rights or for humane treatment of persons with mental illness may engage in illegal behaviors—that is, break the law for ethically principled reasons.

There is a general assumption that human service professionals have an ethical duty to obey the law. However, "in some circumstances, competing ethical principles may be so fundamental that they justify disobedience of the law" (Melton, 1988, p. 944). This dilemma is highlighted by the *Tarasoff* decision (*Tarasoff v. Regents of the University of California*, 1976, 551 P.2nd 334 at 340). The wider implications of this decision will be discussed in detail in chapter 5. Here we will only note that in *Tarasoff* the California Supreme Court held that in some situations the welfare and safety of the community may be more important than the confidentiality principle. Some social workers view this legal requirement to break confidentiality as forcing them to choose in certain cases between the professional helping relationship, professional ethics, and law. Other social workers hold that a law cannot override professional ethical duties. Most, however, have accepted the principles of this decision. The Code of Ethics has been revised to reflect the *Tarasoff* decision (NASW Code, 1999, 1.07c); most social workers no longer think that they have to choose between professional ethics and law in the duty to warn. In other situations, the dilemmas posed by the *Tarasoff* decision are still acute. For instance, consider a social worker whose clients include HIV-positive persons. What are the ethical and the legal requirements when such a client admits to his social worker that he continues to share needles or engage in unprotected sexual relations without notifying his partner of his condition? Must this social worker break confidentiality and warn the endangered partner?

When an ethical social worker discerns a wrong against an individual or a group, she is obligated to act. For example, the Code (6.04a) suggests social workers "should engage in social and political action that seeks to ensure all people have equal access to the resources, employment, services, and opportunities they require to meet their basic human needs and to develop fully." Thus, social workers are concerned not only with what ought to be but also with how to bring what *is* more in line with that ideal outcome. The feminist approach to ethics must include action to achieve equity for women within existing political, social, and economic structures. When such structures are not amenable to equity, they must be altered to be made more just (Brabeck & Ting, 2000, p. 29).

The NASW Code of Ethics, in a discussion of the Code's purposes, approaches this issue in a different manner:

> Instances may arise when social workers' ethical obligations conflict with ... relevant laws or regulations. When such conflicts occur, social workers must make a responsible effort to resolve the conflict in a manner that is consistent with the values, principles, and standards expressed in this Code. If a reasonable resolution of the conflict does not appear possible, social workers should seek proper consultation before making a decision.

Sometimes the conflict between ethical behavior and the law is at such a high governmental level that the conflict may not be resolvable at a local or individual practitioner level. Nevertheless, individual practitioners may decide ethically to act contrary to a law. This possibility arose recently in relation to undocumented immigrants. The Border Protection, Terrorism, and Illegal Immigration Control Bill was approved by the House of Representatives. The legislation as proposed would— among other things—subject to five years in prison anyone who "assists" an undocumented immigrant to remain in the United States. Cardinal Archbishop Roger Mahony of Los Angeles stated that he would instruct the priests of the archdiocese to disobey the proposed law because it is part of the mission of the Church to help people in need. Cardinal Mahony stated that he did not mean that the Church encourages or supports illegal immigration; rather, that from an ethical point of view, denying aid to a fellow human being violates a higher authority than that of Congress (Mahony, 2006).

MALPRACTICE AND UNETHICAL BEHAVIOR

A social worker's activities may be unprofessional, unethical, or both. An activity is unprofessional when it departs from the usual practice that a "prudent professional" would have rendered in the same situation. Such unprofessional conduct may be the result of professional negligence, lack of knowledge and skill, or misconduct. Unethical behavior violates the professional principles and standards promulgated by the profession's Code of Ethics in dealing with clients, colleagues, practice settings, the profession, and the broader society.

Failure to provide proper professional service (that is, rendering unprofessional service) can make a social worker guilty of malpractice liable to civil suits and/or criminal charges. Failure to provide ethical service can make a social worker liable to professional sanctions. In some situations, a social worker faces all three risks. For example, a social worker who has sexual relations with a client may face a civil damage suit, criminal charges, and professional sanctions for unethical behavior (see chapter 9 for a more extensive discussion of the ethical issues involved in client/social worker relations). Having sexual relations with a former client may also be unethical and illegal, but after a lapse of a period of time, there may no longer be a case for civil liability. The length of the period of time differs in various states and also depends on the date of termination of therapy, when sexual contact occurred, and whether the failure to bring an action within the prescribed period was due to the effects of the sexual contact. The basic question, both legally and ethically, is not the elapsed time, but whether such relations still constitute an exploitation of the therapeutic relationship (Perry & Kuruk, 1993). There is little consensus among therapists regarding post-termination sexual involvements. Some therapists call it an "abomination" and others suggest there needs to be provision for individual situations with mitigating factors (Shavit & Bucky, 2004).

Legal remedies for malpractice can be classified into three categories: civil lawsuits (potential monetary damages), criminal complaints (potential criminal sanctions such as jail), and licensing board complaints (potential loss of license to practice for varying periods of times) (Sutherland, 2002). The type of proof necessary for conviction differs according to the charge and the law of a particular state. Among the legal considerations for action in sexual exploitation cases are the wording of the state's sexual exploitation and assault statutes, negligent breach of fiduciary duty, malpractice, negligent infliction of emotional distress, battery, intentional infliction of emotional distress, fraudulent misrepresentation, and breach of contract. Spouses may also assert separate and independent claims for the above and loss of consortium and alienation of affection (Advocate Web, 2002).

Strom-Gottfried (2003) analyzed almost 900 ethics cases filed with the NASW between July 1, 1986, and the end of 1997. Of those cases, 267 were found to be substantiated violations after hearings (cases may include more than one violation; the total number of substantiated violations was 781). Of the boundary violations (dual or multiple relationships with clients), 40% were sexual relationship violations. From 2002 through 2005, the most common complaints and lawsuits against social workers insured by the NASW Insurance Trust were incorrect treatment, sexual misconduct, suicide of the patients (or attempt at suicide), state board complaints, reporting of abuse to authorities, and dual relationships (nonsexual) (NASW, personal communication, October 3, 2006). Daley and Doughty (2006) compared ethics complaints for social workers in rural and urban areas of Texas; contrary to what they expected, social workers in urban areas were more likely to have complaints against them for boundary violations, including dual roles. According to Mittendorf and Schroeder (2004) and others, sexual misbehavior by social workers remains a problem. Because such behavior is a major cause of claims against social workers, the National Association of Social Workers Insurance Trust limited its coverage of social workers found guilty of sexual involvement with clients to $25,000 (Mittendorf & Schroeder, 2004; Shavit & Bucky, 2004).

Civil suits to recover damages resulting from unprofessional actions or inaction are known as malpractice suits. The relatively low premium rates for malpractice insurance that social workers pay (in contrast to the premiums paid by physicians and other high-risk occupations) suggest that successful malpractice suits against social workers are still rare, but their number is increasing every year. In the early 1970s, there were almost no lawsuits against social workers, but since then the number of suits against social workers insured by the NASW Insurance Trust has increased dramatically (Houston-Vega, Nuehring, & Daguio, 1997). It must be remembered that all professions have experienced a growth in lawsuits in recent decades, which is

| BOX 2.1 | NECESSARY CONDITIONS TO BE MET TO WIN MALPRACTICE SUITS |

A client must prove these four conditions in order to win a malpractice suit:

1. The defendant (that is, the social worker) must have a legal duty to provide a professional service to the plaintiff (client). Ordinarily, a social worker has such a legal duty once a person becomes a client (whether in an agency or in private practice).
2. The social worker's performance must have been negligent or below generally accepted professional standards of competence. What would other social workers have done under the same circumstances? "Good intentions" or "ignorance" are rarely an effective defense.
3. The plaintiff (client) must have suffered an injury or monetary loss.
4. The social worker's actions or inaction must have caused the alleged injury or loss.

characteristic of our increasingly litigious society. In the past, there might have been relatively few malpractice suits against social workers because most clients believed in their social workers' selfless dedication to client welfare. The relative scarcity also could have been due to a lack of common law to serve as a cause of legal action (Perry & Kuruk, 1993).

Social workers who want to protect themselves properly should know what is involved in malpractice. By learning how liability develops, they can take precautions that will reduce the hazards they may face. One need not be a lawyer to understand the principles involved, though in specific situations legal consultation is desirable. Nevertheless, it is important to keep one's perspective about malpractice and not panic, while recognizing the potential risks that social workers face. Box 2.1 summarizes the four conditions necessary for a client to win a malpractice suit.

There appear to be few limits to the reasons for which malpractice suits can be initiated. The list presented in Box 2.2 shows the great range of possible malpractice actions (Besharov & Besharov, 1987; Corey, Corey, & Callanan, 2003). Many social workers are familiar with several of the risks of malpractice listed in Box 2.2 and the general principles of malpractice litigation, but fewer are well informed about risk reduction methods (Houston-Vega, Nuehring, & Daguio, 1997). In the following section, risk reduction methods will be introduced. In one research study, 105 New Jersey social workers were asked whether a malpractice suit would be successful in the case of a therapist who asked the police to pick up an emotionally disturbed client. This client had threatened to assault his therapist because he imagined that the therapist had revealed confidential information about him. Only 29 respondents (27.6%) gave the correct answer to this vignette—that there was little or no basis for a successful malpractice litigation based on the therapist's actions. However, 61% gave the correct answer to another illustrative example involving a case where a depressed client threatened to commit suicide and also kill her two children. Social workers were asked whether there was a basis for a successful malpractice litigation against the worker if she failed to inform the client's husband of the threat. The correct answer was that her actions were very likely the basis for a successful litigation. The publicity given to the *Tarasoff* decision in professional journals may explain the higher

BOX 2.2	SOME EXAMPLES OF POSSIBLE BASES FOR MALPRACTICE SUITS

- Treatment without obtaining and documenting consent
- Incorrect diagnosis and incorrect treatment
- Failure to consult with or refer a client to a specialist
- Failure to prevent or causing a client's suicide
- Inappropriate release or detainment of a client in a hospital or confinement
- Breach of confidentiality
- Defamation
- Sexual involvement with clients or other sexual conduct
- Failure to provide adequate care for clients in residential care
- Failure to be available when needed
- Abrupt or inappropriate termination of treatment
- Improper child placement
- Failure to report suspected child abuse or neglect
- Use of unestablished practice methods
- Practicing beyond the scope of one's competence

percentage of correct responses in this instance. Nevertheless, even in this case, 40% of the social workers did not seem to know what is involved in malpractice litigation (Gerhart & Brooks, 1985).

PROTECTION AGAINST MALPRACTICE SUITS

The question remains: How can a social worker defend herself against the possibility of a malpractice suit? Knowledge and good practice are the best defenses against liability. In addition, sound risk management can reduce the degree of risk by implementing a plan for practitioners and agencies that includes having (a) familiarity with "wrongful acts" and possible malpractice actions, (b) a risk management audit (see Box 2.3), (c) a consultative relationship with legal counsel, (d) specialist consultants as needed, and (e) continuing education (Kurzman, 1995).

There are additional means of protecting oneself from malpractice actions. One's practice can be limited to clients for whom the social worker is prepared by virtue of education, training, and experience. Other precautions are honesty and fidelity with clients, knowing one's limitations, and using consultation for difficult situations (Corey, Corey, & Callanan, 2003). Box 2.3 provides a list of how a social worker can protect herself from malpractice actions (Kurzman, 1995).

Furthermore, as our society has become more litigious and accountability is more emphasized, documentation of social work practice interventions takes on greater importance. Documentation that has many uses, ranging from assessment to evaluation of services, also is useful for risk management and prevention or able defense of potential malpractice suits or complaints. Reamer (2005) defined guidelines for risk-management documentation and care recording into four categories: content of documentation, language and terminology, credibility, and access to records and documentation. Documentation—properly done—can be helpful to protect both clients and practitioners in legal situations and complaints to state licensing boards or NASW.

BOX 2.3	PROTECTIONS FROM MALPRACTICE ACTIONS

1. Risk management audit, including

    - Licenses and registrations in order
    - Protocols for emergency situations in place
    - Insurance coverage paid
    - Client records maintained and safeguarded
    - Other factors all in order and up to date

2. Consultative relationship with legal counsel
3. Specialist consultants for

    - Diagnosis and treatment
    - Second-opinion referrals
    - Ruling out organic pathology
    - Psychological testing
    - Evaluations regarding appropriateness of psychopharmalogical interventions

4. Continuing education

In regard to documentation content, Reamer (2005) suggests too much or too little content can be problematic in regard to liability risks. Similarly, loose and inappropriate language and professional terminology can create problems. Careful writing that is logical and mindful of potential audiences is essential. Credibility requires social workers to carefully document, for example, informed consent, assessments, termination procedures, and so forth; in other words, the entire process should be documented. Properly done documentation is supportive of credibility; when it is missing or not well done, questions are raised. Knowledge of legal responsibilities, including statutes and regulations, regarding access to records and documents is necessary for risk management. Certainly, it is important to recognize that not all storage mechanisms are foolproof.

Furthermore, practitioners should be alert to the potential circumstances under which records will be revealed. An ethical practitioner concerned with malpractice and risk management will—if agency employed—be clear about the documentation standards of the agency, including legal responsibilities and liability. Private practitioners have the responsibility to educate themselves through study and consultation to be prepared regarding all aspects of risk management. There are a number of relevant standards in the Code of Ethics which one should review. They notably are included in Privacy and Confidentiality (1.07), Access to Records (1.08), and Client Records (3.04).

WHO NEEDS PROFESSIONAL ETHICS?

Do professional practitioners require special norms and ethical principles to guide their well-intentioned activities? Are not general ethical principles sufficient?

Whenever two ethical principles or two ethical rules provide contradictory directions, social workers need guidelines to help them decide which takes precedence.

Professional ethics seek to provide such guidelines. There are those, however, who see no need for professional ethics. They argue that "common sense" or "practice wisdom" is all a social worker needs in order to make the right decision. While no one should underrate the importance of sound judgment and practice wisdom, many recall the occasions when these simply were not sufficient to arrive at an ethically correct and effective practice decision.

Those who argue that professional ethics are not necessary for social workers may cite one or more of the following arguments:

- *Competence is enough.* Correct practice is based on competence and skill, not on the mastery of ethical principles. Many so-called ethical problems merely reflect poor practice. For example, good contracting will avoid many situations that are presented as ethical problems. Social workers will make more appropriate ethical decisions by becoming more competent.
- *Each case is unique.* Every case is different and every client presents unique problems. No code of ethical principles can provide adequate guidance for every unique situation a social worker faces.
- *Evidence-based social work is value-free.* Evidence-based social work must pay more attention to knowledge and technology than to religion and morality. An exaggerated interest in ethics will deflect practitioners from developing further skill and knowledge, two areas that are most important for strengthening professional practice.
- *There is no time.* Social work practitioners have no time for lengthy ethical reflections because practice demands that they act quickly. They do what they think is best for their clients. A code of abstract ethical principles will not help. If social workers were to analyze each ethical problem, they would never get anything done.
- *Philosophers' ambiguity.* At least since Aristotle's day, philosophers have been unable to agree whether anyone can determine the truth of an ethical principle. Under these circumstances it is not possible to know the correctness of any ethical proposition. It is best not to fool ourselves into believing that professional ethics can help us know what is "right."
- *Relativity.* What is thought to be right varies from country to country and even within a country at different times and for different population groups. In one society it is rude to come late for appointments, in another it is rude to come on time. Which is correct? In one culture a social worker is encouraged to recommend sexual abstinence when appropriate, while in another culture this option is taboo. Which is right? Within American society, different ethnic and cultural groups provide conflicting guidelines to what is correct. In the social welfare field, the emphasis has shifted pendulum-like between individual well-being and societal welfare. Which emphasis best reflects professional social work ethics? Those citing this reason conclude that there are no fixed ethical principles that hold over time or space. Everything is relative, and there is no way of indicating which choice or option is correct.
- *Instinct and "gut" feeling.* Practitioners usually know what is right in any given practice situation without having to turn to an authoritative ethical

guide prescribed by some superior body. It is far better to trust a worker's intuition than to depend on the enforcement of bureaucratic rules.

- *Coercion.* The adoption of a code of professional ethics will result in latent, if not overt, coercion to make practitioners act only in accordance with that document. Such coercion contradicts the basic social work and societal value of self-determination. A code also tends to stifle professional creativity because it places every social worker in the same mold and expects the same routine standard behavior from every practitioner. Personal ethics and regard for client welfare are far more important for ethical behavior than any fear of sanctions imposed by a professional organization.

- *Virtuous persons.* There is yet another argument, made by Aristotle, that all that is required for ethical decisions is that social workers be virtuous persons. When ethical decisions have to be made, people of good moral character will act ethically, based on their virtuous and morally schooled characters (Broadie, 1991).

- *Wasted effort.* There are so few valid complaints about unethical behavior that a code of ethics and enforcement machinery really are wasted efforts. Actually, there is much variability in the number of ethics complaints dealt with by the NASW. In 1987, there were 54 cases nationwide, rising to 99 in 1993; but in 1996, the number was reduced to 70. The apparent decrease may be the result of an actual decrease in the incidence of unethical behavior or the result of the increased scope of state regulation of social work combined with diminished use of NASW processes (Strom-Gottfried, 2003). Is there an acceptable level of ethics complaints? Can any profession be satisfied that it has reduced unethical behavior by its practitioners to a bare minimum number?

These arguments against a code of professional ethics are not entirely persuasive. Some are fallacious, others distort reality. Here a brief response to some of the arguments must suffice. The philosophical and clinical bases for these arguments will be dealt with in greater detail in chapter 3.

Anyone who practices social work knows that social workers seldom take time for drawn-out theoretical debates. Large caseloads and constant client demands for service do not leave time for calm contemplation and leisurely thinking. Ethical decisions, however, need not take a long time. Social workers need help in making correct choices, precisely because they have so little time, and in some cases, ethical choices that will need to be made can be anticipated.

Every social worker knows that each case is unique, yet there are commonalties. Ethical codes address these common elements. Principles and rules in a code of ethics are stated on a generalized level in order to permit adjustment to the unique features of each situation. The voluntary acceptance of professional discipline, including a code of ethics, can hardly be viewed as a violation of the self-determination principle. A person becomes a professional social worker as a result of a voluntary decision. Even though a code of professional ethics does not supply all of the answers (nor should that be its function) that contemporary social workers need, there is a real demand for such a code. In time, improvements will make such a code even more useful.

CODES OF PROFESSIONAL ETHICS

Every occupation that strives to achieve professional status attempts to develop a code of professional ethics. Such a code usually contains a compilation of the ethical principles relevant to the practice of that profession, principles to which the members of that profession are expected to adhere. Many codes of professional ethics also describe the sanctions that will be invoked against those who are unable or unwilling to meet these expectations.

The code of almost every contemporary profession has been written with the following functions in mind:

1. Provide practitioners with guidance when faced with practice dilemmas that include ethical issues.
2. Provide statements of the agreed upon standards of ethical practice, useful for those who evaluate professional conduct and misconduct.
3. Inform clients about what they have a right to expect from their professionals and protect the public from charlatans and incompetent practitioners.
4. Inform other professionals about the kind of cooperation they can give.
5. Protect the profession from governmental control; self-regulation is preferable to state regulation.
6. Enable professional colleagues to live in harmony with each other by preventing or minimizing the self-destruction that results from internal bickering.
7. Protect professionals from litigation; practitioners who follow the code are offered some protection if sued for malpractice.

Because a code of professional ethics tries to provide guidance for every conceivable situation, it is written in terms of general principles, not specific rules. Yet when we compare codes written earlier with those written more recently, we note that the contemporary ones tend to be more specific and try to cover a greater variety of specific situations. Thus, the original 1960 Code contained 14 standards, by 1990 the Code included 66 standards, and the latest version of the Code (1999) contains 155 standards. On the other hand, the American Medical Association's latest code of ethics includes only nine principles (AMA, 2001). One reason for the lack of detail in the current AMA code is the desire to prevent lengthy litigation that resulted from the detailed provisions of the previous code.

Internal inconsistencies between various paragraphs of the same code are one of the possible consequences of greater specificity. When there is greater specificity, various ethical principles often conflict with one another, even though each may be valid. One of the major problems of the 1999 Code is that it avoided the specification of a hierarchy of values, principles, and standards. In effect, every standard in the Code is equal to all others. This avoidance of any formulation of ethical principles in a hierarchical order provides the ingredients for many of the ethical dilemmas that we will examine in the following chapters. Another problem, suggested by Marcuse (1976), is that codes of professional ethics often fail to provide answers to ethical dilemmas because their orientation is more likely to be system-maintaining than system-challenging. At the same time, it must be remembered that codes of ethics "are not intended as a blueprint that would remove all need for the use of judgment or ethical reasoning" (Conte, Plutchik, Picard, & Karasu, 1989, p. 5).

much interest, the adoption of a nationwide professional code had to await further organizational developments. It was only in 1951 that the AASW Delegate Assembly adopted a code of ethics.

When the historic merger of all major professional social work organizations took place in the mid-1950s, work on drafting a new code of professional ethics was started almost immediately, but the NASW Delegate Assembly did not adopt a code of ethics until 1960. Seven years later, this code was amended to include a nondiscrimination paragraph. The absence of such a provision from earlier codes tells much about the change in the moral climate of the country and in the profession.

Before long, many social workers called for a complete revision of the code in order to produce a document that would provide clearer guidance for practitioners and that would be more in tune with the realities of contemporary practice. A completely new code was adopted by the 1979 NASW Delegate Assembly. Soon it became evident that this code did not yet provide sufficient guidance for social work practitioners who sought help when facing difficult ethical issues. In an early discussion of the draft code, one prominent social worker noted that its usefulness was limited because of "its high level of abstraction and lack of practice utility" (McCann, 1977, p. 18).

The revised NASW Code of Ethics placed a much greater emphasis on the welfare of individuals than did the earlier 1967 document. This change may be considered problematic because it tends to shift the focus away from the common welfare. At that time, one analysis of different codes of professional ethics found that all other helping professions (with the exception of medicine) placed a greater emphasis on the common welfare than did social work (Howe, 1980).

Several groups of social workers have prepared codes. For example, social workers affiliated with the National Association of Black Social Workers prepared a code of ethics that gives expression to their belief that individual welfare can be served best by promoting the common welfare of all African American people. Social workers in clinical practice adopted a code of ethics that reflects their special concerns. The Code of Ethics of the Canadian Association of Social Workers reflects some of the special concerns of Canadian society. A Feminist Therapy Code of Ethics is based upon feminist philosophy, psychological theory and practice, as well as political theory. In recent years, the NASW Code has been revised several times in rapid succession (1993, 1996, and 1999) in an attempt to help social workers to better deal with evolving problems. Web sites where these codes are located can be found below.

Exercises

1. In chapter 1, you read about competing values. You undoubtedly became aware of the importance of a social worker's values in the ethical decision-making process. Can you identify some of your personal values that might play a part in how you might engage in such a process?

2. Go to one of the Web sites listed below and locate the code of ethics.

3. Compare and contrast the ethical principles that relate to confidentiality in two of the codes of professional ethics located in Exercise 2. Which code do you consider most helpful when a practitioner must make ethical decisions concerning the principle of confidentiality?

4. Ethical principles and rules are derived from societal values. Identify the relevant social work ethical principles for the following societal values:

- Cultural diversity
- Equality
- Freedom
- Integrity
- Knowledge building
- Privacy
- Social justice

5. Interview a human services professional about whether it is possible and desirable for a social worker to remain neutral and keep her own values from influencing clients.
6. As a social worker, if you had to choose between a child's right to confidentiality and a parent's right to know things that affect the child, how would you go about making this decision? What factors would influence your decision?
7. Look on the Web for the Feminist Therapy Code of Ethics. When you compare that code or guidelines with the NASW Code, can you identify themes not emphasized in the NASW Code but found in the feminist code? Are there any standards that conflict? How congruent are the political stances of the NASW Code and the feminist code?
8. Discuss in small groups whether it is preferable that social workers work only with clients whose values are similar to their own. Are there any potential ethical positives to such a decision? If not, what are the potential ethical negatives of such a decision?
9. Discuss in small groups whether the NASW Code of Ethics should apply to all social workers, as long as they use the title *social worker* and regardless of whether they belong to NASW or not.
10. There are extensive ethics resources available on the Web. Go to your favorite search engine (e.g., Google, Yahoo!, etc.) and type in "social work ethics" to check out several sites. How can you decide which sites are reputable?

SUGGESTIONS FOR ADDITIONAL READINGS

McGowan (1995) examines how values shape professional decision making as well as the history of shifts in social work value preferences and ethical concerns. Reamer (1998) traces the evolution of social work ethical norms, principles, and standards. Excellent introductions to the place of moral philosophy in social work practice can be found in Goldstein (1987, 1998), and Manning and Gaul (1997). Mackelprang and Mackelprang (2005) illustrate how end-of-life circumstances have changed dramatically in recent years, causing social workers to reconsider ethical values traditionally embraced by the profession. Barker (1988b) raises a question that faces social workers who are members of several professional associations: Which code of ethics should they follow? Clark (2006) argues that social workers, among other human service professionals, model ways of life and counseling on morally problematic issues and that value-neutrality is neither feasible nor desirable, concluding that the social work role includes demonstrating virtuous character.

WEB SITES OF INTEREST

Codes of ethics for several professional organizations can be found at the following Web sites:

- National Association of Social Workers: www.socialworkers.org/pubs/Code
- National Association of Black Social Workers: http://nabsw.org/mserver/CodeofEthics.aspx

- Canadian Association of Social Workers: www.casw-acts.ca
- American Association for Marriage and Family Therapists: www.aamft.org/
- There are also several Web sites that provide multiple links to ethics resources; see for example:

  - Lawrence M. Hinman's (University of San Diego) site: http://ethics.sandiego.edu/
  - The Association of Baccalaureate Social Work Program Directors (BPD): www.uncp.edu/home/marson/nlink.htm

3 | GUIDELINES FOR ETHICAL DECISION MAKING: CONCEPTS, APPROACHES, AND VALUES

Social workers must make ethical choices every day. A client tells her social worker that she is planning to commit suicide. A group member who has been unemployed for the past nine months asks his social worker not to tell a prospective employer about his criminal past so that he can get the job, which he needs desperately. Another client has been telling his worker that he embezzled funds from his employer in order to pay for his son's graduate school tuition. A young man threatens to harm a fellow worker who he believes has caused his fiancée to lose her job. Each of these situations confronts the social worker with one or more ethical dilemmas because they involve conflicting obligations. What are a social worker's obligations to her clients, to others who may be harmed or benefited by what the client did or will do, to society, and to her own values? In this chapter and the next we will provide guidelines for ethical decision making. This chapter will discuss the philosophical and practical components of ethical decision making, and the following chapter will provide a model and tools for ethical decision making. We'll begin with an analysis of a practice situation, Exemplar 3.1, to illustrate this approach.

3.1	SERENA ADAMS HAS HERPES

At the Jeanette April residential treatment center for teenagers with emotional problems, the staff became aware that 15-year-old Serena Adams has herpes. Herpes is an incurable disease that lies dormant but is easy to transmit when active at the time of intercourse, sometimes when no symptoms are present. Serena has complained from time to time of itching and sores in her groin and burning sensations while urinating. Although not life

42

| 3.1 | SERENA ADAMS HAS HERPES *continued* |

threatening, genital herpes can affect one's life by making one more susceptible to HIV infection; newborn babies can be infected if herpes is active in the mother at the time of birth; and one may have to explain the disease's presence to future partners. Serena has been sending notes to Donnie, an 18-year-old male resident, suggesting dates for sex. The fact that Serena is infected is known only to the staff members and to Serena.

The treatment team, after discussing this development, asked Jackie LaMartine, Serena's social worker, to explore the situation with her. She was instructed to try to convince Serena to avoid any sexual relations with Donnie, or at the least to make sure they use safe sex methods. Jackie said she didn't mind speaking to Serena but felt someone should inform Donnie of Serena's herpes. Jackie thought that not telling Donnie prevented him from making an informed choice, even to assure his use of a condom. When Jackie spoke to Serena, she told her that she knows she loves Donnie and that she feels Serena would want to protect him and herself. Serena refused to cooperate, arguing that the information must be kept confidential, that she and Donnie love each other, and that how they have sex is their own business. She insisted that no one tell Donnie of her illness. The team members are split as to what to do now.

The facts seem fairly clear, as are several of the ethical dilemmas that face Jackie and the team. There are many questions that arise out of the social worker's professional knowledge and experience, among them:

1. Should Jackie and the team leave Serena and Donnie to make their own decisions despite the risks to them both? Is the duty to protect Donnie more important than the maintenance of confidentiality for Serena? If Jackie tells Donnie the facts, she will interfere with Serena's self-determination and freedom, but if she doesn't tell him, she exposes him to potential infection. Is the social worker ethically justified to discuss the situation with Donnie without Serena's agreement?
2. What is the social worker's duty to protect in this situation and whom should she try to protect?
3. What are the long-term potential costs for Serena and Donnie if the team accedes to Serena's request? Are the costs to the agency, to these two residents, as well as to other residents, worth an effort to prevent a sexual relationship, which may not be preventable in any case?

Ethical decision making does not involve the automatic application of arbitrary rules. What MacIver (1922) wrote more than 80 years ago is still relevant today: "Ethics cannot be summed up in a series of inviolate rules or commandments which can be applied everywhere and always without regard to circumstances, thought of consequences, or comprehension of the ends to be attained" (p. 7). If this were the situation, social workers would find it easier to deal with the ethical problems they encounter.

Social work professionals, like other professionals, make many ethical judgments every day with confidence. They do not think that such judgments are difficult or controversial. The professional Code of Ethics and common sense provide them with sufficient guidance to cope with many of these dilemmas (Beyerstein, 1993). Social workers, however, do not always face simple choices between one good option and one bad option. Instead, they are often confronted by a number of choices, each one of which contains both positive and negative features, as in Exemplar 3.1. In such situations, the skilled worker must assess and weigh all options and outcomes and then select the one that appears to be the most ethical. How does a social worker know which option is "the most ethical?"

FOUNDATIONS FOR ETHICAL DECISION MAKING

Decisions about ethical questions are rarely idiosyncratic and usually follow an individual's consistent behavior patterns. Because such decisions involve questions of right and wrong, they are deeply rooted in the value system that is most important to the decision maker. Though philosophy has had a major impact on the development of ethics, there have also been other influences, including tradition, politics, religion, race, and gender. Contemporary philosophers have identified two major theories that encompass most approaches to ethical decision making: ethical absolutism and ethical relativism.

ETHICAL RELATIVISM

Ethical relativists reject fixed moral rules. They justify ethical decisions on the basis of the context or situation in which they are made or on the basis of the consequences that result. What are the risks and what are the benefits? What decisions will result in the greater balance of good over bad consequences? An option is chosen because it will lead to desired results or is rejected because it will lead to results that are not wanted. The amount of good that is produced or the balance of good over evil (not any absolute standard) serves as the major criterion for reaching an ethical decision.

Ethical relativists differ when it comes to identifying the target or the intended beneficiary of the planned decision. Ethical egoists believe that one should always maximize what is good for oneself, no matter what the consequences for others. Ethical utilitarians, on the other hand, argue that the most important thing is to seek the greatest good for the largest number of persons.

Ethical relativism is not a recent invention but was already known in ancient Greece. Among its early followers were the sophists and Herodotus. In more recent times, John Stuart Mill, Jeremy Bentham, and Sigmund Freud were among those who followed this approach. All three taught that ethical decisions should be made on the basis of maximizing pleasure and avoiding pain.

There are those who are highly critical of ethical relativism, suggesting that this approach to practice is essentially asocial and perhaps even amoral because it assumes that individual satisfaction is the primary value. Others fault ethical relativists because they say that the only thing that matters is the result. If the result is the only thing that matters, is there no difference when someone dies because an armed robber kills a bystander during a bank holdup, a soldier kills an enemy in combat, or a parent kills her child after a social worker determines that the child has not been abused and therefore leaves the child in the home? Different motivations and differing activities lead to the "same" results, but are they really the same?

The search for certainty, a rational and definable truth, is questioned by many persons and even discredited. Some believe there are no universal truths and absolute rules are unacceptable. Various "isms" (such as postmodernism, deconstructionism, and social constructionism) claim that situations, including those that require ethical decision making, are best viewed from their "more truthful" perspectives. Because postmodernists believe there are no independent standards of objectivity, no universal truths, and no absolute rules (Rothstein, 2002), they are included here as a subset of ethical relativism.

According to some persons, our era is a postmodernist age, "the point at which modern untying (dis-embedding, disencumbering) of tied (embedded, situated) identities reaches its completion; it is now all too easy to choose identity, but no longer possible to hold it" (Ulrich & Beck-Gemsheim, 1996, p. 24). Necessity and certainty are being replaced by contingencies. The certainties of God, nature, truth, science, technology, morality, love, and marriage are being turned into "precarious freedoms" in which "nothing that has been binds the present while the present has but a feeble hold on the future" (Bauman, 1996, p. 51).

Ethical Absolutism

Ethical absolutism stresses the overriding importance of fixed moral rules. Philosophers who hold this approach teach that an action is inherently right or wrong, apart from any consequences that might result from it. A specific action or practice is morally right or wrong not because of its consequences or the circumstances but "because of some feature intrinsic to the act or practice itself" (Callahan, 1988, p. 20). Ethical absolutists maintain that ethical rules can be formulated and that these should hold under all circumstances. For example, they will argue that the rule "A social worker shall tell the truth to her client" is always correct and applies in every situation, no matter how much damage may be caused by telling the truth in any particular situation. Philosophers such as Plato and certain religious philosophers who follow this theory are known as **deontologists.** Immanuel Kant (1724–1804) was the first modern philosopher to adopt deontological concepts, which he expressed through the principle of the categorical imperative—that is, one should "act only according to that maxim by which you can at the same time will that it should become a universal law" (Wikipedia, 2004). He insisted that categorical imperatives (anyone in similar circumstance should act in the same way) are morally necessary and obligatory under all circumstances. Based on this perspective, one should never lie; one should always tell the truth whatever the circumstances. But, of course, there can be conflicts between two equal duties. Because one has a duty to perform each, obvious conflicts may occur. According to this perspective, fulfilling one's obligation has a greater priority than weighing the consequences of one's actions.

Jeremy Bentham (1748–1832), one of the earliest exponents of English utilitarianism, accepted "the greatest good for the greatest number" as a binding principle that applies in every situation. It is important to note that many ethical absolutists allow for situations where the fixed rules do not apply. For example, many theologians have accepted the argument, first proposed by the Dutch jurist Hugo Grotius (1583–1645), that one must always tell the truth and never lie, but that it is permissible to speak falsely to thieves because no one owes them the truth. However, there is an important difference between not applying a rule in an exceptional situation and deciding each situation as if there were no rules.

Practitioners may not be aware of these efforts by professional philosophers. Neither do they always know which ethical theory they follow when making ethical decisions. This is especially true because the differences between the major theories frequently are not as clear in practice as they are on the printed page. These theoretical approaches often seem to merge in practice, but it does make a difference in ethical decision making whether a social worker follows one or the other theory, as the following analysis will illustrate.

DIFFERENT APPROACHES OF TWO SOCIAL WORKERS

We will now return to the exemplar from chapter 1 with Basanti Madurai to examine how these different approaches may impact decision making. Recall that the social worker Ellen Ashton had been informed that Basanti was being abused by her husband; however, when Ellen invited Basanti to join a support group, Basanti reported that everything was fine. What did you identify as the ethical dilemmas when you first read this exemplar and what, if anything, would you have done?

As promised, we will now add some more information to this case. Let us assume that in the days or weeks since you read chapter 1, the social worker, Ellen, has invited Basanti to meet with her individually, based on Basanti's initially expressed wish to try to make a better life for her family. During the first meeting, Ellen observed a large bruise on Basanti's arm. When she asked Basanti about the bruise, Basanti admitted that her husband had grabbed her during a disagreement, but that she was sure he did not mean to harm her. During the interview, Ellen established that there has been a pattern of these incidents, but that Basanti does not want to leave her husband and she does not believe her husband needs help. As a new social worker, Ellen was not sure how to respond to this and she was afraid that if she pushed too hard Basanti might not continue to see her, so Ellen decided to consult with more experienced social workers in her agency.

The two social workers—Ruth, an ethical relativist, and Anne, an ethical absolutist—might provide Ellen with different guidance. Our focus will be on learning how these differences might lead to different considerations and decisions. Anne, the ethical absolutist, believes that domestic violence is wrong, and women who are in abusive situations should immediately leave to protect themselves and their children if they have any. Therefore, she encourages Ellen to convince Basanti to leave her husband and take her children to a shelter for victims of domestic violence.

Social worker Ruth views the ethical aspects of Basanti's situation in an entirely different light. Being an ethical relativist, she assesses the consequences of respecting Basanti's denial that there is abuse and her wish to make a better life against the possible harm that Basanti may experience staying in a violent relationship. She provides Ellen with information about domestic violence, including some research on patterns of leaving and returning. She suggests that even when women decide to leave an abusive relationship, many return (often repeatedly), and that it is therefore very important to do further assessment of the situation and consider the consequences of staying versus leaving for Basanti and her family.

The two decision-making scenarios just described illustrate ethical absolutist and ethical relativist decision making. The decisions made by social workers Anne and Ruth are in each case only one of many different scenarios they could choose. The scenarios presented illustrate the general decision-making patterns (absolute rules or weighing the results of actions or omitted actions) connected with each philosophy. The decision as to what is the best course of action in this situation depends upon the social worker's philosophy of life, her values, her commitment to ethical relativism or ethical absolutism, and the degree of immediate and direct danger to Basanti's life. It also depends on the influences of the worker's peer group, family, professional group, neighborhood, and society. The situation, as with all ethical dilemmas, touches on the question of priorities. What is best for Basanti and her family? Furthermore, the impact of any decision must also take into consideration other participants in this situation, including the agency, the society that pays for the care that would be provided, the social worker, and other persons who may be involved.

Not all deontologists follow identical ethical rules with respect to any given problem. Identification of the relevant rules is, therefore, of the greatest importance. For example, some ethical systems consider abortion to be the same as murder and prohibit it altogether, no matter what the circumstances; others permit abortions under specified conditions, such as danger to the mother's life. Still other ethical systems are mute on this issue, leaving any decision to the individual involved. Social worker Anne may face other ethical dilemmas after she has identified the relevant moral rules. One dilemma arises out of a conflict between two categorical imperatives—the professional value and standard that calls for client self-determination and her own value system that may assign the highest priority to the protection of life. There is also another conflict between two competing professional values: confidentiality and client decision making based on full information. Here are situations where the social worker cannot honor both categorical imperatives, but must make a choice about which one to follow. The problems involved in making such choices will be discussed later in this chapter.

CONTEMPORARY APPROACHES TO ETHICAL DECISION MAKING

Philosophers have identified ethical absolutism and ethical relativism as two major ethical theories. Yet these theories are usually presented at so generalized or abstract a level that people do not always find them helpful when coping with the ethical issues they face. In the past, conscience was often suggested as the key to ethical decision making. Some contemporary philosophers have substituted guilt feelings for the older concept, and others have added "feeling good," "democracy," and "empowerment" as current keys.

Conscience or guilt feelings are too idiosyncratic to serve social work professionals as guides for ethical decision making. One person's conscience will not be the same as another's. Professional ethics are common to the entire professional group and should, therefore, be relevant to every member of that profession. What a social worker needs are tools of analysis that will permit a more systematic and rational consideration of the ethical aspects of social work intervention. The Code of the professional association helps social workers handle clear and obvious ethical choices that arise in practice, states the standards of ethical practice by which professional conduct can be evaluated, and promulgates the ethical principles of the profession, all the while assuming there is consensus within the profession about the standards (Beyerstein, 1993). Such models must include knowledge elements, but ethical decision making cannot be based on knowledge alone because ethics deal principally with what ought to be and not with what is. Before presenting our ethical decision-making models in the next chapter, we will discuss various approaches that other social workers have found useful in making ethical decisions.

CLINICAL PRAGMATISM

Many social workers indicate that they are neither philosophers nor specialists in solving ethical problems. Instead, they believe that their primary responsibility is to deliver a high level of professional service. Perhaps they agree with Jim Casey, who, in John Steinbeck's *Grapes of Wrath*, said, "There ain't no sin and there ain't no virtue, there is just stuff people do." They are sure that they will not become entangled in ethical problems if they concentrate their efforts on improving practice. In addition, they suggest that the type of service provided, the nature of the problems dealt with, and the modes of intervention used are determined in the first instance by society so that a worker's personal ethical stance is far less important than societal ethics. Social workers who follow this approach focus on implementing the values of the society that sanctions their activities. For example, one of the functions of social workers in contemporary American society is to help individuals and groups who face various kinds of emotional disturbances and crises. These social workers use societal values as a criterion to identify the types of behavior that require professional intervention, behaviors the society believes to be beyond the norm. They try to resolve any value conflicts that may arise in the practice context by considering the value priorities of the group in which they work.

While this approach seems simple, straightforward, and even supportive of scientific practice, it has a conservative tinge. Radical writers, such as Thomas Szasz (1994) and Ivan Illich (2006), have criticized this approach as unethical because these social workers tend to act as agents of social control on behalf of dominating and exploiting societal institutions. Social workers who follow this approach rarely question society's ethics or its norms (as they understand them). Their practice supports the status quo. These social workers rarely encourage the autonomous development of alternate lifestyles, nor will they be found among those who challenge society's values in other ways. These social workers should remember that social workers have the responsibility and ethical imperative to "not practice, condone, facilitate or collaborate with any form of discrimination on the basis of race, ethnicity, national origin, color, sex, sexual orientation, age, marital status, political belief, religion, or mental or physical disability" (NASW Code, 1999, 4.02). Furthermore, social workers "should advocate for living conditions conducive to the fulfillment of basic human needs ... and ... the realization of social justice" (NASW Code, 1999, 6.01). The question is whether those who follow this approach are aware of the implications of what they are doing. They must seriously consider whether they are in compliance with the professional ethics cited.

HUMANISTIC ETHICS

Many practitioners have found the humanistic ethical approach attractive because it combines a strong idealism with opportunities for individual choices. An idealistic view of human nature as essentially positive, together with an optimistic stance toward the future, provides the basis for this approach. The focus is on causal rather than on moralistic explanations of human behavior.

This approach stresses the capacity, opportunity, and responsibility of every person to make choices that make sense to him or her. The individual client or group, rather than any institution or ideology, occupies the center of attention. Such an approach appears to be particularly suited to contemporary America, with its emphasis on individualism and pluralism.

Self-realization has been at the center of the humanistic theories of Abraham Maslow, Erich Fromm, and other existentialists. Human beings are believed to be innately good and to have the ability to behave ethically. The inner core of the human personality is intrinsically ethical. Individual freedom and responsibility form the basis of social life. Self-expression and self-actualization are postulated as the desired outcome of mature development. Personal identity is defined by each individual according to self-chosen values that are derived, we hope, rationally. The priority of professional intervention at the individual level and group level will be to help people achieve self-actualization, rather than to help them to learn how to adjust to the existing social order. On the societal level, social workers who follow this approach will intervene to change those social institutions that inhibit the growth and self-realization of individuals.

Practitioners following this approach can be found in the forefront of many causes that promote freedom and equality. Some propose and experiment with disrupting the power hierarchies among therapists, clients, family members, and society (Parker 2003), in these ways opposing stable social authority structures; others emphasize hedonistic rather than traditional values (Orovwuje, 2001). All followers of this approach feel that they have minimized the ethical dilemmas they face; by clearly identifying value priorities, they feel that they can cope with the ethical aspects of most practice problems. More important, by emphasizing individual responsibility, the major burden for ethical decision making is shifted from the practitioner to the client.

The selection of humanistic ethics as the major approach to ethical decision making can be criticized on several grounds, primarily because such a choice does not reduce but increases the necessity for dealing with dilemmas. Not everyone comes to social workers seeking help for self-actualization, and the fact is that one person's individual self-realization may very well interfere with another person's self-realization, including the social worker's aims. Conflicts generated by individual self-realization and clashes of will can exist between the client, practitioner, agency, community, profession, and society—all of which will require means of dealing with the dilemmas that arise out of the conflicts.

There is yet another criticism of this perspective. Is it better for social workers as a profession to encourage individualism and hedonism, which in many ways fragment and undermine the social work aim to build a sense of community and alter societal structures so they are more enhancing of people? Such a question raises the reality of conflicts among individuals and professions and society. After all, few, if any, clients or social worker behaviors are devoid of moral questions and considerations. The chief criticisms of self-realization are that not everyone is innately good, one person's or group's fulfillment can clash with other persons and groups, and self-realization without boundaries and responsibility can lead to destructive as well as constructive actions.

RELIGIOUS ETHICS

Religious ethics presuppose a belief in the existence of God. While secularist philosophers teach that men and women are the creators of their own values, religious philosophers maintain that there is a set of divine values that humans must try to discover. Unlike those who deny the existence of absolute truth and absolute ethical rules, those who follow religious ethics declare that there are eternal rules that give direction for correct behaviors at all times. Believers are convinced that religious faith and ethical morality are two sides of the same coin. They cannot conceive of the long-term effectiveness of ethical principles that come from a source other than the divine will. The ethical aspects of interpersonal relations can exist only if one accepts the authority of God. They agree with Ivan in Dostoyevsky's *The Brothers Karamazov* when he said, "If there is no God, everything is permissible." Jacques Maritain, a Christian philosopher, argued that a secular ethics in which the individual becomes the ultimate goal does not deify the person but degrades him or her because "the greatness of man consists in the fact that his sole end is the uncreated Good" (1934, p. 269). For believers, the search for divine meaning is meaningful, while nonbelievers consider this search futile.

One of the consequences of accepting the religious approach is that ethics and law merge into one comprehensive, interrelated system. Because ethical principles are usually stated on a very generalized and abstract level, the authorized interpreters of religious law deduce specific applications to daily problems. These deductions become precedence or law. When this occurs, law is no longer separated from ethics but implements ethical principles in the daily life of societies. This approach provides those who follow it with a powerful tool that helps them cope with many of the ethical issues encountered in social work practice. On the other hand, they face a very serious problem when applying this approach because they practice in what is essentially a secular society and the law/ethic of one religious grouping may conflict with the law/ethic of another societal group.

If you consider yourself to be a religious or spiritual person, you might want to think about your own beliefs and how they are related to the kinds of client and community situations you might encounter in social work practice. How might your beliefs and values relate to the Code of Ethics and to the ethical decision making that will be necessary in your social work practice? If you identify potential conflicts between your beliefs and values and the standards of the Code of Ethics, how might you handle the conflicts when they are significant for potential practice situations?

The Ethics of Caring

According to those who developed the caring ethical perspectives, the experience of women and children in the "private" world of parents and families, professionals, and clients is lacking from traditional models of ethics. Missing are feminine psychological traits and moral virtues that society associates with maternal feelings and women in general. Feminists, from a different perspective, raise questions about Western ethics and view traditional ethics as reflecting masculine culture and masculine ways of reasoning. According to this view, traditional ethical decision making emphasizes universality and impartiality over "culturally feminine ways of moral reasoning that emphasize relationships, particularity, and partiality" (Tong, 1998, p. 261). Much emphasis is placed on an ethic of caring that views individuals as "existing and flourishing only within networks of care...networks of relationships, practices, values, and ways of life" (Manning, 1992, p. 163).

The ethics of caring suggest that people are by their very nature bound up in relation to others and that tensions and conflicts in those relations are at the heart of moral dilemmas. According to this perspective, to resolve such conflicts one must focus on the specific situation of the persons involved, on the web of their relationships, and on how to keep those relations intact without the application of a governing law or principle (Spelman, 2004).

The ethics of caring take as their central focus the compelling moral responsibility of "attending to and meeting the needs of the particular others for whom we take responsibility" (Held, 2006, p. 10). According to Held, when we try to understand what it would be best for us to do and to be, the ethics of caring value emotion rather than ignore or reject it. Sympathy, empathy, sensitivity, and responsiveness are to be cultivated in order to determine what morality recommends. The caring and maternal ethic aims at preserving life—feeding, clothing, and sheltering—as well as fostering growth and training children and others to be committed and concerned citizens (Tong, 2003).

The ethics of caring reject more abstract reasoning about moral problems and, thus, questions universalistic and abstract rules or principles of more traditional theories that value autonomy of moral agents, not being swayed by powerful emotions of the moment, and acting on consistent and impartial principles. In contrast to the "voice of justice" (more typical of men), the "voice of caring" is viewed as more typical of many women's thinking about morality.

An ethic of caring concerns itself with responsiveness and taking responsibility in interpersonal relationships. It is concerned with context-sensitive deliberation that resists abstract formulations of moral problems. An emphasis on rights, duties, and general obligations is downplayed. However, there are at least four criticisms made of the ethic of caring. Can one type of human relationship serve as the model for all human relationships? Does this theory over-idealize women and exclude men and nonbiological mothers from maternal work? How does one choose between those for whom caring is important, especially where needs are relatively equal? Caring by itself does not take into account the oppressive contexts in which women live and work. Accepting the idea that caring is innate to women can be used to determine women's social possibilities and roles, stereotyping them and steering them toward particular occupations and tasks (Bowden, 1997). Thus, women can be guided or guide themselves toward a more limited number of possible professions and roles.

Feminist Ethics

Feminist ethics are also women-centered and focus primarily on women's moral experiences. As a result, they emphasize the oppressive contexts within which women live and work. Feminist ethics are political in that they are committed to the elimination of women's subordination and that of other oppressed persons. Issues of power—domination and subordination—take priority before good and evil, care and justice, or maternal or paternal thinking (Tong, 2003).

Among the aspects of feminist theory that have importance for professional ethics are the following:

- The critique of domination and the concomitant articulation of the value of reciprocity, balancing traditional power differences
- The recognition of the distinctive individuality of the other

- A commitment to an ideal of caring
- A rejection of abstract universality and a model of reasoning that is concerned with context

According to Worrell and Remer (2003), "the social construction of gender relocates women's problems from individual and internal to societal and external. The feminist construction of gender redefines the nature of women's and men's relationship in terms of the expression and maintenance of power" (p. 5). Because domination and oppression in any form are considered morally wrong, feminist ethics are concerned with both particularities of individual situations and a concern with social structural conditions such as racism, classism, and sexism. In ethical decision making, private troubles are viewed within the context of public issues. Personal situations and societal contexts should not be viewed separately (Abramson, 1996).

However, there is no one feminist approach to ethical decision making, and different models (liberal, Marxist, radical, multicultural, existential, lesbian, and others) have been developed. Furthermore, as Glassman (1992) suggests, feminists also will find that "their feminist beliefs come into serious conflict with other deeply respected social work traditions, values, and principles" (p. 161). Can social workers respect the cultural values and customs of some ethnic groups without accommodating and perpetuating oppression? What should social workers who are respectful of self-determination do when clients accept patriarchal or other communal values?

VIRTUE ETHICS

Virtue ethics originated with Aristotle, who argued there are no general rules for good or right action. Only the person in each case can know then and there what is best, the right reason for the particular situation. One does the right thing as a result of virtues that are taught from youth. People will be trained and train themselves to be of good character (act and behave with practical wisdom), thus learning to be good. Moral training is the inculcation of habits, customs, and mores—that is, accepted ways and behavior. A just and honest person is that way because he has become and is that type of person. Human virtues—justice, courage, generosity, temperance, gentleness—are enacted in behaviors as a result of a developed personal character (Broadie, 1991). Character is the determining factor. Morality cannot be codified in a general model of ethical decision making. The right thing to do in any situation is what a virtuous person would do in those circumstances. For example, what would Moses, Jesus, Buddha, or another role model do in this situation?

Whose list of virtues is the correct one? A number of criticisms of virtue ethics have been put forth. Virtue ethics seem to be mainly interested in the acquisition of virtues by the person, thus virtue ethics are viewed by some as self-centered because they are mainly concerned with the person's own character. Virtue ethics fail to provide practical action-guiding help. Finally, right education, habits, and influences can promote virtue, but the wrong influences can promote vice. Some people will be lucky and receive the help they need to become mature and virtuous, others will not. Is it fair to praise the virtuous and blame the others for something that was not within their control? (Athanassoulis, 2006)

SUMMARY OF CONTEMPORARY APPROACHES

Perhaps over time as these developed approaches find means of dealing with various ethical dilemmas, they may challenge and alter more traditional ethical decision-making patterns in social work practice. Just as clinical pragmatism, humanistic, and religious ethics, among other perspectives, have had their particular impact on ethical decision making in social work, so caring, virtue, and feminist ethics may also contribute to contemporary ethical decision making, although their ultimate impact is not yet clear. Meanwhile, traditional models of ethical decision making provide guidance and clearer directions as to what to do. They provide principles by which professional social workers may reason their ways through ethical choices.

PERSONAL, GROUP, SOCIETAL, AND PROFESSIONAL VALUES

Values are a key element in the ethical decision-making process. No wonder Levy (1976b) called ethics "values in action." The purpose of clarifying one's personal and group values, as well as societal and professional values, is to increase one's awareness of the potential conflicts among them and the potential impact these conflicts can have on ethical decision making. Recognition of our own values and those of clients, agencies, communities, and other people—including professionals—involved in various practice situations is an important step in preparation for ethical decision making. Ethical decision making requires being alert to the impact of values in order to reduce conflicts and to assist social workers in making ethical decisions based on client needs and the maintenance of one's own ethical integrity.

Before clarifying the relationship between values and ethics, it may be helpful to differentiate between different levels of values:

1. *Individual or personal values* are values held by one person but not necessarily by others.
2. *Group values* are values held by subgroups within a society—such as religious groups, ethnic groups, and so forth.
3. *Societal values* are values that are recognized by major portions of the entire social system or, at least, by the leading members or spokespersons of that system.
4. *Professional values* are values proclaimed by a professional group, such as social workers.

Generally, these four value sets are complementary or reciprocal, although at times they may be in conflict. Most of the time and in most places, discord among the different level value sets is infrequent, though differences in interpretation, priority, and intensity are not uncommon.

CLARIFYING PERSONAL VALUES

Some social workers question or denigrate the importance of personal values for professional practice. They suggest that a social worker must suspend or neutralize her personal values when serving clients. Charles Levy, who chaired the NASW committee that drafted an earlier Code of Ethics, said: "To be a professional practitioner is to give up some of one's autonomy and to relinquish some of one's right as a freely functioning being" (1976a, p. 113). However, the conflict between personal and professional values is rarely as unambiguous as this. The desirability of professional social workers suppressing their personal values in many situations, although perhaps possible, remains an ambitious, problematic, and very difficult task.

Others suggest that personal values have relatively little influence on ethical professional behaviors. They claim that social workers know instinctively or intuitively what is the right thing to do. Admittedly, feelings and instincts are important and do influence behavioral choices. However, having a strong feeling for something does not necessarily make for an ethical choice. A worker may feel that she wants to have sex with or befriend a client, but this instinctive feeling, strong as it may be, does not make this behavior ethically correct.

Frankena (1980) indicated that a person's cultural experiences and background, including personal values, implicitly direct the ethical decision-making process of that person. Unless these become explicit, however, there is danger that biases and stereotypes, rather than professional values and ethics, will shape professional behaviors. For example, Garb (1994) and Flanagan and Blashfield (2005) report research findings showing the existence of gender biases in personality assessment for both male and female clinicians and student social workers.

Shakespeare gave sound advice when he wrote: "This above all, to thine own self be true. . . . Thou canst not then be false to any man" (*Hamlet*, 1, 3, 78–80). This same advice may also help social workers when they consider their personal values that are relevant for ethical decision making. No matter what approach social workers use, it is essential that they clarify and make explicit their own personal values. Those who agree with Siporin that "there is a moral and ethical imperative that social workers act as moral agents" (1985b, p. 20) know the importance of holding clear, unambiguous, and specific personal and professional values. Only such values are effective in influencing and guiding behavior. In no other way can a social worker be true "to thine own self" and not act as a "hired gun" for a client, an agency, or even the state. It just will not do to speak in generalities. Instead, a social worker must carefully scrutinize and define her values.

For example, it is not enough for a social worker to say that she favors (or opposes) assisted suicide. She must be able to define her values about assisted suicide clearly. Does she believe a person has a right to doctor-assisted suicide if death is expected in the next six months and the person is found by a psychiatrist not to be depressed? Or does she believe that, with palliative care, all terminally ill persons can take advantage of the dying process to search for important values, to reconcile with families, and make some valued use of the time? Does she dismiss assisted suicide under any circumstances and opt for life despite the difficulty of the last days? For any of these, one also has to consider what is meant by assisted suicide, ranging from removing life support to discontinuing a feeding tube, to leaving a fatal dose of pain killers available, to administering a fatal dose of medication, and whether any of these options are more or less acceptable than others. These questions are raised here to emphasize that social workers must first clarify their own value stance in relation to value-laden issues they meet in practice situations if they want to be true to themselves and to their profession.

Clarifying Group Values

Social workers, like all other people, belong to more than one group and derive their values from those of their family, community, profession, religion, and other groups with which they are in contact. Part of analyzing one's value system is clarifying the values of those reference groups with which one identifies. Group membership and context are powerful and often decisive value forces. Like everyone else, social workers act in ways that they might not have chosen except for the influence of groups.

Most Americans grow up valuing a sense of independence. There is, however, a growing diversity of group values and cultural standards that social workers encounter and/or hold. Some groups favor strong interdependence among their members (loyalty, dependence, and connection to the group) and others foster independence (move out, do not be dependent, and steer your own course); what is valued may be different for men and women. Some of these values may be contrary to those held by mainstream America. Independent decision making is valued by Americans in general, but some groups may hold other values. For instance, persons with Pacific Island backgrounds (among other groups) attach a greater value to group-oriented decisions than to individual self-determination (Ewalt & Mokuau, 1995). Without considering those population groups that value group decisions above individual-oriented values, the NASW Code (1999, 1.02) prioritizes self-determination among the ethical responsibilities of social workers. It does so when it encourages social workers to respect and promote this right among clients (Ewalt & Mokuau, 1995), except when clients' actions or potential actions pose a serious, foreseeable, and imminent risk to themselves or others.

Immigrants often share their residence with relatives or other families because their cultures emphasize family closeness and interdependence or for economic reasons. This group value is foreign to many Americans who were raised and live in one-family apartments and homes, valuing their privacy. Many social workers may come from groups that do not value close and interdependent living arrangements. Similarly, a professional may be unhappy when immigrants turn for help to kin and hometown networks rather than to the organizations in which social workers are employed, despite their effectiveness as informal helpers (Chow, 1999; Padilla, 1997).

Just as assumptions cannot be made by social workers about their own group values, it is often difficult to offer generalizations about the values of particular client groups. Social workers should keep the following in mind:

- When there are conflicts between the social worker's values and client values, in some instances the difference may be based on the client's membership in a particular group.
- There are limits to the generalizations that can be made about groups, and social workers must take care to avoid the use of stereotypes. Clients may have values that differ from others in their *own* cultural group by date of immigration, whether they were born in the United States, education level, geographic origin, social class, and even language (Agbayani-Siewert, 1994; Fellin, 2000). Differences within a group may be greater than differences between two groups.
- Professional social workers should not assume their clients will necessarily reflect or follow the values of their group.

Social workers who understand and clarify their values and the connection of those values to the groups that affect them and their clients have a better chance of identifying and handling value conflicts in ethical decision making.

CLARIFYING SOCIETAL VALUES

In the United States, it grows more and more difficult for social workers to identify and use societal values as ethical guidelines in a multicultural, multireligious, multivalues society. The influx of persons and families from so many different cultures and nations has created an expanded pluralism of values. To the extent that ethical behavior in general reflects what society values, nevertheless, a social worker must have accurate knowledge of the current various societal value stances and take them into consideration when assessing a problem situation and when making her decisions. There may be situations, however, when a social worker is justified, even obligated, to act in ways that are contrary to perceived societal norms. In every instance, the worker first has an obligation to clarify the relevant societal values.

The application of societal norms may become problematic when a society accepts values that previously were disvalued, especially when the adoption of the new value occurs unevenly among different groups within society. For example, today many (but not all) Americans accept the value that one may choose one's lifestyle freely, particularly if this does not impinge on the lives of others. Other issues, such as gay marriage, school prayer, abortion, and assisted suicide, still divide Americans because the acceptance of these new values has not been uniform across American society.

CLARIFYING PROFESSIONAL VALUES

Social work professional ethics are based on "social work's core values of service, social justice, dignity and worth of the person, importance of human relationships, integrity, and competence. The profession expresses its values through its primary mission to enhance human well-being and help meet the basic human needs of all people, with particular attention to the needs and empowerment of people who are vulnerable, oppressed, and living in poverty" (NASW Code, 1999, Preamble). Essentially, the social work value system reflects a democratic *ethos* that provides for individual and group fulfillment. It calls for respect of individuals and their differences, while at the same time recognizing the need for mutual aid and societal supports so that all persons can attain their maximum potential.

Finding the correct balance between the rights of the group or community and the rights of the individual is often not an easy matter and is a challenge not unique to social work. Such choices present serious dilemmas for which there are few guidelines. Within this balance, however, ethical decisions clearly require adherence to a democratic *ethos*.

Social work practice always involves ethical decision making. Assumptions about morals and values are basic to social workers' theories, policies, and practice decisions. Ethical dilemmas may arise when there is a conflict between the social worker's personal, group, societal, and professional values that are relevant in a given situation. The "absence" of conflict for the social worker may indicate either that the social worker is unconscious of the moral nature of the choices she faces or that the social worker is so clear about her values and societal priorities that the choice is prima facie correct. Another explanation may be that making the decision is not problematic for this worker because such decisions are routine (Fleck-Henderson, 1991). This does not imply that decisions made in such situations will be ethically correct. When decisions become so routine that they do not cause the social worker second thoughts, the time may have arrived for taking extra care in regard to ethical decision making.

EXERCISES

1. Before moving on to chapter 4 and the ethical decision-making model and tools we'll present there, please rank order from (1) highest importance or priority to (7) lowest importance or priority the following ethical principles:

   a. Autonomy and freedom
   b. Equality and inequality
   c. Least harm
   d. Privacy and confidentiality
   e. Protection of life
   f. Quality of life
   g. Truthfulness and full disclosure

   Please save your rank ordering so that you can use it in chapter 4 when we discuss the ethical decision-making model.

2. Social workers deal with varied situations, which may be congruent or dissonant with their personal values. Can you identify what your personal values are for the following: abortion, genetic screening, religious beliefs or their absence, personal and family responsibility, family planning and contraception, sexual intercourse before marriage, and pornography? From where did you derive your personal values? Can you identify how your values play a part in your personal life and how they might play a part in your professional life? What is said regarding social work practice also holds true for ethical decision making: "As important as self-awareness is value awareness. Helpers cannot be effective if they are not aware of their own values and the impact these can have on the helping process. Many decisions we make as helpers are based on the values we hold" (Alle-Corliss & Alle-Corliss, 1999, p. 11).

3. The legislature of your state has been alarmed by a sharp rise in the number of children born to young adults with mental retardation. Even when these infants are healthy, many of the parents with retardation are not able to give their children the care that they need. As a result, most of these children must be placed in foster homes at great expense to the public. A bill has been introduced by a group of powerful state senators calling for mandatory sterilization of all men and women with mental retardation. The senators argue that this is an effective, efficient, and painless way of taking care of this problem. You have been asked by your local NASW chapter to prepare testimony in opposition to this bill. In your testimony you should be mindful that considerations of efficiency and effectiveness cannot be dismissed out of hand in these days of tight budgets. Yet you might argue that ethical considerations are sometimes even more important. Remember, however, that you are trying to convince legislators, not social workers.

4. Organize a class debate on the proposition: "A true professional must be willing to give up some of his autonomy and some of his rights as a freely functioning individual, especially when there is a conflict between personal and professional values."

5. Tonight's forecast is for below-freezing temperatures. The mayor has ordered the police to pick up all homeless persons and to deliver them to the city shelter. The police have asked the shelter social workers to help them locate the homeless and persuade them to come to the shelter. You are one of the shelter social workers and know that many homeless persons will refuse to go to the shelter. What are the ethical implications of this request? What should you do as a professional social worker?

6. Most professional associations (i.e., physicians, engineers, lawyers) have codes of ethics available on their Web sites. Do an Internet search for the code of ethics of a profession other than those listed in chapter 1. Compare that code with the NASW Code in terms of specificity and usefulness.

7. In this chapter, one of the social workers consulted about Basanti's situation suggested that women in domestically violent situations may be reluctant to leave, and if they do leave, they may return, sometimes multiple times. What do you think of this suggestion? If you are not already familiar with the research on this topic, do a literature search to learn more about patterns of leaving and returning in domestic violence situations. How does what you've learned affect the kind of advice you would give a woman who is experiencing intimate partner violence?

Suggestions for Additional Readings

Klosterman and Stratton (2006) examine the values of Jane Addams, a prominent settlement-house worker and social worker, that influenced her emergence as an internationally known social activist and pacifist who sought a more humane and peaceful society. Clifford and Burke (2005) examine the implications for social work and social work education of developing anti-oppressive ethics in social work education curriculum. Abbott (1999) examines social work values within cross-cultural and geographic boundaries and the implications of value bases. Brill's (2001) "Looking at the social work profession through the eye of the NASW Code" provides one view of social work practice and the ethics of the profession. Panchanadeswaran and Koverola (2005) present the findings from a study of 90 women in India who were abused. Anderson and Saunders (2003) discuss research and theory related to the process of leaving an abusive partner.

Web Sites of Interest

There are many Web sites devoted to "values clarification"—we do not recommend any of them in particular, but you may find it interesting to go to your favorite Web browser and search for "values clarification." Note the specific values and types of activities that some organizations use. For information on values for social work, go to: www.socialworkers.org and enter "values" as the keyword to search.

GUIDELINES FOR ETHICAL DECISION MAKING: THE DECISION-MAKING PROCESS AND TOOLS

In the previous chapter, we examined philosophical components, contemporary approaches, and values as background for ethical decision making. In this chapter, we turn to the practical components of decision making itself. Sometimes a social worker can realize instantly that an ethical decision must be made. More typically, decision making is a process or series of thoughts and activities that occur over time and that result in a person or group acting (or not acting) in a particular manner. The process may not be conscious, but it always precedes making the ethical decision itself. Decisions will be better, more effective, and more ethical to the extent that the process becomes conscious.

Ideally, decisions are approached step by step so that one moves through a series of stages until, at the end of the process, one makes the decision. It is erroneous to assume that only one person, the decision maker, participates in this process. There may be many participants in the decision-making process, but there is only one responsible decision maker. Many different persons present information, react to assessments, introduce additional options, or make changes in the environment; these, in turn, change the nature of the data on which the decision is based or the nature of the decision that is made.

Observing decision making is like watching ocean waves approach the shore. Choices are always influenced by previous decisions that lead to new directions. Ethical decision making is far too complex to permit the development of a "how-to" problem-solving model, but a model may help social workers understand what is involved in ethical decision making. Like all models in science, such a model will simplify reality by focusing on only one decision. A model is a permissible didactic device as long as it is understood that in real life every decision is preceded and followed by other decisions, many of which have a direct bearing on the matter under consideration. In Figure 4.1, we present a general model for decision making that is

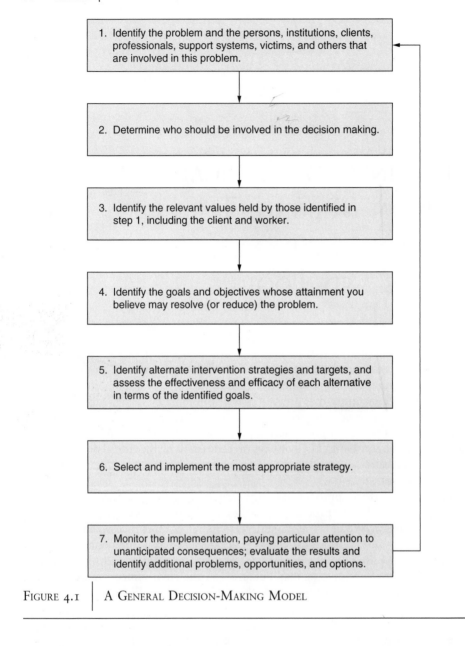

1. Identify the problem and the persons, institutions, clients, professionals, support systems, victims, and others that are involved in this problem.

2. Determine who should be involved in the decision making.

3. Identify the relevant values held by those identified in step 1, including the client and worker.

4. Identify the goals and objectives whose attainment you believe may resolve (or reduce) the problem.

5. Identify alternate intervention strategies and targets, and assess the effectiveness and efficacy of each alternative in terms of the identified goals.

6. Select and implement the most appropriate strategy.

7. Monitor the implementation, paying particular attention to unanticipated consequences; evaluate the results and identify additional problems, opportunities, and options.

FIGURE 4.1   A GENERAL DECISION-MAKING MODEL

applicable to many different situations and is not limited to ethical decisions. This model is based on the assumption that social workers can plan rationally what is needed for intervention in human situations and that they want to minimize the irrational, the impulsive, and the unplanned consequences of actions.

1. Identify the relevant professional values and ethics, your own relevant values, and any societal values relevant to the ethical decision to be made in relation to this ethical dilemma.
2. What can you do to minimize conflicts between personal, societal, and professional values?
3. Identify alternative ethical options that you may take.
4. Which of the alternative ethical options will minimize conflicts between your client's, others', and society's rights and protect to the greatest extent your client's and others' rights and welfare, and society's rights and interests?
5. Which alternative action will be most efficient, effective, and ethical, as well as result in your doing the "least harm" possible?
6. Have you considered and weighed both short- and-long term ethical consequences?
7. Final check: Is the planned action impartial, generalizable, and justifiable?

FIGURE 4.2 | ETHICAL ASSESSMENT SCREEN

ETHICAL ASSESSMENT SCREEN

The social worker who is alert to the ethical aspects of practice will examine and assess the available options and alternatives somewhat differently than her colleague who is not as concerned with those aspects. This becomes clear when we consider various assessment criteria. In Figure 4.2, we present an ethical assessment screen designed to help social workers further clarify and integrate the ethical aspects of decision making in social work practice.

PROTECTION OF CLIENTS' RIGHTS AND WELFARE

The definition of rights and privileges changes over time, and these changes may create ethical problems. What is thought to be a right at one time may not be so defined in another era—for example, social workers were once expected to protect confidentiality, no matter what the obstacles. Today, social workers remain concerned about confidentiality but may not be able to completely protect it for various reasons: changes in laws; court decisions; the introduction of new technologies; managed care and administrative record keeping required by funding and accrediting organizations; participation and consultation with team members, including those from other disciplines; and responsibility to supervisors and courts. In chapter 5, new privacy regulations required by the Health Insurance Portability and Accountability Act (HIPAA, 1996) that became effective in 2003 will be discussed.

Changing definitions of rights may also create ethical problems for social workers. Consider the ethical problems faced by social workers in the adoption field as the right of adopted persons to information about their biological parents is becoming recognized in more and more jurisdictions. At one time, the biological and adoptive parents were assured that such information would remain confidential and would never be shared with the adoptee. Now, when court decisions or legislative enactments in some states support the right of adopted persons to this information, social workers in these jurisdictions have little choice but to reveal it. Is it ethical for other social workers to continue to tell biological and adoptive parents that this information will always remain confidential when they have no way of ensuring this promise? This problem is not limited to courts and adoptees. No social worker can ever assure complete confidentiality because the social worker often cannot control what others (interdisciplinary team members, insurance companies, etc.) will do with the information she appropriately shares.

PROTECTION OF SOCIETY'S INTERESTS

Sometimes it is difficult to balance society's interests with a client's interests. If a client tells his social worker that he has committed a property crime, the social worker must weigh her obligations to the client against her obligations to society. Social control is one of the functions of every social worker, but so is the maintenance of a helping relationship. To which function should the practitioner give priority if she cannot pursue both at the same time? Does it matter whether the law violation harms another person? Can lawbreaking be overlooked when a client makes progress toward attaining identified and constructive intervention goals? Keep these questions in mind as you assess the ethical dilemmas posed in Exemplar 4.1.

4.1	SECURITY OR PROTECTION?

John Newton was a likable young man—22 years old, not steadily employed, but always willing to help. Even before Ray Dunkirk, the community worker, had arrived on the scene, John had organized a number of young adults into a club. This club was well known in the neighborhood for the many helpful services it provided. The community's elderly population was especially appreciative of the security services that the group gave them. Thefts and holdups of older people had ceased ever since this club began to operate in the community. However, Ray became aware that John had intimidated local store owners and obtained regular payoffs from them in return for promising them "protection." What was Ray Dunkirk to do? He considered various options, including the following:

- Overlooking John's protection racket in view of the many positive things he was doing that were benefiting the community
- Reporting John's protection racket to the police, because illegal activities should never be condoned
- Strengthening his relations with John with the view of helping to guide him away from the illegal activity; in the meantime, he would not report the law violation to the police

What are the ethical aspects in choosing the best option? One ethical dilemma is how to balance the best interests of the various persons and groups involved: older persons, storekeepers, the community, the larger society, and others. Another question concerns the ethics of doing something that might result in the return of violence against the older people of this community. The following discussion is intended to help social workers cope with these conflicts and find answers to these questions.

The "Least Harm" Principle

Sometimes social workers are confronted by problems for which there are no positive choices. Regardless of the option chosen by the client and/or the worker, some harm will come to one person or another, perhaps even to the client or to the social worker. What is the ethical choice in such situations? The "least harm" rule suggests choosing the option that will result in the least harm, the least permanent harm, or the most easily reversible harm. These are not always simple decisions, and in some cases, there are complex considerations. A social worker has to consider "the least harm to whom?" A given choice may result in the least harm to one person but major harm to another person.

Consider the options facing Ellen Ashton, the social worker who has to consider the options in the Madurai family situation (Exemplar 1.1). Does the least harm principle offer guidance in choosing the most ethical alternative? How?

Some have suggested that the routine application of the least harm principle may diminish the possibility of choosing the most effective intervention technique. There may be times when it is justified to use an option that has great risks but enhances the likelihood of a successful outcome. However, such a choice should be made only with the full consent and agreement of the client.

Efficiency and Effectiveness

Many people think that *efficiency* and *effectiveness* are synonyms, but there are important differences between the two terms, especially when it comes to ethical decision making. The **efficiency criterion** is concerned with the relative cost (including budget, staff time, agency, and community resources) of achieving a stated objective. Whenever two options will lead to the same result, the one that requires fewer resources is the more efficient one. The **effectiveness criterion,** on the other hand, relates to the degree to which the desired outcome is achieved. When the implementation of one option results in halving the number of poor people in a county, while the second option reduces the poverty population by 80%, the latter option is the more effective one—but its cost may be so high that it is considered inefficient.

Difficult choices arise when the more efficient option is the less effective one or vice versa. In addition, making decisions only on the basis of efficiency and effectiveness criteria may result in unethical decisions. At times, the most efficient or the most effective option must be rejected because of its ethical implications. As early as 1975, Cuba tracked down Cubans who had lived in Africa and tested them for diseases. Cuban officials also committed people to sanitariums when they tested HIV positive, where they were forced to remain, despite human rights complaints by Cubans and other persons. Later, some HIV-positive men and women were allowed to leave if their condom use and hygiene were approved (Aguilera, 2003). In the United States, these actions may be seen as highly effective at controlling the transmission of HIV but questionable from an ethical point of view. For example, sending poor people or people with chronic mental illness to another city or deporting them to another country may be the most effective and most efficient way of eliminating poverty or the expense of long-term or repeated hospitalizations, but such decisions must be dismissed out of hand by anyone who is concerned with the ethical implications of these proposed plans.

More often, the ethical assessment of an option is not as clear as in these examples, so a social worker may find it difficult to make a decision. For example, what are the ethical implications of forcing poor people to work, a more efficient option? Work is highly valued in our society, but *force* means limiting a person's freedom, another important value in our society. The ethical assessment, in this case, demands that we assess work and independence against the loss of freedom. In the past, social work ideology rejected the various "workfare" programs that forced poor people to work. With the implementation of Temporary Assistance for Needy Families (TANF), a change in societal and social work ideology and values is apparently taking place. Although a professional consensus on the issue may be lacking, there appears to be less agreement on whether "workfare" is ethical than was true in the past (Dolgoff, 2002).

Another kind of ethical quandary arises out of the continuing efforts to deinstitutionalize patients of mental hospitals. When this policy was first proposed some years ago, certain professionals supported and implemented the program because they thought it would right a wrong. In some instances, the option of releasing mentally ill patients from hospitals was adopted even though it was known that most communities lacked adequate resources for caring for these people. Many state governments were unable to help communities with the problem because they themselves were facing major budget cuts. How ethical was it to institute a strategy that might result in some long-range improvements, but in the short run might harm many fragile people, as well as others? Was it ethical to do so without first ensuring the availability of adequate community resources? Consider this question by using the ethical assessment screen (Figure 4.2). The ethical assessment screen provides a sequence of questions to be answered systematically that takes a person through the important variables to consider in order to arrive at a thoughtful and careful ethical decision.

RANK ORDERING ETHICAL PRINCIPLES

In the preceding sections we discussed a number of ethical criteria that some social workers have found helpful when assessing decision alternatives. These criteria have not been arranged in any order of priority. More specific guides are needed whenever two or more of these criteria point toward different alternatives. Even though some social workers disagree, we believe that the preferred way of resolving such conflicts among ethical principles is a lexical ordering of these principles—that is, rank ordering them from the most important to the least important. Such ordering is necessary even though "ordering principles is not an easy task" (Christensen, 1986, p. 82).

A lexical ordering of ethical principles can provide social workers with a guide, but such a guide is not meant to be a magic formula that can be applied blindly. As Baier (1958) suggested, the principle of priority should be used when two or more moral rules (standards) conflict. Based on the earlier work of a number of authors including Baier (1958), Kitchner (1984), Joseph (1985), Lewis (1984), Reamer (1983), Siporin (1983), and Zygmond and Boorhem (1989), we have prepared guides for ethical decision making. Social workers rarely make direct use of theoretical knowledge or philosophical principles when making practice decisions. Instead, they have integrated knowledge and values into a set of practice principles, and these are what social workers use at the critical points in the decision-making process. We have

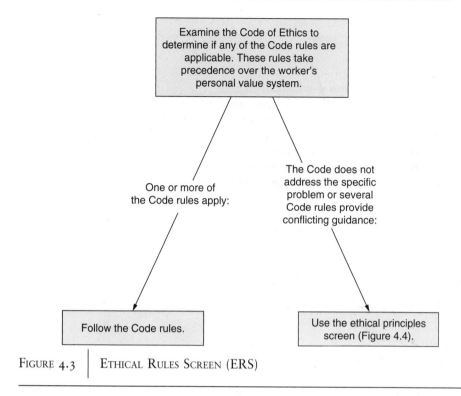

FIGURE 4.3 | ETHICAL RULES SCREEN (ERS)

used the work of the authors mentioned, as well as additional sources and our own practice experience, to prepare the following two guides or screens that we believe will be helpful in making ethical decisions. We call these guides the **ethical rules screen (ERS)** and the **ethical principles screen (EPS)** (see Figures 4.3 and 4.4). These guides are meant to be tools; they should not be applied blindly.

The ERS should always be used first. Only when this screen does not provide any satisfactory guidance should the social worker use the EPS. To be useful, a guide for rank ordering ethical principles must clearly indicate the order of priority of such principles. Once such a priority list has been established, the operating rule is that the satisfaction of a higher-order principle takes precedence over the satisfaction of a lower-order principle. Even though there is not yet any general agreement on the rank order of professional ethical principles, we have developed the EPS on the basis of our perception of what might be the consensus among social workers. All ethical principles are important. When more than one ethical principle is relevant in the analysis of a set of practice options and each of these principles leads to a different outcome, the rank order suggested in the EPS should be used to make a decision. In other words, an assessment based on Ethical Principle 1 is more compelling than one using Ethical Principles 2 or 3. For example, if both confidentiality (Principle 6) and full disclosure (Principle 7) apply, the ethical principle of confidentiality should receive priority. Because the EPS is the key ethical assessment tool for resolving ethical practice dilemmas, we will comment in detail on each of these principles.

FIGURE 4.4   ETHICAL PRINCIPLES SCREEN (EPS)

ETHICAL PRINCIPLE 1   The *protection of human life* applies to all persons, both to the life of a client and to the lives of all others. This principle takes precedence over every other obligation. "The right to life is the most basic of all rights, for if one's right to life is violated one cannot enjoy any other rights" (Kuhse & Singer, 1985, p. 509).

Most physicians follow this principle of saving and prolonging human life, regardless of the resulting quality of life or the economic costs involved. This life-sustaining principle received wide publicity through the cases of Karen Ann Quinlan and Terri Schiavo, whose physicians refused to withdraw life-support systems, even though these patients had been unconscious for many years and there was no further hope for any positive change. Today, physicians keep many Americans "alive" through the use of high-tech life-sustaining instruments. Social workers, on the other hand, tend to place more emphasis on improving the quality of life for individuals, groups, and communities. Most of the time, social workers are not aware of any conflict between the biophysical principle of sustaining life and the psychosocial principle of improving life. At times, however, there is conflict. One example is the case of a middle-aged man with marked hypertension. The medication that brought down his life-threatening blood pressure also caused sexual impotence (Roberts, 1989). Is it ethical for a social worker to support this client's decision to stop taking the medication so that he can once again enjoy sexual relations? Such a decision may lead to an improvement in the quality of his life (Ethical Principle 5), but it may also contribute to shortening his life span (Ethical Principle 1).

ETHICAL PRINCIPLE 2   The *principle of equality and inequality* suggests that all persons in the same circumstances should be treated in the same way—that is, persons in equivalent situations have the right to be treated equally. At the same time, persons in different situations have the right to be treated differently if the inequality is relevant to the issue in question. Unequal treatment can be justified when other considerations such as beneficence (the duty to do good, not harm others) outweigh the equality principle or on the grounds that such unequal treatment will promote greater equality (Frankena, 1973, p. 52). This principle was formulated by Kitchner (1984) and is based on the seminal work of Rawls (1971). Kitchner specifically applied this principle to ethics; she taught that a principle can suggest an obligation, but if there are special circumstances or conflicting obligations, one should always act on the basis of the obligations derived from the higher principle.

This principle applies in situations that involve child abuse or elder abuse because the abused child (or elder) and the abuser are not in an equal position. In these circumstances, the principles of confidentiality and autonomy with respect to the abusing adult are of a lower rank order than the obligation to protect the child or older person, even when it is not a question of life and death. Another situation in which this principle applies occurs when several families apply for limited resources. For example, after a natural disaster, many families may need emergency housing, but higher priority may be given to finding housing for families with small children or frail elderly and lower priority may be given to families with only healthy adults. Should family composition or prior lifestyles be taken into consideration? In situations where one family is demonstrably nearer nutritional or other disaster, the ethical principle permits or even requires the unequal allocation of scarce resources.

ETHICAL PRINCIPLE 3   A social worker should make practice decisions that *foster a person's self-determination, autonomy, independence, and freedom.* Freedom, though highly important, does not override the right to life or survival of the person him- or herself or of others. A person does not have the right to decide to harm someone else on the grounds that the right to make such a decision is his or her autonomous right. When a person is about to make such a decision, the social worker is obligated to intervene because Ethical Principle 1 takes precedence.

The risk/benefit ratio may also help determine when the autonomy principle applies and when it is ethical to ignore a client's "decision." If the condition facing a client is life threatening and if the risk of intervention is minimal (while the potential benefit of the intervention is great), the social worker may consider proceeding even without a client's consent. In this situation, the client's refusal may or may not be considered an indication of his lack of competency.[1] On the other hand, if the risk is great and the potential benefit minimal, the client's refusal is logical and should be accepted.

ETHICAL PRINCIPLE 4   The *least harm principle* holds that when faced with dilemmas that have the potential for causing harm, a social worker should attempt to avoid or prevent such harm. When harm is unavoidable, a social worker should always choose the option that will cause the least harm, the least permanent harm, and/or the most

---

[1]Competency is a legal construct and may vary by state; social workers should know the process and requirements for having someone declared incompetent in the state(s) in which they practice.

easily reversible harm. If harm has been done, the social worker should attempt where possible to repair the harm done.

ETHICAL PRINCIPLE 5   A social worker should choose the option that promotes a better *quality of life* for all people, for the individual as well as for the community. Consistent with the Code of Ethics, "social workers should promote the general welfare of society, from local to global levels, and the development of people, their communities, and their environments" (NASW Code, 1999, 6.01).

ETHICAL PRINCIPLE 6   A social worker should make practice decisions that strengthen every person's *right to privacy and confidentiality*. Keeping confidential information inviolate is a direct derivative of this obligation. Professionals have a duty to protect the privacy of clients and groups to the greatest extent possible consistent with laws and the will and agreement of the clients. Confidentiality, however, is not sacrosanct when the social worker can prevent violence or harm of a serious nature to others.

ETHICAL PRINCIPLE 7   A social worker should make practice decisions that permit her to speak the truth and to *fully disclose all relevant information* to her client and to others. Social and professional relationships require trust in order to function well, and trust, in turn, is based on honest dealing that minimizes surprises so that mutual expectations are generally fulfilled.

APPLICATION OF ETHICAL DECISION-MAKING SCREENS

Let us try to apply these two ethical decision-making screens to analyze Exemplars 4.2, 4.3, and 4.4.

4.2 | WHAT WILL HAPPEN TO JIMMY PREGO?

Jimmy Prego is a passive, deeply disturbed early adolescent who lives in a therapeutic home where he has sometimes had to be protected from other residents. He is now ready to be moved to a less restrictive environment but clearly needs a therapeutic foster home, something your supervisor originally suggested. You have contacted such a home and begun plans to move Jimmy in about two weeks. When you inform your supervisor that you have initiated the move and that everything is proceeding as usual, he tells you that space has become available in an even less restricted group home run by your agency and that it would be appropriate to move Jimmy to the group home instead of the therapeutic foster home.

You tell your supervisor that you will check it out, but he seems a little uncomfortable. When you check out the group home, you discover the residents are older, bigger, and more aggressive than Jimmy. You do not agree that the group home is appropriate for Jimmy, who has had difficulty defending himself where he currently resides. Also, you learn that the agency has placed pressure on the supervisors to boost the group home's census, an action related to agency financial considerations. Jimmy's mother is unable to assist in making the decision because of overwhelming personal and mental health problems. Jimmy's problems and his youth make him incapable of making the decision. Mrs. Prego insists that she trusts you and trusts that you will do what is best for Jimmy.

Several issues are involved in this exemplar. Ethical Principles 4 (least harm) and 5 (quality of life) are particularly relevant here. Will the least harm be done by confronting your supervisor and succeeding in obtaining the placement in the therapeutic home, even if it means reducing the agency income when that is what the agency needs? When you examine the Code of Ethics for applicable standards, you find that your "primary responsibility is to promote the well-being of clients" (NASW Code, 1999, 1.01). Who is your client and to whom do you owe loyalty—Jimmy, his mother, your supervisor, your agency, or yourself—as you make your decision about the correct thing to do? Whose best interest takes priority, that of the client, agency, or worker? In addition, some social workers might argue that Ethical Principle 5 is relevant because the worker wants to promote a better quality of life for Jimmy Prego and the right treatment situation will support that outcome.

Next, who is competent to make decisions? When clients lack "the capacity to provide informed consent, social workers should protect clients' interests by seeking permission from an appropriate third party" (NASW Code, 1999, 1.03c). Jimmy is not capable of making an informed choice. Mrs. Prego trusts you and wants you to make the best decision for her son. Is your supervisor an appropriate third party? He is placing the agency needs before those of Jimmy. In addition, "social workers should not allow an employing organization's policies, procedures, regulations, or administrative orders to interfere with their ethical practice of social work" (NASW Code, 1999, 3.09d). You, the social worker, may be the only one in this situation who is competent to make decisions for the best interest and protection of Jimmy and to advocate for the right treatment plan. Jimmy's needs take priority over the supervisor's, the agency's, and your own needs. Exemplar 4.3 provides another example.

4.3	STARTING IN PRIVATE PRACTICE

Cliff Baxter is an experienced social worker who recently resigned his agency job in order to devote all of his time to private practice. Before Cliff left the agency, Dennis Norton, a colleague in the agency, told him that he would be willing to refer clients to him for a "finder's fee." As in many private practice beginnings, Cliff is having a difficult time making ends meet. His income last month was not even sufficient to pay the rent for the office. Should he give Dennis a call?

We will use the ERS and examine the NASW Code of Ethics to determine if there are any rules relevant to this situation. The NASW Code (2.06c) states: "Social workers are prohibited from giving or receiving payment for a referral when no professional service is provided by the referring social worker." This rule provides such clear and unambiguous guidance that no further screening seems necessary. Cliff should not call Dennis to take advantage of his offer. Are there ethical issues if Cliff calls Dennis and lets him know he would be happy to accept referrals, but he cannot pay a finder's fee? Should Cliff report Dennis's unethical practice?

In Exemplar 4.4, we will apply the EPS.

| **4.4** | THE WRONG MAN SITS IN PRISON |

Raul Lovaas has been enrolled in a drug rehabilitation program to break his cocaine addiction. The program's treatment routine includes pharmacological treatment, group therapy, and individual therapy. You are his social worker. You have succeeded in establishing a good relationship with Raul in the daily treatment sessions. One morning Raul tells you that, some years ago, he accidentally injured a bank guard during a holdup. He was never caught by the police, but another man was convicted for this crime and now sits in prison on a lengthy sentence. For several days you have been trying to convince Raul that he should talk to the police in order to free an innocent man from prison. Raul not only refused to listen to your suggestion but said that he expects you to keep in complete confidence what he has told you. What should you do?

These are some of the thoughts that you have:

1. Raul has neither a legal nor a moral right to have another man serve a lengthy sentence for a crime that Raul committed.
2. The "wrong" that you may cause by breaking confidentiality is hardly of the same importance as the wrong inflicted on an innocent person who is now imprisoned.
3. The effectiveness of the entire program may be compromised if it becomes known that social workers do not always keep confidential the information they receive from clients.
4. On the other hand, your whistle-blowing can cause the release of the wrongly convicted person.

We will focus our analysis on the latter two considerations because the first point, though obvious, does not relate directly to what you, the social worker, should do, but rather to what the client is ethically required to do. At least two ethical principles are involved in the second consideration: Ethical Principle 3, the principle of autonomy and freedom, specifically the freedom of an innocent man who is now imprisoned; and Ethical Principle 6, the principle of confidentiality, specifically respecting the confidence of the information that your client, Raul, gave you. Some may also base their decision on Ethical Principle 2, the principle of equality and inequality, because an innocent man in prison is obviously not in an equal situation and requires additional resources in order to regain access to equal opportunities. Because Ethical Principle 6 (confidentiality) is of a lower order than Ethical Principles 2 and 3, the second consideration leads to the decision that you are ethically justified in breaking confidence and reporting to the police what you have learned from Raul.

From a practice point of view, the third consideration may be especially important because in most situations we would hesitate to do anything that might impede the effectiveness of an intervention. It might be argued that a program that can improve the quality of life (Ethical Principle 5) of many addicts should receive preference over the quality of life of one individual, even if that person is falsely imprisoned. It is likely, however, that such reasoning involves a number of fallacies, including the following:

- We have no information on the effectiveness of this rehabilitation program. How effective is it in improving the quality of life of all/most/some participants?
- We do not know what impact, if any, breaking confidentiality will have on the effectiveness of the program. It may well be that other participants will be happy that the worker was instrumental in freeing an innocent person from prison.
- Statistical probabilities are never a permissible substitute for ethical screening.

In other words, the quality of life principle (Ethical Principle 5) is not relevant in this situation, but even if it were, it would be of a lower order than Ethical Principles 2 and 3. Consideration 3 is therefore not relevant and should be ignored in making an ethical decision. We would conclude that you are obligated to inform the police if you are unable to convince Raul to do so himself.

THE IMPORTANCE OF IDENTIFYING ONE'S OWN HIERARCHY OF VALUES

Although the NASW Code of Ethics (1999) recognizes "the possibility of conflicts among the Code's values, principles, and standards," it does not specify which values, principles, and standards are most important and ought to outweigh others in instances when they conflict. Nevertheless, social workers are frequently faced with conflicting standards and loyalties and a hierarchy may help when choosing among principles. Earlier we introduced our lexical arrangement of ethical principles based on our own work and that of others. Ultimately, each social worker when faced with conflicts in ethical standards or loyalties must utilize such a priority ladder. The reason we emphasized the need for each social worker to carefully clarify her own values is that each social worker, when faced with dilemmas, must depend on her own hierarchy of principles.

Originally, Loewenberg and Dolgoff (1988) based the hierarchy on their perception of what the common consensus might be, and the hierarchical list of principles was changed in the following edition (Loewenberg & Dolgoff, 1992). Beyerstein (1993) suggested that because a professional code of ethics is created through a democratic process, members of the profession can only agree on the obvious and they "fudge" difficult or contentious principles through compromise, leaving the choice of a hierarchy of principles to the individual decision maker.

Over time, the makeup of the profession itself has become more diverse as a result of immigration and other societal and professional factors, including generational and other differences, which may result in more disagreement about the relative importance of ethical principles. We have found that there is little agreement on the rank ordering of the ethical principles, suggesting that perceptions may change over time.

SUMMARY AND CONCLUSIONS

In this chapter, we have examined a series of guidelines and decision-making tools that social workers can use when making ethical decisions. We noted that every social worker is confronted by ethical dilemmas and that these always require choices that must be made before action can be taken. Iserson (1986) suggested that we ask three questions as a final check before moving to the action phase of ethical decision making:

1. *Impartiality* Would you be willing to act the way you have chosen if you were in the other person's place? This question asks the social worker to consider the effect her action would have if she or a member of her family or other loved ones were the recipients of the action. The purpose of this question is to correct for partiality and self-interest and to minimize or prevent the possibility they will play too dominant a part in the decision.
2. *Generalization* Are you willing to undertake this action in similar circumstances? Generalizing a particular decision may reduce bias and partiality, but it also may blind one to the unique qualities of a situation that demands a unique response, one that would not generally be used in many other situations. When one evaluates a particular action in light of its general applicability to similar situations, one is concerned with both the breadth and range of effects and the short- and long-range consequences. The purpose of this question is to make the social worker think of the consequences of an action beyond the short term and to consider it not as a particular instance but as a justified general practice in similar circumstances.
3. *Justifiability* Can you explain and justify your decision to others? The purpose of this question is to make certain that you have, in the available time, consciously and purposefully considered the options and have made certain the client's rights and best interests are served by your professional actions in the context of the values and standards of the profession.

EXERCISES

1. In the previous chapter, we asked you to rank order the seven ethical principles. How does your rank ordering compare to the ethical principles screen (EPS)? After completing this chapter, has your rank ordering changed? Compare your rank ordering with that of others in your class and discuss why you ordered the principles differently.
2. Identify two ethical decisions you recently made or learned of that took place in social work practice. On the basis of the ethical assessment screen and the ethical principles screen (EPS), would you change your or the other social worker's ethical decision?
3. If when you read the NASW Code of Ethics you believe the Code assumes that one particular ethical standard is the highest priority for social workers' ethical behavior, which standard do you think it is?
4. The director of a drug addiction rehabilitation program faces a difficult budget allocation decision. He has sufficient budget to mount only one of the two programs his agency would like to offer. Program A is geared to elementary school students. It will serve 500 children from some of the city's most troubled neighborhoods. Past experience has shown that without such a program 200 children will be addicted by the time they are 16 years old. With such a program, it is expected that no more than 50 will become addicted. Program B focuses on the rehabilitation of adolescent drug addicts. Fifty teens can be served each year, with a 60% success rate. What ethical considerations should the director examine? What ethical rules and ethical principles can he use to help him make a decision? How does the availability of the outcome data provided affect the decision-making process?

5. In Exemplar 4.2 there is a conflict between the needs of the client and the needs of the agency. Social workers who provide direct service may have a different perspective on this dilemma than social workers who are supervisors or agency administrators. Arrange to talk to someone who is in a different position than you are about his or her perspective on this issue; how did this discussion influence your perspective?

Suggestions for Additional Readings

Dean (1998) describes her view of "The Primacy of the Ethical Aim in Clinical Social Work: Its Relationship to Social Justice and Mental Health" concepts. Kurri (2005) in "Placement of Responsibility and Moral Reasoning in Couple Therapy" illustrates the importance of moral and ethical judgments in family and couple therapy. Hadjistavropoulos and Malloy (1999) argue for a philosophical and practical ranking of ethical principles in "Ethical Principles of the American Psychological Association" as does Kitchener (1984) in "Intuition, Critical Evaluation and Ethical Principles: The Foundation for Ethical Decisions in Counseling Psychology." Landau and Osmo (2003) explore "Professional and Personal Hierarchies of Ethical Principles." Smith (2004) argues that social work is more than a series of technical activities based on what works, particular role expectations, and regulatory and legal frameworks. Individual encounters between social workers and those being served are morally charged in regard to their impact on the service users' well-being.

ETHICAL DILEMMAS IN PROFESSIONAL PRACTICE

Confidentiality and Informed Consent

A person's right to privacy is a first-order value in our culture. Every person has a right to determine *when, how,* and to *what* extent he or she wants to share (or have shared) personal information with others. Even though the Constitution does not explicitly mention a right to privacy, Chief Justice Richard B. Hughes of the New Jersey Supreme Court wrote, "Supreme Court decisions have recognized that a right of personal privacy exists and that certain areas of privacy are guaranteed under the Constitution" (*In re Quinlan,* 170 NJ 10, 1976). Privacy is protected under the Constitution in certain circumstances. The Supreme Court in the landmark case *Griswold v. Connecticut* (1965) ruled that the Constitution protected a right to privacy. The case involved a Connecticut law that prohibited the use of contraceptives. The Supreme Court invalidated the law on the grounds that it violated the right to marital privacy. A number of Supreme Court rulings supported this right, although the right to privacy does not appear in the Bill of Rights. Privacy, thus, is a protected value but with some limitations. Privacy of school records is limited, and individuals have no right to sue a school for releasing records covered by the Family Educational Rights and Privacy Act (*Gonzaga v. Doe,* 2002). The USA Patriot Act (2001) served to diminish privacy rights as antiterrorist legislation made it easier for law enforcement persons to conduct electronic surveillance.

The professional ethical principle of confidentiality is derived from the privacy societal value, and confidentiality is highly valued in countries that emphasize individual rights, such as the United States (Congress & McAuliffe, 2006). This principle is not a modern invention but was already recognized in ancient times by Hippocrates. The physician's oath that is attributed to him states, "What I may see or hear in the course of treatment . . . I will keep to myself, holding such things shameful to be spoken about" (Van Hoose & Kottler, 1985, p. 7). In the NASW Code of Ethics this principle appears as a major standard:

Social workers should respect clients' right to privacy. Social workers should not solicit private information from clients unless it is essential to providing services or conducting social work evaluation or research. Once private information is shared, standards of confidentiality apply (NASW Code, 1999, 1.07a).

Seventeen other paragraphs (1.07b through 1.07r) provide additional explanations and limitations. For example, valid consent is required before social workers can disclose confidential information (107b), and clients should be informed to the extent possible of disclosure of confidential information and the potential consequences of such disclosure (1.07d). However, information may be disclosed if compelling professional reasons exist, such as imminent harm to a client. Where disclosure is required, only the minimal amount of information necessary to achieve the goals should be shared (1.07c). Social workers should discuss with clients and other interested parties the nature and limitations of their right to confidentiality (1.07e).

In addition, social workers providing services to couples, families, or other groups "should seek agreement among the parties involved concerning each individual's right to confidentiality and obligation to preserve the confidentiality of information shared by others" (1.07f); they should also inform clients of policies "concerning ... disclosure of confidential information among the parties involved in the counseling" (1.07g). Social workers "should not disclose identifying information when discussing clients for teaching or training purposes unless the client has consented to disclosure of confidential information" (1.07p) or with consultants unless the client has consented to disclosure or there is a compelling need for such disclosure (1.07q). Confidential information should not be discussed in public areas (1.07i), and client records, including electronic files, should be stored in a secure location (1.07l). In addition, "reasonable precautions [should be taken] to protect client confidentiality in the event of the social worker's termination of practice, incapacitation, or death" (1.07o).

PRIVACY AND CONFIDENTIALITY

Privacy and confidentiality are often confused (Congress & McAuliffe, 2006). **Privacy** refers to people's right to decide what, if any, information about them is shared with others. **Confidentiality** means that a social worker or other professional (or bureaucrat) will not reveal to anyone information that she has received from a client without the client's informed consent. However, it is not always easy or possible for a social worker to implement this rule. The Code itself recognizes the possibility that "compelling professional reasons" may require a social worker to reveal information received in confidence "when disclosure is necessary to prevent serious, foreseeable, and imminent harm to a client or other identifiable person" (NASW Code, 1.07c). The nature of some of these compelling reasons will be discussed later in this chapter under the section entitled "Duty to Protect." Even those who are committed to practicing in an ethical manner and who want to observe confidentiality face ethical dilemmas in this area. Social workers may not be able to maintain confidentiality when they have a duty to protect the privacy of a client, participate in interdisciplinary teams that require sharing of information, are required to provide accountability data, or must respond to requests for information from third-party payers. Furthermore, there are situations in which courts order disclosures, and disclosures may be required in some settings such as probation and parole.

Confidentiality is a principle that affirms the explicit promise or contract to reveal nothing about an individual except under conditions known and agreed to by the client, with the exception of those which require disclosure for "compelling professional reasons." Social workers and clients may differ in their perceptions of this issue. Millstein (2000) found in a study of experienced social work practitioners that almost three quarters of them strongly agreed that confidentiality is necessary to maintain therapeutic relationships; however, fewer than half believe that clients expect that confidentiality will be maintained. An ethical dilemma occurs whenever a practitioner has to choose among conflicting claims that may be equally valid, such as choosing between a client's right to privacy and the right of other people and of society to certain information.

Social workers generally assume that a client's reliance on confidentiality promotes trust in the professional practitioner. Many think that this relationship with the professional would be harmed if clients were aware that there are limits to confidentiality. However, empirical studies do not support the assumption that limiting confidentiality necessarily endangers the client/social worker relationship. Steinberg, Levine, and Doueck (1997) found that only 27% of clients of psychotherapists withdrew from treatment immediately or shortly after they became aware that the therapist had made a mandated child abuse report. Retention in treatment was higher when the informed consent procedure was more explicit and when the reported perpetrator was a third party not involved in the treatment. Similarly, Weinstein and colleagues (2000) found that when mental health professionals reported suspected child abuse and maltreatment, three quarters of the patients did not terminate their treatment and, in many cases, the therapeutic process was enhanced.

Confidentiality is an especially problematic issue because this ethical principle is based on an oversimplified practice model that includes only the social worker and the client. The reality, however, is much more complex. For example, a child maltreatment case typically involves not only the child who has been maltreated and the adult perpetrator, but also the child's parents, other siblings, and relatives, as well as society and its agents (such as police and courts), child protective services workers, other social workers, colleagues from other fields, administrative personnel, insurance companies, and third-party payers. Each of these may make conflicting demands for confidential information. The ethical considerations for sharing confidential information with each of these participants will differ from person to person because there are varying legal and ethical obligations to share. Marshall and Solomon (2004) stated that "although the importance of confidentiality policies is clear, the implementation of these policies often impedes communication between providers, consumers, and families." Below we discuss confidentiality issues as they relate to working with various other professional practitioners and various service systems.

OTHER SOCIAL WORKERS

Often we do not give sufficient thought to the ethical implications of sharing confidential information with other social workers. We are not referring here to small talk at a cocktail party (which is clearly a violation of confidentiality), but to formal or informal consultations with colleagues or supervisors, as well as to the transmission of such information to other social workers who have a professional interest in the information (such as a social worker who is working with other members of the same family, the social worker who will take over the case while the worker is on vacation, and so on). This type of information transmission is intended for the client's benefit because it is meant to assure more effective service, but is it ethical to share this information to others without the client's consent? In many cases, a general informed consent agreement may be helpful, but many clients will sign it as a routine matter, perhaps without really understanding its meanings or implications. Taking special care to make certain a client understands the intention of the form and periodically revisiting the issue of confidentiality and informed consent may be required (we will discuss informed consent later in this chapter).

The 1999 Code of Ethics provides some guidance on this issue. The limitations of confidentiality should be discussed with clients early in the professional relationship (1.07e). When a client has been previously served by another agency or colleague, "social workers should discuss with the client whether consultation with the previous service provider is in the client's best interest" (3.06b). These sections of the Code advise that it is generally not ethical to share information about the client with other social workers without the client's prior consent. However, the social worker should also consider the possible harm that may be caused by not providing vital information to colleagues who are now working with that client. It is this consideration that led Taylor and Adelman (1989) to conclude that "keeping information confidential can seriously hamper an intervener's efforts to help" (p. 80). How can social workers balance the need to protect clients' confidentiality with the need to share information so that the best service can be provided?

COLLEAGUES FROM OTHER FIELDS

Many social workers practice on multidisciplinary teams or in settings where information must be shared with colleagues from other professions whose confidentiality practices may differ from those of social workers. All social workers are aware that "timely and effective interagency collaboration can have many benefits for both clients and workers" (Darlington, Feeney, & Rixon, 2005, p. 1086). Even though it is important to protect confidentiality, it is also important to seek consultation from and collaboration with others when needed. Differences in agency confidentiality policies can be a barrier to effective collaboration, but two or more agencies can formalize and coordinate the consent process and establish specific methods for information exchange, perhaps reducing this potential barrier (Darlington et al., 2005, p. 1094). Frost, Robinson, and Anning (2005) found that issues of confidentiality and information sharing policies were key concerns for social workers who participate in multidisciplinary teams. Problems arose both in relation to social workers being unable to access information from other agencies (e.g., health records) and from their inability to share information from their databases with professionals from other agencies.

Some social workers are required to share information with others because of the type of position they occupy. For example, those who provide case management services are obligated to share information about the client. However, the client must consent to what information will be shared with which agencies before the social worker can share confidential information. Before giving consent, the client must be made aware of what information will be shared with whom—otherwise his consent is almost meaningless.

The Community

Green (2003) suggests that confidentiality and privacy raise critical dilemmas especially for social workers in rural communities. In these small communities it may be difficult to protect a client's privacy because neighbors may see him enter the social worker's office. Members of the community may feel entitled to certain information and may pressure the social worker to share information in order to protect community members. For example, community members may feel that they have the right to be notified about sexual offenses, particularly against children. Under Megan's Law and the Adam Walsh Child Protection Act of 2006 (H.R. 4472) communities are notified of convicted sexual offenders through the National Sex Offender Registry and state registries. However, this protection exists only after a person has been convicted of a sexual offense. What is the social worker's responsibility if she knows her client has committed a sexual offense, but has not been convicted?

Administrative and Electronic Records

Social agencies and other employing organizations require that all social workers report information about their clients and client contacts, because they need such data for administrative and accountability reasons. The initial request to supply these data may be entirely proper, but once the requested information has been transmitted, the practitioner is no longer able to protect its confidentiality. As the use of computerized records becomes more common in social agencies, this aspect of the confidentiality issue has become even more crucial. The 1999 Code of Ethics specifically addresses these issues, requiring social workers to "take precautions to ensure and maintain the confidentiality of information transmitted to other parties through the use of computers, electronic mail, facsimile machines, telephones and telephone answering machines, and other electronic or computer technology. Disclosure of identifying information should be avoided wherever possible" (1.07m). The Health Insurance Portability and Accountability Act (HIPAA) (1996) requirements may be helpful in this area as health care agencies are required to develop procedures to protect the confidentiality of client information (HIPAA will be discussed in more detail later in this chapter). It is not simply the electronic transmission of data, however, that requires precautions. Today, when computers are used frequently to store case and process records, serious thought must be given to ensuring their security.

Morin and colleagues (2005) examined older adults' comfort with electronic health records, and found that most were comfortable with having their health data available electronically. Only a few were concerned about errors and confidentiality. Almost all of these patients provided appropriate informed consent for permitting access to their electronic health records, but many did not remember that they could withdraw their consent at any time, suggesting that they may not have fully understood the consent information.

Interestingly, some people like the anonymity provided by the Internet and believe that it actually protects confidentiality. In addition, "the Internet improves access to service for those who may not gain access otherwise. Individuals who are stigmatized, shy, or embarrassed to share personal problems are 'faceless' on the World Wide Web and have been found to be more willing to participate in groups dealing with delicate issues" (Parker-Oliver & Demiris, 2006, p. 130, citing Vernberg & Schuh, 2002). However, it is unclear whether people who feel more anonymous and safe do so because they do not fully understand the potential for being identified in these circumstances.

INSURANCE COMPANIES AND THIRD-PARTY PAYERS

New dimensions have been added to the problem of confidentiality as more and more social workers are required to report diagnoses to insurance companies or other third-party payers in order to qualify clients for reimbursement. While clients may consent to sharing this information because they are interested in having a third party pay for part or all of the services they receive from a social worker, they are not always aware of the diagnosis reported or who will be privy to this information. In addition to the issue of confidentiality, the severity of the diagnosis may be overstated in order to qualify clients for reimbursement. If clients are aware that third-party payers may share confidential information with others, including their employers and future service providers, they may prefer to pay for the services of the social worker out of their own pocket. The 1999 Code of Ethics specifically states that "social workers should not disclose confidential information to third-party payers unless clients have authorized such disclosure" (1.07h).

POLICE

In many states, the law requires that social workers, as well as other professional practitioners, inform the police whenever they acquire information about criminal activities that have taken place or are being planned. For example, a social worker is present when an adolescent street gang discusses plans for a holdup—what is expected of her? Should she have any ethical qualms about reporting the gang's intentions to the police? What is her obligation when a third party (such as a parent or neighbor) tells her about such a plan? At the very least, she must ask herself several questions: How reliable is the report? Can the information be provided without revealing the source? How might such revelation affect the helping relationship? What harm can be prevented or result by informing the police? The situation has a number of legal and ethical elements. To whom does the social worker owe her primary loyalty—to the gang, parents, neighbors, the police, or society? What harm could be prevented by her report? All of these and other questions have legal, professional, and ethical implications. Many social workers are perplexed by ethical dilemmas arising out of various other kinds of law violations, particularly delinquent acts that do not seem to harm others. Exemplar 5.1 describes one such situation that raises a number of ethical questions about reporting possibly illegal behavior.

5.1	FRAUD AND AN AGING MOTHER

Social worker Jean Fisher is a marriage counselor and family therapist in the Old Town Family Consultation Center, a nonsectarian United Way agency. Sue and Dean Kern have been coming to her for marital therapy once a week for the past two months. Though their problem is not critical, they came to seek help while their marriage was still salvageable. They have made good progress toward reaching their goal. During today's session Dean mentioned that he has continued to receive supplemental security income (SSI) payments for his aged mother, who lived with them until she moved overseas two years ago. She now makes her home with his sister, who lives in England.

Should Jean report this case as possible fraud? Does client/worker confidentiality cover this communication? According to the Code, disclosure required by law or regulations is a compelling reason to break confidentiality (1999, 1.07e); therefore, it is important for social workers to know the reporting regulations in their jurisdiction and act accordingly. At the same time, Jean must consider what might happen to the client/therapist relationship if she does report what she has learned. Should she discuss the possible consequences of their activities with the clients in an attempt to persuade them to change their behavior so that she will not have to report them? What would Jean's obligation be if she had learned that Dean had escaped from prison 10 years ago? Or that Sue was pushing drugs? Does the seriousness of the offense change the ethical considerations? Does the degree of harm to the client or someone else make a difference?

RELATIVES

Are the relatives of a client entitled to confidential information that might affect them? What should the social worker do if a son asks whether his father is dying when the father, who is terminally ill, has specifically asked that none of his relatives be told how ill he is? How does the social worker decide whether to keep the confidence or tell the truth? Do the relatives of a person living with HIV have the right to know about the person's health status? Does the type of relationship matter (e.g., a spouse or a sibling)? This is a type of ethical dilemma that may be especially acute for social workers who are engaged in settings such as health care and genetic counseling and who are privy to medical and or genetic information that may affect the health of relatives (Freedman, 1998).

Are parents entitled to confidential information about their children? Does the age of the child make a difference? For example, Planned Parenthood researchers in Wisconsin found that most girls under 18 would stop or limit their use of health services at family planning clinics if their parents had to be told they were seeking prescribed contraceptives (Flaherty, 2002). Consider Exemplar 5.2, which discusses confidentiality in a school setting.

Should Debbie's parents be told about their daughter's pregnancy? Should child protective services be told about the situation? What is the ethical decision in this ambiguous situation? Should the social worker respond differently if Debbie is older, if she is 16 or 18 years of age and is willing to identify the father of the baby?

5.2   DEBBIE ROBERTS IS PREGNANT

Debbie Roberts is a 12-year-old sixth grader who is 10 weeks pregnant. She has been a good student, and her teacher reports that she has never had any problems with Debbie. The school nurse referred Debbie to the school social worker because Debbie refused to discuss her condition with the nurse. At first, Debbie also refused to speak to the social worker, but later she told her that she did not want to have an abortion. Debbie asked the social worker to make arrangements so that she could carry to full term; she repeatedly emphasized that she did not want her parents to know that she was pregnant. Debbie will not reveal who the father is, and the social worker suspects that Debbie may have been sexually abused.

CLIENTS

What are a social worker's obligations when a client wants information about himself, such as wanting to read his own case record? According to the Code of Ethics, "social workers should provide clients with reasonable access to records concerning the clients...Social workers should limit clients' access to their records, or portions of their records, only in exceptional circumstances when there is compelling evidence that such access would cause serious harm to the client" (1999, 1.08a). Ambiguities about what constitutes "reasonable access," "exceptional circumstances," or "serious harm" make it difficult to implement this standard.

There are a number of arguments against sharing confidential information with the client, especially against granting him unlimited access to his own record:

- The case record may contain information supplied on a confidential basis by a third party, such as another social worker, teacher, neighbor, or relative. According to the Code of Ethics, "when providing clients with access to their records, social workers should take steps to protect the confidentiality of other individuals identified or discussed in such records" (1999, 1.08b). This suggests that while the social worker needs to protect the confidentiality of others mentioned in the client's record, this is not a sufficient reason to deny the client access to his records.
- The case record may contain "raw data" that have not yet been checked or evaluated, or test results or other data that may be misinterpreted by a lay person. The Code of Ethics requires social workers to "provide assistance in interpreting the records and consultation with the client regarding the records" (1999, 1.08a). Therefore, this may not be a sufficient argument for denying access to client records.
- The social worker may use the case record to explore various options or to ask herself questions that need further clarification; when the client reads such material, his trust in the worker may be impaired. In this situation, the social worker will need to assess the potential for serious harm to the client that may be caused by his reading the record. If this is the case, then access may be limited or denied (Code of Ethics, 1999, 1.08a).
- Reading or hearing negative information about himself may hurt the client. Again, if the potential for serious harm exists, then access may be denied.

Whenever the social worker denies access to the record, "clients' requests and the rationale for withholding some or all of the record(s) should be documented in clients' files" (Code of Ethics, 1999, 1.08b).

On the other hand, there are also several arguments in favor of giving clients access to their own case records:

- Reading the information gives the client an opportunity to correct mistakes.
- A client can give informed consent to share information with others only if he knows what this information is.
- Knowledge of information may lead to change, while ignorance will result in only maintaining the present unsatisfactory situation.
- Opening the case record will demonstrate the efficacy of client/worker cooperation and may be followed by even greater client participation in the social work process.

We have presented a number of (but not all) arguments for and against opening case records to clients in order to help social workers arrive at an ethical decision. Admittedly, this is a decision that few social workers employed in agencies have to make alone because, generally, agency policy and directives on this point are specific and clear. However, if you were asked to present to an agency board of directors on the issue of client access to records, what would your recommendations be? If you were in private practice, what policies would you decide on regarding client access to records?

LIMITS TO CONFIDENTIALITY

Clearly, there are limits to confidentiality. In one of the first meetings between the client and the social worker, the nature of confidentiality should be explained to clients and other interested parties, including the limitations of the clients' right to confidentiality. This information may need to be reviewed periodically throughout the professional relationship (NASW Code of Ethics, 1999, 1.07e). However, in what detail should these limitations be discussed? Weinstein et al. (2000) found that about 40% of experienced mental health practitioners *did not* inform clients about the limits of confidentiality until information came up that they were required by law to report to the authorities. At the same time, Weinstein et al. found that informing clients about the limits of confidentiality did not deter them from entering treatment. We will discuss these issues in greater detail later in this chapter.

HEALTH INSURANCE PORTABILITY AND ACCOUNTABILITY ACT (HIPAA, 1996)

Social workers and others (health plans, health care clearinghouses, and health care providers who transmit health information electronically) are expected to be in compliance with HIPAA requirements. The Department of Health and Human Services (DHHS) established a standardized electronic format for eight common health care transactions: claims payment and remittance advice, coordination of benefits, eligibility for a health plan, enrollment and disenrollment in a health plan, health care claim status, premium payments, and referral certification and authorization. The 2002 HIPAA privacy regulations (P.L. 104-191; Standards for Privacy,

2002) amended the original act by replacing the requirement for patient authorization with only a notice of the provider's privacy policy for information about treatment, payment, or health care operations. Yang and Kombarakaran (2006) suggest that the 2002 HIPAA provisions provide less protection than the original 1996 provisions and allow greater opportunities for breaches of confidentiality. But this amended rule does not preclude social workers from obtaining a written consent prior to release of information for treatment and payment. Providers are still required to have a separate written authorization from the client for each *nonroutine* use and disclosure of health information (Yang & Kombarakaran, 2006) and there are special HIPAA privacy protections for "psychotherapy notes" (Reamer, 2005, p. 117).

In states where minors can give consent to health care treatments, they also have the right to make their own decisions about the release of protected health information. In those states, their parents are not considered to be their personal representatives for this purpose. In some states, minors are permitted to consent to drug and alcohol counseling, mental health treatment, or health care regarding pregnancy without parental consent. In these states, social workers may exercise their discretion to deny or provide access to the records by a parent. If a parent voluntarily consents to a confidentiality agreement between the minor and the social worker, the minor can also make individual decisions about the use and disclosure of their own protected health information. If a state law has specific provisions that grant or deny access by the parents to minors' health information, the state law applies (NASW, October 1, 2002). HIPAA was passed in 1996, but not fully implemented until April 2003. As with any new law or policy that has the potential to have a major impact on social work practice, social workers are encouraged to stay updated on this issue in terms of federal and state law, as well as agency policy.

CHILD WELFARE AND CONFIDENTIALITY

Social workers and other professionals are required by law to report all cases of suspected child abuse and neglect to the child protective services agency or other designated authority. Although details vary from state to state, such reporting is required in every jurisdiction in the United States and in many other countries. There is less concern with the ethics of breaking confidentiality in cases of child abuse and neglect because of the ethical imperatives on finding ways to assure the safety of the maltreated child.

Surveys have found that one in three professionals have had contact with at least one case of suspected child abuse that they have declined to report, and they reported only about one third of the abuse cases they suspected (Kalichman, 1999). When a report is made to a child protective service, the CPS worker is required to investigate the reported maltreatment and is required to take any necessary action to protect the child. Social workers who continue to be uneasy about the ethical and practice implications of reporting suspected child abuse that involves one of their clients might want to consider the following options when the need to report arises:

1. Work with the client to help him make the report himself; the social worker should follow up with the client to make sure that the report was made.
2. Discuss with the family why a report needs to be made, what the potential benefits and risks to the family are, what procedures will be followed during

the investigation, and if the report is substantiated or indicated, what some of the treatment options are likely to be. The social worker should be aware of the procedures followed in her area so that she can accurately inform clients about what to expect.

3. Report without notifying the family if failing to do so would place the child at immediate risk.

It is important to note that not all parents with mental illness or substance abuse problems will maltreat their children, yet children of such parents are at higher risk for child abuse and neglect (see Darlington et al., 2005; Kroll, 2004). Consequently, professionals working in these areas are more likely involved in reporting suspected child abuse or may be asked to share information about a parent's mental health or substance use with child protective services workers. Kroll (2004) also notes that children may feel uncomfortable or disloyal discussing parents' substance misuse, and that professionals need to be "clear about issues of confidentiality, so that children [know] what would happen to the information they gave and that they would not be punished, judged or blamed for talking about parents' behavior" (p. 137).

Collaboration between child welfare, education, health, mental health, juvenile justice, and other systems is also important because children and youth in foster care "are one of the most educationally vulnerable populations. . .[and] no one agency has [all] the resources or expertise to provide the services and supports required to better serve these young people" (Zetlin, Weinberg, & Shea, 2006, p. 166). Zetlin et al. (2006) conducted focus groups to examine ways to support education of foster care youth. Among the themes that emerged were concerns about the adequacy of educational records (such as not being able to keep track of all the schools the youth attended and what courses they had taken at each), the difficulties of interagency collaboration, and issues about confidentiality. Because each agency often has its own confidentiality and data sharing policies, information about youth is more limited than if all records were kept by one agency (Zetlin et al., 2006). Should confidentiality of records be maintained to such an extent that it interferes with providing effective interventions? How should social workers balance these two goals?

PRIVILEGED COMMUNICATION

Privileged communication is a legal right granted by legislative statute. It guarantees that certain information need not be revealed in court without the consent of the person who originated the communication. Privileged communication is a rule of evidence that allows one party in a legal proceeding (in this case, the client) to limit the admissibility of statements originally communicated in confidence, thus rendering the witness (that is, the social worker) "incompetent" to testify regarding a particular matter. The common law principle that the public has a right to every person's evidence is followed in the absence of a statute of privilege. No person can refuse to testify in court when called to do so. Persons reluctant to testify can be subpoenaed or commanded to testify by the court; failure to appear and testify in response to a subpoena can result in a citation for contempt of court. Historically, privileged relationships have been limited to husband/wife, attorney/client, and priest-confessor/worshipper. Any other relationship is privileged only when so defined by a statute enacted by a state legislature. All 50 states and the District of Columbia have enacted laws concerning privileged communications. Special attention must be paid to this issue by social workers because the specifics of the privilege differ from state to state.

"Every U.S. jurisdiction has recognized some form of evidentiary privilege for statements made by a patient to a psychotherapist for the purpose of obtaining treatment" (Harris, 1999). On the federal level, the U.S. Supreme Court established the psychotherapist/patient privilege in the federal courts with its ruling in *Jaffee v. Redmond* (1996). The Court had not previously addressed this issue, but did so in a case involving a licensed clinical social worker, simultaneously establishing the principle for psychiatrists and psychologists. For practical purposes, the Supreme Court ruling extends the privilege to civil actions in federal courts, thus institutionalizing recognition of psychotherapist/patient privilege. The exact dimensions of the privilege will evolve through case decisions as they unfold. For example, in *United States v. Chase*, the United States 9th Circuit Court of Appeals ruled in August 2002 that there *is* a dangerous patient exception to the *Jaffee* privilege, a ruling opposite to a position taken by the 6th Circuit in *United States v. Hayes*. During 2001 the 9th Circuit ruled that communications between an unlicensed EAP counselor and a patient are protected from compelled disclosure by the privilege established by *Jaffee*. The privilege belongs to the client, not to the social worker. When a client waives the privilege, the social worker must testify in court even if the client does not know or is not certain what information is included in his case record and even if this testimony may harm him. Other interested persons do not control the privilege. For example, a father or husband cannot suppress or waive testimony of a social worker who is treating his child or wife, even when he pays for the treatment (VandeCreek et al., 1988).

In many states, the privilege ceases to exist if a third party was present at the time that the client communicated the confidential information to the social worker. However, some state laws specifically extend the privilege of communications to situations that involve group, marital, and family therapy—that is, to situations where third parties are present (VandeCreek et al., 1988). In other states, the courts decide whether the rule of privilege applies, but no clear trend has evolved regarding communications in the presence of third parties. The Minnesota Superior Court addressed this question in *Minnesota v. Andring* (10 FLR 1206, 1984) and ruled:

> The participants in group psychotherapy sessions are not casual persons who are strangers.... Rather, every participant has such a relationship with the attending professional, and in the group setting, the participants actually become part of the diagnostic and therapeutic process for coparticipants.
>
> An interpretation that excluded group therapy from the scope of the psychotherapist-patient [privileged communication rule] would seriously limit the effectiveness of group psychotherapy as a therapeutic device.... [T]he confidentiality of communications made during group therapy is essential in maintaining its effectiveness as a therapeutic tool.

In the absence of a privilege statute, a social worker who testifies about confidential information that she has received from a client may face a double bind—if she testifies, she may be sued by the client for revealing confidential information; if she refuses to testify, she may be cited for contempt of court. Privileged communication is a legal and not an ethical concept. Although privileged communication raises a number of ethical dilemmas, questions arising out of privileged communications require legal consultation.

INFORMED CONSENT

The professional ethics rule of **informed consent** is derived from the moral principle of autonomy, which states that all persons have the capacity for self-government and self–decision making. This capacity must be respected at all times by all "helpers." Informed consent means that a social worker or another professional will not intervene in a client's life or release confidential information about him unless that client has freely consented. It cannot be assumed that because a client consented in the past he will again consent now. It is therefore important that consent be obtained every time a client starts a new treatment procedure, every time he starts with a new social worker, and every time that confidential data will be released to a third party (Manning & Gaul, 1997). The NASW Code of Ethics (1999) states clearly that:

> social workers should provide services to clients only in the context of a professional relationship based, when appropriate, on valid informed consent. Social workers should use clear and understandable language to inform clients of the purpose of the services, risks related to the services, limits to services because of requirements of a third-party payer, relevant costs, reasonable alternatives, clients' right to refuse or withdraw consent, and the time frame covered by the consent. Social workers should provide clients with an opportunity to ask questions (1.03a).

If a client is not capable of providing informed consent, then permission should be sought from an appropriate third party (1999, 1.03c). If a social worker is serving involuntary clients, then she "should provide information about the nature and extent of services and about the extent of clients' right to refuse service" (1.03d). Further, in cases where a social worker may be required to report findings of an investigation or assessment, such as in a child custody hearing or in probation and parole settings, the client should be warned about the limits of confidentiality as part of the informed consent process (Luftman, Veltkamp, Clark, Lannacone, & Snooks, 2005). Palmer and Kaufman (2003) emphasize the importance of obtaining informed consent in a culturally sensitive manner. The social worker must not assume that such basic values as individualism, self-determination, obedience, and democracy will have the same meaning for her client as they do for her. By keeping this in mind, she can give her clients a meaningful experience in self-determination.

While everyone agrees that clients should provide informed consent before starting treatment or before having confidential information shared, there is little agreement on what information needs to be included in informed consent and whether written consent is needed. In a qualitative review of 37 written family therapy informed consent documents, Haslam and Harris (2004) found a general consistency in the main categories of information included (e.g., process or nature of therapy, confidentiality, insurance issues, etc.), but there was great variability in some of the details, such as indicating the risks of the treatment provided. Pollack (2004) warns of the risk of providing too much information:

> There is no single way to ensure that every potential question a client might have can be adequately addressed. What we can do is be vigilant of paternalism that leaves clients dependent, and be mindful of giving clients so much autonomy that, in the name of good professional practice, they are left unanchored and helpless.... Self-respect, self-direction, and a sense of fair play are at stake (p. 28).

Disclosure of Information, Voluntariness, and Competence

The three issues of informed consent are disclosure of information, voluntariness, and competency (Grisso & Appelbaum, 1998; Moreno, Caplan, & Wolpe, 1998; Palmer & Kaufman, 2003). Problems involving any one or all of these issues make for difficult ethical dilemmas in social work practice. We will discuss briefly the ethical aspects of each of these issues.

DISCLOSURE OF INFORMATION   A person can be considered sufficiently informed to give consent only if he knows what will occur during the intervention or treatment, what the results of the intervention will be, and what will happen if he does not consent. He should know how much better (or worse) he will be if he agrees to the intervention than he will be if he does not agree. He should also have full knowledge about alternate options and their associated risks and benefits. In situations in which the client is being asked to consent to the disclosure of confidential information to a third party, he should know what information will be released, to whom, for what purposes, and with what consequences. He should also know the consequences of not agreeing. Finally, the disclosure of information must be done in a clear and understandable manner (Grisso & Appelbaum, 1998). In some cases, fundamental problems of communication may exist when attempting to communicate technical and value-laden information, particularly to those who are in stressful situations. For example, some persons may have difficulty understanding the idea of probability, while different styles of communication may be intimidating to some clients (Moreno et al., 1998). Much of the required information can be provided by the social worker, but even he may not be cognizant of some of the possible outcomes because there are always secondary and unanticipated consequences. In fact, the nature and consequences of any option are never entirely clear and may be interpreted differently by different experts.

There is much evidence that many people do not pay attention or fully comprehend information presented to them, no matter how carefully the details and possible risks are explained. It is not always clear whether this is a case of selective listening or of suppressing unpleasant information. In a study of patient/physician communication following general physical exams, the patients could not remember almost 70% of the problems physicians diagnosed (American College of Physicians Observer, 1997). Some have estimated that only 20% of adult Americans have the ability to read, fully understand, and act appropriately on health care information they have received (Dent, 2000). Other patients simply do not want to know the risks involved in the procedure or treatment that has been provided. Still others do not hear because they have hearing difficulties.

Social workers differ in many ways from physicians, but many social workers also report that their clients really do not want to know all the details. They have a problem and want help from an expert whom they trust. Yet the social worker is ethically committed to the principle of providing services and treatment only on the basis of informed consent. One of the ethical dilemmas facing the social worker in this area is that she does not want to overwhelm the client with too much information, yet is obligated to provide sufficient information to enable the client to make a meaningful decision. Should the worker be satisfied and proceed when the client has given permission, even though she suspects that this client does not fully understand the information and its meaning or should she delay help so that she can give the client additional information that she believes is necessary to obtain informed consent?

VOLUNTARINESS   Consent is meaningful only when it is not coerced, but given freely. Though there is wide agreement with this ethical rule, some social workers practice in settings where the client has little or no freedom. Prisoners, parolees, and patients hospitalized with mental illnesses are classic examples of involuntary clients. When working with court-mandated clients, there are three barriers to informed consent. First, the risks and benefits of the court-ordered assessment cannot be fully anticipated. Second, the power imbalance results in client vulnerability that undermines voluntariness of consent. Third, while the "ability to form a therapeutic alliance and obtain relevant information is valued by the court, the therapeutic alliance may not always serve the best interest of the client, who may not be aware of the complexity of the relationship" (Regehr & Antle, 1997, p. 301).

Consent may also be less than voluntary in some settings. Voluntariness is often presented as a dichotomous value—a decision either is or is not voluntary. However, closer inspection will suggest that there is a wide range between the two extremes. For example, how voluntary is the consent of a client who believes that it is important to gain the worker's goodwill in order to obtain the services or goods desired? A destitute single mother may agree with almost everything her social worker suggests because she desperately wants to qualify for assistance. The man who is eager for reconciliation with his estranged wife may agree with everything his social worker mentions because he believes that in this way he may be able to salvage his marriage. The family that desperately needs help and services for their autistic child knows they can obtain these only through the social worker. While these people are not forced to come to a social agency or to agree with the social worker's assessment and recommendation, is their "informed consent" really voluntary?

The importance of developing client trust may lead to another ethical dilemma. Research has demonstrated that trust or faith in the practitioner is a key component in furthering effective change. Yet faith or trust may result in a surrender of decision-making participation. Instead of giving voluntary consent, the client who has blind faith in her social worker will agree to everything this worker says. Developing and encouraging trust, while strengthening voluntary consent and decision-making participation, is a challenge for every social worker. Grisso and Appelbaum (1998) comment that "encouraging patients to pursue a particular option is not coercion, unless unfair threats are involved. Clinicians need not simply lay out the alternatives for patients. They can distinguish among the options they consider more or less viable" (p. 9).

COMPETENCE   Informed consent presupposes that the person who gives consent is competent to do so. However, many social work clients are less than fully competent. Persons with dementia, Alzheimer's disease, or mental retardation, and the seriously emotionally disturbed, as well as young children, may not be competent to give informed consent for some or all decisions. However, even clients with serious mental or physical illness may be competent to provide consent. Moser and colleagues (2002) found that 80% of participants with schizophrenia and 96% of persons with HIV had adequate capacity to provide informed consent. Only a court of law can declare a person incompetent, but there are many situations in which a social worker must make an informal assessment of a person's competency to participate in decision making.

The ethical problem is complicated because ostensibly the issue of competency is raised only when a client disagrees with his social worker's recommendation. Rarely does the social worker question his competency when he agrees with her. Ethical problems that arise in this area are especially well known to social workers who are working with adoption, foster placement, custody, abortion, contraception, and end-of-life decisions. The social worker's dilemma may become a difficult one, particularly when young children are involved. While there is no agreement about how old a child must be before he or she is considered competent, everyone agrees that an infant is not competent to make decisions. Children, like adults, may not always mean what they say or say what they mean. Stated preferences may not reflect actual preferences.

The decision to intervene in a person's life must never be taken lightly. To limit a person's freedom by removing her from her home and placing her in an institution is a very serious decision, which ordinarily should not be made without the person's consent. At the same time, it may be a mistake to always accept that person's consent or refusal at face value. A client may be temporarily depressed, may not understand the reality situation or the dangers involved in it, may change her mind upon further reflection, or may be reacting to a situational fear. Consider the ethical issues involved in Exemplar 5.3.

| 5.3 | Archie Walker's Golden Years |

Muriel Palmieri is an outreach worker for the Downtown Elderly Program (DEP). She has organized a group of volunteers who regularly visit with homebound older people. These volunteers have been trained to identify older people who need additional help so that they can report their names to the DEP. One of the volunteers recently told Muriel that she had discovered a bedridden older man in a cold and dirty fourth floor walk-up apartment.

Archie Walker was probably not as old or as feeble as he appeared, but the volunteer thought that he required more care than the occasional help provided by his 79-year-old neighbor, who brought him food whenever he thought of it. When this neighbor forgot to come, as happened not infrequently, Archie subsisted for days on cold water and bread. It had been years since Archie last saw a doctor. He seemed delighted with the volunteer's visit and begged her to come again soon. Muriel told the volunteer that she would see what could be done to make Archie more comfortable.

When Muriel visited Archie, he welcomed her warmly. She was able to confirm the volunteer's observations. Archie seemed relatively alert. Muriel thought that his dissatisfaction with his present condition was realistic and a hopeful sign, indicative of a capacity to participate in developing plans for the future. Archie explained that his only income came from Social Security. He had never heard of the federal Supplemental Security Income (SSI) program. Muriel suspected that he would qualify for SSI. Archie said that he could not afford to move to another apartment, but he insisted that he did not want to go to an "old folks' home." Muriel explained about many of the programs that were available to help persons in his situation. She listed the advantages and disadvantages of each and indicated the time it might take before each program or service would start for him. She also noted how she could help him qualify. Among the programs they discussed were SSI, Meals-on-Wheels, health visitors, homemakers, Title 8 housing, and the Manor Apartments. Archie seemed bewildered by the many programs from which he could choose and by the many decisions he had to make. He asked Muriel to do whatever was best for him.

If you were in Muriel's place, what would you have done? Here are some of the ethical issues that may arise in trying to help Archie:

- What did Archie mean when he told her to do whatever was best for him? Does this mean that he gave his consent for her to make all kinds of arrangements on his behalf? Is this a satisfactory way of giving informed consent? If not, in what ways does it fall short?
- Instead of overwhelming Archie with so many choices, should Muriel have simplified the decisions he has to make by presenting only a few options or programs at a time? Perhaps it would have been better to have Archie decide first whether he really wanted to stay in his present apartment or move somewhere else. Can he make this decision without having a full knowledge of all options? Do social work ethics require that a client have full knowledge of *all* the relevant options?
- Muriel tried to present all of the advantages of every option. Did she really know *all* of the consequences? Does Archie really care about *all* of the consequences? Is he not much more interested in what will happen to him in the next few months? How much knowledge must a client have before the social worker can be sure that she has met the demands of the Code of Ethics?
- Would it be ethical for Muriel to design a package of relevant services on the basis of her assessment—and on the basis of Archie's wishes—and then ask Archie whether this package was acceptable?

Additional questions could be asked, but it is already clear that in social work practice informed consent is beset with many difficulties and that these difficulties often lead to ethical dilemmas.

COMMUNITY ORGANIZING AND INFORMED CONSENT

The ethical dimensions of obtaining of informed consent are especially problematic when the client is a community or neighborhood, as may be the case for social workers engaged in community organizing. A social worker involved in a neighborhood renewal program must consider whether the elected representatives really represent all residents. Does their informed consent suffice or must every resident consent? What is the situation when the initiative for intervention comes from the outside? What does it mean "to obtain informed consent" when the social worker's initial objective is to raise the residents' consciousness to the fact that there is a problem in their community and that they can do something about it? Requiring every person's consent in this latter situation may be tantamount to ruling out any intervention activity, yet intervening without informed consent is a violation of professional ethics. What should a social worker do in these circumstances? Hardina (2004) suggests that the best method for ensuring that most participants agree with an approach is to hold a "meeting in which all members debate risks and benefits of the proposed action and attempt to reach a consensus" (p. 599). This approach can be time consuming, and there is no guarantee that consensus can be reached, however "constituents should be fully informed about the consequences of their actions, especially when personal sacrifices (such as job loss, arrest, or social stigma) are great" (Hardina, 2004, p. 599).

WAYS OF CONSENTING

Oliver Goldsmith (1764) wrote that "silence gives consent," but social workers have learned that silence and other nonverbal signals, such as a nod, or even a verbal yes may be deceptive and may indicate something other than consent. Clients may be ashamed to withhold consent or simply not understand what they have been asked to agree to. A social worker is obligated to offer a full explanation of what the intervention involves, what the projected benefits and risks will be, what other options may be available, and what might happen if the client does not consent. All this must be presented in a language that the client can understand. Language per se is important but even more so may be how the social worker presents the information. Many clients have short attention spans. Exceeding that time span may mean "turning the client off," even if the language is simple.

Aside from questions of disclosure of information, voluntariness, and competency, the various forms of consent also make for ethical problems. Consider the following possibilities:

- *Direct or tacit. Direct* refers to the client's verbal response, while *tacit* means that the client remained silent. Is it ethical for the social worker to assume that the client agrees when he does not respond to her suggestion?
- *Oral or written.* Written consent is often preferred, but is the use of oral consent necessarily unethical? Does using written consent forms automatically eliminate all unethical dilemmas? Should services that are typically provided via telephone (e.g., suicide hotlines) be withheld until written consent can be obtained? Can other forms of documentation that consent was obtained (e.g., audio recordings of the verbal consent or copies of e-mail messages) substitute for written consent?
- *Past/present.* Does current dissent invalidate all past consents? Is this a case of change of mind, diminished competence, situational fear, or something else? To state this dilemma differently, how much credence should a social worker give to a person's change of mind when she knows that in the past the client consistently expressed a contrary view?
- *Present/future.* Can a social worker assume that the client would (or will) agree with her decision if he were (or when he becomes) more aware of what is involved? Can a social worker wait to obtain informed consent until the client and the process is far enough along so the client understands fully the consequences of the decision?
- *Forced consent.* One way to obtain a client's consent is to frame options in such a way that the client will consent, no matter what the response. For example, the social worker may ask, "Do you want to move to the nursing home this week or next?" Is this an ethical way of obtaining consent? Another form of "forced consent" is by threatening undesirable consequences unless the client consents. Clearly, everybody agrees that this is not ethical. What if the agency provides only one kind of service and if the client does not agree, he cannot be served? In this situation, is a "threat" of no-service-unless-you-agree ethical?

As we have indicated repeatedly, each of these forms of consent presents ethical problems and dilemmas. One thing is certain: Involving the client in providing informed consent cannot be a one-time activity, but must be an ongoing process. Some have suggested that all of the problems around informed consent can be avoided or resolved by employing good clinical practice. For example, if a client is fully involved in the decision-making process, questions of consent will not arise. It is a fact, however, that even formal contracting does not resolve all the problems involved in obtaining informed consent. The power gap between client and worker inevitably results in contract negotiations between unequals. Some unintended coercion may be brought into play, leading the client to agree to choices that are not entirely of his choosing.

DUTY TO PROTECT

The ground rules that govern how all mental health professionals, including social workers, must deal with violent or potentially violent clients were fundamentally changed by a landmark legal decision (*Tarasoff v. The Regents of the University of California*). This landmark legal case started when a murder took place in 1969 in California. A young man—Prosenjit Poddar—who was a voluntary outpatient at the student health service at the University of California, Berkeley, told his therapist that he intended to kill his former girlfriend just as soon as she returned from an out-of-town trip. Shortly thereafter, the young woman— Tatiana Tarasoff—was killed by the young man. The young woman's parents subsequently charged the therapist with neglect. The therapist argued that he was not guilty because his relationship with the young client/killer was confidential. However, the judge held that:

> Public policy favoring protection of the confidential character of patient/psychotherapist relationship must yield in instances in which disclosure is essential to avert danger to others; the protective privilege ends where the public peril begins.
>
> When a therapist determines, or should determine, that his patient presents a serious danger of violence to another, *he incurs an obligation to use reasonable care to protect the intended victim* against such danger. This duty may call for him (1) to warn the intended victim or (2) [to inform] others likely to apprise the victim of the danger, (3) to notify the police, or (4) to take whatever other steps are reasonably necessary under the circumstances (*Tarasoff v. The Regents of the University of California*, 1976, 551 P 2d 334 at 340; emphasis added).

We have cited at length from the *Tarasoff* ruling because it has become very important for all mental health professionals, including social workers. Although it was a California court case, this case has had a nationwide impact. The case changed the ground rules for mental health professionals when dealing with violent or potentially violent clients and stimulated anxiety among mental health professionals. Major concerns were expressed at the time by many professionals who feared the decision would undermine the practice of therapy by destroying its confidential nature.

Since 1976, mental health practitioners have been required to take reasonable measures to protect potential victims from a client's foreseeable violent acts. Subsequent court decisions further defined the *Tarasoff* doctrine. One decision explained that under the *Tarasoff* doctrine, a social worker or other professional (1) must be able to predict "pursuant to the standards of his profession" that the client is violently dangerous and (2) must be able to specify one or more clearly identifiable victims (*Brady v. Hopper*, 1983, 751 F 2d 329).

In another decision involving the murder of the victim's minor children, the California Supreme Court extended the *Tarasoff* doctrine beyond the identified intended victim to others who also might be in danger. In the same decision, the court ruled that a therapist's failure to use reasonable care to protect a third party from harm constituted "professional negligence," rather than "ordinary negligence." This definition allows suits to be initiated for up to three years after the injury occurred, rather than the usual one-year limitation (Butz, 1985, p. 87, citing *Hedlund v. Superior Court,* 1983, 669, P 2d 41).

In recent years, the duty to protect (sometimes called the duty to warn) has been further extended by various legal decisions, but practice applications are not always entirely clear. New decisions by various courts clarify some questions that professional practitioners face. For example, a 1994 "California appellate court case, *Gross v. Allen,* expands the *Tarasoff* duty to include suicide threats. It also makes explicit that a psychotherapist's 'duty to warn' includes informing a subsequent therapist about a patient's known dangerousness" (Meyers, 1997, p. 365). Recently, in *Ewing v. Goldstein* (120 Cal. App. 4th 807 [2004]) and *Ewing v. Northridge Hospital Medical Center* (120 Cal. App. 4th 1289 [2004]), a California Court of Appeal found that family members' reports of threats could also trigger a clinician's duty to warn, suggesting that the clinician does not need to have heard the threats directly in order to have a duty to protect (Ewing, 2005).

Yet other important issues remain open, undecided, or ambiguous (Almason, 1997). Social workers must become aware of and remain up to date on the current laws in their states. In *Rost v. State Board of Psychology,* a Pennsylvania court held that ignorance of the law is not a sufficient defense for not protecting confidential records. The court stated that "a psychologist cannot claim ignorance of the ethical obligations of her profession, and if there was a conflict between her ethical duty to maintain confidentiality and the subpoena, she should have sought legal advice" (Beck, 1998, p. 378). Although this case deals with confidentiality, rather than duty to protect, it suggests that ignorance of legal responsibilities is not a defense for illegal actions, even when these are committed in an attempt to follow the profession's ethical rules.

The duty to protect varies from state to state (Beck, 1998) and may be ill defined in states where laws regulating professions (or legal decisions interpreting these laws) do not make reference to the *Tarasoff* duty. Some states have enacted *Tarasoff* legislation and others have not. Some states have adopted and extended the *Tarasoff* principle; others have "contained" third-party liability within the context of the state's protective disclosure law. The laws of still other states (including Florida, Mississippi, and Texas) do not make any reference to the duty to warn. Some states acknowledge circumscribed duties to warn or protect (Felthous & Kachigian, 2001). Even the state of California in a criminal case (*People v. Felix,* Court of Appeals, 2001) revisited these issues and tested the limits of the duty to protect. This court held that applying the duty to protect principle without limitations would mean that those who need therapy for homicidal thoughts would not seek it because they would incriminate themselves while in the therapeutic relationship. Mental health professionals praised this ruling, but law enforcement personnel claimed it undermined the rights and safety of potential victims (Ewing, 2002).

Social workers should be alert to the legal dimensions regarding the duty to protect because these differ from state to state and from profession to profession. Some professions may receive the benefit of immunity from liability for breaches of confidentiality and others do not. Some state laws create legal confidentiality as a right of the client but do not provide liability waivers for mental health practitioners who warn a potential victim. There is no wide agreement on what is meant by "serious threat of physical violence," nor on the meaning of "intended" or "capable of being carried out." However, "most state statutes require an actual or serious threat; thus therapists in these jurisdictions no longer have to attempt to predict dangerousness" (Almason, 1997, p. 481).

Different states also vary in their requirements in regard to how the duty to protect should be discharged: warning the potential victim or someone close to the victim, notifying the police, starting commitment proceedings, or informing mental health evaluators of the nature of the threat. Each of the alternatives may present new ethical dilemmas. Reporting to the police, for example, may fulfill the duty to protect, but the police may use this information in ways that social workers would consider unethical (Egley, 1992). Does a social worker who practices in a state without a legal duty to warn have an ethical responsibility to do so when her client presents a danger to another person?

In addition to varying state legislation and court decisions concerning the duty to protect, a fundamental issue of concern is the assessment of the probability of violence. Consider, for example, the situation described in Exemplar 5.4.

| 5.4 | AN IDLE OR SERIOUS THREAT? |

Rufus Hall is seeking help with his four-year marriage. According to Rufus, his wife, Sara, refuses to come to counseling with him and has been threatening to get a divorce. Rufus reports that on occasion he gets very angry with his wife and has "slapped" her once or twice. During one session, he said that he loves his wife and would kill her if she goes through with her threat to get a divorce. His social worker, Jillian Adams, who lives in the same community as Rufus and Sara, knows that Sara recently saw a lawyer about a divorce. To date, Rufus has only spoken of a couple of slaps, but Jillian is uncertain how to respond to his comment that he would kill Sara if she divorces him.

Should Jillian report the husband's comment as a threat? If yes, to whom? How can she assess the seriousness of his statement? Would it matter if she knew his "slaps" had been more violent than he reported? What information would be helpful in deciding whether the threat to Sara's safety is real and should be reported?

Admittedly, the prediction of violence is not a hard science. While some personality characteristics have been found to be related to a higher probability of violent behavior, potential violence cannot be predicted with any certainty. Beck (1998) comments on the difficulty of predicting violent behavior, especially for clients who are likely to be impulsive, such as those with certain mental disorders. Until now, "when violence appears to be impulsive for whatever reason, courts are reluctant to find the defendants negligent" for not warning a potential victim (Beck, 1998, p. 381).

Some ethical problems that arise in regard to the *Tarasoff* duty are not readily answered in the NASW Code of Ethics. Social work ethics prohibit revealing confidential information, but this ethical imperative may be overridden "for compelling professional reasons. The general expectation that social workers will keep information confidential does not apply when disclosure is necessary to prevent serious, foreseeable, and imminent harm to a client or other identifiable person" (1999, 1.07c). However, there remains much ambiguity about the precise meaning of "foreseeable and imminent harm."

Currently, there is no statute or model law that provides a comprehensive definition of all the components of the duty to warn. The major question is under conditions do social workers have a duty to protect potential victims. Because the legal situation changes so frequently in this area of the law, even social workers who practice in states where there is no clear precedent would be well advised to use legal and professional consultations where the situation makes it possible to do so.

There are those who hold that the *Tarasoff* doctrine does not present social workers with any new ethical problems because the requirement to break confidentiality and warn the intended victim applies only in specific instances. Beck (1998) suggests that the legal and ethical issues surrounding the duty to warn are "remarkably congruent with good clinical practice" (p. 375). When the duty to protect does apply, the ethical decision screens in chapter 4 provide guidance because saving human life from direct and immediate danger is a higher-order ethical principle than confidentiality. The ethical issue becomes problematic only because the risk to life is often ambiguous.

Since the initial establishment of a clinician's duty to warn in order to protect third parties from violence, courts have adopted and expanded *Tarasoff*-like duties. At the same time, although more gradually, limits have also been placed on this duty by courts. These limits on the duty to protect have often been codified in state statutes that explicitly make reference to the *Tarasoff* duty and the acceptable ways of discharging this duty. Given the "mixed" and changing legal definition of the duty to protect, social workers should be certain they know the law in their state and utilize professional supervision and legal consultation to determine appropriate actions (Walcott, Cerundolo, & Beck, 2001).

Exercises

1. Investigate the laws in your state (or neighboring states or your home state) concerning confidentiality, privileged communication, and the duty to protect, as they apply to social workers.

2. Prepare a brief to be presented to your state legislature, urging that the privileged communication rule be extended to the client/social worker relationship and that it include group, couple, and family therapy.

3. Divide the class into groups of two. In each group, have one person assume the role of the social worker and the other the role of an applicant who is seeking help for coping with an alcoholic and physically abusive significant other. The specific task is for the social worker to inform the applicant/client of the limits of confidentiality. Students should try several different approaches and report to the class the one they think is most effective and best meets the demands of the Code of Ethics.

4. Divide the class into groups of two. In each group, have one person assume the role of the social worker and the other the role of an applicant who is seeking help with parenting issues. The specific task is for the social worker to inform the applicant/client of the limits of confidentiality, especially given the possibility of the need to report child maltreatment to the appropriate agency. Students should try several different approaches

and report to the class the one they think is most effective and best meets the demands of the Code of Ethics.

5. Your agency is reviewing its policy on giving clients access to their case records. Almost all staff members agree to abide by the Code of Ethics, but there is a difference of opinion on how to define "reasonable access" and "exceptional circumstances when there is compelling evidence that such access would cause serious harm to the client" (1.08a). Try to define these in ways that are congruent with both professional ethics and clients' rights. If there are differences of opinion in your class, organize a discussion to examine the strengths and weaknesses of each position. Can the class reach consensus on how to best define these issues?

SUGGESTIONS FOR ADDITIONAL READINGS

Palmer and Kaufman (2003) explore informed consent and how it applies to the multicultural context of many therapy and other situations. Galambos (2005) examines issues related to confidentiality in rural social work practice and maintaining confidentiality in the face of dual relationships. Reamer (2005) reviews the current situation regarding confidentiality issues in practice with children regarding ethics risk management. Schlossberger and Hecker (1996) discuss the *Tarasoff* ruling as it relates to family therapists working with clients who are HIV-positive. Beck (1998) discusses the *Tarasoff* duty as it relates to working with impulsively violent clients, and Meyers (1997) discusses the *Tarasoff* duty to subsequent caregivers. Harris (1999) discusses the *Tarasoff* duty and the *Jaffee* decision on psychotherapist/client privilege. Slaughter and colleagues (2007) provide guidelines for obtaining consent and assent to participate in research from people with dementia; while these guidelines were developed for research, many of them could be adapted for practice as well. Zayas, Cabassa, and Perez (2005) report on a tool developed for screening capacity to consent.

WEB SITES OF INTEREST

- For extensive information on HIPAA, including the statute and consumer information: www.hhs.gov/ocr/hipaa/
- For information on Megan's Law, which requires sex offender registration and community notification, as well as links to state laws: www.klaaskids.org/pg-legmeg.htm
- For information on the Adam Walsh Child Protection and Safety Act of 2006: www.whitehouse.gov/news/releases/2006/07/20060727-7.html
- For an extensive list of publications on legal issues, including the *Tarasoff* duty and Megan's Law (this site is password protected, so you will only have access to these articles if you are a member of NASW): www.socialworkers.org/ldf/legal_issue/

6 | CLIENT RIGHTS AND PROFESSIONAL EXPERTISE

WHO IS THE CLIENT?

The question "Who is the client?" may be the source of several ethical dilemmas. In the classical professions, such as law and medicine, a client was traditionally defined as the person(s) who engaged the practitioner and paid her a fee. Alternatively, the client is the person (or the system) whose behavior is to be modified or changed by the professional's intervention. However, these definitions may not be entirely appropriate for most social workers, especially for those who are employed by an organization, such as a social agency, a department of government, or an institution. According to the traditional definition, the organization that pays the social worker's salary would be considered the client. But is the school really the client of the school social worker? Is the prison the client of the correctional social worker? Nowadays, the traditional definition may be too narrow, because it was originally devised for clients of independent professional practitioners in private practice.

The alternate definition also is problematic because it is not always accurate to say that the client is the person or system whose behavior needs to be changed. Often social work intervention involves changes in systems other than the client system, such as a court, employer, social agency, or local housing authority. The worker does not intend to change the client, but instead helps the client by advocating with or attempting to change other systems that impact on the client in order to gain access to needed resources. In the past, the social worker automatically considered the person(s) who applied for help as her client(s); however, today the answer to the question "Who is the client?" is not quite so simple, as Exemplars 6.1 and 6.2 illustrate.

Who is Robin Osborn's client—Arlene Johnson or the premature infant? Whose interests should be accorded priority? Exemplar 6.2 is quite different, but it raises similar questions.

| 6.1 | ARLENE JOHNSON'S ABORTION |

Arlene Johnson, 18 years old and single, is nearly six months pregnant. Yesterday, she came to the Women's Counseling Center to request help in getting an abortion. At the time of the abortion procedure, the fetus was considered viable and was placed in the neonatal intensive care unit as a high-risk premature baby. Arlene was most upset when she learned that the "abortion" had resulted in a live infant. She refused to look at the baby or take care of it. Instead, she threatened to sue the doctor and the hospital if the infant survived despite her expressed wish for an abortion. Arlene asked Robin Osborn, the hospital social worker, to make sure that the baby not be given intensive care, but rather be left alone so that it would die quickly.

| 6.2 | MRS. LINDEN'S CLASSROOM |

Mrs. Linden is a fifth-grade teacher in the Abraham Lincoln Elementary School. The school is located in a neighborhood into which a large number of Central American families have moved recently. Joan Ramirez is the social worker assigned to this school. She is the social worker responsible for several children in Mrs. Linden's class. Yesterday, Mrs. Linden asked Joan for help in keeping her pupils quietly in their seats. She told Joan that never in her 20 years as a teacher has she had as much trouble as this year. She thought that her troubles were caused by the many children who do not speak English well. Surely Joan could advise her how to handle these children so that they would be quiet and stay in their seats.

Again, who is the client—Mrs. Linden, the pupils, their parents, or the school? Whose interests should be accorded priority? What if Joan believes the problem stems from a different source, such as racism or inflexibility? The two problem situations in Exemplars 6.1 and 6.2 seem quite different, but in each case the request made by the applicant for service creates a dilemma that has ethical implications for the social worker. Arlene Johnson does not want to have a baby, but now that a live infant has been born, her expectations of the obstetrician (and the request she made to the social worker) conflict sharply with the rights of the infant and with what society expects from these professionals. Joan Ramirez is approached by Mrs. Linden, but the students are already her clients. Is the problem with the students, Mrs. Linden, or the school setting? What should Joan do about the role conflict? To whom does she owe loyalty? The social worker is not at all sure that the problem is with the pupils; perhaps the teacher is the real problem. What is the ethical thing to do?

One of the reasons why the question "Who is the client?" causes so many ethical dilemmas is that the question itself is based on an oversimplified and not entirely accurate model of the professional relationship. The traditional model included only the practitioner and the client. An updated model might include the applicant, client, target, beneficiary, practitioner, agency, community, and others. Each of the four positions noted in Figure 6.1 can be occupied by one or more persons or institutions. Sometimes the same person is the applicant as well as the client, target, and beneficiary. At other times or in other situations, different persons occupy each of these positions.

Applicant	The person(s) or system that requests help with a defined or felt problem
Client	The applicant who enters into a formal, contractual, goal-focused relationship with a social worker
Target	The person(s) or system(s) that must be modified in order to achieve the desired outcome to which client and worker have agreed
Beneficiary	The person(s) or system(s) that will benefit from successful goal achievement in which the resolution of the ethical issues may not fully coincide with the legal requirements

FIGURE 6.1 | SOME PARTICIPANTS IN THE SOCIAL WORK PROCESS

The applicant may not be the client (e.g., when a mother applies for services for her child) and the client need not be the target (e.g., the target may be an employer or school principal), nor is the client necessarily the beneficiary of the intervention.

Social workers who engage in genetic counseling are constantly faced by difficult problems that involve ethical issues. Modern medical procedures such as amniocentesis and chorionic villus sampling make it possible to detect hundreds of different genetic disorders *in utero*. When there are positive findings, the social worker must help the parents think through all of the implications for all involved so they can make the best decision. However, some physicians routinely expect the social worker to persuade the pregnant mother who has received positive indications of a genetically defective fetus to abort, while other doctors expect the social worker to persuade the mother not to abort based on their own religious or other principles. Should the best interest of the as-yet-unborn child play a part in the decision? What is the best interest? Should the social worker stress arguments in favor of abortion, even if it is evident that the parents do not want to terminate the pregnancy? What is the ethical stance that the social worker should adopt? Should the decision of the social worker depend on knowledge of more or less certainty of the predicted consequences of genetic effects—that is, mild or severe effects leading to a degree of independence or to the need for constant care and assistance? How would your decision in such a situation be affected by your own values and religious beliefs?

Social workers in the criminal justice system face similar ethical issues. In the probation service, social workers regularly prepare reports for the court judge. The judge takes these reports into consideration when making a final disposition of the case. The ethical dilemma here is that the social worker has responsibilities both toward the alleged delinquent and toward the court. She is helper and judicial fact finder. The client/worker helping relationship started during the first contact with the offender, long before the social worker has completed her evaluative assessment or presented her report to the judge. To whom does the social worker owe priority consideration—to the detainee or to the judge? Who is her client? Note that in the criminal justice system social workers will often face situations in which the legal requirements may not fully coincide with professional ethical principles. Does it help if the social worker explains her court responsibilities to the client?

An ethical dilemma arises out of a conflict between two values: (1) the self-determination or autonomy guide, which states that the person most affected by a decision should make that decision, and (2) the benefit guide, which posits that since the professional social worker has the knowledge and skill necessary to best assure a positive outcome, she is responsible for making the decision that will secure the optimum benefit for the client.

Social workers have always believed that every person has a right to make his or her own decisions. Veteran social worker Charlotte Towle (1987) noted many years ago that "a person has a right to manage his own affairs" (p. 15). The NASW Code of Ethics states, "Social workers respect and promote the right of clients to self-determination and assist clients in their efforts to identify and clarify their goals." (NASW Code, 1999, 1.02). This rule seems clear and unambiguous. The Code also states "social workers may limit clients' rights to self-determination [only] when, in the social workers' professional judgment, clients' actions or potential actions pose a serious, foreseeable, and imminent risk to themselves or others" (NASW Code, 1999, 1.02).

At one time, this ethical conflict between the client's right to self-determination and the social worker's expertise was less severe because there was a great deal of uncertainty about the adequacy of social work knowledge and about the effectiveness of social work intervention. However, recent studies have shown that the application of professional knowledge and appropriate professional skills does result in positive client outcomes (Lundahl, Nimer, & Parsons, 2006; Reid, Kenaley, & Colvin, 2004; Rizzo & Rowe, 2006; Roseborough, 2006; Rosen & Proctor, 2003). The ethical problem with potentially critical ethical implications is how to combine client self-determination with the use of professional knowledge and skill. Is it ethical for a social worker to refrain from using professional knowledge—known by her to be effective—if the client chooses an option with which the social worker cannot concur because it is not consistent with evidence-based recommendations?

The social worker may know what strategy will best achieve the objectives that the client has chosen. Is it ethical for the social worker to implement this more effective strategy when the client prefers another approach? The social worker may understand what the client needs or wants even before the client is aware of this. May the social worker follow the strategy suggested by her knowledge and insight when the client has made another, less beneficial decision based on ignorance or partial knowledge?

Some social workers do not hesitate to give priority to their professional knowledge and skill even when this means ignoring a client's input. Recently, Taylor (2006) studied 320 clinical social workers with an average of 25 years experience in mental health services about their views regarding self-determination and involuntary treatment. They reported that, over their careers, they maintained positive attitudes about the importance and utility of self-determination. However, they indicated that over time their attitudes changed so that they became relatively untroubled when practice situations conflicted with the value of self-determination, such as when the client was in need of involuntary treatment interventions. They understood that there are some situations for patients or clients for whom informed decision making and judgments based on reality are not present (i.e., not based on valid information or poor reality assessment) and beneficent and paternalistic actions by the worker are necessary. Earlier ideas concerning conflicts between self-determination and paternalistic interventions are being reexamined. A British study of community care (Clark, 1998) similarly uncovered clearer justification in some situations for beneficent and paternalistic interventions by social workers.

Nevertheless, social workers believe not only in the right but also in the effectiveness of client participation in as many phases of the social work process as possible.

The potential conflict between the value of client self-determination and the worker's use of professional knowledge and skills is often complicated by the question as to who is the client for whom knowledge and skills will be applied. We will turn now to consider this question.

SELF-DETERMINATION

Immanuel Kant, one of the early giants of modern philosophy, insisted that a person's right to determine his or her own destiny is unconditional. He taught that persons are always ends in themselves and should never be treated as means. Kant would have taught that the social worker must provide professional services for the client and not take advantage of the client. Self-determination is also a first-order principle in American society. Though not specifically mentioned in the Constitution, the U.S. Supreme Court, in a series of due-process cases, equal protection cases, and privacy cases, developed the rule that self-determination is a fundamental right that is protected by the Ninth and Fourteenth Amendments.

The individual's right to make his or her own decisions is the source for the social work value of self-determination. Many hold that self-determination is an absolute right. Yet most social workers would agree with Rothman (1989) that when used as a practice principle, its application is limited. For practitioners, the principle of self-determination can raise as many questions as it answers. No wonder that Rothman (1989) states "self-determination is accorded utmost esteem in the profession [but] its meaning and application are clouded" (p. 598). The right of self-determination can become the source of common and perplexing dilemmas. How can a practitioner respect and uphold client self-determination when working with a client whose concept of what is good for him or her differs from that of the social worker or is at variance from the needs or desires of those who will be affected by the client's decision? What if the client who has many positive attributes wants to make self-destructive or criminal decisions? Should a mentally ill person (or any person) be allowed to refuse treatment or be permitted to live on the street? What degree of mental instability calls for limiting self-determination?

Hartman suggests that many social workers believe that in their practices they always honor the client's right to self-determination, but this is often an illusion because many clients cannot fully exercise this right. Since true self-determination requires "access to resources, access to opportunity, and access to power," she supports the idea there are real limits to self-determination. This is especially true because real self-determination requires power and resources, something that many clients lack (Hartman, 1997, p. 216).

Ethical dilemmas become more frequent and increasingly perplexing as major life decisions involve highly technical and specialized considerations that often are beyond the comprehension of untrained people. Reliance on professionals who have the necessary expertise has become more common so that directiveness as a helping technique seems to have become more acceptable. There is an urgent need to reexamine issues of self-determination and autonomy as social workers respond to new mandates and demands in relation to persons with disabilities and to those who are especially vulnerable. In some cases, clients are unable to take care of themselves. In such situations social workers often intervene protectively, despite the client's objections. For example, is it ethical for a social worker to act when a suicidal client requires hospitalization, but does not want to be admitted to the hospital? The use of directive methods raises an ethical question as to whether the ends ever justify the means. Should a client be pressured into doing things he does not want to do even when his social worker is certain that this will contribute to solving or reducing his problem? Is it ethical for a social worker to deceive a client in order to have him participate in a treatment that he would reject if he knew all the facts? Perhaps the key to answering these and similar questions is not whether directiveness by the social worker is permissible but rather who has the right to decide whether a client can or cannot manage for himself in given circumstances.

Some professionals do not hesitate to use their superior knowledge and power to move the client in the "right" direction. Thus Dworkin (1985) states that control of the client by the worker occurs in all professional relationships, no matter what theoretical framework is used. Usually, this control is not manifest but occurs in an implicit or unconscious way. Dworkin suggests that it would be better if this control were acknowledged and exercised in a systematic and explicit way. A professional should consider whether (a) her intentions are in the best interests of the client, (b) her personal investment in the situation is clear and not motivating her actions, and (c) because of the power differential, there is no conflict between her best interests and those of the client. Berlin assumes that social workers express their power for basically compassionate reasons and suggests that "recognizing the other person's autonomy and capacity tempers the controlling aspects of compassion, thus enhancing the client's self-determination and autonomy" (Berlin 2005, p. 485).

Control and manipulation are not acceptable professional methods. Social workers must consciously avoid these methods and frequently reassess the meaning and practice of client self-determination. What are the ethical considerations that should guide a social worker who is convinced that an older adult client (who can no longer cope alone at home) should enter an assisted-living facility very soon, but who knows from past experience with this client that every worker suggestion elicits a "no" response? If this client has close relatives, should they be asked to make the decision? If there are no close relatives, should the worker make the decision without fully involving the client? To do so limits the client's freedom of choice.

As another example, consider an aging person in a nursing home who is physically disabled, confined to a wheelchair, incontinent, and eating poorly. This woman, who has been fiercely independent throughout her life, now wants to return to her home, even though she will need special care. Her aging sister says she will be able to care for her at home. Although this resident has the law on her side (the 1990 Patient Self-Determination Act and the 1993 Uniform Health Care Decisions Act), her social worker could oppose her voluntary discharge if it appears to be life threatening (Sasson, 2000). Such interventions in the life of the client can range from one-time to ongoing, with minor or major involvement, and must be related to the degree of rational impairment or incapacity for decision making demonstrated by the client, as well as the amount of risk or danger present in the situation.

There is some evidence that class-related or age-related criteria are sometimes used to assess the capacity of different client groups to make autonomous decisions. Those who work with aged clients are very much aware of this problem, but this ethical quandary is not limited to the aged. Stereotypes exist about teenagers, racial and ethnic groups, genders, rich and poor, and other groups as well. A situation involving both the problem of "Who is the client?" and the problem of self-determination is illustrated in Exemplar 6.3.

6.3 SHOULD ELEANOR POMER COME HOME?

Eleanor Pomer is 8 years old, the youngest of six siblings. She has been diagnosed with Down syndrome. For the last three years she has been a resident in a special school. According to her cottage parents, psychologist, teacher, and social worker, she functions on a moderate level but needs assistance with certain daily activities. Both of Eleanor's parents are employed. They rent the downstairs apartment of a two-family home in a working-class neighborhood about one hour's drive from Eleanor's school. The Pomers visit Eleanor once a month; for the past year, Eleanor has successfully spent one weekend a month at home. Both Eleanor and her family look forward to these monthly visits.

The school's staff feels that Eleanor now is ready to leave the school and live at home. The social worker has acquainted Eleanor's parents with this staff assessment. She has told them about the community resources that are available in their city and has urged them to take Eleanor home. However, the Pomers disagree with the staff recommendation. They are satisfied with the present arrangement since they feel that it would be too much of a strain on their other children if Eleanor again lived at home. The social worker is convinced that it would be best for Eleanor to leave the school and resume a more normal home life. She is aware that Eleanor is excited about the possibility of again living with her parents and brothers and sisters.

The ethical problem in this situation arises out of the conflict between applying professional knowledge and respecting the client's right to make decisions. It is further complicated by the question of who is the client. How much weight must the social worker give to the Pomers' and Eleanor's wishes? Should the most important criterion in reaching a decision be what is best for Eleanor? Who decides what is best for Eleanor? What about the welfare of the other Pomer children? Does the social worker have an ethical right to manipulate the environment (e.g., by raising the tuition fee) in order to "help" the Pomers reach the decision that staff thinks is best for Eleanor? Are there standards in the Code that will help her decide what the correct decision is? Does the ethical principles screen in chapter 4 provide any guidance?

Another basic ethical dilemma in social work practice arises out of two—at times contradictory—professional principles that all social workers have accepted: (1) the principle to provide professional help when needed or requested by a client in order to assure or improve that person's welfare, and (2) the principle to not interfere with a person's freedom. Ideally a social worker should not experience any conflict between these two rights (or principles), but what if a person's well-being can be achieved only at the expense of his or her freedom? Who defines well-being? Who defines the need for professional help? Who can legitimately request professional help for another person?

Unless there are serious indications to the contrary, no social worker will want to interfere with another person's freedom, even if that person is her client. It is, however, generally agreed that there are occasions when intervention becomes necessary even if it is at the expense of freedom. Most people agree that a person's right to self-determination should be limited when its exercise will result in harm to another person, but what if the harm is only to the person himself or herself? Though the conditions that justify intervention may seem clear, a social worker will discover many ambiguities. What is *clear and present danger?* How can it be demonstrated? When is harm sufficiently grave to warrant coercion? Who may coerce? How certain must the social worker be that her intervention will prevent the harm before she is justified in curtailing a person's freedom? Consider the situation in Exemplar 6.4.

6.4	How Immediate Is the Danger?

Social worker Maria Espinosa has been working for one month with Allison Bode, an extremely thin, almost gaunt, reserved 17-year-old college freshman. Allison was referred to the Family Counseling Center by her pastor after she told him of her loneliness and obsessive thoughts. She came for help with the agreement and support of her parents. Allison is doing passing work academically but has been unsuccessful making friends at school. This afternoon, Allison told Maria that her menstrual cycle has stopped. When Maria explored the situation, she learned that Allison is on an extremely restricted diet and exercises two to three hours a day to lose weight. She is slightly depressed but still able to concentrate on her school work and reports she is seldom irritable. Based on all of this information, Maria is quite certain that Allison has anorexia and suggests she go to the college health service to consult with a physician. As soon as Allison heard the suggestion, she rejected it.

Is anorexia a case of clear and present danger that requires immediate action? What harm would be done if a few more weekly sessions are used to help Allison act to protect her health and her visit to a physician is delayed? Or should Maria call on the authority of the college and medical personnel to coerce Allison to attend to her illness? What is the ethically correct choice?

More crucial than the type of problem or the chances of rehabilitation or recovery is the question of the client's capacity to make decisions. As long as she can make informed decisions, the social worker has no mandate to interfere, unless (a) it is a question of life and death for the client, or (b) there is serious danger to others in which case she has the duty to warn. The social worker's task is to enable the client to make an informed decision to the maximum extent possible.

An additional dimension of the social worker's ethical mandate arises from his professional obligation to do more than merely observe the negative injunction of not interfering with a person's freedom. Instead or in addition, positive action designed to strengthen or promote the client's freedom is required. If promoting a client's self-determination and not interfering with the client's freedom is to be more than empty rhetoric, social workers must understand that a person is truly autonomous only when all of the following conditions prevail:

- The context provides more than one option from which a person can make choices.
- There is no coercion by the social worker or others professionally involved in the case to choose one or another option.
- The person is aware of all the available options.
- The person has accurate information about the cost and consequences of each option so that he or she can assess them realistically.

- The person has the capacity and/or initiative to make a decision on the basis of this assessment.
- The person has an opportunity to act on the basis of his or her choice.

No extensive research is needed to discover that the freedom of most social work clients is quite limited. Social workers must be concerned when anybody's freedom is limited. Americans enjoy more freedom than the citizens of many other countries, but the social and economic conditions limit some of the freedom of most people in almost all contemporary societies. Inequality, racism, sexism, and ageism are especially blatant conditions that limit people's freedom. As Stevens (1998) reminds us, the freedom to choose and the right to make decisions are profoundly cherished rights; however, "self-determination is grievously restrained when opportunities for social mobility are blocked" (p. 294).

Social workers are committed to use their professional skill and know-how to help not only their clients but all people gain full freedom. This ethical commitment may explain why many social workers have been in the forefront of struggles for more freedom and greater equality for all people. This ethical concern for greater autonomy must also find expression in the day-to-day practice of social workers.

The ability to engage in self-determination also varies with the dependency of the client on the benefits he receives from his social worker. The more essential and valuable the goods or services received, the greater the client's feelings of dependency on the worker and the less likely it is that he will choose an option that he believes his social worker will disapprove. Thus, public assistance recipients, especially those who believe that they themselves are personally responsible for being on "welfare," are less assertive about their rights, less likely to disagree with their caseworker, and less prone to appeal a decision. Stigma, loss of self-esteem, psychological and economic hardship, and a lack of options undermine the ability to be self-determining (Goodban, 1985). Fewer options become available for public assistance clients as the rules demanding work become ever more rigorous (Pear, 2006; Soss, Schram, Vartanian, & O'Brien, 2004). For example, under the Personal Responsibility and Work Opportunity Act (1996), women who do not comply with work rules can lose all or some of their cash assistance, food stamps, and Medicaid; any one of these losses, even a partial one, can have serious consequences for these women (Lens, 2006).

The limited knowledge and/or capacity of many clients to engage in autonomous decision making places a crucial ethical obligation on the social worker since she is obliged to help them make reasoned choices that will maximize their benefits, while at the same time preserve and strengthen whatever autonomy and freedom they possess. The ethical dilemma remains even when it is recognized that, in the final analysis, the center of gravity in the helping process remains with the professional. As Rothman (1989) stated, "the prime responsibility for making professional decisions about means of helping the client falls to the practitioners" (p. 608).

AMBIGUITY AND UNCERTAINTY

The degree of ambiguity and uncertainty encountered in practice situations can increase the probability of ethical dilemmas. Three types of ambiguity and uncertainty make for ethical problems in social work practice: (1) uncertainty about values and goals, (2) uncertainty about scientific knowledge and about the facts relevant to any specific situation, and (3) uncertainty about the consequences of the intervention.

Ambiguity may be a more critical problem for social workers than for many other professional practitioners because the issues with which social workers deal are often nonspecific, and because social workers generally have less control over the outcome of their intervention than do practitioners in many other professional fields. There may be ambiguity about the nature and assessment of the problems that persons bring to a social worker. Frequently clients, despite their experience of pain and discomfort, do not really know what their problem is, what their goals are, or how to achieve them. They and the social worker may not know the precise nature of their troubles and there may not be any way to help the client. In addition, there may be many different participants in the situation, such as clients, family members, neighbors, other mental health professionals, and insurance companies, all of whom may have different perspectives about the desired outcome (Kirk & Kutchins, 1992).

So many different factors impinge simultaneously on a person that it is often difficult for a social worker to assess the specific impact of her intervention. An unsuccessful outcome may be (but need not be) due to something that the social worker did or did not do—or it may be the result of factors over which the social worker had no control. The same intervention activity in two seemingly identical problem situations may lead to two entirely different outcomes because of factors over which the social worker has no power. Nor will any member of any profession ever know what might have happened had she not intervened or used a different intervention strategy. For example, in a case of suspected child abuse, a social worker cannot predict with any certainty what might happen if the child stays with his parents, nor will the worker know for certain what might happen if the child is forcibly placed in out-of-home care. One such situation with many ambiguities is explored in Exemplar 6.5.

| 6.5 | A VICTIM OF CHILD ABUSE |

Several months ago, Wendy Gillis told her public welfare social worker that she suspected that an upstairs neighbor, George Hill, regularly and brutally beat his 2-year-old son, Leroy. She heard the most frightful noises several evenings each week. When she saw the boy at rare intervals, he always wore bandages and looked so sad. The worker noted these remarks in her case report, but took no further action.

Last month, George's wife, Anne, brought Leroy to Lakeside General Hospital emergency room. Leroy suffered from multiple fractures, which according to his mother, occurred when he fell down the front stairs. The attending physician did not believe her story because the X-ray revealed a large number of previous fractures in addition to the current ones. As required by law, he notified child protective services (CPS) that he suspected child abuse. Andre Conti, an experienced CPS social worker, was sent to the Hill home to investigate. He talked at length with both parents, who admitted beating Leroy occasionally when he misbehaved, as their way of disciplining him. Andre suggested that there were other ways to teach a boy to behave properly but concluded that the boy was in no immediate danger. Two weeks later, another social worker made a follow-up visit to the Hill home. This worker, Millie Walker, agreed with Andre's assessment that for the time being there was no need to remove Leroy from his home. Ten days after Millie's visit, Anne Hill called for an ambulance, saying that her son was having difficulty breathing. When the ambulance crew arrived, they found Leroy unconscious. Twelve hours after he was brought to the hospital, he was pronounced dead. The postmortem confirmed that death was caused by a severe beating with a blunt instrument.

This exemplar gives rise to a number of questions with ethical implications, including the following: Did Wendy Gillis's social worker pay sufficient attention to the report of suspected child abuse and was Wendy's concern sufficient reason to warrant interfering in the Hill family? How can Andre Conti or any social worker know for certain that "a clear and present danger" existed for Leroy's life? When does parental discipline become child abuse? Under what conditions is the removal of a child from his family justified? How certain must a social worker be of the consequences before deciding to leave an endangered child with his family?

It should be noted that there are three sets of ambiguities in the Leroy Hill exemplar:

- Ambiguities resulting from a lack of clarity of societal norms (e.g., what are the limits of parental discipline?)
- Ambiguities resulting from a lack of knowledge (e.g., what evidence is sufficient to warrant intervention?)
- Ambiguities resulting from an inability to know what the future will bring (e.g., what will be the consequences of intervention?)

The social workers involved in this case made professional judgments that Leroy was not at risk. As a consequence of their mistaken judgment, Leroy is now dead. The mistake could also have gone the other way—identifying a risk when there was no danger to the child's welfare and thus removing the boy from his home needlessly. Every social worker in this situation faces a critical ethical dilemma because both types of mistakes cannot be avoided at the same time. Ambiguities and uncertainties are endemic conditions in social work practice. Neither the social worker nor anyone else can know for certain that a given parental behavior will lead to the child's death. The test of an effective social worker is that she should retain the ability to function even while coping with the ethical dilemmas that result from ambiguity and uncertainty.

EXERCISES

1. Role-play the situation described earlier in this chapter where the social worker has determined that her older adult client is no longer able to live alone in his home. We know that this client responds negatively to every worker suggestion. Try various approaches to this problem situation. Keep in mind the ethical aspects.
2. Rothman (1989) and others have stated that the primary responsibility for making professional decisions falls on the social work practitioner. On the other hand, many social workers argue that the client has the exclusive right to make decisions about his life. Interview a social worker about these two professional perspectives. Ask them what ethical factors they consider when they decide to take the primary responsibility for making professional decisions about the client's personal life situation.
3. Assume that you are the child protection social worker sent to investigate the report of Leroy Hill's abuse (Exemplar 6.5). What criteria would you use to arrive at a decision to remove or not to remove Leroy from his parental home? Keep in mind the ethical aspects.

SUGGESTIONS FOR ADDITIONAL READINGS

Healy (2004) explores the degree to which practitioners try to influence clients to accept a course of action preferred by the practitioner and the means they use to do so. Moody

There are critical questions about this value-neutral stance that must be considered, including whether value neutrality or value suspension is a realistic option for social workers. Turner (2002) suggests "it is impossible to interact with another human being ... without making a series of judgments and observations about them that shape our responses to them" (p. 61). What are social workers to do with the values they hold when working with clients who hold contrary values? Can social workers really avoid introducing or imposing their own values by subtle or nonverbal communications?

There are no easy answers to these questions, but these are considerations that must be made by every practitioner. Many believe that suspension of judgment, a basic concept in social work, has been so misinterpreted that it has caused rather than prevented much unethical professional behavior. Siporin (1985a) writes that "in being of help to people, there is need to make moral ethical judgments, and to help clients do so as well" (p. 202). Goldstein (1998) suggests that the social work profession cannot be concerned only with what works but also must develop a moral orientation. Since the situations and problems of social work practice present difficult moral dilemmas, Goldstein believes that social workers have an ethical obligation to act as moral agents—they cannot ignore what is good and ethically correct, what is "right" and "wrong." There is no possibility to avoid moral and ethical issues that exist at each step of the social work processes. Maslow (cited in Bergin, 1980, p. 99) believed that "to study human behavior means never to ignore concepts of right and wrong ... the question of right and wrong behavior is essential." Furthermore, he suggested that a science that "is morally neutral, value free, value neutral is not only wrong, but extremely dangerous" (1969, p. 724). Therefore, in practice it is wrong and potentially dangerous to assume that value neutrality is a true characteristic of social work.

Value neutrality may actually cause damage in the following situations:

- Attention is not paid to potentially self-destructive or other-destructive acts.
- Social workers fail to distinguish between what is functional or dysfunctional, normative or pathological behavior.
- Failing to challenge a client's behavior may result in that client thinking that the social worker approves of what he does. The worker may intend her silence to be an expression of value neutrality, but her silence may be interpreted as a signal of acceptance of that behavior.

Value neutrality is itself a value. Sometimes social workers do not acknowledge their own moral judgments. The contemporary social worker who bases her practice on value neutrality may be avoiding all moral dilemmas by accepting the client's absolute right for self-determination. Historically, value suspension became a professional response to the moralistic paternalism that was practiced by the Friendly Visitors (the volunteers who preceded professional social workers in the last decades of the nineteenth century); such an approach was modeled after the early psychoanalytic view that therapy should be a value-free scientific activity (Holmes, 1997). Originally, suspension of judgment meant that the social worker related to the client's whole person and to his strengths, instead of only to his weaknesses and problems. It meant trying to understand this person in terms of his total personal history, environment, culture, and community. If the client's behavior was problematic, then the social worker was ready to help him change that behavior without condemning him. This was often expressed as "I accept you, but not your behavior." Can we honestly say that we do not care what a client does? Can we accept child molestation, neglect, violence, cheating, stealing, or lying? Dare social workers not condemn physical and sexual abuse, rape and beatings, irresponsible sexual activities, and similar antisocial behaviors?

According to Clark (2006), "key values such as respect and self-determination have to be actualized in practical contexts that inevitably favor one credible interpretation over another...the expression of key values cannot be independent of personal sympathies" (p. 76). Bergin (1980, 1991) argues that therapeutic neutrality is a myth, that even the most "nondirective" of therapists maintain strongly held values that are communicated in one way or another to clients. Carey (2006) concluded "none of us can help having a personal take on any issue a patient is discussing, and there is no way for us to think about any issue—let alone intervene—without that being influenced by our own very personal psychology" (p. D2).

In today's practice context, social workers have to balance the notion of the client's right to self-determination against being directive. There is more clarity about directiveness or paternalism when clients do not have the capacity to make informed decisions and when there is the likelihood of potential harm and danger to the client or to others (Kelly, 1994). More directiveness by practitioners may be demanded by managed care, pressures to maintain agency funding or income, and productivity measures.

Rothman and colleagues (1996) found that all social workers, even those using psychodynamic as well as cognitive-behavioral, task-centered, and brief treatment focuses, used a broad range of directiveness modalities in their practices. Although the directiveness modalities they used were influenced by specific contextual factors, they avoided either extreme—paternalism or client self-determination—as their only practice pattern. However, this flexibility and consistency reflects one of the practical limitations to social worker neutrality, in that it discounts the social worker's ethical and legal responsibility to "promote the well-being of clients" (NASW Code, 1999, 1.01).

VALUE IMPOSITION

Much of what social workers do involves helping people choose between available options. Both the worker's and the client's ethical principles are important considerations in making this choice. Can a social worker provide this help without imposing her own values? This question takes on special urgency because social workers often grapple with strategies that are designed to modify or change the behaviors, beliefs, and values of clients.

Some approaches to helping people with problems assume that it is desirable to systematically change their values and thought patterns by substituting more sensible and rational thoughts and values, such as those held by social workers. The rational/emotive therapy (RET) developed by Ellis is one school of therapy that recommends this view. The therapist's values always should influence client values. For example, RET "shares the views of ethical humanism by *encouraging* people to emphasize human interest (self and social) over the interests of deities, material objects, and lower animals" (Dryden & Ellis, 1988, p. 232, emphasis added). While those following this school suggest that these values be used in a conscious and controlled manner (Frank, 1991), many others disagree with any attempts to impose values.

Even when a social worker does not want to impose her own values, she may do so unintentionally. Covert messages about value, such as body language, facial expressions, and tone of voice, are often more powerful than overt ones. The social worker may be unaware that she is subtly communicating her preferences or values commitments in these ways. A social worker may also define the goals and outcomes of the treatment without once saying what she deems appropriate, but by not presenting options he considers "inappropriate" she has effectively imposed her values. How can one ethically justify such worker control? Some have suggested that an explicit communication of the social worker's values would safeguard the client against such potential misuse of power by the worker. Sophie Freud (1999) went so far as to suggest "it might even be best to admit our own biases to our clients and engage in honest debates with them . . ." (p. 338). Such self-disclosure of the worker's values may enhance the client's comfort with and sense of trust in the practitioner. However, value self-disclosure may be harmful when used inappropriately or at the wrong time, especially early in the professional relationship. Spero (1990) and Strean (1997) concluded that any short-term advantages of a worker's value disclosure may be cancelled by long-term harmful effects.

The problem facing the social worker of Bess and Todd Moore, described in Exemplar 7.2, illustrates the range of ethical dilemmas around the issue of imposing values.

| 7.2 | SAVING A MARRIAGE |

Bess and Todd Moore have agreed to seek help to "rescue" their marriage. Bess recently discovered that Todd has been having sex with several other women over the past few years. Todd has told the social worker that his sexual relations with other women are only physical. He has greater sexual needs than Bess and therefore cannot give up these relations. Yet he loves his wife and wants to continue this marriage. Bess is ready to forgive the past, but cannot bring herself to live with Todd knowing that he will continue to have sex with other women.

Different social workers hold different values about marriage and extramarital relations. Should the social worker keep her own values to herself so that she will not influence the Moores' decision? Is this possible? Or should the social worker openly state her own values and then let Bess and Todd work on a solution to their problem? Which is the more ethical approach?

A recently developed school of thought suggests a third approach, challenging the assumptions of objectivity, value neutrality, and scientific expertise. Using assessment as their focus, Iversen, Gergen, and Fairbanks (2005) suggest the importance and validity of engaging in dialogue and collaboration with clients; rather than assuming she knows what the problem is, the social worker should engage in active negotiation with the client to define the problem. From this perspective, they propose understanding assessment as a collaborative deliberation concerning various possibilities for the client's life, relationships, and the future. However, the social worker cannot evade making decisions about assessments and any conflicts of values by simply engaging clients in collaborative assessments.

Do social workers have a responsibility to examine together with the client the ethical nature and quality of the problems that people bring to them? Or is it more helpful to overlook the moral aspects of the situation? Society, with near unanimity, condemns child sexual abuse and incest. Should a social worker assume a value-free stance and listen to her client's report of what could be incestuous behavior with the same equanimity as she would to any other problem he may raise? Should she communicate the community's valuation of incest? Does it make a difference whether the abuser or the victim is the worker's client? Are there cultural factors that might make a difference in assessing the ethical implications of this type of behavior? What if the client's ethnic culture does not proscribe father/daughter relations that do not involve penetration? What if the incestuous relations occur between consenting adults? What about legal requirements to report abuse? To what extent would keeping quiet translate into condoning such behavior? What is the social worker's role as a societal agent?

MAKING JUDGMENTS ABOUT VALUES

The three types of value situations that have been discussed in this chapter—client/worker value gap, value neutrality, and value imposition—form a matrix of ethical considerations (client/social worker differences, neutrality, imposing values). Even those social workers who attempt to maintain a value-free stance will abandon this behavior beyond a certain point. To give an obvious example, no social workers will sit by quietly when a father describes how he threw his 1-year old child from a third-floor balcony. But the ethical dilemma is more serious than such unusual examples suggest because, in fact, ethical quandaries involving the social worker's values and judgment occur at every step of the social work process. The social worker who suspends her judgment when a client relates a promiscuous episode or an aggressive behavior incident may be as judgmental as her colleague who does not hesitate to indicate disapproval. When a client expresses guilt about a certain behavior but continues to engage in that behavior, he may conclude that the worker considers such behavior acceptable if the worker addresses only the problem of guilt. One psychiatrist summed up this latter point of view when he stated, "I'm a shrink, so I'm more interested in his motivation than his morality" (Lipsyte, 2002, p. 5). Is such a stance ethical for a social worker?

It has been suggested that in these and similar situations a social worker can avoid making judgments by letting the client decide what he wants—whether he wants help with his "guilt" or with the "deviant" behavior. At first glance this appeal to the principle of client self-determination seems to solve all ethical problems. On second thought it may turn out that this is an irresponsible and perhaps even an unethical response to a client who desperately seeks help. Even when the client's request for help is specific, the worker may have a societal responsibility that she dare not shirk. For example, should a social worker help a client manage and reduce his feelings of guilt so he can continue an extramarital affair, continue abusing his wife, or continue stealing money from his employer?

As the population of the United States grows more diverse through changing patterns of immigration, social workers are faced more frequently with behaviors that generally lie outside their experiences. Consider Exemplar 7.3.

| 7.3 | Loyalty to Self or Family? |

Rosa Arriga, a social worker at a family service agency, has seen Adira Salima for three sessions. Adira has been depressed, has experienced much conflict at home with her parents and other relatives, and has been subject to much anxiety on her job as a packer. All family members, including Adira, are recent immigrants to the United States. All must work because everyone's paycheck is necessary to maintain a marginal existence. Her supervisor, who likes her, referred her to the agency for help. Adira told Rosa that her family will not allow her to have a normal American social life. Her parents, who want to arrange a marriage for her, do not allow her to date. She cannot leave home because her earnings are insufficient to support herself. Her knowledge of English and her other skills are not sufficient to qualify her for a better job. Adira vacillates between feeling pride at doing what is expected in her family's culture, and wanting to become more Americanized by dating and deciding for herself whom she should marry.

What should be Rosa's approach? Should she support loyalty to Adira's family because they are all dependent on each other and they are her only relatives in the United States? Should she support Adira's struggle toward more independence? If Adira has the possibility of living with extended family members or friends she knows from her past, should she be encouraged to leave home and live with them? How should Rosa, who is a feminist, respond to this situation, and would it be possible or appropriate for her to be value neutral when discussing options with Adira? Would it make a difference if Rosa was from the same culture as Adira's family and a member of their community? Value neutrality seems neither helpful nor possible.

It seems that suspension of judgment is an impossible demand. The Code of Ethics and social work practice stress self-determination, but doesn't Adira have some obligation to her family and group? Some social workers try to avoid the ethical dilemma by suggesting to a client that they approve or disapprove only of a specific behavior, not of the client. This is a fine, almost legalistic distinction that may seem to avoid the ethical issues posed here. Such a solution, however, creates other practice problems and does not really avoid the ethical issues raised. Perhaps a more realistic way of phrasing this ethical obligation is to demand that the social worker's own value judgment never become the sole criterion for making a decision. There is no relationship that is free of values. At the same time, we must remember that it is the client's responsibility to identify the values that will guide her behavioral choices; the social worker can never assume this responsibility (Frankl, 1968).

THE INEVITABILITY OF VALUES

In this chapter, we have included sections on value neutrality, the imposition of values, and client/worker value gaps. One must remember that practice should reflect the value principles of the social work profession that are expressed in the Code of Ethics.

Goldstein (1998) describes the ethically grounded social worker as "alert and responsive to questions of moral choice, social justice, prevailing moral codes of conduct, and, not the least, personal accountability whether she is doing research, applying theory, planning, or engaging in practice—any professional activity that

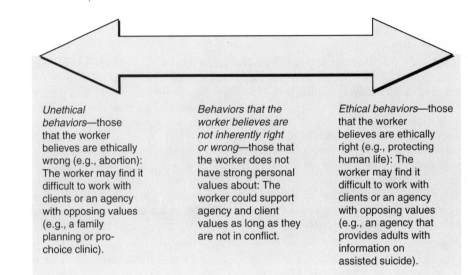

| Unethical behaviors—those that the worker believes are ethically wrong (e.g., abortion): The worker may find it difficult to work with clients or an agency with opposing values (e.g., a family planning or pro-choice clinic). | Behaviors that the worker believes are not inherently right or wrong—those that the worker does not have strong personal values about: The worker could support agency and client values as long as they are not in conflict. | Ethical behaviors—those that the worker believes are ethically right (e.g., protecting human life): The worker may find it difficult to work with clients or an agency with opposing values (e.g., an agency that provides adults with information on assisted suicide). |

FIGURE 7.1 | CONTINUUM OF WORKER VALUES

impinges on the life and well-being of others" (p. 246). Ethical decisions by social workers have importance at every level of practice—from the individual case to societal and political action. One means of selecting from the multitude of ethical issues for clients and oneself in practice is through a screening device. Behavior can be considered along a continuum. Knowing where one falls on this continuum can help in deciding when one can anticipate value conflicts. One can observe in the continuum of worker values shown in Figure 7.1 that a social worker can find it inadvisable in some situations to work with clients whose values are significantly contrary to her own. This continuum is intended to assist social workers in a systematic way as they consider differences in values concerning themselves, clients, and agencies.

But the ethical dilemmas posed by the social worker's values and those of a potential employer are not encountered just in relation to particular client individuals or groups. In Exemplar 7.3, conflicting cultural values are in play. The question was raised as to how a social worker who is committed to strong feminist values might deal with the value conflicts in the situation. Whose values should take priority?

There are, however, prior implications for the social worker, derived in the continuum of worker values. If information is known to them about the values of a potential employing agency, should social workers (given their own conflicting values) seek employment or accept jobs with employers who only will or will not hire lesbians, oppose family planning or are pro-choice, overtly or covertly discriminate against particular groups, and view stern "discipline" of children as appropriate? Thus, even before engaging in the work of the agency, social workers have to consider whose values take priority.

Situations as described in this chapter may present painful dilemmas for both clients and social workers but—for example—neglect, abuse, and violence also raise questions as to whom the social worker represents, whose welfare is at stake, and social workers' roles as moral agents. The Code of Ethics (1999) states that "social workers should promote the general welfare of society" (6.01) and "social workers should act to expand choice and opportunity for all people, with special regard for vulnerable, disadvantaged, oppressed, and exploited people and groups" (6.04b).

EXERCISES

1. It has been said that even when a social worker does not declare her values publicly, her lifestyle and her nonverbal communications will usually indicate the values she holds. Identify how your own lifestyle and nonverbal messages might inform Adira Salima as a client (Exemplar 7.3) of the values you hold. What problems might this create for maintaining a professional relationship?
2. The risk of acquiring HIV from sexual activities has been compared with the risk of a fatal automobile accident. Does such a comparison communicate a value, or is it an example of value neutrality? Defend your answer.
3. Your client feels very guilty about engaging in certain behavior. Assume that this behavior is not illegal. He asks your help, but he does not specify whether he wants help in dealing with his guilt or in extinguishing the behavior. Discuss the ethical implications of choosing either approach. Will the specific behavior make a difference in your ethical assessment? Try to assess the two approaches with the following types of behavior: overeating, smoking, gambling, masturbation, eating foods his physician suggested he avoid for medical reasons, having an extramarital affair, or taking the time to work out for an hour five times a week.
4. How would you respond to the telephone call that Jeff Butz received (Exemplar 7.1)?
5. Can a social worker be neutral and value free concerning issues such as suicide, adultery, use of drugs, or engaging in illegal behaviors? There are social workers who might support a person's right to engage in these behaviors because they believe they should take a value-free approach. In group discussions, decide which view is right, and identify the implications of each approach for ethical decision making. What options are available for a social worker in dealing with such issues? Who will decide and what values will prevail?

SUGGESTIONS FOR ADDITIONAL READINGS

Clark (2005) suggests that the place of values in social work practice is crucial, and social workers have to be moral agents. Simon and Gutheil (1997) defend the duty of neutrality for therapists. Bisman (2004) discusses social work values as "the moral core of the profession." Iversen, Gergen, and Fairbanks (2005) trace the assessment procedures in social work to empiricism, suggesting they are based on assumptions of objectivity, measurement accuracy, value neutrality, and scientific expertise.

WEB SITES OF INTEREST

Using any Internet search engine to search for "social work values," you are likely to get thousands of hits (www.google.com found over 102,000 hits in January 2007). If you are very interested in this topic, you may want to do just that to get a sense of the incredible amount of information available on the Web. If you don't want to start that broadly, you might want to visit the following sites.

- Scottish Executive Publications for an article on "The Role of the Social Worker in the 21st Century, Professional Values and Ethics": www.scotland.gov.uk/Publications/2005/12/1994633/46349

- The Association of Baccalaureate Social Work Program Directors (BPD) has an Information Technology Subcommittee on Curriculum Resources for Social Work Values and Ethics: www.uncp.edu/home/marson/nhome.htm
- The Center for the Study of Ethics in the Professions at the Illinois Institute of Technology provides links to hundreds of professional codes of ethics and information on the function of codes of ethics, including a case study for using a code of ethics: http://ethics.iit.edu/codes/
- The International Federation of Social Workers presents their social work values: www.ifsw.org/en/p38000208.html
- The Bureau of Labor Statistics (BLS), U.S. Department of Labor, *Occupational Outlook Handbook, 2006–07 Edition*, Social Workers provides the occupational outlook for social work and other disciplines; note that the discussion of social work includes values: www.bls.gov/oco/ocos060.htm

EQUALITY, INEQUALITY, LIMITED RESOURCES, AND ADVOCACY

Every person has an equal right to obtain social benefits and an equal obligation to carry social burdens. This principle is based on the first-order societal value of equity and suggests that goods should be distributed as widely and as equally as possible. Persons in similar situations should be treated in the same way unless this equality of treatment is outweighed by other considerations such as fairness and beneficence. Those in the most needy and most vulnerable groups need to receive greater resources and more services in order to obtain their "fair share" and "fair opportunities" (Rawls, 2001). From this societal value, social workers have derived the professional rule that obligates them to distribute available resources on an equal basis to all clients, unless unequal distribution is indicated for the reasons suggested by beneficence and fairness.

COMMITMENT TO EQUALITY

All social workers will agree that everyone is entitled to an equal share of available resources, yet an ethical problem occurs when the available resources are so limited that an equal distribution is not possible and choices must be made about to whom to allocate these. In other words, some will receive these resources and others will not, thus resulting in unequal treatment. For example, when a county has only 20 beds for chronically ill older people, these cannot be distributed on an equal basis to 30 clients who desperately need this service. The equity value may create ethical problems even with respect to goods and services that lend themselves to an equal division (e.g., the social worker's time or the department's budget), because another professional value may obligate the practitioner to allocate more of her time or resources to meet the specific needs of a certain client. In the sections that follow we will discuss how time, inequality, diversity, and discrimination are related to a commitment to equality.

TIME

Time is a very limited and precious resource in the social work process. For example, a social worker in a family agency is available 30 hours each week for direct service to clients. Is each of her 30 clients entitled to a one-hour session every week? For some clients, an hour a week may be more than what they need, while for others it may not be sufficient. Is it ethical for a social worker to devote several hours to one client this week to help him cope with an unexpected and sudden family crisis, even if this results in less time being available for other clients? Many social workers recall situations when a client could have received more effective service if only there had been more time available. Ethical dilemmas can occur both in regard to fairness (equity) and equality (equally situated persons receiving equal treatment). For example, the attempt to observe equity in the allocation of time to clients results in several ethical dilemmas, one of which is illustrated in Exemplar 8.1.

8.1	INCEST IN THE SCHILD FAMILY

Doreen Schild is a 13-year-old with a history of school truancy, alcohol and drug experimentation, and several attempts at running away from home. Her parents appear warm and accepting, but the family agency worker who has been meeting with Doreen for the past four weeks suspects that the real problem is Doreen's home life. Today was the fifth session with Doreen. The conversation was routine, and little of significance was said until three minutes before the next client's scheduled appointment. Suddenly, Doreen said that both her father and older brother have tried repeatedly to have sexual relations with her, but thus far she has not let them go all the way. When she told her mother about this, she was told to forget it had ever happened. As Doreen related this information, she became noticeably more upset.

The social worker realized that this interview could not be terminated just because time was up. Doreen was agitated, and the session could not be ended at that point. Later, the worker would need to make a report of suspected child abuse to child protective services. She was not sure how long the discussion with Doreen would take and was worried about how long she could keep the next client waiting. Doreen could easily use all of the next client's hour, but that would not be fair to the other clients scheduled for that day, who may also be experiencing serious difficulties.

What would you do? What other ethical issues, in addition to the equity issue, does this worker face? What are the social worker's obligations to Doreen, her parents, other clients with whom she has appointments scheduled, and the community? How should a social worker be prepared to deal with such unexpected situations?

INEQUALITY AND THE DISTRIBUTION OF SCARCE RESOURCES

Americans have accepted as a self-evident truth that all persons are created equal. From this first-order value, social workers have derived the ethical rules of "equal distribution of resources" and "equal access to opportunities." Equality is often equated with democracy. Those raised in this tradition often find it difficult to understand how anyone can raise questions about it. They are upset when it is suggested that an equal distribution of resources is not always ethical and may result in serious injustices.

It is self-evident that all people are entitled to the best medical services, but some have asked whether it is right that medical resources, especially scarce and expensive life-extending technologies and instruments, are distributed equally to all, regardless of a patient's age. Daniel Callahan (1987), a philosopher and medical ethicist, does not seem to think that such an equalitarian approach is ethical. He writes that medicine should "resist the tendency to provide to the aged life-extending capabilities developed primarily to help younger people avoid premature and untimely death" (p. 24). He suggests that age be used as a decision criterion for allocating life-extending therapies. Does this mean that open-heart surgery should not be available only to people over a given age, such as 80? Is not the life of an 84-year-old person as important and valuable as that of a 74-year-old person? Some would argue that the chances of a successful operation decrease rapidly as people grow older. Others avoid this statistical argument by noting that it is preferable to use limited resources to add 20 years of life rather than one or two years, particularly when the younger person can still make a valuable contribution to society, while the aging person may be totally dependent on others for the rest of his life. In recent years, a version of this problem has been noted in Oregon, which uses a prioritized list of health services for its Medicaid program. Services are listed from most important to least important for their comparative benefit to the population served, resulting in rationing of health services for those who receive Medicaid based on the funds available (Oregon Health Services Commission, 2006).

Deciding the allocation of societal resources on the basis of potential returns to society gives rise to other serious ethical problems. The social contribution of highly intelligent people may be more valuable than that of people with a lower intelligence and perhaps more significant than that of persons with mental retardation. But does this give society the ethical right to provide open-heart surgery only to those whose IQ is above 140 or some other arbitrary line or to people with a college degree? Is it ethical for society to limit such open-heart surgery to those with sufficient income to be able to pay for this life-saving operation? This diabolic argument can be pushed even further by arguing for the elimination of all undesirables, a policy implemented by Nazi Germany in the 1940s. While few will maintain that the "final solution" was ethical or moral, the implication of this approach for the unequal distribution of resources demands further careful thought. While these examples come from the health field, parallel problems occur in social work situations. Can you think of any?

Even if you have not yet encountered such situations, many social work resources in health, mental health, and child welfare are not distributed equally. Members of minority groups suffer disproportionately from mental illness because they often lack access to services, receive lower quality care, and are less likely to seek help when in distress (Goode, 2001). In a review of child welfare research, it was found that "children of color and their families experience poorer outcomes and receive fewer services than their Caucasian counterparts" (Courtney et al., 1996, p. 99). A similar conclusion was reached by Rodenborg (2004), who found that when African American children were child welfare clients, they received fewer and lower quality services, fewer parental supports were made available, and these children were more likely to be placed in institutional placements. It is urgent that, wherever such unequal distribution of resources exists, this issue be reexamined and, if necessary, corrected by providing unequal (i.e., more and better) services.

The provision of unequal treatment can be overt but more often occurs in social agencies in more subtle and less formal ways. Exemplar 8.2 illustrates how unequal treatment can take place unofficially.

8.2 | **A FRIEND IN NEED IS A FRIEND INDEED**

Latoya Jefferson is a volunteer social worker in an emergency food pantry where persons come to obtain needed food for themselves and their families. The only requirement is that people answer several questions: name, household size, and source of income, not subject to verification. No one asks about living situations (a place to cook, ages of children, or special dietary needs). There are not enough paid staff and volunteers to run the pantry as well as is needed. Because of the shortage of supplies, families can only receive food once a month, but over time the staff and volunteers still get to know individuals and their situations.

Latoya, the paid director of the pantry, recently discovered that Keisha Attlee, another volunteer social worker, favors some clients over others. She chooses favorites who are especially friendly or who have well-disciplined and cute children with them. She also identifies those she thinks "abuse" the system; when food is in short supply, she refers the "abusers" to another pantry while assisting her favorites. When Latoya complained to Keisha about her discriminating so that some get needed supplies and others are referred elsewhere, Keisha replied, "In my view I am giving food to those who are most needy and cooperative. Aren't they entitled to the help? Because they have it together I know they will make good use of the food. Those I refer elsewhere may be selling the food and buying beer and whiskey. Furthermore, as a volunteer I don't want to be supervised. If you keep bothering me, I will just leave and you can do the job."

What should Latoya do? If she "bothers" Keisha, the pantry loses a volunteer worker whom they need because they are short of staff. Do the so-called abusers actually misuse the food? Does it make a difference if they do so? If Latoya keeps quiet, some families receive supplies while others don't. As it is now, who gets food often depends on who the volunteer is and only the luck of the draw determines who gets what.

As noted in chapter 4, there is another side to inequality. Those who are not equal should receive special help (both services and resources) in order to gain equal access to life opportunities. It is this consideration that often justifies the unequal allocation of resources. Children with disabilities, for example, may receive more attention and greater resources than other children in order to compensate for their disabilities. A blind child will not have the same access to education as a sighted child unless society provides the blind child with extra resources, such as talking books and/or a reader. In other words, unequal allocation of resources to those who are not equal or who do not have equal access to life opportunities is more ethical than sticking to equality at all costs!

DISCRIMINATION AND DIVERSITY

Despite the efforts of many social workers and other citizens, discrimination continues to exist in America. In what has become increasingly a multiracial, multiethnic, and highly diverse society, competition for various resources undoubtedly exacerbates conflicts between groups, especially during times of recession, economic changes, and increased international economic competition. But discrimination is not only the result of competition for various resources; discrimination can also be the result of prejudices and stereotypes, such as prejudging others on the basis of unproven assumptions about individuals and groups, and preexisting feelings and attitudes unrelated to the actual persons. For social workers, discrimination is a societal problem that directly affects their practice, the availability of resources, and the delivery of social services. The NASW Code of Ethics states that:

> Social workers should not practice, condone, facilitate, or collaborate with any form of discrimination on the basis of race, ethnicity, national origin, color, sex, sexual orientation, age, marital status, political belief, religion, or mental or physical disability (NASW Code, 1999, 4.02).

Discrimination is contrary to the ethical standards of the profession. Whenever and wherever discrimination interferes, social workers cannot achieve their professional aims.

The ethical principles enunciated in the Code of Ethics call on social workers "to help people in need and to address social problems," to "pursue social change, particularly with and on behalf of vulnerable and oppressed individuals and groups of people," to be "mindful of individual differences and cultural and ethnic diversity," and to "promote, restore, maintain, and enhance the well-being of individuals, families, social groups, organizations, and communities" (NASW Code, 1999, Ethical Principles). There is a whole range of activities that are needed to fight discrimination, ranging from individual interactions to confrontation of institutional and societal racism. Some have suggested that there is a difference between the individual social worker's obligation to fight discrimination and the profession's obligation to fight discrimination. However, both individual social workers and the profession as an organization have a responsibility to address discrimination.

The NASW Standards for Cultural Competence in Social Work Practice (2001) call on social workers to become proficient "to respond respectfully and effectively to people of all cultures, languages, classes, races, ethnic backgrounds, religions, and other diversity factors in a manner that recognizes, affirms, and values the worth of individuals, families, and communities and protects and preserves the dignity of each" (p. 11).

The Council on Social Work Education (CSWE) addressed the issue of discrimination in social work by including as an educational purpose for social work education the preparation of "social workers to practice without discrimination, with respect, and with knowledge and skills related to clients' age, class, color, culture, disability, ethnicity, family structure, gender, marital status, national origin, race, religion, sex, and sexual orientation" (Educational Policy and Accreditation Standards, 2004, p. 5). Prior to this, all schools of social work had made serious efforts to become antidiscriminatory institutions.

The social work professional associations—including NASW and CSWE—have responsibilities to eliminate discrimination through advocacy, social action, legal, and other efforts within their organizations and in society. Discrimination in society and the profession makes it difficult to achieve social work's goals and ethical aims of equal access—equitable services and resources—for the fulfillment of individuals and the society. Discrimination is unethical and its existence tends to make for additional social problems. Individual social workers also have an ethical responsibility to work toward the elimination of discrimination in their practice, employment, and in society, first because it is unethical and second because it contributes to the creation of additional social problems.

Earlier in this chapter, we reviewed reports that suggest that discrimination exists in provision of health, mental health, and child welfare services. It has been suggested that in these services some social workers may have been responsible for serious ethical breaches. Even though they did not necessarily engage in deliberate unethical activities, their behavior was unethical if they remained silent in the face of systematic institutional discrimination. The single child welfare worker may not be able to change the entire system, but this is hardly an excuse to avoid attempts to change as much of one's local system as possible. What are the ethical obligations of social workers who encounter such ethics violations by systems or institutions? What advice does the NASW Code of Ethics (1999) provide social workers who find themselves in these situations?

What should you do if you are on the staff of a training program for young adults whose funding will be cut unless the program serves both White and African American persons? At present few Whites are enrolled. In order to meet the demands of the funding agency, staff are now making strenuous efforts to recruit qualified White applicants, even though there is a waiting list of eligible African American candidates. In these circumstances, is it ethical to give preference to Whites? Should you report the situation publicly, even though as a result the program will lose its major funding base? If you do not serve more White young adults, funding will stop, and no one—neither White nor African American young adults—will receive the service they now receive. If you do comply and recruit more White participants, the result will be that the program will serve fewer African American young adults. Weigh the alternatives: What is the ethical thing to do?

DISCRIMINATION AND ADOPTIONS

Many more children are available for adoption than there are families to adopt them. Child welfare agencies usually seek adoptive families from heterosexual two-parent or single-parent families. Gay men and lesbians often encounter legal and other barriers when they attempt to adopt children. This discriminatory pattern prevails even though the traditional heterosexual two-parent nuclear family has decreased and now is a diminishing percentage of the various types of American families. As of 2006, while the total number of married couples is higher than ever before, less than half of the nation's households were made up of married couples (with and without children) (Roberts, 2006). The effect of excluding nontraditional families from adopting means that some children will remain in foster care longer before they are placed in permanent adoptive homes. Yet social workers who advocate placement of a child with a homosexual person or couple may be subjected to ridicule, ostracism, and other career-damaging reactions (Ryan, Perlmutter, & Groza, 2004). Pressures to deselect gay men or lesbians as adoptive parents can come from peer and/or supervisor influences. In such cases, a social worker may have to choose among loyalty to herself and her career, loyalty to her supervisor, and loyalty to her professional values and agency policies.

Child custody disputes may be complicated by parents' sexual orientations—for example, between a formerly married parent who now identifies as homosexual and the former spouse, or two gay people who agreed to co-parent but are now separated. When two gay individuals co-parent they may both be adoptive parents or one may have conceived the child through artificial insemination while the other has shared in the caregiving without adopting the child. If the couple separates, who receives custody of the child may depend on the prevailing community attitudes toward homosexuality and toward homosexuals as parents, as discussed in Exemplar 8.3.

| **8.3** | **FAILURE TO ADOPT** |

Janice McNally, a highly successful attorney with a very busy professional life, including frequent work-related travel, and Virginia Barker, a sales clerk in a mall who frequently changes jobs, have been in a long-term relationship. They agreed to have a child to be conceived by Janice as the biological mother. When Susan was born, Virginia began but failed to complete the adoption process. Both Janice and Virginia loved the child and at first shared equally in the parenting. Janice's high income made possible many "extras" for Susan such as play groups, day camps, arts and crafts classes, and music lessons. For a number of years, the couple remained compatible and cared for Susan together, and the child bonded with both of them. When Susan was 8 years old, Virginia and Janice separated; Virginia asked for joint custody of Susan, which Janice refused to provide.

Judge Watson assigned Roberta Stevenson, a social worker employed by the court, to study the situation and to make recommendations to him as to what he should decide. Roberta, who had special training regarding lesbian adoptions, recommended to Judge Watson that Virginia should have major visitation rights because she has been a significant parental figure and that the best interest of the child is best served by a two-parent relationship.

However, the judge has views not supported by the history and behaviors of all involved. The prevailing community belief is that children raised by lesbians suffer harm, and Judge Watson believes that having a lesbian parent—whatever the legalities—will by itself affect a child's sexual identity, lead to peer rejection, or expose the child to "unusual" images of family life. He thinks that to allow Virginia visitation rights would only make more problematic a "bad" situation, and there is room in the law for leeway for his decision.

What should Roberta do? She is an employee of the court but has dual loyalties—to the child Susan and to the court. As long as she is employed by the court, her duties are clear. She can try to persuade the judge, but in the final analysis, the judge makes decisions to be implemented by social workers and others. If Roberta believes the judge's decision is contrary to her professional and ethical judgments, how should she respond? What is in the best interest of Susan? How should Roberta respond to Judge Watson's request, and what should she recommend about Susan's future? What ethical dilemmas can you identify? Where can guidance be found for dealing with this situation?

LIMITED RESOURCES

The ethical problems resulting from the equality-and-inequality principle are often aggravated by limited resources. If resources were unlimited, in theory there would be no problem in providing all persons with the help they need. In the real world, there are never enough resources to do everything that should be done. Life is a zero-sum game—allocating a scarce resource to one person means that another will not receive it. The concept of limited resources, however, may be a manipulation of language, used to conceal certain deliberate decisions. Often it means that the available resources have already been allocated elsewhere or that commitments or priorities have been shifted. During George W. Bush's presidency, tax cuts, Iraq and Afghanistan, and the "war on terrorism" have become top priorities. It has been argued that success in the war on terrorism makes it necessary to assign a lower priority and make fewer resources available to other important programs, including social programs designed to eradicate poverty, eliminate discrimination, and improve human services. Even though overall societal resources are limited, it is possible to assign vast resources to particular programs when such a policy decision is made at the highest level. If there is a wide consensus that a certain program deserves the highest priority, or powerful decision-making forces conclude it is necessary, it will receive funding even at the expense of limiting allocations for other important projects.

If this is the meaning of limited resources, the focus of ethical decision-making shifts from the micro to the macro, from the specific case to societal allocations. This process occurs on the organizational and agency level when one program has been prioritized. As a result, other programs may not receive the support necessary. Even on the individual level this process operates when a worker makes a decision that a certain project or population group or intervention method should receive priority at the expense of all other projects, populations, or methods.

On one level, the ethical problem facing the social work practitioner will be how to allocate the resources she controls. On another level, the profession as an organized group and individual social workers as citizens have an ethical responsibility to become involved in the societal allocation process—that is, the political process. For example, home health care, a major segment of community-based long-term care, is especially important for frail elderly persons. When budgets for this program are cut back because of soaring costs, many of these elderly people are pushed into nursing homes and hospitals, even though it creates unnecessary dependency and is more costly. Social workers have a responsibility on ethical and other grounds to advocate for continued home health care services (Beder, 1998).

Much of what social workers can and cannot do is determined by political decision makers. When the legislature passes budgets, it determines to a large extent priorities and resources available both for public and voluntary agencies and institutions. Other political decisions have a major impact on the nation's economic health, rate of economic growth, availability of jobs, and other indicators that have a direct or indirect impact on what social workers are or should be doing. Are social workers merely passive observers of these political processes? Or is there an "ethic of responsibility" that obligates social workers to take an active part in these societal processes? We agree with Siporin (1985b) and Goldstein (1998) that social workers are moral agents who have a responsibility to influence organizations and communities. Priorities and commitments determine resource allocations. Significant resources have been allocated to drug "wars" and rehabilitation programs, while considerably less money has been allocated to solve the problems of the homeless. What are the ethical implications of such decisions? What can social workers do about this?

ETHICAL PROBLEMS IN ALLOCATING LIMITED RESOURCES

Many allocation decisions are made at the highest political level in Washington or at a state capitol, settings in which most social workers do not feel at home, but which nevertheless require the ethical attention and skills of social workers. At other times such decisions are made much closer to home. Consider the decision facing the social workers of Centro Latino, a United Way agency in Westport, a community that has always had a large concentration of Spanish-speaking immigrants. Centro Latino was started as an indigenous self-help group in the 1960s by immigrants from Latin America. Today, its budget is met largely by the United Way and supplemented at times by specific state and federal grants. Though volunteers are still used, most assignments are now handled by professional staff members. The decision-making powers are vested in the agency's board of directors, made up largely of Spanish-speaking residents of the community. At a recent staff meeting, the staff discussed an issue (Exemplar 8.4) that many felt had ethical implications.

| 8.4 | REFUGEES IN WESTPORT |

Early last year, more than 400 new Central American refugee families arrived in Westport. Centro Latino was able to generate a special onetime $100,000 grant to help in the adjustment of these refugees. The board of directors decided after lengthy discussion to allocate 20% of this grant to employ two more part-time social workers and to distribute the remaining funds directly to families to help them in their adjustment.

The detailed rules for distributing these funds were to be developed by the agency's staff. The current staff meeting was devoted to developing criteria for distributing the funds. The agency's director, Sandra Lopez, argued that equity demanded that each of the families receive an equal cash grant of approximately $190, which each family could use as it wished. Several staff members agreed with Sandra. But others urged that the limited funds be used where they could do the most good. Since the basic needs were already met, the new monies should be earmarked for special needs where an intensive use of resources could best achieve the desired objective. Each staff group believed that its proposal was supported by the professional ethics code.

If you had been participating in this staff meeting, which position would you have supported? Look at the NASW Code of Ethics. Do you find guidance there for your proposal? Following your review of the Code, look at the ethical principles screen in chapter 4. What ethical considerations, including those of equity and equality, should be weighed before making a decision? What would you say is the ethically correct decision? Why?

Although social workers have an ideal of equality of treatment for those similarly placed, the distribution of scarce resources often reflects discrimination against various groups. The Code of Ethics takes a strong stand for social workers to be proactive against discriminatory behaviors both formal and informal, as individual professionals and for the profession itself. But there also can be ethical dilemmas connected to the distribution of scarce resources. In some instances, it is more ethical to make distinctions that favor those who are most needy rather than simply defending the idea of equality of treatment. Special situations can require special treatment.

ETHICAL DILEMMAS IN ADVOCACY

The NASW Code of Ethics requires social workers to "advocate for living conditions conducive to the fulfillment of basic human needs and ... promote social, economic, political, and cultural values and institutions that are compatible with the realization of social justice" (NASW Code, 6.01). Other circumstances that call for a social worker to serve as an advocate include situations where clients are served by an impaired, incompetent, or unethical social worker (Code, 2.09a, b; 2.10a, 2.11a, d) or when the practitioners of the employing organization are inconsistent with the NASW Code of Ethics (3.09, c, d). The purpose of advocacy should always be "to ensure that all people have equal access to the resources, employment, services, and opportunities they require to meet their basic human needs and to develop fully" (Code, 6.04a).

To be an advocate and to engage in advocacy is to adopt a particular stance about an issue of concern, advance a cause, and attempt to produce a result on behalf of an interest of a person, group, or cause (Cohen, 2004). Hoefer (2006) defines social work advocacy as taking "action in a systematic and purposeful way to defend, represent, or otherwise advance the cause of one or more clients at the individual, group, organizational, or community level, in order to promote social justice" (p. 8). Admittedly, there is no end to the issues that confront social workers and suggest their serving as advocates, either individually or in groups. Any person who lives in our society can easily recognize that there are ever-present human needs that require advocacy for clients, patients, and others. Because the social worker's time and resources are limited, serious thought must be given to determining priorities in this area.

CASE ADVOCACY

On the individual case level, the objective of advocacy intervention is to obtain a needed resource or service for an individual client or group of clients. On the class level, the goal is to alter the environment through social policy changes or concessions from resistant or unresponsive systems (Mickelson, 1995). The ethical principle of equality and inequality provides the ethical justification for engaging in the advocacy role. Empowerment techniques are necessary in order to give disadvantaged groups and individuals a chance for equal access to life opportunities. However, this ethical justification does not mean that social worker advocates automatically avoid all ethical dilemmas.

Suppose there is only one bed available in the only home for senior citizens in your community. Your client needs to enter this institution because he can no longer cope at home. You also know that there are other elderly people (not your clients) whose situations are even more critical. Should you become an aggressive advocate on behalf of your client, knowing that his admission will be at the expense of other older people who have a greater need for this service? Should you advocate his admission even if you are fairly certain that your success will result in irreversible harm to others? How do the "who is your client" considerations discussed in earlier chapters affect your decision? Are there other ways in which you can meet your ethical obligation to all the elderly persons who need this service?

In Exemplar 8.5, an example of case advocacy, we turn first to a request for advocacy by an elderly client who is a resident of a nursing home.

8.5	A "SQUEAKY WHEEL" GOES UNHEARD

Thomas Wayland is a resident of Room 209 in the Serenity Nursing Home. His roommate has a serious cognitive impairment, is generally incompetent, is incontinent, and makes continual repetitive noises that Thomas finds deeply disturbing. He spoke to a nurse's aide a week ago requesting that his room be changed. He repeated his request to that aide and several others, but so far there have been no changes. This morning he asked that his social worker, Kelli Forsbeck, come visit him. When Kelli arrived, Thomas was quite disturbed and angry; he explained to her that he had asked several times over a full week for a change of room, but nothing had been done to correct his situation. All of his requests have been ignored. He is still in the same room with the same roommate and the same noises. Kelli said she would speak to the head nurse to ask if his room can be changed. When she did so, she was told that the home has no beds available to meet Thomas's request. There are a number of people waiting to be admitted to the home. Other residents also have made requests that cannot be met at this time. Furthermore, she noted, the problem is not unique to Thomas and his current roommate. Other residents also have disconcerting and annoying characteristics, so there is no assurance that if Thomas is moved he will go to a room without some disturbance. She suggested impatiently that Kelli "cool out" Thomas as best she can. This is what the nursing home administration needs to be done. Kelli is torn. Was the nurse's comment a threat about her job? Other residents also have needs that are unmet. Kelli understands that the power of social workers in this home is quite low. In fact, all human service professionals with the exception of physicians are subordinate to the administration and its focus on dollars.

What are the ethical dilemmas present in this situation? How much autonomy does Thomas or Kelli really have? What does Kelli's professional role demand she do? Should she try to reassure and calm Thomas in the hope that a bed will open up in a few days, strongly advocate for him, or explain to him that there is little to no chance he will be placed in a different setting but that she will continue to work on his situation? When she persisted in advocating with the head nurse, the nurse was visibly upset. To whom does Kelli owe loyalty? Thomas, the nursing home, the head nurse, herself and her family? What is the correct ethical decision? Are there other possible options?

CAUSE/CLASS ADVOCACY

Another ethical dilemma a social worker advocate may encounter is illustrated by Exemplar 8.6, which is an example of cause or class advocacy in which a social worker confronts an issue of importance to a group of persons.

8.6	NO WINTER CLOTHING

Three children in a family receiving public aid are sent home from school because they are not adequately dressed. There is no money available at home because their mother has used every last cent she has to pay off more pressing bills. You, the family's social worker, have no emergency funds available to help these three children obtain winter clothing.

What should you do? Should you become an advocate to press for institutional changes, such as more adequate public welfare allowances or special clothing allowances? Should you mobilize your volunteer network to locate suitable clothing donations so that the children can return to school as quickly as possible? Or should you do both? The former option will likely take time and will not get the children dressed appropriately so that they can return to school before the end of winter, while the latter option will get the children appropriately dressed and back in school quickly, but will not address the underlying problems. What are the ethical implications of causing short-run harm to your client (i.e., not getting the children back to school quickly) in order to gain an uncertain ultimate benefit (i.e., getting policies changed)? This situation is complicated by the fact that in one strategy (i.e., advocacy to change the policy) the cost is certain (the children will not attend school for a number of weeks or even months) while the benefit is uncertain since there is no guarantee of success, but if successful such advocacy will help many people. The other strategy (i.e., depending on volunteers to contribute winter clothing to these specific children) may result in early benefits for your clients, but will not solve this problem, which many other children also have.

Social worker advocates will encounter many ethical problems when their practice role is not fully supported by the employing agency, as is demonstrated in Exemplar 8.7.

8.7 | TRAFFIC IN SHADY HILL

Shady Hill was a quiet residential neighborhood until last year, when a new expressway exit brought a great amount of traffic onto its streets. As a result, there are now several very dangerous intersections. Last month, three children on their way to school were seriously injured when crossing one of these intersections. Parents and neighborhood residents are enraged and demand that the city close the exit or put up traffic lights. A meeting with the mayor has not produced any results. Lou Seward is the neighborhood worker who for the past two years has been staffing the Shady Hill Neighborhood Council, an arm of the Bay City Community Development Department. Under Lou's guidance, the council has undertaken several projects that have improved the quality of life in the neighborhood; everyone has been happy with the results achieved by these projects. Since the current problem has become acute, Lou has helped council officers organize a coalition of all neighborhood groups that are interested in this problem, including the PTA, churches, and fraternal organizations.

At last night's meeting of the coalition, it was agreed that ways must be found to put additional pressure on city hall. It was decided to call a news conference tomorrow morning to announce that a protest rally would be held across the street from city hall next Monday afternoon. If no positive response is received, the residents plan to block the exit the following week. Lou participated in last night's meeting by raising a number of questions, by encouraging the group, and by providing technical information and advice. In this morning's conference with his supervisor, Lou reviewed the Shady Hill situation to see if there were additional ways he could be helpful. His supervisor, the assistant director of the Community Development Department, thought that Lou had not done enough to calm the neighborhood. Though agreeing that the problem demanded attention, his supervisor did not think that an aggressive conflict strategy was helpful. He and the agency expected Lou to use his influence to keep the neighborhood quiet. That, after all, was the major reason why the city allocated monies to this department. The message was clear and so was the problem.

To whom does Lou Seward owe loyalty—to the Neighborhood Council that has successfully improved life in the neighborhood, to his supervisor and the agency, to his profession, or to himself as a professional who wants to place service to clients as his highest priority but who also wants to retain his job?

ADVOCACY AS WHISTLE BLOWING

In addition to case and class advocacy, there are situations in which social workers engage in whistle blowing (reporting or informing on a superior's or organization's ethical or legal misconduct) as a special type of advocacy. However, this is a rare phenomenon in social work (Green & Kantambu, 2004). Examples of such actions might include protecting clients or patients from abuse by staff members, relatives, custodians, or others, or attempting to protect social workers or other staff members from unwarranted vindictive retribution by other employees or administrators. Protecting an organization against the misuse of funds by administrators or others with access to funds could result in depleting the availability of funds for human services as well as exposure to legal actions and depressed fund-raising ability. Whistle blowing to protect clients against those who are abusing them requires great care and skill. It can expose the agency to potential public criticism or expose misuse of funds, both of which may be harming services. By exposure, better services may be provided, but this action also raises issues of loyalty to the agency. Although there are laws at both the federal and state levels to protect whistle blowers from retaliation, social workers anticipating such advocacy need to take special care to consult with an experienced employment/labor lawyer (Whistleblower.org, 2007). According to a survey by the National Whistle Blower Center, most employees who expose wrong-doing in the workplace face some form of retaliation, despite existing laws (*New York Times,* Whistle-Blowers Being Punished, 2002).

Greene and Latting (2004) reviewed social work's stance on advocacy to protect clients' rights, explained whistle blowing as a type of advocacy, and offered guidance to social workers on handling whistle blowing when it is a relevant option for action. Exemplar 8.8 focuses on an organizational problem in a community fund-raising agency with implications for the organization, the human service agencies it serves, the staff, and the social worker.

8.8	THE SITUATION IS NOT GOOD AND WHO WILL BLOW THE WHISTLE?

Julie Greenacre is employed by the Alliance for Human Services Fundraising, a community-wide effort to raise dollars to fund human services. Recently, in discussion with the executive director's secretary, Lillian Radkin, a long-time friend who also attends her church regularly, Julie learned that the executive director has been skimming funds by manipulating his expenses. He also established a business with his son as a subdivision of the organization with a separate legal status and IRS designation. The executive director and his son are receiving excessive salaries and using the resources of the Alliance to operate this business. Lillian explained that she needed to tell someone she trusted because it has been bothering her since she found out about these illegal activities, but there is nothing that she can do about it because she desperately needs her job. She asked Julie if she would do something about the situation.

Should Julie believe these charges, even though Lillian did not provide any corroborating evidence? How should Julie respond? Should she find a way to communicate with the executive director to let him know that some staff members are aware of what is happening, even if this means risking her own job or putting Lillian's job at risk (since the executive director can easily figure out who provided information on his activities)? Would it be more effective and safer to inform people outside the organization, such as the district attorney? Or should she just wait, hoping the information will come out eventually? To whom does Julie owe primary loyalty: the agency, the community, herself, her friend Lillian, or her profession and its ethical stances?

In this chapter, the fact that social workers are constantly forced to make ethical decisions about the use of scarce resources to help individuals and communities was explored. Resources such as available time, health and mental health care, child welfare services, and food are not in limitless supply. In fact, they are usually in short supply. As we have seen, social workers frequently have to make ethical choices about how the resources available will be distributed. Discrimination also enters the picture. To serve one group may mean other groups receive less than they legitimately also need. Advocacy necessary to attain equitable distribution of resources was introduced through case advocacy, cause and class advocacy, and whistle blowing.

EXERCISES

1. What would you do if you were the neighborhood worker in Shady Hill (Exemplar 8.7)? What are the ethical problems this neighborhood worker faces? How would you resolve them? Do you think that the supervisor's comments are in accord with the Code of Ethics? What are the supervisor's ethical dilemmas, and what would you do if you were the agency director?

2. The East Side Neighborhood Council has received a small grant to mount an educational program for Central American refugees now settling in large numbers on the East Side. The board is considering two projects: One would fund supplementary classes in local schools; the other would establish English classes for adult refugees. There is a need for both projects, but there is barely enough money to mount one. What are the ethical problems facing the social worker who staffs the board? What ethical considerations should the social worker keep in mind? How can the social worker find guidance that helps to make an ethical decision? If the social worker makes an ethical choice about the programs, does she have a responsibility to tell the board what the relevant professional ethics are, her stance, and how the decision was reached? Suggest ways this social worker can reach an ethically correct decision and what ethical actions should be implemented.

3. In addition to the NASW advocacy efforts (see Web Sites of Interest) many of the state chapters of NASW have local or state level advocacy efforts. Go to the Web site for your local NASW chapter and examine the advocacy activities they are engaged in. Do you agree with the issues identified as the most important and with the actions being taken?

SUGGESTIONS FOR ADDITIONAL READINGS

Schools of social work and the Council on Social Work Education have made strenuous efforts to eradicate racism in individual schools and in social work education (Trolander, 1997). See Basham, Donner, Killough, and Rozas (1997), who describe the efforts and process by which the Smith College School of Social Work moved to become an antiracist institution. Courtney and colleagues (1996) report on discrimination in child welfare and its effects. Dodd and Jansson (2004) argue that contextual barriers often prevent social workers from ensuring that clients' and patients' perspectives are sufficiently represented in ethical deliberations in multidiscipline settings. They propose that social workers, in addition to rational ethical reasoning, should be prepared with strategies and skills to engage in effective ethical advocacy.

Web Sites of Interest

- Check out the National Association of Social Workers' advocacy efforts, including grassroots, national, and legislative efforts: www.socialworkers.org/advocacy/
- The Action Network for Social Work Education and Research (ANSWER) "coalition's mission is to increase legislative and executive branch advocacy on behalf of social work education, training, and research. This goal is accomplished through collaboration among social work education, research, and practice organizations, social work education programs, and other interested groups": www.socialworkers.org/advocacy/answer/
- For extensive information on whistle blowing laws, visit: www.whistleblowerlaws.com
  Note the disclaimer in the lower-left corner of the following page—although this site is not specific to social work, it provides a great deal of information on state and federal law: www.whistleblowerlaws.com/whistleblower.htm

9 THE PROFESSIONAL RELATIONSHIP: LIMITS, DILEMMAS, AND PROBLEMS

The essence of social work practice can be found in the relationship between the social worker and her clients. Trust is a central element in this relationship because a helping relationship requires that the client will be able to trust his social worker and the social worker must be able to trust her clients. However, it is important that the social worker recognizes that for the client "to trust is to become vulnerable and dependent on the good will and motivations of those we trust" (Pellegrino, 1991, p. 69). Going to a social worker or to any other professional for help requires that the helpseeker or client believes that the professional will act morally, will perform professional functions competently, and will be concerned about the problems the client brings to the situation. The client is dependent upon the prudence of the professional. In order for the client to receive any service, it is often necessary that he remove the protective cover that his privacy normally gives him. The client will do so only when he believes that the professional will use her good judgment and skill for his welfare.

PROFESSIONAL RELATIONSHIPS AND SPECIAL DUTIES

The "link between the professional and the client is a professional relationship. The client who trusts the professional entrusts his total self (not just his possessions) to the professional" (Sokolowski, 1991, p. 31). The professional presents herself as trustworthy because she is certified as a professional. This means that she is obligated both to the client and to the profession. Actually most clients cannot evaluate the trustworthiness of the social worker to whom they have been assigned or to whom they turn; instead they place their trust in the reputation of the employing agency, governmental licensing, and professional certifications. We do not personally check out every airplane pilot or railroad engineer with whom we travel; we depend on the employer to select qualified professionals. Similarly, we trust that our vulnerability will not be exploited by the social work professional for her own purposes such as power, profit, or pleasure.

The social work professional's relationship with the client assumes special duties that arise because of the trust or confidence the client places in the social worker. The professional role introduces a power imbalance—in this relationship the client has certain needs and the social worker has various powers. The professional's knowledge, as well as her power, can dominate and influence the client. It is crucial, therefore, that the social worker act in the best interest of the client and not take advantage of the client to promote her own (or her agency's) interests. The confidentiality and informed consent obligations are intended to prevent the abuse of power by the professional practitioner. Basic to this relationship is the requirement that the social worker be honest. Likewise it is important that social workers recognize the ethical nature of the professional relationship and the limits it places on social workers in their dealings with clients. These ethical duties are found in the Code of Ethics, but social workers should be aware that recognizing the ethical nature of practice does not avoid all conflicts of interest.

Many social workers assume clients trust them and the social agencies that employ them, even though the distrust of professionals and of many social agencies is widespread. Many people are wary about placing their trust in any professional, including social workers. Trust, while necessary, is not enforceable. Clients cannot be compelled to trust a worker or a social agency, even when they have no choice about the service they need. It is also a fact that social workers cannot be required to trust their clients, even when practice theory demands that they do so. Today, the caution of clients may reflect not only their own questions but also the skepticism and climate of distrust found throughout society. Several additional factors have affected the trust relationship, including limitations on professional judgments, democratization and the rights revolution, and the growing lack of privacy.

LIMITATIONS ON PROFESSIONAL JUDGMENTS

The advent of managed care of health and mental health services, where specialized skills and professional judgment are required, has tended to undermine the professional authority and powers of clinicians and others by limiting their control over treatment choices, instituting productivity reporting systems that intrude upon professional decision making, and skewing treatment choices and options. Hall and Keefe (2006) in a national study of social workers, psychologists, and psychiatrists found these professionals did not see themselves as having adequate skills to interact effectively with managed care organizations to ensure the care they are providing is certified and follows best practice guidelines. Professionals can have difficulty defending their intervention choices. Furthermore, because of managed care, social workers often cannot make decisions about what services they can provide, thus conveying to the client the existence of a hidden, unapproachable, and unaccountable presence affecting his life. From an ethical point of view, managed care—at its best—may protect the client and society from exaggerated or distorted professional decisions, from providing "treatments" that may be profitable to the practitioner but not effective for the client. However, clients may not know who is making decisions— the clinician or someone at the insurance company. This raises the issue of honesty.

When the social worker does not make the decision, is she obligated to tell this to the client? How does doing so affect the professional relationship?

DEMOCRATIZATION AND THE RIGHTS REVOLUTION

The consumer rights revolution followed in the footsteps and flowed out of the civil rights movement and legislation, the development of self-help organizations, demedicalization and self-care, deinstitutionalization of the mentally ill population, and the independent living movement of physically disabled people (Tower, 1994). These consumer movements often criticized professionals. Two aspects of these criticisms are (1) a desire by clients to affect the quality of services they receive and (2) their desire to participate in gaining some control over standards. As a result of the rights revolution, professionals now have to explain to clients how they can help, how long it will take, and what the expected outcomes will be, with an emphasis on effectiveness of treatment and accountability. Decisions and notes previously not shared with clients are now open to inspection by clients and others. These changes empower clients and democratize to a greater extent the delivery of services. For every change, however, there is a cost. The question is how this greater accountability affects the client, the worker, or the effectiveness of the helping system. These accountability systems may be interpreted by professionals as indicating a lack of trust in their judgment, while the social worker's caution about what to place in a record may potentially reduce the record's usefulness as a tool to help the social worker analyze and plan.

A DISAPPEARING SENSE OF PRIVACY

At one time personal privacy was absolute. Nowadays almost everyone is aware that personal privacy is limited. Supermarkets and other businesses track purchases made by individuals; "identities" are stolen (e.g., social security numbers used, purchases made with credit card information obtained illegally, hackers invading hospital individual health files); Internet surfing is recorded; electronic messages are retrieved by persons other than the intended recipients; and mishaps are reported where information being sent to one recipient (such as an insurance company) can be received by others. This is the background in which citizens in general no longer trust the professional's claims that confidentiality will be respected. No professional today can make such a claim. Both clients and professionals recognize that the professional does not control the data provided by the client.

LIMITS OF THE PROFESSIONAL RELATIONSHIP

Primary relationships, especially those within the family or between friends, have few limits. The professional relationship between the client and social worker, on the other hand, is not a primary relationship because it is limited and focused on the problem for which help is sought. The professional assumes responsibility for helping the client with his problem(s), and traditionally, the relationship terminates once these objectives have been achieved. Thus, it is a limited relationship in contrast to the broad primary relations that most people treasure. We will focus on the ethical problems and dilemmas that social workers face because of their commitment to certain values within the professional relationship. One of the major causes for ethical problems in this area arises whenever a social worker determines that her client needs help that goes beyond the limits that the traditional professional relationship allows. But there are other, equally perplexing ethical dilemmas, as the discussion in this chapter will show.

The limits of the professional relationship can raise a number of issues. Some social workers prefer to hide behind the limited professional relationship because they are uncomfortable with their clients' lifestyles and cultures. At the same time many social workers want to identify with their clients by expressing empathy with their fate. Without wanting to imitate a lifestyle that is not authentic for them, they want to learn about and participate more fully in their clients' lives because they know that they cannot be effective and helpful without such knowledge. But this type of knowledge cannot be achieved if the workweek is limited to 9 a.m. to 5 p.m., Monday through Friday. Many conscientious social workers are not entirely clear about what the correct professional conduct is. Is it ethical for a social worker to accept an invitation for Sunday dinner in the client's home or to join the client on Friday evening in the local bar? May a social worker reciprocate and invite a client for supper at her home or in a restaurant? Is it appropriate for a social worker who wants to learn about a particular culture to accept an invitation from a client to explore the client's ethnic neighborhood with him so as to understand better the culture from which he has come? Until recently practice wisdom has given fairly clear and generally negative answers to all of these questions, but increasingly, social workers express discomfort with the barriers that have been erected between them and their clients.

The Code of Ethics (1.06 a, b, c, d) suggests that dual relationships and conflicts of interests can be accommodated within sound social work practice if professional discretion is used and there is no risk of exploitation or potential harm to the client. Dual relationships occur when a social worker "assumes a second relationship with a client that may cause actual or potential conflicts between their professional duties and their social, religious, or business relationships" (Johner, 2006, p. 2). Boland-Prom and Anderson (2005) explored this issue and suggest that proper decision making can—in certain cases—provide for such dual relationships. Aside from prohibiting any sexual relationships with clients, they suggest much depends on the legal and other contextual factors, type of social work practice, history of the relationship, and degrees of dependence and vulnerability.

Though the relationship is supposed to be a limited one, social workers often have an emotional reaction to their clients. Such feelings may be natural, but the consequent worker behavior may cause ethical problems. When a worker's own needs become entangled with the professional relationship, emotional feelings may become destructive. In such situations, the social worker may lose her sense of objectivity; instead of helping the client, she may cause harm.

CLIENT INTERESTS VERSUS WORKER INTERESTS

Giving priority to a client's interests is one of the cornerstones of every professional code of ethics. The Code of Ethics expresses this professional obligation as follows: "Social workers elevate service to others above self-interest" (1999, Ethical Principles, p. 5) and "Commitment to Clients: Social workers' primary responsibility is to promote the well-being of clients. In general, clients' interests are primary" (NASW Code, 1999, 1.01).

This ethical rule is meant to safeguard the client from exploitation because most clients can neither control nor evaluate practitioner activities. Providing unnecessary treatment is one example of a violation of this ethical principle. From time to time, professionals (psychiatrists, social workers, and others) as well as social agencies and institutions are charged with needlessly extending the period of service or providing unnecessary services for financial or other reasons. Some hold that this practice hardly presents an ethical problem for the majority of social workers who are employed by social agencies because the workers themselves do not gain any economic advantage when they offer these unnecessary services. This may be an ethical problem for an occasional social worker in private practice who may be tempted to place financial gain above client interests, but even agency-employed social workers might face this ethical dilemma if urged by their supervisor to keep a child in a more restrictive treatment setting than needed so that treatment facility will have enough clients to remain open.

There are other ethical dilemmas of this type that do not involve financial gain for the individual or an agency. For example, a social worker is in the middle of preparing supper for her family when she receives an emergency call for help from one of her clients. Should she drop everything and rush out to help her client, even if this means that her family will once again have to make their own supper? Another social worker has a very important date whom she is to meet within the hour when she is notified that one of "her" foster children has run away. What should she do? What is the ethical thing to do?

Social workers face critical ethical problems when there is a threat to life. For example, must a social worker give priority to client interests, even when this may result in physical injury to the worker or her family? Do considerations of self-preservation and survival legitimize actions that ordinarily might be considered unethical?

Gewirth's (1978) Principle of Generic Consistency may be helpful when considering these problems. He stated, "Act in accord with the generic right of your recipients (that is your [clients] *as well as yourself*" (p. 135, emphasis added). Gewirth suggests that there is no need for the worker to abdicate the right to her own welfare, even when this right conflicts with the client's right to professional services. Because Gewirth's principle was not developed to guide professional activities, some people argue that it does not apply to professional practitioners. Instead, they hold that a professional should always be guided by the ethical obligation to give priority to a client's interests, no matter what the consequences to herself. They take this position because the Code (1999, Ethical Principles) requires that "Social workers elevate service to others above self-interest."

Those who would follow Gewirth's lead must consider whether ethics are relative. Do ethical obligations change according to their consequences? What must be the degree of potential harm before it is permissible to disregard the ethical rule that demands giving priority to a client's interests? Or must social workers serve their clients' interests at all times, regardless of the consequences? Is it ethical for them to declare that under certain unusual circumstances the professional obligation to serve their clients' interests is no longer primary? How did you respond to Exemplar 1.3, where the social worker is asked to leave her family in a potentially dangerous situation so she can respond to clients' needs? Would you still give the same response now that you gave when you first read chapter 1?

Consider Diggs's (1970) observation that "there is an important difference between interpreting a rule or violating it in *special circumstances,* and deciding each individual case just as if there were no rules" (p. 267). This formulation permits retention of the client-priority ethical rule except in special circumstances, such as when the life of the worker is threatened, because in such a case absolute adherence to the rule (client's interests above all) would be unrealistic and unwise.

DUAL ROLES WITHIN THE PROFESSIONAL RELATIONSHIP

In this section, we will examine issues related to dual-role relationships. By **dual-role relationships,** we mean the social worker interacts in any capacity beyond the social worker's professional role, for example, as a teacher, member of church committee, sexual or business partner. Please keep in mind there are differences between conflicts of interest and dual roles. A **conflict of interest** occurs when a social worker advances her own interests or the interests of others in ways detrimental to clients' or others' interests. Social workers may be parents, members of religious groups or political parties, or members of other groups. Conflicts of interest can occur when the social worker has conflicting personal interests—her interests as a parent, as a member of a religious group, or as a business person. Consequently social workers can be faced with personal conflicts of interest. In addition, social workers face conflicts of interests when they seek the attainment of their own interests ahead of those of their clients. The Code (1.06 b) cautions against taking unfair advantage of any professional relationship to exploit others in order to further one's personal, religious, political, or business interests.

Social workers reside and practice in communities, and they have social, business, financial, religious, or other roles in addition to their professional roles with clients. There are a number of situations where it is clear the avoidance of dual relationships is difficult. The possibility of dual relationships may be minimized in large urban areas and dual relationships encountered more frequently in small towns and rural areas. However, even in urban areas dual relationships may be difficult to avoid in particular smaller subcommunities such as religious, political, sexual orientation, new immigrant groups, and self-help groups associated with physical illnesses and chemical dependency. Here are some examples of dual-role relationships:

- You discover that your client Bertha Martins is your dentist's mother.
- Kathleen Olds, your daughter's new teacher, is the mother of Tom Olds, a troubled teenager whom you have been treating for the last year.
- Lorraine Simkins, the wife of Al Simkins, stockbroker, is your client and inadvertently discloses insider information about local businesses in which you own stock.
- Your client, Cynthia Goddard, joins a recreational basketball league, and her assigned team plays regularly against the team to which you belong.

In such dual-role situations, it is always possible for a client to be confused by the existence of the dual roles, for the professional to exploit or harm the client in some manner, or for the additional role to interfere with the professional relationship by creating conflicts of interest for the practitioner and ambiguities and confusion for the client. The Code of Ethics states "social workers should not engage in dual or multiple relationships with clients or former clients in which there is a risk of exploitation or potential harm to the

---

6 CHAPTER 9

...ddition, the lack of agreement may ...ssue.

...al workers and clients is not simply an ...o grounds for legal action in all 50 states, practitioner's d.ry, malpractice, intentional and negligent uggest the nee...al abuse. Abuse of clients can result in

Sexual int...stress disorder, that are disturbing, harmful, ethical breac.e effects on family, friend, and work relation- where the s.t the practitioner is not avoided by the formal infliction ...ip, while in other states sexual contact following symptom...llegal for a one-, two-, or three-year period (Perry & and em. clients, current as well as past, is unethical, illegal, ships. .are dependent on their social worker; exploiting this term.ual or nonsexual, is prohibited, regardless of whether the .ts the therapeutic outcome.

Ku. professional admonition against sexual contacts with a.r, even if at a diminishing rate. However, there are some ...her ways of viewing such relationships. Maidment (2006) ...rspectives should be considered within the framework of ...ognizes that "client-worker relationships [have] focused on ...f sexual contact in professional practice." She states that she ...existence of sexual relationships between workers and clients," ...ciferous nature of moral condemnation regarding such cases has ...any debate about alternative models for managing this aspect of ...p. 118).

...workers have questioned the ethical rules that prohibit any sexual ...nts, pointing out that many problems brought to their attention involve ...ual dysfunction. In some cases the professional intervention, they argue, ...ally include sexual techniques and activities. There have been therapists ...and practice the notion that sexual involvement with a client is advanta- ...y note that this is not a new helping technique; Freud's colleague Sandor ...helped" his clients express their physical affections toward him as a way of ...ating for their childhood deprivations (Van Hoose & Kottler, 1985).

...se who say there is no problem when sex takes place between social work ...sionals and their clients are underestimating the impact of such behavior both ...ofessional relationships and on the lives of their clients. These relationships ...een social workers and clients are serious because of the consequences for the ...sons involved. The consequences for the therapist are malpractice and possible ...gal suits; in addition the behavior distorts the professional relationship, affects the ...ractitioner's thought processes, and puts objectivity at risk, so that professional treatment is undermined. The consequences for the client include ambivalence, guilt, emptiness and isolation, sexual confusion, impaired ability to trust, confused roles and boundaries, emotional lability, suppressed rage, increased suicidal risk, and problems in cognitive functioning, including concentration and memory, flashbacks, intrusive thoughts, unbidden images, and nightmares (Pope & Vasquez, 1998; Pope, 2000).

Sexual relationships between social work students and their field instructor... also cause damage and have the potential for later imitative behavior by the student...

client. In instances when dual or multiple relationships are unavoidable, social workers should take steps to protect clients and are responsible for setting clear, appropriate, and culturally sensitive boundaries" (NASW Code, 1999, 1.06c). These same guidelines apply to social workers who are supervisors (Code, 1999, 3.01b, c), or educators and field instructors of students (Code, 1999, 3.02d). These standards highlight the issue of dual-role relationships and require that social workers take steps to limit such relationships or to avoid them altogether whenever this is possible, thus avoiding actions that are detrimental to clients, supervisees, and students. The major focus of these standards is to avoid exploitation or harm to clients, former clients, supervisees, and students.

Must dual-role relationships necessarily interfere with professional relationships? Do they always result in conflict? In modern society where everyone fills multiple roles, there are many opportunities for social workers and clients to participate in dual or multiple relationships. Both may be members of the same political party, church, mosque, or synagogue, or their children may attend the same school or be classmates. There is no reason for a social worker to withdraw from these activities simply because the client also engages in them. The issue is to separate the professional relationship from other relationships. Among the relationships with clients that should be avoided are dating, bartering services, buying products, investing work or money in businesses, and endorsing or recommending a client's business to potential buyers. For example, the used car salesman who is a client may offer to sell you a car at a discount. Why should these relationships be avoided or—if unavoidable—minimized? What are the ethical implications for the social worker?

Reconsidering and Further Defining Dual Relationships

Essentially, dual relationships are problematic because they can be harmful. Recently, questions have been raised whether it is necessary to forbid all dual relationships. Zur and Lazarus (2002) offered arguments for and against dual relationships with clients or patients, thus implying that dual relationships are often inevitable, especially when the social worker is in private practice or in a denominational or special-group agency. They argue that boundary violations sometimes are harmful and exploitative but at other times or in other situations they may be constructive (e.g., a home visit to a bedridden client or attending a family event such as a wedding). Rigid boundaries can reflect distance and coldness. Furthermore, there is no reason to assume that a hug, home visit, or acceptance of a gift will inevitably lead to exploitation. These may strengthen the professional relationship if they occur within that framework. Clients, particularly in mental health settings but not only there, can profit from a "sense of belonging, connectedness, and meaningful relationships with others, including workers" (Maidment, 2006, p. 117).

Dual relationships can occur in both clinical and other social work practice settings. Boland-Prom and Anderson (2005) suggest that as the size of the community decreases, the possibility for contact other than the professional relationship increases. In addition, there are communities (e.g., rural, religious, feminist, gay, and ethnic minorities) in which it may not be desirable to maintain rigid separations from dual relationships. Social workers recovering from chemical dependency may find themselves at self-help meetings with present or former clients.

Dual relationships are a fact in many situations, potentially involving many clients. In fact, there are treatment situations that can call for practitioners to have

informal encounter
library with a client,
client make progress
such relationships sho
documented, and ultim
(Boland-Prom & Anders
issues is crucial: mental hea
and self-help communities,
policy and planning, evalua
sideration of the ethical, legal,
is essential.

SEXUAL RELATIONS WIT

The Code of Ethics is quite clear that
engage in sexual activities or sexual cor
is consensual or forced" (NASW Code,
codes of ethics of most professions. In ad
activities "with clients' relatives or other
close personal relationship when there is a ris
client" (1.09b) or "with former clients becaus
(1.09c). In addition, social workers "should no
with whom they have had a prior sexual relati

Nevertheless, sexual misconduct with patient
claims against social workers covered by the NASW
incorrect treatment, and followed by suicide and by
patients (Imbert, 2006). Sexual misconduct accounte
NASW members from 2002 through 2005 (NASW, 2
interpreted with caution because they only represent com
bers, and this may underestimate the problem because co
and malpractice insurers are not included here. In addition,
do not report social worker/client sexual contact is unknov

In regard to sexual relations with a former client, it is a
that is unethical today continues to be unethical at a later da
or former client model for the client the idea that sexual
expected in subsequent psychotherapy? For those social worker
relationships with former clients or claim that an exception
warranted, the burden is on them to demonstrate "that the former
exploited, coerced, or manipulated, intentionally or unintentionally
1999, 1.09c). A study of 654 NASW members' definitions of who is a cli
approximately half of them believe once a client, always a client. Others
while the other half believe "clienthood" ends when service is
periods following service defined whether a former client remained a client. A
lack of consensus was found among MSWs regarding the definition of former c
and what is appropriate behavior at what times regarding various dual relationship
(Mattison, Jayaratne, & Croxton, 2002). This lack of consensus suggests a need for
caution by practitioners because these situations can be affected by state laws as well as

Such sexual relationships can be replicated and reinforced in subsequent practice with clients. A national study of 481 psychologists found that a student's engagement in a sexual relationship with a supervisor is statistically linked to the likelihood that this pattern will repeat itself with future clients, students, and supervisees (Barnett-Queens, 1999). Of those who reported sexual contact with an instructor, almost one in four (23%) reported subsequent engagement in sex with a client compared to only 6% of those who while students had no sexual experiences with their teachers (Bonosky, 1995).

How frequently does this problem occur in social work practice? No differences were found among the behaviors of psychiatrists, psychologists, and social workers (Pope & Vasquez, 1998). During the period 2002–2005, sexual misconduct was the second most frequent cause for legal suits against NASW members covered by the Insurance Trust (NASW, 2006). Therapists who ignore sexual boundaries are likely to repeat the behavior.

One factor that undoubtedly affects this type of unethical conduct is the prior life experiences of practitioners. In a national survey of psychologists' sexual and physical abuse histories, Pope and Feldman-Summers (1992) found a significant number who reported that they themselves had been abused. Among their findings were: (a) almost 6% of male therapists and 21% of female therapists reported sexual abuse by a relative during childhood or adolescence; (b) 26% of male therapists and 39% of female therapists experienced at least one type of abuse (relative, teacher, physician, thera-pist, nonrelative other than those listed above) or nonsexual physical abuse; (c) 21% of female therapists had experienced attempted, acquaintance, or stranger rape; and (d) of 958 patients who had been sexually involved with a therapist 32% had experienced incest or other child sexual abuse, and 10% experienced rape prior to sexual involvement with the therapist (Pope, 2000).

Attitudes of practitioners about having sex with clients seem to be changing. Among psychologists it was reported in 1977 that 5.5% of male psychologists and 0.6% of female psychologists had sexual intercourse with patients (Holroyd & Brodsky, 1977). A decade later, Borys and Pope (1989) reported that only 1.3% of therapists reported sexual involvements with clients. Each year there are about 10% fewer self-reports of patient/therapist sex than the prior year, regardless of the mental health profession (Pope & Vasquez, 1998). It may be that this marked drop in reported sexual activity reflects a broad acceptance of the ethical rule prohibiting sexual relations with clients. What is not entirely clear from the data is whether therapists now refrain from having sex with their clients or whether they are less willing to admit that they behave in unethical ways.

Jayaratne, Croxton, and Mattison (1997) studied six domains of social work practice: intimate relationships, dual-role relationships, mixed modalities, advice giving, boundary behaviors, and financial transactions. The study was based on a large sample of the membership of the Michigan Chapter of NASW. Some of their findings are summarized in Table 9.1. While only a small number of practitioners report they have dated a former client, over 6% think it appropriate to do so. Similarly, a small number report they have had sex with a former client, while almost 5% believe that such behavior is appropriate. Very large percentages report they have dual-role relationships with clients (e.g., friendship, serving on the same boards or committees). Only a few social workers use massage in their practices, however, more than one in eight believe to do so is appropriate; almost 40% believe it is appropriate to touch a

TABLE 9.1 | FREQUENCY AND PERCENTAGES OF INCIDENTS AND PERCEIVED
APPROPRIATENESS OF BEHAVIOR OF SOCIAL WORK PROFESSIONALS

Behavior	Done		Perceived as Appropriate	
	N	%	N	%
Go on a date with a former client	7	.8	53	6.4
Have sex with a former client	9	1.1	37	4.6
Develop a friendship with a client	174	21.2	170	21.0
Have clients with whom you have another relationship	185	22.5	270	33.5
Serve on community boards or committees with clients	187	22.6	471	58.7
Use massage	15	1.8	107	13.7
Touch a client as a regular part of therapy process	253	31.2	319	39.9
Give financial investment advice	37	4.5	64	7.7
Advise clients to do something that may be illegal	25	3.1	30	3.7

Source: Adapted from S. Jayaratne, T. Croxton, and D. Mattison (1997), "Social Work Professional Standards: An
Exploratory Study,"*Social Work, 42,* 187–198.

client as a regular part of the therapy process. Maidment (2006) argues that alternative
views of ethical standards need to be considered and suggests that "respectful and
appropriate physical contact between the client and worker conveys a sense of
connectedness unparalleled by verbal assurance and empathy" (p. 118).

Exemplar 9.1 raises a critical ethical issue that all social workers need to analyze
before they meet the situation in practice.

9.1 | TREATMENT OF AN INFERIORITY COMPLEX

Jill Jordan, a 35-year-old divorcee, has been a client of the Family Consultation Center for
a number of months. Her presenting problem is that she feels inadequate, unattractive, and
stymied in her career. She feels her negative self-image contributed to her divorce and has
become a barrier to advancement on the job. Finding fulfillment in her career and
developing more rewarding relationships depend on her becoming more positive about
herself and being more optimistic.

Bob Temple, an experienced social worker, was assigned as her therapist. A contract
was established with the presenting problem as the focus. During the course of treatment,
Bob was very understanding and warmly responsive to Jill. His objective was to restore
Jill's faith in herself. As treatment proceeded, Jill did not hesitate to express her admiration
of Bob. At the end of one session, she spontaneously hugged him and said how
appreciative she was for all his help. As she experienced more successes in her life, she
would ask for a hug as a sign of his support for her. Still later, she made it evident that she
was attracted to Bob and would not reject his interest in her. Bob was also attracted to Jill.
He very much wanted to further express his feelings toward her and have sexual relations
with her, but he knew that the professional ethics demanded that he not do so.

What is the most ethical way of handling this problem?

1. He can deny his feelings and continue treatment but discontinue the hugs; chances are that these emotions, if controlled, will not interfere with the treatment.
2. He can maintain a professional relationship in the office and join her church, where there will be opportunities for them to meet after hours, outside the office.
3. He can accept his emotional attraction to Jill, but at the same time realize that a professional social worker cannot have a personal relationship with a client. Next time Jill broaches the subject, he should tell her that he likes her and that if he were not her social worker he might become involved with her. However, because he is her social worker, his task is to help her professionally; no other relationship is possible.
4. He realizes that he cannot control his emotions. Therefore, it is best to terminate the relationship and refer Jill to another social worker.
5. He realizes that he cannot control his emotions. Therefore, it is best not to deny his attraction for Jill and instead do what comes naturally—that is, have sex with her; at the same time, he can continue to be her social worker.

Option 5 is clearly not acceptable. In most jurisdictions this behavior is judged as illegal, even criminal. The NASW Code of Ethics prohibits it, as do the ethical codes of all other professions. Though there is no ethical or professional justification for this choice, we mention it because we are aware that a small number of our colleagues do engage in such behavior, a behavior that is blatantly unprofessional and unethical. But some of the other options are also unethical and/or go against the Code. Use the two ethical decision screens to determine which might be the preferred approach in the situation facing Bob Temple.

According to Schoener (1995), sexual misconduct and other boundary violations by professionals (unless they are adjudicated by the courts) should be dealt with through a combination of reprimands and/or temporary privilege suspension, followed by personal therapy and possibly some sort of ongoing supervision.

TOUCHING

Touching became a widespread practice technique during the late 1960s and early 1970s as a result of the popularity of the encounter movement. Some have questioned the ethical propriety of touching, believing that such behavior is only a first step that will inevitably lead to full sexual relations. Others reject this assumption, suggesting there are many types of touching, including therapeutic touching (Durana, 1998). Durana, in a comprehensive review of empirical studies of nonerotic touch in psychotherapy, found there were few such studies, most of the emphasis having been placed on erotic contact. Although Durana concluded that touch has become "an integral part of the clinical practice of many psychotherapists" (p. 15) and that it has beneficial uses in certain circumstances, nevertheless he suggested that legal and ethical considerations combined with transference and countertransference issues make touching in psychotherapy a sensitive subject. The available research evidence is limited and does not provide unambiguous guidance; therefore clinicians should use caution when employing this technique. The Code recognizes physical contact as a practice modality but cautions that "social workers should not engage in physical contact with clients when there is a possibility of psychological harm to the client as a result of the contact (such as cradling or caressing clients). Social workers who engage in appropriate physical contact with clients are responsible for setting clear, appropriate, and culturally sensitive boundaries that govern such physical contact" (NASW Code, 1999, 1.10).

OTHER SOCIAL RELATIONS

While almost all social workers agree with the ethical prohibition against engaging in sexual activities with clients, there is less agreement about the ethical propriety of engaging in other social relations. The findings presented in Table 9.1 clearly indicate the lack of agreement that exists among professional social workers as to what are appropriate professional behaviors. Some of the results highlight the lack of consensus about which social relations should be considered unethical. Although not included in Table 9.1, Jayaratne, Croxton, and Mattison (1997) found that large percentages think it appropriate to hug or embrace a client (see NASW Code, 1999, 1.10), pray with a client, recommend a religious form of healing, comment to clients about their physical attractiveness, discuss one's religious beliefs, or accept goods or services from clients instead of money (see NASW Code, 1999, 1.13).

TRUTH TELLING AND MISREPRESENTATION

The NASW Code of Ethics states that "social workers should not participate in, condone, or be associated with dishonesty, fraud, or deception" (1999, 4.04). Telling the truth and avoiding deceptions are basic ethical obligations. Every human interaction is based on the premise that each side in the interaction intends to tell the truth. Deceiving—that is, deliberately misrepresenting facts in order to make another person believe what is not true—violates the respect to which everyone is entitled. Telling the truth to a client is an even stronger professional obligation than the generalized obligation of truth telling because of the professional's fiduciary responsibilities. This professional ethic is anchored in the specialized client/practitioner relationship and in the obligations that a practitioner owes to her clients.

Some practitioners may believe that it is ethical to use dishonesty when it is in the client's interest, but such a stance requires further thought before it can be accepted. For example, is it ethical for a social worker to present a wrong diagnosis so as to be able to provide a service that otherwise would be not be available? Bayles (1981) concluded that the obligation to be honest with clients does not require honesty toward a third party when acting on a client's behalf. Is honesty always the best policy for a social worker? Haley (1976) raised a number of questions about the efficacy of always being honest, including the following:

- Do social workers (therapists and nontherapists) have an ethical obligation to be honest in their professional relationship when the professional situation is not an honest human experience, but a paid relationship?

- Can any therapist, no matter what her orientation, claim that she is willing to share with a client all of her observations and understandings?
- Must a therapist answer all questions that a client has about the therapy that the practitioner plans to use? How will understanding the theory used by the therapist help this patient to achieve autonomy?
- Will an "honest sharing" of understanding solve the problems for which the patient is paying his money to get help? (p. 208)

Haley presents one point of view, but not everyone agrees. In addition to Haley's questions, there are a number of ethical dilemmas that the attempt to tell the truth may provoke. Consider the ethical problems facing Gail's social worker in Exemplar 9.2.

| **9.2** | GAIL FINDS A JOB |

Gail Silva is a single parent who is raising two daughters, ages 7 and 6. She has been trying to find a part-time job to supplement her meager child support income ever since her younger daughter started kindergarten two years ago. She has been repeatedly refused a job because she has had no prior work experience. By now she has become very frustrated and has developed a very negative self-image.

She believes that nobody wants her—neither as a spouse nor as a worker. This morning she told you excitedly that she thinks she has found a job. As she describes the job, you realize that she is telling you about an employer who is known to exploit his workers and who pays below the minimum wage, when he pays at all. Should you tell Gail the truth about her prospective employer? Or should you share her enthusiasm, hoping that things will work out? What is the ethical thing to do?

Several options might be considered:

- Don't say anything.
- Tell her everything and urge her not to take this job.
- Point out the advantages (a job, an employment history) and disadvantages (low pay, exploitation) and let her make the decision.

Which option would you choose and why?

Deception has become so common in our world that we hardly pay attention to the little lies and half-truths that everyone uses and knows how to justify. Nyberg (1996) suggested that deception is a necessary part of our world: ". . . deception is not merely to be tolerated as an occasionally prudent aberration in a world of truth telling; it is rather an essential component of our ability to organize and shape the world, to resolve problems of coordination among individuals who differ, to cope with uncertainty and pain, to be civil and to achieve privacy as needed, to survive as a species, and to flourish as persons" (p. 187). Or, as he suggests: "to live decently with one another we do not need moral purity, we need discretion—which means tact in regard to truth" (p. 202).

What are the ethical implications for a social worker who uses "lies?" What is the ethical question involved in telling another person a bit less than the full truth? When a social worker decides to withhold the truth from a client or to deceive him, she usually thinks that she is doing so for the client's benefit. Whether her decision was ethically justified cannot be assessed empirically. Are the following reasons sufficient justification for why a social worker might deceive her client or not tell him the full truth?

- To make a client-selected goal less desirable
- To create new goals
- To obscure options
- To increase options
- To change the cost/benefit estimate for one or more options
- To increase or decrease client uncertainty
- To increase or decrease client anxiety
- To protect the client from a "damaging" truth
- To protect the effectiveness of the current intervention strategy
- To obtain the client's "informed" consent
- To protect confidential information received from a third party
- To strengthen the relationship with a client by lying at his request to a third party
- To increase the worker's power over a client by withholding information
- To make the worker look good by "papering over" mistakes she has made

Are any of these reasons applicable in Exemplars 9.3 and 9.4 ? If applicable, does this make dishonesty ethical?

9.3   A GROWTH ON THE FOOT

Art Elder, age 34, is a high school teacher. At present he is a patient in University Hospital because he has a growth on his foot. His physician told him that there are two ways of treating this problem. Both involve some risks. When Art asked what he would advise, the physician suggested surgery. Sally Brown is the social worker in the surgical department. From her discussion with the resident, she learned that Dr. Kutner, the physician, did not tell the patient all the available choices and that he withheld information about the option with the least risk. Evidently, he weighted his presentation in favor of the experimental surgical treatment method that he is just now developing.

Here we are not concerned with Dr. Kutner, but with Sally Brown. Should she discuss the issue with Dr. Kutner, tell Art the truth, mind her own business and leave the giving of medical information to the medical staff, or suggest that Art get a second opinion? It may be that such behaviors by physicians are uncommon but Sally still faces an ethical dilemma. On what basis can she decide the ethical course of action?

Social workers in direct practice are not the only ones who may have ethical problems with truth telling. Exemplar 9.4, from the field of social work administration, also raises questions about the ethics of truth telling.

9.4 | THE FRANS MUSIC APPRECIATION ROOM

The Frans family contributed a considerable sum of money to the Uptown Community Center to furnish and equip a music appreciation room in memory of their mother. An appropriate plaque marks the room. Since the center accepted the contribution, the neighborhood has experienced a large influx of immigrants from Southeast Asia. Because of their needs, the room is now used for purposes other than those designated by the donors.

You are the center's associate director. You know how important the music appreciation room is to the family. There is a good possibility of obtaining additional donations for other projects from this family, but if the family discovers that their room is no longer used for music appreciation activities, they may lose interest in the Uptown Community Center. At the monthly meeting of the United Way board of directors, you meet Gerald Frans. He asks you how the music appreciation room is doing.

How should you reply? Do you tell the truth? Do you try to avoid the issue by shifting the conversation to another area? Do you tell a little untruth, such as "the immigrants love music"? Or not? What is the ethically correct response? How do you decide?

Social workers at every level sometimes have to choose between loyalty to a friend or colleague and telling the truth. In Exemplar 9.5, a supervisor has to make a choice concerning truthfulness.

9.5 | A SUPERVISOR DECIDES

Karl Samil is a supervisor in a large department of social services. Roger Lewis, a colleague, applied for promotion and Karl has been asked to provide a reference. He is aware of instances when Roger acted in ways that were harmful to the agency, including inappropriately criticizing the agency at several interagency committee meetings, which may have injured the reputation of the agency's elder-abuse team. For over a year, Karl has noted that Roger has been distracted and jumpy about his current job responsibilities. Most of his local colleagues have been aware of his behavior but out of loyalty have kept quiet and have often covered for him. To confuse matters further, Karl and Roger have played cards together in a weekly game since they graduated from college. Even there, Roger's behavior has been somewhat erratic. When Karl spoke to Roger to say he seemed unusually upset and distracted, Roger brushed it off. If promoted, Roger will move to another part of the agency.

Should Karl give a positive reference because of personal loyalty, thereby passing Roger Lewis on to another setting without letting them know of his limitations? Should he risk his own reputation if the promotion is gained but Roger does poorly at the job? What about loyalty to himself and his family? Should he turn his back on the agency and the profession? Or should he speak to Roger again and suggest that Roger defer promotion and take care of his own problems?

The question of truth or deception involves the intention of the speaker and not the factual accuracy of the statement. Knowing the truth does not necessarily result in

TABLE 9.2 | INTENTIONS AND FACTS

The statement is factually:	The speaker intends to be truthful	The speaker intends to be deceptive
True	The speaker intended to tell the truth and did so.	The speaker intended to deceive, but unknowingly spoke the truth. While her intentions were not ethical, her actual behavior does not raise any ethical issues.
False	The speaker intended to tell the truth, but failed to do so because she did not have the correct information. The problem here may be lack of competence or lack of skill, or both, which *although unintentional, may be unethical.*	The speaker intended to deceive and did lie. *This situation involves questions of unethical behavior.*

telling the truth, while not knowing the truth does not always result in a deception. The relations between the objective situation and a speaker's intentions are summarized in Table 9.2.

Some practitioners who abhor lying have suggested that it is possible to deceive without lying by exaggerating or manipulating. One social worker, for example, wanted to dissuade a client from placing his daughter with mental retardation in an institution. She arranged for the father to visit the worst possible institution but did not mention the availability of other alternatives. This social worker would never lie, but did she tell the truth? A social work administrator exaggerates the benefits that may result from a new program so that the agency will receive a larger budget allocation next year. Are these social workers acting ethically? Or is this yet another version of the ends-justifying-the-means quandary?

DIAGNOSIS AND MISDIAGNOSIS

The controversy about the place of diagnosis in social work practice has a number of ethical aspects. Many social workers believe that diagnosis is an essential element in every professional intervention, but others reject its use because they consider it an inappropriate application of the medical model to social work practice. For many, the problem of diagnostics has become even more critical in recent years as use of the *Diagnostic and Statistical Manual of Mental Disorders* (DSM-IV-TR) of the American Psychiatric Association (APA, 2000) has spread rapidly among social workers. Many social workers are required to use the DSM-IV-TR because many government programs authorize service or reimburse for service rendered only on the basis of an appropriate DSM-IV-TR diagnosis; likewise most insurance companies require such a diagnosis before they will authorize third-party payments (Schamess, 1996). Often, authorization and reimbursements are limited to certain diagnostic categories; in other instances, the amount of reimbursement (or the length of the treatment authorized) depends on the diagnosis submitted. These requirements put pressure on social workers to use this diagnostic instrument even though they may not think it is an appropriate diagnostic instrument for social work practice. Some engage in deliberate misdiagnosis in order to meet the stated requirements for reimbursable social work treatment. Exemplar 9.6 illustrates one of the ethical problems that this creates.

9.6	LET THE INSURANCE COMPANY PAY THE BILL

Christine Sales is seeing a private practice social worker. At their initial session last week, she mentioned that she hoped her insurance company would reimburse her for these sessions. Today, Christine brought in the insurance forms and asked her social worker to complete them. The social worker, who was familiar with the requirements of this insurance company, realized right away that she would have to report a more "serious" diagnosis than was clinically indicated if she were to qualify the client for reimbursement.

Under what circumstances is it ethical for a social worker to lie about a diagnosis? What are the potential risks for both the client and the social worker? What is the ethical thing to do if the only way the person will receive services is for the social worker to "fudge" the diagnosis? Earlier we noted that Bayles (1981) suggests that the obligation to be honest with clients does not require honesty when acting on a client's behalf. Do you accept his point of view?

While some social workers will report a more serious diagnosis to obtain third-party payments, others may report less serious diagnoses and justify it as harmless or in the client's best interest. Generally, social workers use "the least noxious diagnosis" (also known as the mercy diagnosis) because:

- It minimizes the communication of damaging and confidential information to nonsocial workers, especially to insurance companies and others.
- It avoids the labeling effects of a more severe diagnosis.
- It limits the adverse impact on a client's self-esteem if the client should become aware of the diagnosis.
- It can protect the future employment prospects (and possibly protect a current job) for the client, as well as the potential for future insurance coverage.

These reasons are used to justify underdiagnosis by suggesting that this is in the client's interest. Some social workers admit that sometimes they deliberately report an underdiagnosis. For example, they might use the category adjustment disorders when a more serious diagnosis would have been more accurate. On the other hand, there are social workers who at times overdiagnose. They may use an Axis 1 diagnosis when this is not warranted in order to qualify a client for reimbursement. Though claiming that overdiagnosis is done for the client's benefit, the real beneficiary may be the social worker or agency whose payments are now guaranteed by a third party.

Misdiagnosis of any type may result when managed care and third-party payers intrude into the professional relationship. While this may provoke such responses, the misdiagnoses are the responsibility of the social workers who make these reports. However, not all misdiagnoses result from an attempt to gain benefits for the client; some misdiagnoses are the result of practitioner incompetence, influenced by the ambiguity of some diagnostic categories, failure to consider biological and physical factors, or failure to ensure medical review when indicated. Competent social work practice is an expected ethical norm.

Another ethical problem arises when a social worker reports a diagnosis for one individual when the primary problem is located in the family system. Since DSM-IV-TR allows only the diagnosis of the problems of an individual, this deliberate misdiagnosis is usually used to qualify for insurance reimbursement.

Even under the best of circumstance, social workers, like all other professionals, will at times make mistakes and err in their diagnosis. Mistakes, though unfortunate and regrettable, but probably inevitable, often have ethical implications. Among these mistakes in diagnostics are the following:

- Lack of sufficient knowledge in using diagnostic instruments such as DSM-IV-TR
- Poor professional judgment
- Deliberate misdiagnosis, often in connection with third-party insurance reimbursement claims and/or reimbursements by government programs

These mistakes may involve both illegal and unethical behaviors. Examine Exemplar 9.7 and consider the ethical aspects involved in arriving at a diagnosis.

9.7	BARRY HAS A LEARNING PROBLEM

Barry is a first grader. He has two older brothers, ages 8 and 10. His oldest brother is doing very well in school, but the middle brother has been identified as a "slow learner" and is in a special education class. Barry's teacher reports that Barry also has some learning problems and finds it difficult to keep up with the rest of his class. The school social worker and the educational psychologist have been discussing what to do with Barry. His tests indicate a relatively low score but within the "normal" range. The social worker knows that Barry would benefit from special attention that his regular classroom teacher cannot give him. However, sending Barry to an ungraded class might label him for the rest of his life, result in his being stigmatized, perhaps being insufficiently challenged, and potentially placing real limits on what is possible for his future.

In this situation, as in many others, the "simple" technical task of diagnosis has a number of ethical aspects that every thoughtful social worker must consider seriously before arriving at a decision. Consideration has to be given to the potential short and long-term effects on the persons immediately involved, including Barry and his brothers, as well as other members of their family, the school, the social worker and teachers. Furthermore, a "simple" decision seemingly affecting only those immediately involved may have potential effects for others who are not so closely involved.

COMPASSION FATIGUE, SECONDARY TRAUMATIC STRESS, AND PSYCHOLOGICAL INDIFFERENCE AS ETHICAL LIMITATIONS

Today, almost everyone experiences sensory overload. Information comes at us constantly by word of mouth, pagers, cellular phones, computers, television, radio, and other advanced technologies. We live in an era of sound bites and brief messages intended to convey complex information. Social workers, along with all other human service workers, also experience immense stress on the job, critical stress in their personal lives, and constant pressures to be even more productive, along with a myriad of other stressors. In many cases this invasion of our personal and professional spaces results in burnout, both as personal alienation and as a coping mechanism in response to these stresses. Social workers upon occasion will tune out, deal only with the surface of things, experience a sense of impotence, and distance themselves from clients, colleagues, and their work (Powell, 1994; Soderfeldt, Soderfeldt, & Warg, 1995).

There are costs that come from being in caring professions. Offering professional help to people in crisis, to persons who suffer from post-traumatic stress disorder, to people who have been abused, to those who are experiencing major and chronic mental health difficulties, depression, or other chronic illnesses can demand a heavy toll in emotional, physical, and social costs. Acker (1999) examined the relationship between the degree of involvement with clients with chronic mental illness and social workers' job satisfaction and burnout. Greater involvement (emotional, extent of direct work with client, percentage of time delivering concrete services) by a social worker with the clients was related to significantly higher levels of emotional exhaustion and depersonalization. The caring social worker can experience physical exhaustion (feeling tired and run down), emotional exhaustion (feeling depressed and without hope), and mental exhaustion (disillusionment, resentment).

When social workers in their roles as helpers hear about traumas, compassion fatigue or secondary traumatic stress may be one "consequence of working with suffering people" (Figley, 1999, p. 4). People can be traumatized without actually being harmed or threatened with harm. Just learning about the traumatic events endured by others can affect helping professionals. Learning about violent personal assaults, serious accidents and injuries, sudden deaths, or the deaths of young children, all can wreak havoc emotionally on helping professionals (Figley, 1999).

One result of psychological distancing may be paying less exact attention to the ethical dilemmas that one encounters in practice, Hannah Arendt in *Eichmann in Jerusalem* (1977) characterized this human ability as leading to "the banality of evil." Americans learned about the potential insidious impact of this kind of banality at My Lai in Vietnam and once again at Abu Ghraib in Iraq. Such psychological distancing can lead a social worker to avoid responsibility by distancing herself from clients, to treat clients with less individualization and dignity, or to serve the organization or society when the right action is to serve the individual. What should the administrator in Exemplar 9.8 do?

| 9.8 | AN ADMINISTRATOR DECIDES WHAT TO DO |

Joseph Parocha is the overworked and stressed-out executive director of a Meals-on-Wheels program. Drivers recently have begun reporting seeing longer and longer lines at several soup kitchens as they travel to deliver meals to shut-in elderly people. Also, drivers have discovered mothers with young children without sufficient food at several of the houses where they deliver meals. In speaking to the president of the board, Haakon Query,

continued

| 9.8 | AN ADMINISTRATOR DECIDES WHAT TO DO *continued* |

Joseph suggested that the agency also has a responsibility to try to help these other people. After all, their job is helping feed people who are hungry, no matter what their age. Haakon responded sharply that the agency has trouble enough maintaining itself and that he and others on the board would oppose any attempt to assist either the soup kitchens or the young families. The homeless and the young parents are the responsibility of other agencies. The agency should focus on its primary mission of feeding the elderly. Joseph was torn by his feeling that something should be done to help all hungry people. He knew that the staff could be doing more, although he personally didn't need any further pressures. When he talked this problem over with his wife, she reminded him that his health is also important, that their son is to start college this fall, and that their daughter needs braces. Joseph was upset but eventually decided that at this time it was better not to attempt to redefine the mission of the agency by trying to move it in new directions.

Is Joseph's decision not to act the result of protecting himself and his family, burnout, or a pragmatic decision? What should Joseph have done? After all, he doesn't have accurate data on the people whose problems are being reported to him by his drivers, nor is it his agency's responsibility to help support all of the city's poor. He is convinced that "anyone in my position would do the same thing." Was his decision correct? Was it ethical? Joseph was confronted with a problem situation in which he decided to tolerate the inadequate condition of young women and their families and of the homeless while concentrating on maintaining the Meals-on-Wheels program and, incidentally or otherwise, protecting his family. To whom does he owe first loyalty? His agency? The president and board members? The soup kitchens? The homeless? The young women and their families? Himself? His family?

PRACTITIONER IMPAIRMENT

There are social workers who suffer from some type of impairment, including substance abuse, psychological stresses due to aging, physical illness, financial hardship, extreme working conditions, marital and family difficulties, or chronic psychological disorders. These problems can affect a social worker and her family, friends, and colleagues, and, most importantly, may result in a social worker's inability to provide professionally competent services. Social workers are thought to have about the same rates of alcohol and substance abuse problems as members of other stressful health professions. A survey of all Indiana NASW chapter members reported that 53% knew a social worker whose performance was affected by emotional or mental health problems, substance abuse, burnout, or sexual misconduct (Hiratsuka, 1994). Earlier, the New York City Chapter of NASW reported that 43% of the respondents to a study knew at least one social worker with a drug or alcohol problem. A self-evaluation study of active North Carolina NASW members found that 19% of the respondents reported having depressive symptoms and 14% were currently depressed, (almost half the respondents reported past depression). Some social workers were currently taking medications for depression and a number reported they had considered suicide at some point in their lives (Siebert, 2004). In a report based on the study of the same North

Carolina population, 12% (one in eight) of the study group scored at the time of the study above a threshold on more than one measure of alcohol or drug use and were at high risk for alcohol and drug abuse (Siebert, 2005).

It is an ethical imperative for the profession to ensure that every professional practitioner is able to provide quality professional services and respect all ethical norms, including confidentiality. However, impaired social workers may act in undisciplined, insensitive, erratic, unprofessional, and unethical ways. Sometimes they use inappropriate language or behavior with clients and colleagues, pay haphazard attention to their clients, fail to follow through on assignments, or engage in excessive absenteeism. Impairments can lead to inadequate and even unethical behaviors, which result in actions detrimental to clients and others, can lower the public's estimate of and trust of the profession, and present ethical problems for other social workers.

The Code of Ethics includes four standards directly related to the impairment or incompetence of professional social workers. Social workers who have direct knowledge of such impairment or incompetence should consult with the impaired colleague where feasible and assist the colleague in taking remedial action. When the colleague has not taken adequate steps to address the impairment, they are expected to take action through appropriate channels established by NASW, licensing and regulatory bodies, employers, agencies, and other professional organizations. (NASW Code, 1999, 2.09a, b; 2.10a, b). However, these standards do not provide answers for all the ethical dilemmas that occur in this area. Consider the situation presented in Exemplar 9.9.

9.9 | MY FRIEND, MENTOR, SUPERVISOR, AND ALCOHOL

You are a social worker assigned to a satellite unit of a family service agency. You and Davis Jones, your supervisor, are the only two social workers who work in the unit. Your relationship with Davis goes back at least 15 years; he has been very important in your life at several junctions. He helped you get into social work school; he recommended you for an advanced treatment institute; and once when your child was ill, he helped you obtain medical care from the best specialist in town. Recently, however, Davis, who is also responsible for evaluating you for pay and possible promotions, has been late arriving for work and has missed some meetings. You have had to cover for him more than a few times with his clients. You are still somewhat in awe of Davis and owe him a lot, but you suspect that his current erratic behavior may be related to alcohol and family difficulties.

So far Davis has done little, if any, harm. At what point must you act? What about loyalty to a mentor, friend, and colleague from whom you have learned much? What about loyalty to yourself, your career, and your family? What about the risks to which you may expose yourself by acting? What should you do? What would be the ethical option? Consider the ethical implications for each of the following options you may select.

- Encourage one of the clients for whom you have had to replace Davis for several sessions to register a complaint with the agency.
- Call in sick one day and ask for a substitute to cover cases so that another social worker also becomes aware of the problem.

- Ignore the situation. Wait for someone else to "blow the whistle." Meanwhile, cover his cases.
- Ask a mutual friend to call Davis and say that he has heard about his behavior on the job and suggest that it is important that he do something about his problems.
- Report the situation to a high-level agency administrator.
- Speak to Davis directly. State that you want to keep quiet about the situation, but that he must go for help before things become worse.

SOURCES OF HELP

Social Workers Helping Social Workers (SWHSW), founded in 1980, is a national association that provides confidential assistance to colleagues primarily through e-mail, listservs, and by telephone. Social workers can contact SWHSW at (773) 493-6940 (confidential) or swhswil@aol.com. In 1995, NASW published a *Chapter Guide for Colleague Assistance for Impaired Social Workers*. According to NASW (2006), "Unfortunately, NASW members are averse to reporting troubled colleagues despite an ethical mandate to intervene" (p. 1). NASW and some chapters offer materials on helping social workers identify colleagues with chemical dependency problems and ways to intervene with these colleagues.

Exercises

1. If there is an NASW chapter in your area, invite the chair of the Chapter Committee on Inquiry to discuss with your class how they handle complaints about ethical misconduct. You might want to examine with the chair how effective these procedures are.
2. Sexual activities with clients are prohibited by the NASW Code of Ethics (1999, 1.09). Some social workers have argued that there is no scientific evidence that such activities are necessarily harmful. They say that a rule of this kind is no longer relevant in a society that permits a wide variety of lifestyles. Present arguments both for changing and for retaining this rule.
3. The "limited professional relationship" characteristic of the client/social worker relationship baffles many clients. It is a relationship that is quite unlike the formal, bureaucratic relationships with which they are familiar, yet it is also different from the informal primary relations they maintain with friends and relatives. How important is this principle from an ethical point of view?
4. In teams of two, develop two lists: (1) social relations with clients that are ethical and permissible, and (2) social relations with clients that are definitely unethical and therefore prohibited. Compare your lists with those of other teams. Discuss those areas where you find disagreement.
5. Are there cultural issues that influence the profession's definition of what is considered acceptable and what is considered unethical?

Suggestions for Additional Readings

Koenig and Spano (2003) explore sexual boundary violations (which are unethical, harmful, and often emotionally devastating to the parties involved) between educators and students and supervisors and supervisees. Strozier, Kmzek, and Sale (2003) examine the use of touch in social work practice and suggest that its use is not without potential harm. Johner

(2006) discusses the legitimization of nonsexual dual relationships in social work practice. Adams, Boscarino, and Figley (2006) examine caring professionals and their emotional exhaustion (compassion fatigue) from working with traumatized clients. Mittendorf and Schroeder (2004) report on the results of an exploratory study examining social workers' attitudes, beliefs, and involvement with their clients and their knowledge of the prevalence of this behavior. Jayaratne et al. (1997) report on research on dual-role and intimate relationships and on boundary behaviors.

Web Sites of Interest

- For an extensive set of resources on burnout and compassion fatigue, including self tests and ideas for combating burnout, see: www.friedsocialworker.com
- Sexual issues in psychology training and practice have parallels in social work. Much information related to sex with clients is examined at: www.kspope.com/sexiss/
- A wide variety of topics related to social work, including issues related to sex: www.nyu.edu/socialwork/ip/

10 # ORGANIZATIONAL AND WORK RELATIONSHIPS

So far, our discussion has focused on ethical problems and ethical dilemmas occurring in the professional relationship between social workers and clients. In this chapter, our attention will be directed to ethical issues arising out of the relationships among social work colleagues and between social workers and their employers, agencies, supervisors, and administrators.

We noted in chapter 2 that one of the functions of professional codes of ethics is to permit colleagues to work together in harmony. The NASW Code of Ethics "informs other professionals with whom the professional must work about the kind of cooperation they have a right to expect from the professional and the limits to the cooperation that a professional ought to give" (Beyerstein, 1993, p. 420). This information reduces bickering and infighting that might lead to professional self-destruction. One section of the NASW Code deals with the social worker's ethical responsibilities toward colleagues, and another section with her ethical responsibilities to employers and practice settings. Several additional ethical rules dealing with relationships with colleagues are found in the section devoted to ethical responsibilities toward the profession.

Strom-Gottfried (2003) examined 894 ethics complaints filed with NASW for the years 1986 to 1997. Of the 894 complaints, 93 (10.4%) were filed against persons identified in the study as colleagues, an additional 40 (4.4%) complaints were filed against an employer or supervisor, and 174 (19.4%) complaints were filed against employees or supervisees. Thus, one third of the complaints were filed against colleagues, employers, or supervisors, all of whom are work associates. In an earlier published report based on the same 1986 to 1997 data cited above, Strom-Gottfried (1999) found that the most commonly occurring violation concerned poor supervision—involving failure to maintain or share performance standards with workers, using insufficient investigation and documentation in performance review processes, not holding regular supervisory sessions, or holding sessions that were unclear and ineffective. The second most common violation involved employee dismissals that were judged to have been based on insufficient or absent personnel policies, or that diverged from accepted processes of progressive discipline, such as counseling or disciplinary actions. These complaints may represent only the tip of the proverbial iceberg because many unethical behaviors of this type are not filed with NASW, but are handled in other ways, as will be discussed later in this chapter and in chapter 13.

RELATIONS WITH PROFESSIONAL COLLEAGUES AND ETHICAL DILEMMAS

What is a social worker to do when she discovers that a colleague engages in unethical or unprofessional conduct? How should she respond when she realizes that a fellow worker provides poor quality client services? What are her obligations when she believes that another social worker harms a client? What is her responsibility when she discovers that another worker engages in activities prohibited by their agency? What are her responsibilities when she learns that a colleague has violated the Code of Ethics?

The ethical rule obligating social workers to treat colleagues with respect (NASW Code, 1999, 2.01a) is one of those rules that ordinarily does not create an ethical quandary. Social workers face relatively few ethical problems as long as the rules governing relations with professional colleagues are unambiguous and not challenged by other ethical rules. However, as accountability to clients and others becomes more important, the unspoken rule to "protect your own" becomes increasingly problematic. Some examples of unethical behavior that might arise include knowing a colleague is: (a) having sexual relations with a client or a supervisee; (b) an alcoholic and is berating some clients; (c) sharing confidential information about a colleague with other colleagues; or (d) "bad mouthing" a team leader after failing to convince an interdisciplinary team to proceed with a particular treatment plan.

Today, most social workers are no longer willing to overlook their colleagues' unethical behavior, but it is not always clear what should be done. On learning that a colleague has engaged in unethical behavior, a social worker may choose one or more of the following options:

Option A. One can decide not to report the violating behavior because reporting it may be too troublesome, past experience suggests that nothing will be done about it even if it is reported, or the conduct may be so widespread that it is unlikely that anyone will take the complaint seriously.

Option B. An informal approach to the colleague may resolve the problematic behavior, especially if the violation is of a minor or technical nature or appears to be the result of lack of experience or knowledge. The situation differs if your colleague is a peer, a supervisee, or a supervisor.

Option C. If the alleged unethical conduct also violates agency rules, it may be brought to the attention of one's supervisor or it may be raised formally by using agency procedures established for this purpose.

Option D. The alleged unethical behavior may be brought to the attention of the NASW Committee on Inquiry. In order to use this procedure, the colleague who allegedly engaged in the unethical behavior must have been an NASW member at the time of the alleged violation, the complaint must charge a specific violation of the Code of Ethics, the complainant must have personal knowledge about the alleged behavior, and the complainant must be able and willing to provide the Committee on Inquiry with relevant and reliable testimony (NASW Procedures for Professional Review, 2001). The National Committee on Inquiry has primary administrative responsibility in all professional review matters. The NASW professional review procedures will be discussed in more detail in chapter 13.

Option E. Where a state licensing board regulates social work practice, unethical conduct harmful to clients can be reported to the board.

Option F. The unethical conduct may be brought to the attention of the general public (whistle blowing), with the expectation that an aroused public will demand appropriate action to bring an end to the violation.

There are a number of possible alternatives within each option. Option A is problematic. Options B, C, D, and E are sanctioned by the Code of Ethics. Are there times and occasions when going public is the only way to proceed (Option F)? The decision to go public should never be a routine one and should be taken only after careful consideration of all possibilities. Before choosing which option to follow, the social worker should attempt to clarify what she hopes to achieve by the action she intends to initiate. Loewenberg (1987) suggests the following as possible objectives:

1. Ensure discontinuance of the unethical behavior.
2. Punish the offending social worker.
3. Identify the unethical practitioner so that potential clients and/or employers will avoid this person and turn to another, more ethical practitioner.
4. Prevent others from engaging in this behavior by warning them that it is unethical and will result in sanctions against the practitioner.
5. Protect the good name of the profession by declaring publicly that the unethical behavior is not approved by the profession.

Exemplars 10.1 and 10.2 highlight some of the problems involved in this ethical issue.

10.1 | SEX WITH CLIENTS

Your colleague Mitchell Moore has been hospitalized quite suddenly. While he is on sick leave, you have been assigned to cover some of his cases. You learn from one of his clients that Mitch has been having sexual relations with her. She says that she was uncomfortable but felt something bad would happen if she had objected. She also asks you to protect her confidentiality and that she will handle the situation when he returns. This behavior is clearly in violation of the Code, which states, "Social workers should under no circumstances engage in sexual activities or sexual contact with current clients, whether such contact is consensual or forced" (NASW Code, 1999, 1.09a).

The violation of the Code of Ethics as reported is obvious, but what you should do is not clear because there are many conflicting demands on you. Your most serious consideration is: How trustworthy is this client's report? Can you/should you act if you have questions about what happened? However, assuming you believe the client's report, let us examine some things to consider, one by one, but not in any order of priority.

- Your obligation to promote the well-being of clients (NASW Code, 1999, 1.01).
- Your obligation to respect confidential material received in the course of the professional relationship, except for compelling professional reasons (NASW Code, 1999, 1.07c).
- Your obligation to "not engage in physical contact with clients when there is a possibility of psychological harm to the client as a result of the contact..." and your obligation "for setting clear, appropriate, and culturally sensitive boundaries that govern such physical contact" (NASW Code, 1999, 1.10).
- Your obligation to "take adequate measures to discourage, prevent, expose, and correct the unethical conduct of colleagues" (NASW Code, 1999, 2.11a).
- Your obligation to uphold the values, ethics, knowledge, and mission of the profession (NASW Code, 1999, 5.01b).
- Making a fuss about it will only result in making you look ridiculous.

The last consideration argues against your taking any action (Option A—Not report), while the earlier considerations suggest a more active response (perhaps Option B—Informal approach, Option C—Use agency procedures, Option D—NASW and professional review, or even Option E— Report to the state licensing board). (The descriptions of these options were provided earlier in this section.) How can a social worker prioritize these considerations by importance? Does the ethical principles screen (EPS) help you in unraveling this conundrum? Which is the priority ethical obligation?

Let us consider another situation that presents the social worker with ethical quandaries in her relation to colleagues in Exemplar 10.2.

10.2	FAILURE TO REPORT A CASE OF CHILD ABUSE

Jake Dember, a frail 5-year-old, was brought to the emergency room of Mt. Ebal Hospital unconscious, covered with blood from head to toe, with severe internal injuries. His father, Hiram, said that Jake fell from their second-floor apartment and landed headfirst on the cement sidewalk. The medical team was able to save Jake's life, though serious brain damage could not be reversed. Now, two weeks later, Jake is still in the hospital's critical care unit. The attending physicians are determined to report this as a case of child abuse. Before doing so, they have asked the hospital social worker, Josie Perry, to pull together all the relevant information they possess so that it can be provided to child protective services (CPS) at the time of the report.

Erica Dember, Jake's mother, did not want to talk to Josie. She said that she and her husband were already in family therapy at the family service agency, and if Josie wanted to know anything about them, she should talk to their therapist, Ed Custer. Josie arranged to meet with Ed on the following afternoon. He was willing to share his assessment of the Dember family because both parents had signed the customary consent forms when Jake was admitted to the hospital. In the course of their conversation, Ed acknowledged that he had been aware of ongoing child abuse in this family, but because he thought that it was not too serious, he did not file a report. He feared that such a report would have interfered with the therapeutic relationship that he was trying to develop with this family.

There are similarities and differences between this exemplar and the previous one. In both cases, one social worker became aware that another social worker may have violated ethical standards. In the first case, continuation of the unethical behavior (sexual relations with a client) might result in further harm to the client. In the present case, the harm to Jake had already been done and perhaps will not be repeated with Jake, but Ed Custer's criminal conduct and his failure to report other cases of child abuse may cause harm to other clients. Are the conflicting claims on Josie Perry similar to those that faced Mitch Moore's colleague? How valid is Ed's fear that reporting a client's child abuse may interfere with the therapeutic relationship?

Research findings do *not* support the claim that reporting child abuse interferes with maintaining a therapeutic relationship. A national survey of psychologists who are psychotherapists and who had filed at least one mandated child abuse report found that clients remained in treatment when such reports were made, especially when certain factors were present. Important for maintaining this relationship was the explicit involvement of the client in the informed consent procedures. It was also important that the limits of confidentiality were fully discussed with the client. Moreover, clients were more likely to continue when there were positive therapeutic relationships prior to the report and when the perpetrator was a third party (someone not engaged directly in the treatment). Most surprising, clients reacted more positively when sexual abuse—rather than other forms of abuse—was reported (Steinberg, Levine, & Doueck, 1997). How should Josie Perry resolve the ethical dilemma facing her? Should she report Ed's negligence to the NASW chapter? Ignore it? Choose another action?

So far, our consideration of the ethical quandaries arising out of this issue has focused on social work colleagues. Social workers also interact with practitioners from other professions and with nonprofessional human service workers. Although the nature of these relations may be different, the NASW Code of Ethics states that the same respect and cooperation that is extended to social work colleagues should also be extended to colleagues of other professions (NASW Code, 1999, 2.01a). In one sense, the ethical problems arising out of these relationships will be the same as those that occur in relationships with social work colleagues. In other ways, the ethical dilemma may be more critical because these non–social work colleagues are not subject to the provisions of the NASW Code of Ethics. They may follow other norms of confidentiality or may routinely engage in behaviors that professional social workers define as unethical. What should social workers do if their values and ethics are in conflict with the values and ethics of team members from other professions when the respective ethical obligations have not been clearly established as suggested by the Code (1999, 2.03a) or the disagreement cannot be resolved through appropriate channels (2.03b)? Which other avenues should be pursued to address their concerns consistent with client well-being?

If a social worker learns of the incompetence of a team member from another discipline, what is one's ethical responsibility? What if social workers are working in cooperation with educators, psychologists, lawyers, physicians, or other disciplines? Is the ethical responsibility of the social worker always the same in whatever setting concerning abuse, confidentiality, sexual impropriety, inadequate professional performance, conflicts of interest, and the like? Suppose as a social worker you are employed in an agency led by lawyers. In some states they may have no legal responsibility to report child abuse that is discovered in the course of their professional activity with clients; a social worker finding out about similar situations has a legal and ethical responsibility to report the situation. In the face of these conflicts and obligations, to whom does the social worker owe responsibility—the client or patient, the team, herself, the social work profession, the other involved professions, or society?

ADHERENCE TO AGENCY POLICIES AND REGULATIONS

The fact that most social workers are employed by bureaucratic organizations makes for another set of ethical dilemmas. Every organization has rules and policies. Those individuals who accept employment voluntarily agree to abide by these regulations. The NASW Code of Ethics considers this commitment to the employing organization a basic ethical obligation: "Social workers generally should adhere to commitments made to employers and employing organizations" (NASW Code, 1999, 3.09a). The goals and objectives of some organizations, even of some social service agencies, however, are not always congruent with the values of the social work profession. Organization maintenance and survival demands may result in rules that contradict the primary obligation of social workers to give priority to their clients' interests. Efficiency measures may limit intervention options so that the most effective option for a given client may not be available. Budgetary considerations may result in service cutbacks that will not be in the client's best interest. This is the type of ethical dilemma that is especially demanding for social work administrators. They must resolve a critical ethical dilemma—whether to give priority to adherence to agency rules or to service to clients.

One response to these situations is collusion with clients to violate agency policies. This approach is often rationalized by the social worker by defining her activities as promoting the client's welfare or contributing fairness and social justice. Is it ever ethical to violate agency policies? For example, what should a social worker do upon learning that a client has occasional additional income, which she is supposed to report to her public assistance worker so that part of this income can be deducted from the following month's welfare check? Or a Supplemental Security Income (SSI) beneficiary also is working "off the books" and not reporting the extra income that would cause her to lose support? If the social worker does not report this income, all of the extra money will be available to the clients. In the first case, the additional cash may help her to return to employment and independence and, in the second case, enable the beneficiary to live at a relatively minimal subsistence level. Keeping quiet may be in the best interest of both clients. Do the amount and the regularity of the extra income make a difference? In each case, what about the worker's obligations to the law, her employer, and society?

A particularly difficult ethical dilemma is faced by social workers when they discover that their agency's policies or regulations are unethical. For example, a hospital social worker discovers soon after employment that it is hospital policy to pressure social workers to encourage mentally competent patients to move into nursing homes. Intended to counter excessive concern by the hospital staff about patient safety following discharge, these actions override patients' rights to autonomy and self-determination (Clemens, 1995). As another example, what if the administrator of a child protective agency hires inadequately trained paraprofessional workers to investigate complaints of child abuse because of insufficient funds to hire professionally trained workers, even though this assignment requires a particularly high skill level?

The examples in the previous paragraph present a question as to what are ethical responses to budget cuts for the administrator and direct practitioner. Exemplar 10.3 provides another example where the purposes of the staff are served without due consideration of the needs of the client.

10.3 | PREGNANT WOMEN NEED SUPPORT

Terry Newton is a social worker in a private organization, Upward Strivers, that performs contract work for a local Department of Social Services (DSS). The clients receive public assistance under the Temporary Assistance to Needy Families (TANF) program as long as they are enrolled and active in a program that is designed to prepare them for regular employment through job readiness training. When needed, clients also receive GED preparation or literacy classes. After completing the three weeks of job readiness, those clients not enrolled in training programs must begin job searches with the help of a placement specialist and may be enrolled part time in GED preparation or literacy training. The Department of Social Services frequently refers pregnant women to the job readiness program. None of these women are able to find employment following the training because most employers won't hire pregnant women. The pregnant women are enrolled in GED preparation in order to avoid the loss of their financial support. Both Upward Strivers and the DSS created this informal policy, which enables both DSS and Upward Strivers to receive payments from the state.

The purpose of these informal policies is to maintain payments for the client, the Upward Strivers, and the DSS. The client needs financial support as do the two agencies, both of which are engaged in many important and constructive activities. If you were a social worker who discovered this pattern of behavior, where would you look in the Code of Ethics for guidance on how to choose in an ethical manner among the clients and their needs, Upward Strivers, and the DSS? To which persons, organizations, or institutions do you have an ethical commitment? How would you implement your ethical decision?

A different aspect of the conflict between agency interests and client interests that results in ethical quandaries is illustrated by Exemplar 10.4.

10.4 | A CASE OF A BOY WITH ADHD

David lives a in a residential institution. He has been diagnosed with severe attention deficit hyperactivity disorder (ADHD) and in the last few weeks, he has been acting out. He frequently tosses food during meals with other children, "short sheets" other children's beds, turns on fire alarms, arrives late wherever he is expected, throws pencils in class, and other such behaviors. Although he is not physically harmful to himself or others, he has been highly disruptive of the institution's daily routine. The consulting physician has prescribed medication to calm David and make him easier to manage, but the cottage social worker has refused on ethical grounds to administer this medicine to David. She feels strongly that such pharmaceutical control will interfere with the child's welfare and freedom and will be counterproductive in any therapy attempted. Her social work supervisor supports this decision. The physician insists the medication prescribed be given to David. The institution's director, a psychologist, supports the doctor against the decision of the social worker.

The agency executive requires an institution that runs smoothly. He also needs a physician who is willing to cooperate with the institution's staff. The social workers in this case argue that David has engaged in some asocial behavior—behavior they believe can be controlled more productively in other ways. Whose welfare takes priority? Is their responsibility to David and their own treatment plans, the executive director, the physician, or the other children in the institution who also have rights the social workers are obligated to support?

Non–Social Work Employers

When a social worker is employed by an organization outside the human services field, she may face even more perplexing ethical problems. Today, social workers are employed by hospitals, industry, police, prisons, the military, colleges, long-term care facilities, and a variety of other organizations that are not social work oriented. To whom do these social workers owe their *primary* loyalty? Who is the client of these social workers? For example, the employees of a large manufacturer may consult about personal problems with the social worker whom their employer has hired. Should the employer be informed when a worker's problems may affect the production schedule of a factory or may have security implications? Should detectives have access to confidential information that a prison social worker has obtained from her contacts with prisoners?

The problem of identifying who is the client may be especially difficult for social workers in military service. Consider Exemplar 10.5.

10.5	THE MILITARY IS A SPECIAL ENVIRONMENT

Sergeant Richard Mozart recently discussed some personal difficulties with Captain Emilio Pacifico, a social worker on an army base. Sgt. Mozart is assigned to hazardous duty and told Capt. Pacifico that he is a moderate alcohol user. Capt. Pacifico was recently transferred to a new duty station. As a result, he transferred Sgt. Mozart's case file to the new social worker assigned to the base. When the newly assigned social worker—Lt. Ted Maddox—read the file, he reported Sgt. Mozart and had him taken off hazardous duty; he did not consult with Capt. Pacifico or talk to Sgt. Mozart before making this report. As a result of this, Sgt. Mozart filed an ethics complaint against Capt. Pacifico.

What are the ethical dilemmas in this case situation? Should Capt. Pacifico have made a report earlier and had Sgt. Mozart removed from hazardous duty? Was Lt. Maddox's action appropriate? Would it make a difference if these events were taking place in a war zone? What difference would it make if Sgt. Mozart were not assigned to hazardous duty?

As social workers in the military, Capt. Pacifico and Lt. Maddox have to adhere to the NASW Code of Ethics *and* to the guidelines of the Department of Defense. These two sets of guidelines view confidentiality differently. This conflict can create difficulties for the social worker who may find his decisions in the military contradict the standards of the professional Code. Should Capt. Pacifico and/or Lt. Maddox be reprimanded by a social work ethics committee? Should signed verbal consent or signed consent forms have been obtained from Sgt. Mozart by either or both social workers prior to the transfer of the case file?

Confidentiality in a military clinical setting is guided by federal legislation, Department of Defense regulations, and service specific regulations. Although privacy is to be respected, these regulations mandate access to confidential files by military personnel on a "need to know" basis. The "need to know" basis, admittedly ambiguously defined, does not require the patient's signature for release. While there may be ambiguity in certain situations about what "need to know" means, where safety is involved in a military environment, confidentiality does not take priority (Jaques & Folen, 1998).

Similar dilemmas related to issues concerning confidentiality can occur, for example, in employee assistance programs. Exemplar 10.6 describes an EAP situation and its ethical dilemmas.

10.6	CONFIDENTIALITY AND THREATENING BEHAVIOR

You are a social worker in a state employment assistance program (EAP) and friendly with Margaret Di Constanza. Margaret recently told you that a male colleague—Ethan Starkey—has been "hanging around" her work space and making "strange sounds." Ethan is an average employee and the only reports of inappropriate behavior by him concern his keeping piles of magazines and other printed materials in his work space. These piles of printed materials only intrude in the area around his desk, but they are unsightly and may be a fire hazard. He has been asked several times to remove the materials. He does so and then shortly after the piles return. His job performance otherwise has been generally adequate. Margaret told you that she feels threatened by his behavior; she doesn't know what to expect next. She asked you to do something about the situation but not tell anyone else. When you attempted to observe Ethan when he was near Margaret, you were unable to confirm her observations and complaint.

To whom do you owe loyalty in such an ambiguous situation: to the EAP, your friendship with Margaret, Ethan Starkey, or yourself as the EAP social worker? Could Ethan's behavior escalate, and what are the implications for others in the workplace? Should you believe and trust your friend and report the incidents to management by revealing her confidence? Should you avoid reporting the incidents but raise what could be a regular concern about Ethan, a concern that would at least keep attention focused on Ethan for a period of time? What is the ethical thing to do?

Exemplar 10.7 describes an ethical dilemma that a social worker involved in international service may encounter, but it has implications for workers in many other settings.

10.7	SERVING ONLY THE GOOD PEOPLE OR...?

Amanda Frankel is a social worker for an international aid organization in a war zone. The forces of one side of the conflict are particularly cruel, attacking civilians, raping young girls and older women, and murdering groups of men and burying their bodies to do away with evidence. Until yesterday, Amanda was happy and proud to serve those in need who were being attacked. Then her supervisor sent a message that she was going to be transferred to the other side to serve the people there. Just as here, she would serve all people, including military and paramilitary personnel. She was awake all night considering what she should do.

What is the ethically correct choice in this situation? In what way is Ethical Principle 2 (equality and inequality) relevant to Amanda's situation and dilemma? In what ways do her personal values conflict with her employing agency's values and requirements? Does the Code of Ethics suggest there is a correct choice for Amanda? Can you identify in your local community situations in which social workers might have their personal values challenged by similar decisions by the agencies for which they work?

Noteworthy for social workers in military and homeland security settings is the struggle of the American Psychological Association and the American Psychiatric Association in response to reports of harsh interrogations of detainees at Abu Ghraib, Guantanamo Bay, and other locations. According to the American Psychological Association, there is a role for psychologists in the interrogation of detainees by the American military and government but they also warn of the ethical dangers of such activities (Lewis, 2005). Their report said that psychologists can serve in consultative roles in interrogation and information-gathering processes for national security-related purposes. In addition to other guidelines, psychologists should not engage in, support, facilitate, or offer training related to torture or other cruel, inhuman, or degrading treatment, and they should not use a detainee's medical information to the detriment and harm of the individual. Psychologists serving as consultants to interrogations involving national security should be aware of factors unique to these roles and contexts that require special ethical consideration. The report avoided explicit answers to the question of whether psychologists may advise interrogators on how to increase stress to make detainees more cooperative if the advice is not based on medical files but only on observation of the detainee (Lewis, 2005; *Psychiatric News*, 2005). The American Psychiatric Association prohibited psychiatrists' participation in interrogations of detainees at Guantanamo Bay and elsewhere. Direct participation includes being present in the interrogation room, asking or suggesting questions, or advising authorities on the specific techniques of interrogation with particular detainees (News Release, American Psychiatric Association, 2006). Behnke (2006), director of the American Psychological Association's Ethics Office, summarized the stances of the American Medical, Psychiatric, and Psychological associations on these issues: "Military psychologists, physicians, and psychiatrists following orders, abiding by clear prohibitions against coercive interrogations, acting strictly as consultants to interrogations and not as caregivers, and reporting coercive or abusive acts to the appropriate authorities, will not be subject to discipline from their professional associations" (p. 4).

Ethical problems arising out of adherence to agency policies occur in all settings. Some of our illustrations are taken from non–social work settings because the ethical dilemmas may be more evident there. Social workers employed by social agencies, however, should not think these problems cannot happen to them, as Exemplar 10.8 illustrates.

10.8 | APPLE HILL YOUNG ADULT SOCIAL CLUB

The Apple Hill Community Center is a group service and recreation agency in a changing neighborhood. When it was established almost 50 years ago, it served an immigrant population and was instrumental in the Americanization of many thousands of newcomers. It now sees "character building" and "strengthening democratic decision making" as its

continued

| 10.8 | APPLE HILL YOUNG ADULT SOCIAL CLUB *continued* |

major contribution to the community. As a matter of policy, it avoids all political activities. Neither staff nor groups affiliated with the center are allowed to take a public stand on controversial issues.

Otto Zupan, a social group worker, staffs the Young Adult Social Club. This group is composed of 25 young men, ages 18 to 21, almost all of whom are high school graduates. They spend much time at the community center because most of them are unemployed. Lately, they have talked a lot about why there are no jobs for them. Some thought that the recession was to blame; others felt it was because they were African Americans. Otto urged them to do some research and see if they could come up with some answers to their question. The results of their field study left little doubt that they were the victims of discriminatory hiring practices. Otto urged them to go public because discrimination in hiring was against the law. Letting the public know about their findings might help them get a better break when applying for the next job. They thought that Otto's idea was great and decided to call a news conference. They asked Otto to arrange for a room at the center for the news conference.

When Otto talked over their plan with the center's director, he was flatly rebuffed. Not only could they not have a room for the news conference, but as a center social club they could not engage at all in this type of action program. Furthermore, Otto must do everything to bring the group back to its original objectives as a social club. The center director added that if Otto could not do this, he should ask for another assignment.

Loyalty to agency rules or meeting client needs—these are two conflicting professional obligations that create a serious ethical problem for social worker Otto Zupan. Is it ethical for him to abide by the agency's directives and abandon the young adults at this critical point in their development? Should he ignore his obligations to his employer and help group members organize outside the center? What is the ethical stance demanded of a social worker who faces this situation?

Another type of ethical dilemma occurs when an agency channels clients into programs that are not beneficial for them. For example, what are the ethical issues faced by social workers when a large number of unskilled men and women are directed into job-training programs that lead only to dead-end or nonexistent jobs? Should social workers act against agency policy and tell their clients all that they know about these programs? Is it more ethical to follow organizational directives and keep quiet? How does a social worker make ethical decisions of this type?

What are the ethical implications when a social agency engages in discriminatory practices? There was a time when such practices were blatant and open; now they are less obvious but may be equally damaging. One child welfare agency places white children in adoptive homes and minority children in institutions "because there are no adoptive homes for them." In another agency, homosexual AIDS patients receive one type of service, while heterosexual AIDS patients receive another type of service. Whatever the reason, discriminatory practices never benefit the client who is being discriminated against. The Code of Ethics clearly states, "Social workers should not practice, condone, facilitate, or collaborate with any form of discrimination on the basis of race, ethnicity, national origin, color, sex, sexual orientation, age, marital status, political belief, religion, or mental or physical disability" (NASW Code, 1999, 4.02). What does this mean in practice? Should a social worker refuse to accept employment in an agency that practices discrimination? Must she resign when she discovers such practices? Should she ignore such agency policies and, whenever possible, not follow them? Or should she accept a job with the intention to change the agency? What would you do if you had Dale Jenkins's job in Exemplar 10.9?

| 10.9 | SOCIAL WORK IN A BANK |

Social worker Dale Jenkins is employed by a large bank as a community representative in a minority neighborhood. Dale is African American and part of his assignment is to be visible and become accepted in the community. He has been very successful in meeting this objective. He is accepted by the neighborhood's residents and is liked by nearly everyone. In the past year, he has been able to help a number of residents qualify for business loans and mortgages. Nick Stamos, vice president of the bank to whom he reports, recently told Jenkins that the bank has decided to direct less money and services to this neighborhood, but that his job is safe. Nick implied that in a few years the bank might again direct monies to this neighborhood. In the meantime, Dale should be more selective in referring residents to the bank for loans and mortgages.

Dale understood this message as meaning that the bank no longer would give mortgages to minority group applicants. He considered the options he had, including the following:

- Making sure that he had understood correctly. If he hadn't, then he could discuss with Nick how the misunderstanding had occurred and how to avoid it in the future. However, if he had understood correctly, then he could consider other options, such as:
- Try to persuade Nick and other bank officials to change the new and discriminating policy.
- Ignore the new policy and operate as he had in the past.
- Tell community leaders about the new policy and encourage them to apply political pressure on the bank to change its policy.

What are the ethical implications of each of the options that Dale is considering?

ETHICAL DILEMMAS IN SOCIAL WORK ADMINISTRATION AND SUPERVISION

Social work administrators and supervisors have an ethical responsibility to protect clients' rights and to foster an atmosphere in which workers will do the same. At the same time, they are accountable to the agency's sponsors for productivity and for operating within the authorized budget. With diminishing budgets and rising demands, this can be a most difficult task. In addition to ethical obligations toward the agency, an administrator also has responsibilities toward his or her employees.

Many administrators think that the line between ethical and unethical behavior is crossed only when their activities result in personal gain. They feel that it is ethical to do whatever is necessary as long as their activities benefit clients or the agency. If a government contract provides money for staff training but not for staff supervision, they do not hesitate to "redefine" supervision as training. Recreation services are renamed "respite services" if government funding for recreation is dropped. In such cases, an illusion of compliance is achieved by playing semantic games. But is this ethical?

Another ethical dilemma that some administrators face occurs when there is a conflict between their responsibility for organizational maintenance on the one hand and professional or communal responsibility on the other. Take the case of the director of a children's home that for decades has provided institutional care for infants aged three days to one year. From a professional point of view, there is no longer any justification for continuing this service, yet the director has responsibilities to the sponsors, to staff, and to others for ensuring that the agency continues to function. How would you respond to the ethical dilemma facing this social work administrator?

A dilemma of a different nature is presented in Exemplar 10.10.

10.10	THE GOOD OF THE AGENCY, COMMUNITY, OR THE STAFF?

John Meenaghan is a social planner in a United Way community fund-raising and social planning agency. Over lunch, Melissa Bridgewater, a longtime friend and a member of the executive staff, told him that the executive director—who is not a social worker—and several favored members of his personal staff have been living lavishly on their expense accounts and padding their expenses. All the information she provided in the past has been completely accurate. The executive director is tyrannical and punitive but has been extremely creative and improved productivity many times over. The fund drive has reached new heights. Later, in his office, John spent almost an hour contemplating why Melissa shared this information with him. Why doesn't she go public herself? What should he *do*, if anything?

John Meenaghan understands that "whistle blowing" can do good as well as harm. If he goes public with the information about agency corruption, he could do much harm to the agency and undermine its fund-raising capacity for some time into the future. Alternately, if he goes public with the information (for which he has no direct evidence), he could perform a public service, protecting the community's resources while ensuring that funds will be spent on the problems for which they were intended. At the same time, the element of trust that generally exists in the agency will be destroyed. The authority structure of the agency will be damaged, at least for a time, thus potentially creating havoc in the administration. If he reports the problem to his supervisor or to a member of the board of directors, he might further his good relations with some superiors and colleagues, and perhaps with members of the board, but the executive director and others will be angry and will be liable to legal actions. Finding successful executive directors is not an easy task.

A number of standards in the Code are relevant to this situation: "Social workers' primary responsibility is to promote the well-being of clients" (NASW Code, 1999, 1.01). "Social workers should treat colleagues with respect and should represent accurately and fairly the qualifications, views, and obligations of colleagues" (2.01 a, c). In addition, "social workers should take adequate measures to discourage, prevent, expose, and correct the unethical conduct of colleagues" (2.11 a, b, c, d); and "social work administrators should take reasonable steps to ensure that the working environment for which they are responsible is consistent with and encourages compliance with the NASW Code of Ethics. Social work administrators should take reasonable steps to eliminate any conditions in their organizations that violate, interfere with, or discourage compliance with the Code" (3.07d). Finally, "social workers should be diligent stewards of the resources of their employing organizations, wisely conserving funds where appropriate and never misappropriating funds or using them for unintended purposes" (3.09g).

Who is the client or what is the priority in this situation—Melissa, who shared the information; the executive director, who has done an outstanding job for the agency, maintaining the viability of the United Way; the community agencies that benefit from the United Way; or those being served by communal agencies? What does John owe Melissa? Lacking detailed information about the improprieties, would he be treating any of his colleagues with respect if he were to move forward? Does he have the right to correct a non–social worker, someone who is not bound by the Code? What would you advise John to do? More generally, both supervisors and administrators have a responsibility to support workers' ethical behaviors and to stop workers' unethical behaviors.

DUAL-ROLE RELATIONS

Supervisors and agency administrators are powerful persons because they have considerable influence over the social workers and students whom they employ or supervise. They make assignments, evaluate work, decide on promotions, and at times terminate employment. They are obligated to use this power in ethical ways. This rule has a number of implications. Any relationship with employees or students in which an administrator/supervisor takes advantage, exploits, or harms persons with less power is unethical, even if the initiative comes from the employee or supervisee. This holds not only for sexual relations but also for other types of relations that create bonds that may negatively affect the professional relationship. Several standards in the Code of Ethics provide clearer guidance for social workers in regard to dual/multiple relationships. This area of unethical behavior has received increased attention in recent years. Here we wish to highlight the need for social workers to consider seriously the ethical problems that may arise in work settings among persons with different degrees of power.

How would you assess the following supervisory situations:

- Your supervisee's husband is an insurance broker. She tells you that her husband will give you a large discount on your automobile insurance. Will you avoid the dual-relationship problem if you place your insurance with him but pay the full insurance rate?
- Your supervisee, a BSW social worker, just enrolled in a graduate school of social work. The school is ready to appoint you as a field instructor and have you supervise your employee's field instruction.
- Your agency is employing your wife as a caseworker and assigns you to work on a team with her.
- Your supervisee has a summer home in the mountains. She invites you and your children to use it this summer while she and her husband are vacationing elsewhere.

In each of these situations, there is a potential for an ethical difficulty. Do the standards give clear answers to these problems?

OTHER CONFLICTING OBLIGATIONS

Social work supervisors are often in the position of the person "in between" with multiple pressures and obligations, as Exemplars 10.11, 10.12, and 10.13 illustrate. Supervisors have many roles and obligations in social agencies. In addition to their primary responsibility to ensure the delivery of high-quality services, their responsibilities include committee meetings, assignments representing the agency in the community, phone calls, emergencies, and other demands on their time and energy.

10.11 | FRIEND, SELF, FAMILY, AGENCY—LOYALTY TO WHOM?

Thomas Kinane recently was promoted to supervisor, a job that pays much more than his prior position. His teenage daughter has been in therapy, and he feels lucky because the money is arriving just when the family needs it. He is responsible for the supervision of 12 workers who are on a task force to implement a new service in Gordonsville, a satellite location. He has an enormous amount of record keeping and report writing to do. Because of demands of the job on his time, both in Gordonsville and at central headquarters, he frequently has to cancel supervisory sessions with individual workers, not fulfilling his responsibilities to supervisees and clients. Yet he does not feel ready to use group supervision, which would help him to better control his time and do his job.

Thomas's situation is not unusual. He wants to succeed in his job, needs the money, and has a responsibility to his employer. But he also has a responsibility to his supervisees' clients, to his family, and to his supervisees. How would you choose among these conflicting obligations? What would you choose to do?

10.12 | THE ETHICS OF MOONLIGHTING

The employment contract of the Bay City Human Services Agency states: "Social workers may not work for another employer in their professional social work capacity, even outside of their regular working hours." Every new social work employee in the agency is made aware of this provision and acknowledges her agreement to it in writing. The other evening, Ellen and Bill Stock rushed their infant daughter Sharon to the hospital because she had a very high fever. While Ellen stayed with the baby in the emergency room, Bill handled the admission routines.

Later on, Bill told Ellen that among the people with whom he had to speak in the admissions office was a social worker. He had been very impressed by her warm and sympathetic interest in their sick child. Ellen asked Bill if he recalled the worker's name and was surprised to learn that it was Joan Gilligan, one of the social workers she supervises. On the way out of the hospital, Ellen peeked into the admissions office to make sure that this was the same social worker she supervises. It was. Because Ellen did not use her husband's name at work, she was sure that Joan did not realize that she had been helping her supervisor's husband.

Ellen did not know what she should do about her discovery. On the one hand, Joan's moonlighting was in violation of the commitment she made to the agency. The Code of Ethics states clearly, "Social workers generally should adhere to commitments made to employers and employing organizations" (NASW Code, 1999, 3.09a). On the other hand, Joan's moonlighting did not harm anyone. As a matter of fact, her presence in the hospital admissions office benefits many patients at a time when they are in a state of crisis. What are Ellen's obligations to her employer, to her colleague, and to the profession? Are there other ways to address this dilemma, such as working to change the agency policy?

Exemplar 10.13 deals with yet another work-related issue.

10.13 | A CARIBBEAN CRUISE

Wilma Stevens supervises a unit of six social workers, of whom Carla Bick is the most qualified and most effective. Last week, Carla was not at work. Her boyfriend called in to say that Carla had a bad case of the flu and would probably be out all week. Today, she returned to work, bringing a note from her doctor stating that she had been sick all week. Aside from the note, there was no evidence of her having been sick. She explained that yesterday she went to the beach, and this accounted for her suntan. Wilma's cousin had been on a Caribbean cruise last week. When they had supper together, her cousin told Wilma all about the trip and about the many interesting people she met onboard the cruise ship. One of those people was a young social worker—Carla Bick. The cousin wondered whether Wilma happened to know her.

As Wilma thought about Carla's absence from work last week, she noted the following points:

- Carla's absence was not authorized and was in violation of agency policy.
- Carla's behavior was unethical and unprofessional.
- Carla may have harmed her clients by failing to provide them with regular service.
- Carla had not told the truth when she claimed that she had been sick.
- Carla was her best worker and Wilma did not want to lose her.
- Other workers probably also misused sick leave but were not caught. Would making an example of Carla persuade others to desist from this unethical behavior? If Wilma does so, what will be the cost? Would making an example of Carla be unethical because her privacy and respect would be violated?

It will be difficult to differentiate between Wilma's administrative/supervisory responsibilities and her professional social work responsibilities. Any decision she will reach will necessarily include both aspects. Whatever her decision, it will have ethical implications.

One of the assignments of an agency director is to staff the board of directors, the agency's policy-making group. Establishing a good working relationship with board members is essential for every successful agency director. At times, the agency director will encounter ethical dilemmas because of conflicting ethical principles. Consider Exemplar 10.14.

| 10.14 | THE BOARD OF DIRECTORS OF THE ALZHEIMER'S ASSOCIATION |

The Alzheimer's Association is a local, voluntary United Fund agency established about 10 years ago to provide a wide range of community services to caregivers of people with Alzheimer's disease. At last night's meeting, the board of directors voted to eliminate all homemaker services because the insurance carrier had again raised the premium for liability insurance that homemakers must carry. You, the agency director, know that the demand for homemaker services has always exceeded the staff available. It is not only a popular service, but a resource that has enabled many families to keep their relative with Alzheimer's disease at home instead of placing him or her in an institutional facility. You know that the agency provides other services for which there are fewer demands; reducing these services could pay for the higher insurance premiums. These other services, however, are of special interest to several board members; they will do anything to protect their favorite services.

What are the ethical problems that this exemplar raises? For example, to whom does the director owe loyalty?

SUPERVISOR ETHICS AND LIABILITIES

Ethics complaints and legal actions can be brought by clients and employees against supervisors that allege ethical breaches or negligence by the supervisors and by those whom they supervise. Supervisors are affected by two types of liability. **Direct liability** may be charged when harm is caused by the supervisor's acts of omission or commission, such as when the supervisee is assigned duties for which the supervisee is inadequately trained or experienced, or when supervisors do not follow supervision guidelines promulgated by their state boards and/or professional associations.

Supervisors may also be charged when the supervisee makes mistakes. Some claims may implicate supervisors under the legal doctrine of *respondeat superior*—"let the master respond." This doctrine—also known as **vicarious liability**—means a supervisor is responsible for the actions of a supervisee that were conducted during the course of employment, training, or field instruction, including potential ethical lapses. Worthington, Tan, and Poulin (2002) conducted an exploratory study of ethically questionable behaviors among 230 graduate counseling psychology supervisees. Among the ethical lapses they identified as unique to supervisees (which could be true also of professional employees) were the following: intentional nondisclosure of important information, mismanagement of case records, actively operating at an inappropriate level of autonomy, failure to address personal biases that impact counseling, inappropriate methods of managing conflict with supervisors, and failure to engage in necessary professional development activities. Two actions were viewed as the most unethical behaviors by both supervisors and supervisees: intentionally fabricating information about a client in supervision and forging a supervisor's signature. Supervisees covertly seeking approval from another person to justify acting on a plan his or her supervisor had rejected was the action with the widest discrepancy between the views of supervisors and supervisees. A similar discrepancy was found regarding the failure to complete documentation of client records within the required time. Otherwise, supervisor and supervisee rating reflected a considerable amount of agreement.

This chapter makes clear that ethical dilemmas can be encountered in direct practice, as well as in relations with professional colleagues, in relationship to agency policies and regulations, and can also occur in the work of supervisors and administrators.

EXERCISES

1. Does your state have a list of unethical professional behaviors that are actionable by your state social work licensing authority? What are the unethical professional behaviors on the authority's promulgated list? Are there actions that you would add to the list? What sanctions or punishments are available to this authority? Are there other sanctions you would like to add?
2. Review the employee handbook for the agency where you are employed or in field instruction. Are any of the agency policies inconsistent with the Code of Ethics? How would you address these inconsistencies?
3. In a community organization, you are a member of the staff at a staff meeting when several employees advocate that only African American professionals should work with African American groups and neighborhoods and that only lesbian and gay persons can be successful in working with lesbian and gay communities (Shillington, Dotson, & Faulkner, 1994; Tully, Craig, & Nugent, 1994). What should you do?
4. Verschelden (1993) argues that social work values and ethics suggest social workers should be pacifists. Do you join Verschelden in the belief that social work ethics require a social worker to be a pacifist?

SUGGESTIONS FOR ADDITIONAL READINGS

Egan and Kadushin (2004) report on a survey of home health social workers and their job satisfaction. Among the issues examined are ethical conflicts between patient access to services and agency financial priorities. Compromising professional ethics contributed to significantly less job satisfaction. See Frost, Robinson, and Anning (2005), which examines how child and family interdisciplinary teams work together. Among the issues explored are models of professional practice, status and power, and confidentiality and information sharing. Desai (2003) in *Ethical Decision Making within the Bureaucratic Context: A Case Study* illustrates how the expectation of transparent decision making in bureaucracies forces practitioners to seek guidance in ethical decision making.

WEB SITES OF INTEREST

- The Association for Community Organization and Social Administration (ACOSA) site includes a number of resources and links for social workers involved in administration and community organizing: www.acosa.org
- The National Network for Social Work Managers site offers information on the organization as well as links to articles and presentations: www.socialworkmanager.org
- For information about social workers in the military: www.todaysmilitary.com/app/tm/careers/supportservices/officer/socialworkers
- The U.S. Air Force Academy Web site includes a link to an article about ethical challenges and training implications for social workers in the military: www.usafa.af.mil/jscope/JSCOPE00/Tallant00.html
- Also provided by the U.S. Air Force Academy Web site is the International Symposium for Military Ethics: www.usafa.af.mil/jscope/

CHAPTER II

SOCIAL WORK WITH SELECTED CLIENT GROUPS

In this chapter, we cover a medley of topics related to ethical issues and dilemmas in areas that are frequently encountered in direct practice situations, as well as several rapidly evolving concerns, such as intimate partner violence; elder abuse; end of life decisions; HIV and AIDS; religion and spirituality; and a plurality of identities and client groups.

INTIMATE PARTNER VIOLENCE

Intimate partner violence (IPV) is also known as domestic violence or spouse abuse. We use the term to refer to violence between adults who are intimates, regardless of their marital status, living arrangements, or sexual orientations. Domestic violence comes in several forms: physical, sexual, psychological, economic, social isolation, stalking, and coercive control (Austin & Dankwort, 1999).

Violence against women and men continues as an epidemic in the United States. Women are more likely to be murdered by intimates than by any other assailant. Homicide by intimate partners is the seventh leading cause of premature death for American women (Hines & Malley-Morrison, 2005). The American Medical Association suggests that domestic violence injures more women than car accidents, muggings, and rapes combined. These acts of violence cause lasting damage to the victims and have serious immediate and long-term "sleeper" effects on children. There are also societal costs for providing medical, judicial, police, shelter, and counseling services and programs (Cavaiola & Colford, 2006).

Licensed therapists often fail to identify—or minimize the significance of—domestic violence in their clients' relationships. Clients may not report violence because:

- They view the violence as trivial or tolerable.
- They see violence as a way to resolve conflict.

- They fear what will happen to their public image if the violence becomes known.
- They feel shame.
- They fear further victimization.

Therapists also fail to ask about violence or may only ask one partner (Hamel, 2005).

Although the occurrence of family violence hinders therapy and harms the quality of family life and welfare of clients, clients may need time to develop a trusting relationship with a social worker before domestic violence may be revealed. Even if someone denies the occurrence of domestic violence early in the client/social worker relationship, the social worker needs to be aware of possible signs of domestic violence and willing to bring the issue up again later in the relationship. What should a social worker do who is working with a client she suspects is in a violent relationship when the client denies this and the professional contract has been time-limited, such as in Exemplar 1.1 about Basanti Madurai? After all, the clients determine what information they will share. Should the social worker use valuable time to come back to this issue again? When IPV is suspected, how can the social worker balance the need to probe for information (because she knows about reluctance to disclose early in the helping relationship) and an ethical responsibility to respect the client's right to self-determination?

Studies on the effectiveness of couple therapy for IPV confirm that therapy results in temporary decreases in violence, but generally, therapy does not result in stopping violence in the long term (Jory, Anderson, & Greer, 1997). Many agencies are understaffed. Others have long waiting lists. All give priority to serving those currently in treatment. Remember this when you consider the ethical implications of not providing frequent follow-up services to present and past clients who have been involved in domestic violence. In Exemplar 11.1 we return to Basanti Madurai and Ellen Ashton, the case we have been following throughout the book.

| **11.1** | **LEAVING AND RETURNING** |

Basanti Madurai has been attending the South Asia Women's Support Group for several months. After some initial resistance, her husband's family decided that it would be good for her to get out once in a while, and they have supported her attendance at the group meetings. Her mother-in-law has even been watching the children so that Basanti can attend the meetings without looking for child care.

As Basanti has become more comfortable with the group, she has admitted that her husband, Prajeet, often yells at her, sometimes hits her, and has occasionally left bruises. Whenever she suggests that he might need help, Prajeet becomes very angry and says that he wouldn't have to yell and hit her if she would just do what she is supposed to. Last month they had a fight and Basanti had to go to the emergency room for a broken arm. She was afraid that the children will become aware of the violence or that her husband would strike out at the children next, so she took the children and moved into a shelter. Prajeet was very upset that his wife and children had moved to the shelter, and he agreed to attend a treatment program. Now that he has completed the treatment program, Basanti is planning to return home.

What is social worker Ellen Ashton's ethical responsibility in this situation? If you were in Ellen's position, how would you balance your desire to protect Basanti with her right to self-determination? Would your choice differ if there were no children involved? Would it make a difference if you don't agree with her view that a woman's place is with her husband?

ELDER ABUSE

In this section, we will briefly discuss some of the ethical issues that can arise in situations where older people are victims of abuse. According to the National Center for Elder Abuse (2005), there are estimates that for every case of elder abuse, neglect, exploitation, or self-neglect reported to local authorities, about five cases go unreported. There are estimates that annually 2 million older Americans are maltreated by family members, an estimate which probably reflects underreporting (Hines & Malley-Morrison, 2005). In addition, in 2003 state long-term care ombudsmen programs nationally investigated 20,673 complaints of abuse, gross neglect, and exploitation on behalf of nursing home and board and care residents. Physical abuse was the most common type reported (Bonnie & Wallace, 2003; National Center for Elder Abuse, 2005).

Approximately two thirds of all elder abuse perpetrators are family members, most often the victim's child or spouse and in many cases, they are financially dependent on the older person's resources and have alcohol and substance abuse problems (National Center for Elder Abuse, 2005). Caregivers of many kinds are responsible for much of the abuse of elders. Bergeron and Gray (2003) discuss the ethical issues that can arise for social workers who facilitate caregiver support groups, and make the following recommendations:

1. Know the elder abuse reporting law; "be
   nal laws, some social services benefits ar
   charge . . . if a report is filed" (p. 102). T
   the caregiver.
2. Develop rapport with elder abuse protec
   tential ethical dilemmas that arise in car
   tive answers, and developing rapport wi
   advance can help the facilitator be prep;
3. Develop clear expectations of confidenti
   to be informed of the limits of confiden
   reporting requirements.
4. Facilitators need to "monitor the group
   being shared prematurely and to ensure
   edge about the outcome of their disclos
5. Prepare support group members for the
   formed of the policies for working with
6. Cultivate peer supervision and mentori
7. Contribute to the research in this area.

These recommendations provide some g
caregiver support groups. If one of the purp

allow members to vent frustrations and concerns, is there a possibility that the "normalization of feelings may send subtle messages to members that certain levels of consistent abusive actions, such as yelling, isolating the elderly person, or not obtaining adequate in-home services, are acceptable" (Bergeron & Gray, 2003, pp. 103–104)? In earlier chapters, we raised the "who is the client" issue; who is the client for these recommendations? Does the elderly abused person who is not physically present ever become the group facilitator's client? Is the facilitator's only responsibility to make the report to an elder abuse protection agency?

Questions have been raised about the priority of self-determination in regard to elder abuse (Bergeron, 2006). Bergeron argues that social work's subscribing to self-determination as the premier principle of practice is an American notion based on the high value of individualism in the United States. However, concentration on individual choice elevates consideration of the individual over consideration of community needs in regard to the situation. That is, individual choice can be elevated over community good and can serve to minimize one's understanding of clients within the context of their environments.

Bergeron (2006) suggests further that "professionals entrusted with the duty-to-protect victims of elder abuse absolutely cannot use the principle of self-determination as the primary reason to leave elder victims in life-threatening situations, or to unconditionally accept victims' refusal for services" (p. 99). Clients who are depressed may refuse treatment out of a concern that no treatment can help, a person can be so abused and "beaten down" that she believes her situation is unsolvable, or an elderly parent can refuse help to protect the family's good name. Is the acceptance of an abused victim's refusal of help a rejection of the Code of Ethic's standard that "social workers act on behalf of clients who lack the capacity to make informed decisions, [and] social workers should take reasonable steps to safeguard the interests and rights of those clients" (NASW Code, 1.14)?

Social workers should bear in mind that they are responsible ethically *and* legally when confronted by abuse of elderly persons. Aside from ethical issues, social workers should know that legal remedies for difficult situations may have to be employed. Most physical, sexual, and financial abuses are considered crimes in all states because these acts violate laws prohibiting assault, battery, rape, theft, and other criminal acts. Under certain circumstances, emotional abuse and neglect may also be subject to criminal prosecution depending on the perpetrator's intent and the consequences for the victim.

END-OF-LIFE DECISIONS

The NASW policy statement on "End-of-Life Care" (2007) provides policy guidance to social workers and is based on the principle that client self-determination should apply to all aspects of life and death. This policy statement states:

> Decisions regarding end-of-life care should be considered numerous times during a person's life, not just at the diagnosis of a terminal illness or in an acute, life-threatening event. End-of-life decisions encompass a broad range of medical, spiritual, and psychosocial determinations that each individual should make before the end of his or her life.... NASW does not take a position concerning the morality of end-of-life decisions, but affirms the right of any individual to direct his or her care wishes at the end of life (Social Work Speaks Abstracts, 2007, p. 1).

The policy statement contains the following ideas:

- The social work profession strives to enhance the quality of life, to encourage the exploration of life options, and to advocate for access to options, including providing all information to make appropriate choices.
- Social workers have an important role in helping individuals identify the end-of-life options available to them.
- Competent individuals should have the opportunity to make their own choices but only after being informed of all options and consequences. Choices should be made without coercion.
- Social workers should not promote any particular means to end one's life but should be open to full discussion of the issues and care options.
- Social workers should be free to participate or not participate in assisted suicide matters or other discussions concerning end-of-life decisions depending on their own beliefs, attitudes, and value systems. If a social worker is unable to help with decisions about assisted suicide or other end-of-life choices, he or she has a professional obligation to refer patients and their families to competent professionals who are available to address end-of-life issues.
- It is inappropriate for social workers to deliver, supply, or personally participate in the commission of an act of assisted suicide when acting in their professional role.
- If legally permissible, it is not inappropriate for a social worker to be present during an assisted suicide if the client requests the social worker's presence.
- The involvement of social workers in assisted-suicide cases should not depend on race or ethnicity, religion, age, gender, economic factors, sexual orientation, or disability.

There are several ambiguities suggested by the last guideline above. Although social workers should not discriminate, different racial and ethnic groups have nevertheless been found to have differences in end-of-life decision making that imply differential interventions by group.

In addition to the statement on end-of-life and self-determination, the NASW published NASW Standards for Palliative and End of Life Care. This publication includes 11 standards for social workers dealing with palliative and end-of-life care. Among the standards included are ethics and values, knowledge required, assessment, and intervention/treatment planning, as well as other features of social work in such situations (NASW, 2007). Reybould and Adler (2006) examined the Standards for Palliative and End of Life Care in regard to end-of-life care for culturally diverse older adults and their families. They emphasize the fact that people from diverse cultures have different perceptions of medical and health care personnel and can have various traditions, beliefs, values, and desires. They can have different values about autonomy and self-determination, death and dying, uncertainty or certainty about whether one is terminally ill, communication (including languages and language barriers), truth telling or not, level of care desired, and other culture-bound perceptions and values.

Gross and Mukamel (2005) argue that any decision-making model focused on the individual practitioner omits the organizational and other contexts in which the decisions have to be made. They studied the process of advance care planning of 3,548 participants in managed care programs. When all the known participant characteristics were accounted for, program effects were found to account for 36% of the variation in do-not-resuscitate choice, 66% in the choice of artificial feeding, and 50% relating to the presence of healthy care proxy. These findings suggest that individual professionals as well as program and organizational factors can have a large impact on individuals' decisions about advance care planning.

Essentially, end-of-life decisions focus on three different stages of ethical concern: life-palliative care, death by choice or otherwise, and grief among survivors. Social workers have a long history of care with persons involving life-limiting illness, the process of dying, and dealing with grief and bereavement following deaths. The end-of-life policy promulgated by the NASW is a relatively new development in social work, which is met by social workers and others with differing sets of values. Little is known about these phenomena. Some social workers believe that promulgation by the NASW of guidelines regarding social workers' potential roles in physician-assisted suicide in effect suggests it is ethical to do so. Others oppose providing assistance in ending-of-life situations (Manetta & Wells, 2001). In some states, assisting in a suicide is against the law.

Werth and Rogers (2005) emphasize the duty of social workers to protect clients who are identified as "suicidal." They propose that the duty to protect should apply whenever a client is engaging in a behavior that may lead to serious self-harm or death within a reasonably short period of time. To do so requires an assessment of impaired judgment followed by appropriate interventions following the evaluation. The values of the mental health practitioner and the values of the client are both considerations in the situation. Werth and Rogers set forth a summary of the issues to consider when exploring end-of-life decisions. The scheme includes four major issues with a number of subquestions to be considered: (1) assessment of capacity to give informed consent to participate in the review and the capacity to make informed health care decisions; (2) the decision-making process, including physical pain and suffering, fear of loss of control, financial concerns, cultural factors, underlying issues, overall quality of life, and so forth; (3) the person's social support system; and (4) systemic and environmental issues. Even if all the above issues are assessed positively, a social worker must decide what her perspective and values are in relation to end-of-life decisions.

Though the NASW policy statement is based on the principle of self-determination, many doubt whether meaningful self-determination and voluntary consent prevail in situations in which a person wishes to harm himself or commit suicide, because "only abysmal ignorance or deep emotional trauma can lead persons to extreme measures like these" (Gewirth, 1978, p. 264). But there are those who criticize this view. They claim that mental illness per se does not preclude competence (Mishna, Antle, & Regehr, 2002). Others also take issue with the autonomy (self-determination) argument by suggesting that active physician-assisted suicide is more than a matter of self-determination. From this point of view, it has been suggested that it is a mutual decision by two people, one of whom is to be killed and the other is to do the killing (Callahan, 1994, cited in Csikai, 1999). In certain situations, medical treatment for palliative care or harsh treatments such as chemotherapy reach a limit beyond which there is no ultimate benefit to the patients and no enhancement of quality of life. Some persons feel that quality of life is ethically irrelevant, and the ethical issue is to take or not take a life. If a social worker is faced with such a situation, does the ethical principles screen (EPS) introduced in chapter 4 provide any help in clarifying the ethical choices being faced and in what priority order?

The policy statement raises many questions, among which are the following: Whose quality of life is supported by assisted suicide? Whose life is harmed? What is competence in such a situation? How does one judge competency? Is coercion entirely absent when people are considering suicide? What should one do if the option chosen creates issues for other family members, significant others, friends, or other professionals? What should one do if there are conflicts among those involved—some wanting to maintain life at all costs, others supporting the person's decision? What does it mean to be present but not participate; is this just another form of approval of the act? The definition of terminal illness is not always clear. Sometimes even the best of medical practitioners makes a mistake, and persons judged to be terminally ill live beyond the projected time. Can "comfort care" and the control of pain offset the desire to end one's life?

Assisted Suicide

Physician-assisted suicide has been legal in Oregon since 1997 when Oregon voters approved the Death with Dignity Act for the second time (an earlier approval's implementation was delayed by legal injunction). After an initial increase in physician-assisted suicide during the first five years the Act was in effect, the number of Oregonians who use physician-assisted suicide has remained relatively stable since 2002. During the first eight years the physician-assisted program was in effect, the 246 patients who took lethal medications differed from the many thousands of Oregonians who died from the same diseases. Rates of participation decreased with age (however, 65% of physician-assisted suicide users were 65 or older), and rates were higher for those who were divorced or never married, those with more years of education, and those with amyotrophic lateral sclerosis (Lou Gehrig's Disease), HIV/AIDS, or malignant neoplasms (Oregon Department of Human Services, Eighth Annual Report on Oregon's Death with Dignity Act, 2006).

As of early 2007, Oregon remains the only state that allows physician-assisted suicide. Forty states explicitly prohibit physician-assisted suicide; six states prohibit suicide through common law; and three states (North Carolina, Utah, and Wyoming) do not have laws prohibiting physician-assisted suicide (Sherer, 2004). Supreme Court rulings on physician-assisted suicide for terminally ill persons left the door open for individual states to define their own statutes in this area and suggested the Court could revisit the issue. Physician-assisted suicide remains quite controversial.

U.S. Attorney John Ashcroft challenged the assisted-suicide program through reinterpretation of the Controlled Substance Act, which would prohibit physicians from prescribing controlled substances for use in physician-assisted suicide. In response to a lawsuit filed by the State of Oregon in 2001, a U.S. District Court issued a temporary restraining order against Ashcroft's ruling. After a series of lawsuits and court cases—including the issue being heard by the U.S. Supreme Court (*Gonzales v. Oregon*, 2006)—the Death with Dignity Act remains in effect (Oregon Department of Human Services, 2006). Two basic ethical issues have to be weighed: one concerns the society, the second concerns the social work profession itself. In regard to society, there are those concerned about the "slippery slope" effect of condoning assisted suicide. In at least one nation where assisted suicide has been permitted, the definition of who is eligible has grown looser and outside the specific guidelines over time (Citizen Link, 2003).

The assisted suicide laws in Oregon and the Netherlands differ in important respects. In Oregon the physician prescribes a lethal dose of a medication; in the Netherlands, a physician may prescribe or directly administer a lethal dose. When is the assistance justified? In Oregon, termination is justified when the person has a terminal illness that will lead to death within six months.

Callahan (1994) argues that "the ethical position for social workers—most in keeping with the spirit and overall content of the NASW Code of Ethics—[is] to oppose assisted suicide and especially to oppose legislation that would change our social policy to one of condoning suicide instead of preventing it" (p. 243).

Mackelprang and Mackelprang (2005) further suggest that Standard 1.02 of the Code asserts that social workers have a responsibility to limit self-determination when people pose a serious risk to themselves or others. These perspectives are at variance with NASW Standards for Palliative and End of Life Care (NASW, 2006). The question then is, how is one to choose and on what basis?

As far as social work is concerned, there are additional questions. Will social workers' participation in assisted-suicide situations result in their being less trusted by those groups that reject assisted suicide? Assisted suicide requires assistance being provided only for those who are undeniably competent to make such requests and for whom there are no alternative ways of relieving their suffering through palliative care. One observer suggests that there are two essential ethical requirements of professionals: to seek to deliver the kinds of services they profess to provide and to be trustworthy. To be trusted as a profession, social work must be viewed as honest, fair, and just (Jackson, 2000). It is against these ethical standards that assisted-suicide participation needs to be weighed.

CLIENTS LIVING WITH HIV AND AIDS

The HIV (human immunodeficiency virus) infection has now spread to every nation in the world and has infected millions of people worldwide. Since the first AIDS case was diagnosed in 1981, the world has had to struggle with its rapid spread, its extent, and its impact. At the end of 2004, there were estimates that 20 million people had died and an estimated 40 million people were living with HIV. In 2004 alone, an estimated 5 million persons worldwide became newly infected with HIV (Hankins, Stanecki, Ghys, & Marais, 2006).

HIV disproportionately affects racial or ethnic minorities, men who have sex with men, and people who inject drugs intravenously (IV drug use [IVDU]). The proportion of cases due to heterosexual contact was estimated at 34%. The proportion of women infected with HIV has been growing and increased from 13% of cases in 1990 to an estimated 27% in 2003 (Morgan & Levi, 2006). In the United States, the estimated number of persons living with HIV in 2004 was 850,000 to 950,000, with an estimated additional 40,000 new infections annually (Morgan & Levi, 2006).

The United Nations in a long-term forecast claims 65 million persons will die from AIDS-related illnesses worldwide by 2020, more than triple the number who died in the first 20 years of the epidemic (Altman, 2002). The number of people living with

HIV has been rising in every region with the greatest recent increases occurring in East Asia, Eastern Europe, and Central Asia. In sub-Saharan Africa the overall population percentage of adults living with HIV recently has remained steady, but the number of such persons is increasing as the population grows (Hankins, 2006). In the United States the HIV epidemic has slowed from a period of rapid growth to a more stable 40,000 new infections annually (Morgan & Levi, 2006).

The progression of the disease varies widely; some individuals may be symptom-free for more than 10 years. The introduction of highly active antiretroviral therapy (HAART) is one of the great success stories of modern medicine, and its impact on HIV-related morbidity and mortality is similar to the effect of penicillin on pneumococcal pneumonia 50 years earlier. However, in contrast to pneumonia, HIV infections are chronic, HAART is not a cure, and antiretroviral therapy is lifelong. In developed nations such as the United States, the introduction of HAART has led to reductions in HIV-related morbidity and mortality (Lange, 2006). The fact that antiretroviral therapy needs to be continued for a lifetime presents its own difficulties. There is a problem of patient adherence (Lange, 2006); many people are unable to follow through on the very demanding drug regimen because of their own limitations, the costs of drugs, or the fact that they have HIV infections resistant to the drug combinations (Altman, 1999). Some patients die of HIV infection and its complications either because they do not have access to such therapies or despite the available treatments. People living with HIV may also experience problems related to social stigma and isolation; the unpredictable course of the disease; and changing treatment approaches (Oppenheim, Hay, Frederich, & Van Gunten, 2002).

Biases About AIDS

AIDS is not an "ordinary" disease. People who have AIDS or who test HIV positive cannot be discussed in quite the same way as people who suffer other kinds of diseases. AIDS is a life-threatening disease; and people living with HIV/AIDS have to come to terms with their own potential mortality, frequently at an early age. Although there are other diseases that are also life-threatening at early ages, there is a very high degree of stigma associated with AIDS, more stigma than is true for almost any other illness. This is because AIDS was first discovered among groups that are traditionally labeled as deviants—gay people, drug users, and prostitutes. Because of this stigma, many people with AIDS do not want others to know they have the disease. They often go to considerable lengths to conceal the illness, even from those who are closest to them. They need support to ask for the help they desperately need.

The AIDS epidemic has become widespread. Many persons have become infected, including spouses and significant others of infected persons, recipients of infected blood, newborn babies of infected parents, persons who shared needles, and others. Some of these persons may share the general public's biases about HIV and AIDS, and the stigma associated with HIV/AIDS may keep them from asking for the help they need when they know they are HIV positive. Social workers must find ways to open communication channels with all of these people, both those who are diagnosed as HIV positive and those who have developed AIDS.

SOCIAL WORK ADVOCACY FOR CLIENTS LIVING WITH HIV

There are many other ethical dilemmas and problems that social workers face when working with clients living with HIV. "Rationing" medical care presents one set of ethical problems that require a social worker's advocacy services. Childless adults living with HIV infection typically only qualify for Medicaid coverage once they become eligible for SSI. Becoming eligible for SSI or Social Security Disability depends on becoming disabled—that is, severely limited in his or her ability to work (Federal Globe, 2007). Those persons with asymptomatic HIV infection are not eligible for Medicaid until the condition has become fully developed AIDS. As a result, childless adults who are HIV positive are ineligible for Medicaid except in several states with Medicaid waivers to extend benefits to nondisabled persons living with HIV. These states conduct demonstration projects to evaluate the cost effectiveness of expanding services to this group in order to slow the progress of the disease and prevent opportunistic infections (Human Rights Campaign, 2003). Does a social worker have an ethical obligation to advocate for such services? Should social workers advocate for other services or rights for persons living with HIV or AIDS?

TECHNOLOGY IN DIRECT PRACTICE

Called by a variety of names, online therapy is a developing method of delivering services. There are a number of methods, including typed text messages without any visual or auditory experiences for the social worker or the client; auditory telephone discussions; and videoconferencing with visual and audio components taking place as distance communication. With some methods, neither the therapist nor client can observe the other. There are very few published studies on the provision of individual or group therapy in online settings.

There are controversies about the pros and cons of online practice, and questions have also been raised about ethical and legal issues. One concern is about the protection of confidentiality and the misdirection of electronic transmissions, as well as the possibility of hackers who can invade the communication. The NASW Code recognizes the limitations of services using technology. As a result, social workers who provide services via electronic media (such as computer, telephone, radio, and television) are advised to inform recipients of the limitations and risks associated with such services (Code, 1999, 1.03e). Encryption of online communication may offer adequate protections, but many individual service providers and clients may not have access or know how to use the necessary software. Confidential e-mail can be misdirected to a wrong person or even to an entire address book or list of people.

A second issue is the appropriateness of treatment services. Which presenting symptoms are appropriate for online treatment? Is online therapy therapeutic? Can therapeutic alliances be developed online? What are the differences between online and face-to-face therapy? To date, no conclusive research exists as to which topics are inappropriate for online therapy. Some topics that might be included in such a list are sexual abuse as a primary issue, violent relationships, eating disorders, and psychiatric disorders that involve distortions of reality (Helton, 2003). Even if there were agreement and evidence about which difficulties can be assisted by online treatment, how can adequate assessments be made without visual and auditory, as well as other, cues?

Even if the therapist and client can see each other via videoconferencing, it is likely that experience will be different from traditional treatment methods and require different skills.

A third concern is whether social workers are sufficiently trained to provide these services. Are the knowledge and skills of traditionally trained and educated social workers transferable to online interventions? A fourth issue is whether there are credentialing and cross-state issues. Is a therapist in Maryland licensed for therapy in California? Where is the service taking place, Maryland or California? California law, for instance, states that online mental health practitioners cannot practice outside California. What national organization would best standardize credentials and provide licenses and credentials? Finally, what if any issues are there for providing professional insurance coverage for those practicing online?

On the positive side, some of the benefits of online therapy are accessibility for rural and isolated areas and home-bound clients; anonymity for those reluctant to see a therapist; 24/7 availability; low cost; and screening and follow-up care. Scheduling problems can be minimized because of the flexibility of the Internet, which can be used day or night, weekday or weekend. Ease of recording for the practitioner may also be increased. There are those who believe that clients may be even more open about self-disclosure in an online setting (Abney & Maddux, 2004).

Although there are claims that social workers who provide these services do so at low risk, there are ethical issues involved. For example, in some crisis situations (such as suicidal ideation) the social worker and the client can be dependent on distant and perhaps unknown persons for assessment and provision of emergency treatment. Where in the Code would you find support suggesting that providing services in this way is ethical or unethical? As with all therapy situations, there are "housekeeping" matters, including completing intake forms; obtaining informed consent; explaining the limits of confidentiality and mandated reporting laws; describing how any grievances will be handled and by whom; providing the fee structure; and covering record keeping, security measures, and termination policies. How can these issues be ethically addressed in online sessions?

Web cameras may further alter the way online therapy is provided. Clients can go to their computers, key in a password, and begin talking to their therapists with full-screen video and audio. Still in their infancy, Web camera therapy efforts need improvement and greater availability, both of which are dependent on technical engineering matters in order to grow as a method of providing therapy (O'Neill, 2001).

O'Neill (2002) found that some social workers thought it a mistake and unethical for social workers to offer online therapy prior to the establishment of practice standards and before the liability issues have been clarified. Other social workers were critical of the criticisms and claimed that online therapists are equally as well prepared as those who provide offline therapy, relative anonymity can increase willingness of clients to participate in the therapy, and both client and therapist can be freed from preconceived notions about each other (O'Neill, 2002).

It is likely that regardless of the undecided practical and ethical issues, Internet services will continue to expand. In 2001, Medicare expanded its coverage of tele-health services for Medicare beneficiaries to include certain individual psychotherapy services. Eligible clinical social workers can receive reimbursement for specified services. However, the services are reimbursable only if clients receive the services at "originating sites" such as physician and practitioner offices, hospitals, and rural health care clinics. In general, these sites must be in rural areas designated as health professional shortage areas or counties that are not part of a metropolitan statistical area (a city with more than 50,000 people) (Ballie, 2001).

Although as this is being written the social work profession has not developed systematic guidelines, for the reader's consideration we are including guidelines prepared for the National Board for Certified Counselors. Among the suggested guidelines are:

- Ensure client confidentiality through encryption methods
- Check on liability issues
- Inform the client how long session data will be saved
- Check on client and counselor identities through codes
- Verify identities of adults when consent is needed for minors
- Establish local on-call counselor or crisis resources
- Screen out problems not appropriate for Internet counseling
- Explain and have contingency plans if technical problems occur
- Explain how to cope with potential misunderstandings that arise due to lack of visual cues
- Discuss what to do if the counselor is offline or when there are delays in sending and receiving messages (Fukuyama, 2001)

The increasing use of e-mail makes unsought information available that may confront a practitioner with critical ethical dilemmas, such as the case presented in Exemplar 11.2.

11.2 | E-MAIL FROM EUROPE AND SUICIDAL THOUGHTS

A university student used an electronic mail discussion group to inquire about a drug that could be used for a painless suicide. A professor in Europe who read this request communicated his concern to the sender's university, which forwarded this message to the university's counseling department. The counselor assigned to this case obtained more information before deciding what to do. She contacted the director of the computer center, who broke into the student's account where additional messages on suicide were discovered. At this point, the counselor decided to contact the student's parents. (This situation was described on a social work electronic discussion list and is used with permission of Steve Marson of Pembroke University. The counselor was not a social worker.)

Exemplar 11.2 has been presented because it reflects the rapidly expanding use of e-mail and because it raises some issues that social workers must consider. One issue facing the counselor is whether to act on the basis of third-party information from someone unknown to her. Because the situation was potentially life threatening, this counselor decided to take the information conveyed by the third party seriously, but she also wanted to obtain verification of the facts, if possible. Here, the worker decided that intervention was justified. More generally, questions can be raised regarding the circumstances under which a social worker should seek access to a confidential electronic file. Is there any issue short of life-threatening situations that might support such an action? Under what circumstances does the computer center or a social agency have a right to examine someone's personal computer account?

What should the counselor have done if the computer center (or agency) stated such an invasion was illegal or against the rules? Although the counselor felt justified in asking the computer center for verification because of the potential life-threatening nature of the situation, was it ethical for her to enter the student's computer account without obtaining his permission? Because the student is at the university and the counselor is a university employee, she has some responsibility for his welfare, especially after she gained information about what was in his file. What should she have done if the student's account did not include life-threatening materials?

We do not know the counselor's reasons for contacting the student's parents rather than the student himself. Is telling the parents about their son's behavior an improper invasion of the student's right to privacy and confidentiality? What should the counselor do if, instead of contacting the student's parents, she spoke to the student, and he simply stated that he has an intellectual interest in painless suicide as a chemical problem? Which standards in the Code of Ethics provide guidance in this type of situation?

RELIGION AND SPIRITUALITY

Historically, religious content was sparsely included in social work education and in social work literature. Little information was conveyed on spirituality and religion as part of the educational preparation of practitioners, and there was—for long periods— an almost complete exclusion of such content from journals, textbooks, and course outlines (Hodge, 2004). Canda, Nakashima, and Furman (2004) surveyed 2,069 NASW members about spirituality and religion in their educations and practices. The majority of the respondents pointed out the inadequacy of their social work educations about the two topics. The need to engage more specifically with notions of spirituality and religion has more recently begun to occupy a growing presence in social work education and practice.

Although agreement about definitions of "spirituality" and "religion" remains scarce, nevertheless, their place in social work and social work education has steadily broadened. We will use the definitions of Canda et al. (2004), who define religion as "an organized, structured set of beliefs and practices shared by a community related to spirituality" (p. 28) and spirituality as involving "the search for meaning, purpose, and morally fulfilling relations with self, other people, the encompassing universe and ultimate reality, however a person understands it" (p. 28).

Religion and spirituality inform clients' and social workers' worldviews. As Sherwood (1997) points out: "Everyone operates on the basis of some worldview or faith-based understanding of the universe and persons—examined or unexamined, implicit or explicit, simplistic or sophisticated" (p. 115). Sherwood's point is that these worldviews affect our approach to social work practice and how we understand people.

Several authors have drawn attention to the ways in which spiritual matters can be introduced into social work practice. Among these are uses of ritual; exploration of sacred stories and symbols; incorporation of art, dance, and poetry; meditation and prayer; and a focus on caring for the body (Maidment, 2006). Canda et al. (2004) explored other dimensions concerned with spirituality and religion in social workers' practices. There was very high agreement that making referrals to clergypersons and collaborating with them was appropriate. Lesser numbers agreed to the appropriateness of using prayer, meditation, visualization, rituals and symbols, inspirational readings, touch for helping purposes, spiritual narrative and dialogue, or religious language. The major disagreements focused on the use of prayer, healing touch, and worker self-disclosure; some thought their use appropriate and others inappropriate.

Although there is little empirical research about if and when to use spiritual interventions and the ethical decision making involved, there are prior questions. Apparently, these questions are being answered in a pragmatic and incremental fashion without being challenged legally: What are the constitutional questions concerning the use of religious interventions in public governmental and voluntary agencies and what are the related religious liberty issues? In the United States there is a careful balance between not establishing religion and the religious liberty provisions of federal and state constitutions. Moberg (2005) suggests that focusing on spirituality and not on religion only partly solves the dilemma. Although spirituality may be viewed by some persons as separate from organized religious groups, the concept of spirituality remains open to argument as to whether it refers to the establishment of religion. However, many clients served by social workers have spiritual or religious orientations that are important to them and can be helpful in treatment. Omitting consideration of these basic beliefs and their effects may limit the effectiveness of the social worker's efforts.

Hodge (2005) reports that the largest health care accrediting body in the United States—the Joint Commission on Accreditation of Health Care Organizations (JCAHO)—now requires in mental health settings the administration of an initial exploratory spiritual assessment. Hodge (2005) also describes the "spiritual life map" and its use for spiritual assessment. He introduces several value conflicts that can emerge with the use of spiritual assessment. First, client self-determination and autonomy must be protected. Second, social workers must be alert to the issue of religious countertransference, both as a result of their own developmental issues and decisions as well as the beliefs and values of their clients and patients. Third, even when the value systems of practitioners and clients are congruent, there exists the possibility of the social worker falling into spiritual guidance instead of focusing on the client's problems.

In a subsequent article, Hodge (2006) provides social workers with guidelines for the implementation of spiritual assessments. He suggests four principles, each of which has ethical implications: (1) respect for client self-determination; (2) the practitioner's ability to provide culturally competent services; (3) the degree to which the norms of the client's faith tradition relate to service provision; and (4) the salience of spirituality to the client's life. As part of his discussion, Hodge introduces research that indicates a link between spirituality and religion and mental and physical health outcomes. Arguably, this knowledge supports the ethical correctness of competently utilizing spiritual assessments and interventions specifically designed for particular groups.

A major ethical dilemma in the sphere of religion and spirituality has arisen in relation to the Code of Ethics. In regard to discrimination, the Code states: "Social workers should not practice, condone, facilitate, or collaborate with any form of discrimination on the basis of race, ethnicity, national origin, color, sex, sexual orientation, age, marital status, political belief, *religion,* or mental or physical disability" (4.02, emphasis added). Some religious and minority groups are viewed by other groups as being discriminatory. Both religious and minority group discrimination are unethical. There is an ongoing debate and discussion about this dilemma. How can the claims of different minority groups where they are in conflict be accommodated within the parameters of freedom of speech and freedom of conscience to which both groups are entitled?

For the individual social worker and client, perhaps the most difficult issue regarding spirituality and religion focuses on the authority of the social worker and the vulnerability of the client. There are few ways to avoid exerting the social worker's authority, which has been gained from licensing, education, agency-granted authority, and skills. The client needs help and is vulnerable and needy. Aside from issues of the psychological transference of the client, the authority of the social worker is at play. Is teaching religious ideas by example or through words appropriate in the service relationship? Is it appropriate to encourage a person raised in one religion to drop out or change to another? What are the effects of suggesting that a client pray with you, the social worker? What are the effects of subtly demeaning religious beliefs and practices that differ from yours?

A PLURALITY OF IDENTITIES AND CLIENT GROUPS

American society is growing more and more diverse, leading to an increasing number of group identities in the United States. Such identities serve as political and social forces, as a means of personal expression, and as a way of achieving meaning in people's lives. One result of this increasing diversity is that social workers deal with a growing number of people who come from a variety of cultures that differ from mainstream American society and whose lives are affected by their own cultures and those of other persons and groups.

Among general American society and among social workers, there is an affirmation of diversity. Enunciated in the Code is the expectation that "social workers treat each person in a caring and respectful fashion, mindful of individual differences and cultural and ethnic diversity." The Code standard on cultural competence and social diversity (1999, 1.05) requires that ethical social workers understand culture and its function in human behavior, and have a knowledge base of and be sensitive to their clients' cultures. Furthermore, social workers are expected "to obtain education about and seek to understand the nature of social diversity and oppression with respect to race, ethnicity, national origin, color, sex, sexual orientation, age, marital status, political belief, religion, and mental or physical disability" (NASW Standards for Cultural Competence, p. 13).

People may belong to several groups and have multiple identities. Even when a person is strongly identified with a single culture, his identity can be based on additional characteristics such as national origin, gender, social class, sexual orientation, disability, and age. In the process of learning much about many different groups, there are dangers of stereotyping persons by a primary group identity. Cultures are varied and complex, and social workers need to create methods to avoid false generalizations or overgeneralization about groups (Walker & Staton, 2000). A

White woman, for example, can be poor, Baptist, 80 years old, lesbian, and have been born and raised in Africa.

Illustrative of this point, Fellin (2000) proposed a way of assessing cultures of identification and participation, which emphasizes the multiple groups and degrees of group membership and participation an individual may have. Clients belong to various racial and ethnic groups and subgroups, religions, social classes, and sexual orientations, and may have disabilities of various types. When dealing with these differing persons and families, a social worker has to determine the degree of identification each person has with the groups they belong to, the level of their psychological sense of membership, and their level of participation in the groups.

Thus, a person can hold membership in various groups, identify themselves psychologically more or less with various groupings, and participate socially to varying degrees in each of the groups. We have introduced this conceptual scheme because it enables social workers to more correctly/ethically understand and assess the clients and families whom they serve from a multicultural and complex perspective. To think a person possesses only one identity is to engage in stereotyping, as each person belongs to many groups and the strength of his identities may shift over time. To understand each person as an individual requires being sensitive to and informed about a client's series of identities.

Because there are often major cultural differences within different cultural groups, it is difficult to offer generalizations that apply to a community as a whole. For example, the Filipino community is a diverse population itself. Individuals and their families differ in respect to when they arrived in the United States, socioeconomic background, educational level, language, factors surrounding their immigration, dialect, geographic orientation, social class, and level of acculturation. There is diversity among groups and within groups.

In addition to the treatment of cultural competence in the Code of Ethics, a milestone in this area of concern was the promulgation in 2001 of the NASW Standards for Cultural Competence in Social Work Practice (2001). Historically, culture and diversity have been associated in social work with race and ethnicity. However, diversity in today's America includes "the sociocultural experiences of people of different genders, social classes, religious and spiritual beliefs, sexual orientations, ages, and physical and mental abilities." (NASW, 2001, p. 8).

DISCRIMINATION AND MISDIAGNOSIS

Understanding of a particular person and culture can be informed and accurate, but discrimination exists at many levels, including at the practitioner level. Discrimination may affect diagnosis and treatment; for example, Leach and Sullivan (2002) found:

- People in lower socioeconomic classes consistently receive more frequent and severe diagnoses than individuals in other class levels.
- Blacks and Hispanics are more likely than Whites to be diagnosed with personality disorders or schizophrenia.
- African American children are more likely to receive a diagnosis of hyperactivity than White and Asian American children.
- Racial-ethnic minorities are more likely than Whites to be diagnosed with chronic disorders rather than acute disorders.

Discrimination in mental health services has been linked to racial and cultural factors, socioeconomic class, and the gender of clients (Toporek, 2002).

At least two theories are suggested to explain these discrepancies. Misdiagnosis is a result of different cultural expressions of symptoms or clinician bias. These kinds of misdiagnoses based on misunderstanding or on bias are unethical. Is the practitioner's intention to misdiagnose necessary before a person can be held guilty of an ethical violation?

CULTURE AND TREATMENT

A social worker can also encounter ethical dilemmas related to confidentiality and respecting a client's culture. For example, a young Asian American woman might be extremely shy about truth telling and disclosure. In her culture, many important decisions may be made by elders and not by the young client. On the other hand, social workers are trained to encourage disclosure and honesty in their clients. For a social worker to report bad news (e.g., that they need to make a report for child abuse or suggest HIV testing) to clients from some cultures could be interpreted as contributing to the illness, depriving the client of hope, and even casting a curse on the client and her family, in addition to bringing shame to them. Is it ethical to explore for more information when the client is culturally protective of family and personal secrets? What should one do if the client does not want you to report abuse because that would shame her family and ruin their life in their community? Consider the situation described in Exemplar 11.3.

11.3 | HOW MUCH TO TELL HYUN CHO?

Hyun Cho, an Asian American and recent immigrant in her early 50s, was referred to the Western Neighborhood Counseling Center by a non-Asian friend whom she admired and who had been helped at the Center. Hyun explained to Haley Traylor, her social worker, that she started having stomachaches, accompanied by becoming quite anxious, following her husband's being laid off. A visit to a physician found no physical problems. As treatment proceeded, things went quite well for a time, and Hyun began to feel better and more in control of her life.

At that point Hyun told Haley that although she is feeling better, a woman at her church told her she should not be using the Western Neighborhood Counseling Center but should use Asian methods and Asian persons to deal with her problems. Hyun announced that she appreciates the help she has been given, but she thinks her friend is correct and intends to go to a "healer" who emphasizes meditation and green tea. This decision surprised Haley because she had heard that the particular "healer" Hyun is going to visit is not helpful and that several persons had their physical problems worsen after his treatment.

What is the ethical choice for Haley? Should she tell Hyun what she knows about other persons' experiences with the neighborhood "healer"? Would that lead to an informed choice? Should she remain silent about her knowledge and accept without question Hyun's decision?

Sensitive and informed social work practice can demand that social workers practice in various and counterintuitive ways, ways that may be considered unethical. For example, people of Chinese backgrounds who are under the influence of Taoistic concepts of mental health can see the world in ways very different from what social workers are accustomed to meeting. Yet as Yip (2005) explains, social work practice stresses cognitive and emotional change of the individual in order to face their problems. Persons of Chinese background and influenced by Taoistic concepts seek change through inaction and regressive self-preservation. According to Tao thought, inaction is not static or passive but suggests insight into the laws of nature, and the client is allowing her mind or behavior to occur naturally. Is it ethically correct to remain silent and accept the person's behavior? Does this mean choosing between ordinary accountability to the agency and loyalty to the client?

There are "culture-bound" syndromes that practitioners may encounter in their practices. For example, social workers in certain locations may be confronted with client symptoms, such as *ataque de nervios* (out of consciousness state resulting from evil spirits); amok (outbursts of violent and aggressive behavior); and *dhat* (extreme anxiety associated with a sense of weakness and exhaustion) (Castillo, 2007). These unfamiliar syndromes when confronted raise several ethical issues: (a) Does the practitioner have sufficient training to recognize and deal with them? (b) What should one do when managed care will not reimburse unless a practitioner assigns a DSM-IV-TR (Diagnostic and Statistical Manual of Mental Disorders) diagnosis? (c) What should one do when managed care refuses to reimburse treatment for the symptoms identified? (d) Can a social worker raised in American culture accept these as valid symptoms even though they are not part of her own cultural experience? (e) Finally, how much multicultural training is required for a practitioner to practice ethically with diverse populations?

EXERCISES

1. If you were confronted as a social worker with the issue of assisted suicide, can you identify your personal values about such actions? What would be your position? What justification would you provide for your decision?
2. The legislature in your state has been alarmed by a sudden sharp increase in the incidence of HIV-positive findings among several populations. A bill has been introduced calling for mandatory HIV screening for all persons applying for a marriage license. The problem is a real one; the solution may or may not be effective, but it does raise a number of ethical issues. Your local NASW chapter has asked you to discuss these questions at the next membership meeting.
3. The agency at which you are employed wants to begin offering services over the Internet. In a group, discuss what you see as the ethical dilemmas for the agency and for social workers. Identify how these dilemmas could be avoided and/or dealt with ethically. How are HIPAA requirements being addressed?
4. If you were the social worker in the situation described in Exemplar 11.3 and Hyun Cho was your client, what would be your decision? What is the basis of your decision?

SUGGESTIONS FOR ADDITIONAL READINGS

Palmer and Kaufman (2003) highlight the importance of self-determination in social work and the United States. It is viewed as a core value and ethical standard. They explore how practitioner and institutional biases about diverse populations relate to informed consent in a multicultural context. Yip (2005) illustrates how traditional Taoism impacts on the mental health of Chinese people. They may not be in favor of empowerment or environmental change, and may favor inaction instead of cognitive and behavioral change, as well as question values such as self-actualization. Hodge (2004) examines the development of cultural competence (attitudes, knowledge) with evangelical Christians, suggesting that unresolved issues of the practitioner may play out in practice situations. Similar issues exist in regard to many and diverse populations.

WEB SITES OF INTEREST

- Georgetown University's National Center for Cultural Competence: www11.georgetown.edu/research/gucchd/nccc/
- Extensive information on cultural competence for health care providers (including assessment tools and training curricula) is available at the USDHHS Health Resources and Services Administration (HRSA): www.hrsa.gov/culturalcompetence/
- The USDHHS Centers for Disease Control and Prevention (CDC) provides information on IPV: www.cdc.gov/ncipc/factsheets/ipvfacts.htm
- The World Health Organization (WHO) provides information on IPV: www.who.int/violence_injury_prevention/violence/world_report/factsheets/en/ipvfacts.pdf
- Additional information from WHO on the link between IPV and HIV/AIDS is available at: www.who.int/hac/techguidance/pht/InfoBulletinIntimatePartnerViolenceFinal.pdf
- Extensive information about elder abuse is available from the National Center on Elder Abuse: www.elderabusecenter.org/
- Information about the Society for Spirituality and Social Work: http://ssw.asu.edu/spirituality/sssw/

CHANGING WORLD, CHANGING DILEMMAS

In this chapter, we discuss ethical dilemmas that result from factors that impact on practitioners and influence the kinds of interventions and decisions that can be made, including managed care and mental health; technology; research and evaluation in practice settings; evidence-based practice; private practice issues; and neighborhoods, society, and macro practice.

MANAGED CARE AND MENTAL HEALTH

For several decades, a number of factors combined to escalate health care costs beyond the rate of inflation in the United States. Among these factors are a growing aged population, technology and costly new treatments, an emphasis on acute care rather than preventive services, and varying standards of treatment according to geographic locations. As a result, there has been an increasing demand to control expenditures and to use managed health and mental health care systems as cost savers wherever possible. Managed care is one major strategy developed in an attempt to control health and mental health costs by monitoring access to and the type of health care patients receive from health care practitioners or health maintenance organizations (HMOs). Costs are reduced by placing controls on health practitioners and by fostering competition among HMOs. Managed care plans also attempt to reduce costs through controlling the type of health practitioners used, limiting access to service, and prescribing the type and length of service provided.

Managed care has been described as "any type of intervention in the delivery and financing of health care that is intended to eliminate unnecessary and inappropriate care and to reduce costs" (Wineburgh, 1998, p. 433) In 2004, almost one fourth of the U.S. population, or 67 million people, were enrolled in health maintenance organizations (managed care) (U.S. Census Bureau, 2007). There are a number of ethical issues that arise out of managed care services.

Managed care challenges the autonomy of both the social worker and the patient, and requires a high degree of accountability (Hall & Keefe, 2006). Professional service

199

stresses the importance of practitioner assessment and judgment, and the Code of Ethics promotes "clients' socially responsible self-determination" (Code, 1999, Ethical Principles). But autonomy for both the practitioner and the patient may be diminished in managed care settings. The choice of treatment can be determined by the practitioner alone or together with a managed care reviewer. However, the managed care reviewer may reduce the autonomy of both practitioner and patients through quality assurance, utilization review, and selection of appropriate forms of treatment (Wineburgh, 1998).

Practitioners must accommodate their treatment choices to those made by the managed care organization. To not do so risks a decrease in referrals, which can mean a potential loss of status and income. Brief therapy appears to be the preferred mode of intervention (Cohen, 2003), and long-term therapy may only be available to those who can pay privately for treatment.

Many social workers may be pressured by managed care organizations to provide group therapy for their clients in place of individual treatment because group service is time and cost efficient. One practitioner can treat many people with similar problems at the same time, thus reducing the number of billable hours. The insurance companies stress that outpatient services in time-limited groups have been found to be very effective. For example, persons with panic disorder who received cognitive-behavioral group therapy in addition to medication "had lower posttest anxiety scores than those who received medication alone" (Mitchell, 1999, p. 188). What is the ethical responsibility of a social worker inexperienced with groups who has a client whom a managed care entity has only approved for group treatment? Should she offer group service (even while learning how to do this) or should she tell the client that he must look for help elsewhere?

Practitioners in private practice may be tempted to agree to emphasize group treatment because this can result in greater income—even when professional judgment counterindicates this mode of treatment. Here, the social worker faces another ethical dilemma: how to juggle the demands of her own professional judgments, those of the insurance company, and her desire for economic security. This dilemma is not limited to workers in private practice; it also occurs in agency practice, as shown in Exemplar 12.1.

| 12.1 | WHAT THE PINE TREE INSURANCE COMPANY WANTS |

Dr. Felicia Montevideo, director of social work clinical services for Family and Children's Services of Pleasant City, was surprised when she received a letter from the Pine Tree Insurance Company (Managed Care Division) and later a phone call, both of which subtly suggested that more of the agency's treatment services be offered in time-limited groups. When she raised the issue with the agency's administrative executive committee, some argued in favor of complying because the money received from the insurance company made up a substantial part of the agency's income. Others were concerned that such a change in operating procedures would upset the staff. Still others wanted to know what would be most helpful to clients, and some argued that compliance would mean yielding their professional judgment to the Pine Tree Insurance Company.

Among the options suggested by committee members are the following: (a) ignore the suggestion because it had not been explicitly stated; (b) comply as soon as possible with the suggestion; (c) refuse to comply and begin to advocate with Pine Tree Insurance for the current mix of service modalities; (d) examine and review research on the relative effectiveness of various treatment methods; and (e) meet with Pine Tree representatives to explore ways to slowly phase in more group treatment. What are the ethical implications of each option?

We see that the influence of the managed care organization affects the practitioner's choice of intervention, the length of service, and the expected outcome of the service. Gibelman and Mason (2002) reported that managed care influenced practice decisions about treatment planning, the amount and types of treatment, limiting who could be seen in treatment, elimination of collateral visits with other family members, lawyers, teachers, employers, and premature discharge of patients. Uncertainty about the reaction of the managed care representative can lead practitioners to "fudge" the diagnosis in an effort to get approval for the treatment needed. Many practitioners have reported that patients whose care has been denied often reappear later with the same complaints that led to their seeking treatment. Such experiences can lead to the view that managed care organizations can be capricious in their decisions. A national study of 582 social workers, psychologists, and psychiatrists found that they do not see themselves as having the requisite skills to interact adequately with managed care organizations to ensure that appropriate care can be ensured (Hall & Keefe, 2006).

The Code of Ethics has several standards that are of special relevance in managed care situations: (a) "Social workers should use clear and understandable language to inform clients of the purpose of the services, risks related to the services, limits to services because of the requirements of a third-party payer, relevant costs, reasonable alternatives, clients' right to refuse or withdraw consent, and the time frame covered by the consent" (NASW, 1999, 1.03a); (b) "Social workers should not disclose confidential information to third-party payers unless clients have authorized such disclosure" (1.07h); and (c) "Social workers should take reasonable steps to avoid abandoning clients who are still in need of services" (1.16b).

Other standards may also be relevant to managed care settings. Consider, for example, the issue of informed consent (1.03). Clients may have limited financial resources that force them to choose their health plan on the basis of cost. As a result, in certain situations, they are not free agents and may not understand the possible rationing of services that may occur when managed care organizations use cost-saving devices. Similarly, there may be limits on refusals by clients to participate in the managed care organization's recommended treatment that minimizes their sense of voluntariness. Managed care programs may place the social worker in situations in which their compliance with standard 4.04 ("Social workers should not participate in, condone, or be associated with dishonesty, fraud, or deception") (NASW Code, 1999) may become questionable. For example, in order to provide a "reimbursable service" for a client, the practitioner may have to consider fudging the diagnosis in some way.

There are many other ethical dilemmas practitioners can encounter in regard to managed care situations. Difficult issues arise when the cost containment goals of managed care place limits on the length of treatment, deny care, or insist on certain treatments. When a client's situation is not improved or the problem is unresolved, managed care may deny further reimbursed treatment. Nonetheless, the client may require a continuation of services. This problem becomes accentuated for a practitioner when two similarly situated clients both need professional social work service but have different benefit packages. On what basis does this social worker decide how to distribute services when both have equal needs? Should the client with the more generous benefit package receive more service?

Certain ethical dilemmas arise from the requirement to continue treatment if it is needed (Code, 1999, 1.16b) or terminate treatment once it is no longer needed (Code, 1.16a). What should the practitioner do if the client who needs continued treatment has reached the maximum on his annual or lifetime benefits and is unable to pay? A practitioner can state at the beginning of treatment that the family agency policy limits the number of sessions. What if during treatment the client resolved several of the problems that had brought him into treatment but another problem had emerged, and the social worker's supervisor denied permission for additional sessions? What is the ethical thing to do?

Davis (1997) discusses the need to ensure the availability of culturally competent standards of care and diagnostic and treatment services to underserved groups. In addition, managed care organizations need to provide accessible services "located within reasonable geographic distance to Black neighborhoods" (Davis, 1997, p. 636). What should the social worker do in Exemplar 12.2?

| 12.2 | WHERE ARE THE SERVICES? |

Anita Dee is a social worker in a state psychiatric hospital that primarily serves low-income people of color. The Medicaid recipients are served through a managed care system that is privately operated. Generally, administrators and supervisors in this public hospital seek harmonious relationships with the managed care organization, located in another state. Anita recently realized that when chronically ill psychiatric patients are discharged, the managed care company refers them to outpatient sites that are seldom near where they reside; transportation to the treatment sites is not provided. Consequently, the discharged persons are not receiving the help they need. Anita believes the managed care company is discriminating against poor and minority persons, but her supervisor says her job is to help prepare persons to leave the hospital and anything after that is not her concern.

It is clear from the Code of Ethics that a practitioner should advocate for her client to receive appropriate services. The issue of advocacy raises several questions. How does one balance advocacy for one client versus the services that other clients need? Advocacy for one client can be time consuming and deprive others of services they need. How far should one appeal? How much unpaid time should be devoted to such efforts? Should one appeal when there is little chance for success? Furthermore, one can advocate once too many times and risk being removed from the managed care panel (Wineburgh, 1998).

TECHNOLOGY

In chapter 11 we discussed technology in direct practice, specifically the delivery of services online and through other technologies; in this chapter we will discuss other ways in which technology can produce ethical dilemmas. Social work, like many other professions, has been affected by computers and other modern technologies. Many people, including social workers, believe that things, unlike people, are value-free. However, because technology exists within a human context, it reflects and shapes human choices, which always involve value choices and ethical priorities.

Initially, social workers were concerned that the introduction of information technologies into social agencies and social work practice would result in more critical ethical dilemmas because these technologies were thought to be insensitive to variations in human needs and individual differential values and cultures. For example, electronic technology used by organizations to provide services for HIV-positive persons may provide support, empowerment, and practical advice about how to cope with the disease. But these patients may be especially vulnerable if the system is unable to protect the confidentiality of communications to and from them (Benotch et al., 2006).

As coordinating agencies, grant-funding agencies, third-party payers, and others create large, interconnected computerized databases, methods are needed to guarantee the confidentiality of records from hackers and other intruders. When multiple agencies become linked in networks in order to promote collaborative case management, new problems arise. Is client permission needed for one agency or worker to share or receive the information held by another agency about a common client? To what extent should agencies limit the client data they have computerized? How can clients be sufficiently informed about data sharing between agencies? How well informed should clients be about the realities of the information networks to which agencies and their personal records are tied? The increased ease and speed of information transfer make these ethical issues ever more critical in social work practice.

Other issues arise from the use of computers. For example, employees in social agencies can work at computer monitors whose screens face a hallway path and are exposed to view by anyone who passes by. Furthermore, if an agency's computer system can be accessed externally, it is potentially open to hackers, even when security systems are in place. Just as anyone can observe what remains in view on an employee's monitor, organizations have the ability to monitor employees' activities: phone calls, e-mail messages, Internet connections, and computer files. Video surveillance also exists for security reasons in many agency locations. Electronic communications accessed through employers belong to the employer, not the employee. Social workers employed in governmental agencies may find that their electronic messages are public records that can be monitored without prior notice (Levine, 2000; Lorenz, 2006). How do these practices affect social workers' and clients' privacy rights? Should a social worker inform her clients that her agency may monitor phone calls and e-mail messages?

Concerns about computer security are not limited to interorganizational electronic communications. Caputo (1991) set forth an ethical framework for information systems that asserts the primacy of clients as citizens. The ethical framework fulfills the following functions:

1. It provides a way to inform clients about the existence of a computerized client-information system.
2. It enables clients to give informed consent in regard to the uses of information about themselves.
3. It offers an opportunity for individuals to inspect, correct, or add information about themselves, allowing them to expunge all or parts of their records, except where such records are legally required.
4. It develops an information-needs matrix to guide unit allocation decisions on the basis of critical success factors.

5. It holds professionals to a professional practice that is mindful of ethical standards, including respect for clients' autonomy, their right to information and privacy, the need to weigh the efficacy of demands for efficiency against the principle of human dignity, and adherence to confidentiality regarding the use of routinely collected information about clients.

Although Caputo (1991) developed this framework a number of years ago, the recommendations are still relevant today and are likely to continue to be so as long as computerized databases are used.

Other ethical issues arise out of still newer developments. Among these are computerized screening and assessment; selection of practice and service recommendations; expert systems for evaluating various risks, such as foster care, parole, and suicide; and interactive treatment games and various forms of therapy. Among the ethical dilemmas that have developed as a result of these technologies are questions of beneficence (autonomy versus paternalism), equity of access to scarce resources (ensuring equality of opportunity), and the promotion of the common good (ensuring that the maximum number of individuals benefit from the introduction of information technology). The assumption of many advanced software and expert systems (computerized decision making) is that there is always one "right" decision that should be followed. As a result, problems concerning client autonomy and worker flexibility have become more critical. How can the worker simultaneously defend the autonomy of the client, meet the expectations of the agency, and avoid paternalism and control of clients?

The introduction of information systems into social agencies with very tight budgets may mean that scarce resources must be deployed to pay for the new technology and for staff with specific expertise even while other agency programs and client supports will be reduced or eliminated. Work patterns and organizational structure will change, and some resources will not be available for some kinds of client services. Consider the common dilemma that confronts the social worker in Exemplar 12.3.

12.3	COMPUTERIZED INFORMATION SYSTEM OR SERVICES?

Miri Neidig, a social worker, is a member of the board of directors of a neighborhood service center that provides counseling and other services, including services for low-income minority teens at a local shopping mall. This service has recently been instituted and is highly valued by community members concerned about sexually transmitted diseases and by teenagers because of the privacy afforded by the location and the likeable staff. The agency recently purchased several computers, and some members of the board are pressuring the executive director to computerize its operation. They believe it is essential for agencies to become technologically up to date. According to the United Way, the current funding situation has become precarious and expenses must be reduced. The board will meet tonight to review the agency budget.

The board and Miri are faced with the question of what services to reduce or cut. Some argue that it is more important to upgrade the technology in the agency, and others argue there are too few services provided now. There are waiting lists for almost all services. The board, including Miri, is faced with difficult choices. For the future, improved use of computers by the agency will be a positive step. If they vote in favor of further computerization, other services will be diminished. A vote for computerization will deny the community services that are desperately needed. What recommendation would you make to Miri about her vote? How would you choose?

RESEARCH AND EVALUATION IN PRACTICE SETTINGS

In addition to keeping up to date with current research findings, social workers are encouraged to "promote and facilitate evaluation and research to contribute to the development of knowledge" (Code, 1999, 5.02b). Many funding sources now require that agencies provide outcome data in order to continue receiving funding. While this requirement is not inconsistent with the Code of Ethics, it may create a number of ethical dilemmas for social workers. Consider the situation in Exemplar 12.4.

| 12.4 | FUNDALOT FOUNDATION WANTS EVIDENCE |

The Sidestreet Agency provides services to runaway adolescents; for the past three years, over 80% of their funding has been provided by the Fundalot Foundation. The board of directors of the Fundalot Foundation recently voted to change the criteria for continued funding; specifically, they now want all programs to provide evidence of their efficacy. They have not been specific about what type of evidence will be acceptable, but rather, they have decided to let each agency determine what types of data should be collected and reported. Funding will be discontinued if programs have inadequate data collection and reporting, or offer findings that do not support the program's efficacy.

Kathleen Hall is the social worker for the Sidestreet Agency. For the past three years, she has written the funding proposal for the Fundalot Foundation. Given the new requirements, Kathleen has asked to meet with the other members of the staff to discuss how they will address them. During the meeting, a number of issues are raised: (a) Should the agency respond or not respond to these requirements? (b) Is informed consent required to collect this sort of outcome data? What if clients refuse to give consent? Will they be dropped from the treatment program? (c) If the agency's clients are children and adolescents, at what age can they give informed consent, and how can it be obtained for those clients who are too young or not competent to give consent? Is the consent of their parents required? (d) What if the findings are not good enough? (e) If "we know it works," why isn't that enough proof for the foundation? (f) Who or what takes ethical priority here: the agency that needs funding, the clients being served, the staff who want to retain their jobs, or honesty that requires accurate recording? How should a social worker respond to these issues?

If an agency decides to evaluate its services, there are a number of potential ethical issues. Among these issues are the use of deception, confidentiality and privacy, conflicts of interest, reporting results, and disclosing the results to the research participants (Grinnell & Unrau, 2005).

The collection of outcome data raises a number of ethical dilemmas. The NASW Code of Ethics (1999) has standards for evaluation and research (see 5.02 a–p), including an injunction against dual relationships (5.02o). Despite this injunction, the current priority given to establishing the efficacy of clinical programs through research is demanding that clinicians include research in the scope of their practice. The dual role of clinician and researcher, although advantageous, poses risks to the self-determination of clients who are potential study participants (Antle & Regehr, 2003, p. 140).

Is the clinician-researcher dual role avoidable for a social worker in an agency that requires the collection of outcome data? If this dual role is unavoidable, how can the social worker protect the client's rights, including self-determination, while meeting the needs of the agency to establish its efficacy? What should a social worker do who works for an agency that will not provide services without the client's agreement to provide outcome data? Finally, let us consider the case of an agency that has collected the outcome data required by its funding agency, but the results are not positive (e.g., there is no evidence that the agency's services are effective). What would you do in this situation?

Although most evaluation and research activities do not call for deception, there can be situations in which deception is used. For instance, the real reason for evaluating client satisfaction might be kept from the clients. Perhaps honest explanations would bias the results in some way. The protection of confidentiality may also be a problem. Who will have access to the responses and data? In addition to personal failures to protect privacy and confidentiality, there can be security problems associated with computers and electronic transmission of data. In Exemplar 12.4, we saw potential issues regarding conflicts of interest and reporting of the results. Involving clients in research efforts may also create potential conflicts of interest of a different type, by creating stress and discomfort for clients because they feel they have no free choice to participate or not. This discussion of research and evaluation in practice leads directly into concerns about accountability, effectiveness, and the recent emphasis on evidence-based practice.

EVIDENCE-BASED PRACTICE (EBP)

What is evidence-based practice? The following are two definitions. Evidence-based practice

> is an approach to care wherein professionals use the best evidence possible, i.e., the most appropriate information available, to make clinical decisions for individual patients. ... [it] promotes the collection, interpretation, and integration of valid, important and applicable patient-reported, clinician-observed, and research-derived evidence. The best available evidence, moderated by patient circumstances and preferences, is applied to improve the quality of clinical judgments and facilitate cost-effective care (Wikipedia, 2007).

Gambrill (2006) suggests that evidence-based practice "is a new educational and practice paradigm for closing the gaps between research and practice to maximize opportunities to help clients and avoid harm" (p. 339). Keeping in mind the ethical obligations described in the Code of Ethics, she suggests evidence-based practice is "a philosophy and process designed to forward effective use of professional judgment in integrating information regarding each client's unique characteristics, circumstances, preferences, and actions and external research findings" (Gambrill, 2006, p. 339). Certainly no ethical practitioner would dismiss the use of empirical, scientific, and relevant information that can be helpful in providing effective and efficient services.

Public and private organizations and third-party payers increasingly are pressuring social workers and human service organizations for evidence that they are accountable and their services are beneficial to those they are serving. This trend is reflected in the Code of Ethics where several standards are relevant to discussions of evidence-based practice and the use of research findings: "Social workers should critically examine and keep current with emerging knowledge relevant to social work ... [and] should routinely review the professional literature" (NASW Code, 1999, 4.01b). In addition, "social workers should base practice on recognized knowledge, including empirically based knowledge" (NASW Code, 1999, 4.01c). Furthermore, social workers are also encouraged to "fully use evaluation and research evidence in their professional practice" (NASW Code, 1999, 5.02c). There are social workers, especially students, who are not convinced that research is relevant to what they do. But more and more demands are made on social workers that they be accountable for their methods and the outcomes of their services. These demands can create ethical dilemmas for social workers.

There has been a great deal of discussion about evidence-based practice and how it should be used in social work (see Gambrill, 2003; Howard, McMillen, & Pollio, 2003). There have been many earlier developments and changes in social work practice that engendered debates. For example, the introduction of behavioral and cognitive therapies and time-limited and task-structured interventions were the occasion of debates, followed by research and gradual acceptance. Evidence-based practice has been touted as another among the major advances in social work with the promise of achieving major change in the profession and its services. Whether evidence-based practice will prove revolutionary for social work or will simply be integrated into the profession with a more emphatic stress on empirical and scientific evidence in the choice of interventions remains to be seen.

How might a social worker use evidence practice? Research knowledge, clinical expertise, and client values are all integrated in evidence-based practice, which involves five steps:

1. Convert information needs related to practice decisions into answerable questions.
2. Track down the best evidence with which to answer them.
3. Critically appraise that evidence in terms of its validity, clinical significance, and usefulness.
4. Integrate this critical appraisal of research evidence with one's clinical expertise and the patient's values and circumstances.
5. Evaluate one's effectiveness and efficiency in undertaking the four previous steps, and strive for self-improvement (Thyer, 2004, p. 168).

Many social workers feel unprepared or unable to perform these five steps and/or they may feel that they are already overburdened and do not have the time to perform them. A social worker may even wonder if evidence-based practice is really ethically necessary. The Code (1999, 4.01) suggests that clients have a right to expect that social workers will be competent in their area of practice. Can a social worker remain competent if she does not stay up to date with current developments in the field? Consider Exemplar 12.5.

<table>
<tr><td>12.5</td><td>CLAIRE JOHNSON IS DEPRESSED BUT DOESN'T WANT TO TAKE ANTIDEPRESSANTS</td></tr>
</table>

Sheryl Adams is a social worker in a solo private practice. One of her clients, Claire Johnson, was referred to her after Claire's physician, who often makes referrals to Sheryl, made a diagnosis of depression. Claire's physician wanted to prescribe an antidepressant, but Claire refused to take the medication prescribed. She is afraid that the medicine will harm her 3-month-old baby because she is breastfeeding, and she previously had been prescribed medications for depression that made her life miserable with headaches, dry mouth, and sweating. Because of Claire's refusal to take the antidepressants, her physician referred her to Sheryl for counseling. He expected Sheryl to convince Claire to take her medication. The physician expressed great concern about the infant's health. Sheryl has little experience treating depression, but there are no other licensed social workers in the area. At the first session, Claire stated that she is very concerned that due to the depression she is not adequately caring for her baby and that she needs immediate relief so she can be a better mother, but she cannot manage to cope with the medications.

What are the ethical dilemmas facing Sheryl? Who is her client—the infant, Claire, the physician, her practice? How can she decide who takes priority? What additional information is needed so that Claire can give informed consent for the treatment? Are there nonmedication treatments for depression? Is this situation a repeat of Claire's earlier depressive episode or postpartum depression? How much time will it take to find and review the relevant research literature? What harm can be done in the interim? Should Claire be told about the available treatment options, the risks and benefits of each, and the likely efficacy of each, including the fact that Sheryl is not experienced in delivering some of these treatment options? What should Sheryl do if she cannot learn the most effective new treatments easily or if Claire refuses to participate when informed of the situation? Review the Code of Ethics (1999) for relevant standards.

Let us consider how Sheryl could apply the five steps of evidence-based practice (Thyer, 2004) described above to this situation. First, she could develop "answerable questions," such as what non–medication-based treatments are available for depression. Also, given that Claire has a 3-month-old son, what distinguishes major depression from postpartum depression, which is the most appropriate diagnosis for her, and are the treatment options different?

Once Sheryl has developed answerable questions, she can move to the second step, "track down the best evidence." How should Sheryl proceed? Assuming that she is a busy professional, does she have time to find and review all the relevant research literature? There are a growing number of Internet-based resources available that provide summaries and critiques of the research literature in a number of areas. What if Claire has heard about a treatment for depression called transcranial magnetic stimulation (given the ease with which information can be obtained from the Internet, it is possible for clients to find information on treatments that the social worker is not familiar with) and has asked Sheryl to convince the insurance company to pay for this treatment? Should Sheryl do so? How could she decide if this is an appropriate referral? Sheryl could check with a library or look for Internet-based resources, such as the Cochrane collaboration, which provides systematic reviews on a number of health-related topics, including depression (for example, see Martin et al. [2002] in the Cochrane Library at www.cochraneconsumer.com for a review of transcranial magnetic stimulation).

Once Sheryl has found the relevant research evidence, she needs to move to step 3 and "critically appraise that evidence." Some social workers find research intimidating and/or have difficulty evaluating research methodology—how should they proceed with this step? Is it ethical to uncritically accept the conclusions of study authors without examining the adequacy of the research methodology used? Is this step easier if one has reliable and trustworthy sources of information?

In step 4, the results of steps 1 through 3 are applied, including considerations of whether what has been found is relevant to the client's issue and how these findings relate to the client's values. What should Sheryl do if after all of this she finds that the most effective treatment is one she does not know how to provide or is unacceptable to Claire? Finally, in step 5, the effectiveness and efficacy of steps 1 through 4 are evaluated. For most social workers, this evidence-based practice process may be quite time consuming, especially the first few times it is used. Does this cause any ethical dilemmas?

Philosophical criticisms have also been expressed. Those who make these arguments suggest that "an evidence based, rational model of decision-making does not fit the realities of individualized, contextualized practice, especially where problems are less well defined" (Mullen & Streiner, 2004, p. 114). The Code requirements include that "social workers should strive to become and remain proficient in professional practice" (4.01b) and they should "base practice on recognized knowledge, including empirically based knowledge, relevant to social work and social work ethics" (4.01c). Reflecting this point of view, Howard and Jenson (1999) advocate for guidelines to direct practice in the most effective and proven ways, faulting the professional association for failing to implement practice guidelines. Others argue that solving human problems through the use of an "approved list" of techniques would violate the richness and dignity of human struggles and triumphs. Social workers "deal with enormously complex and difficult issues. To do this well, they must be analytical, reflective, and compassionate in their approach to human suffering. They must recognize that they often know very little about the lives of those they serve and that, therefore, they must listen and learn from them" (Witkin, 1998, pp. 79–80).

PRIVATE PRACTICE ISSUES

In this section we will address a few issues that may be particularly relevant in private practice or in agencies that have very tight budgets, where social workers are forced to make difficult decisions based on finances. Later in this chapter we will also address issues that are more common in macro practice settings.

CLIENT DUMPING

What is the ethical thing to do when, during the course of treatment, a client's situation changes and he can no longer pay the fee? Consider the situation of Larry Firth in Exemplar 12.6.

| 12.6 | A DIFFICULT FAMILY SITUATION |

Larry Firth came to consult with you about a difficult family situation. His wife has left him and their two sons in order to live with her boyfriend. He himself has formed a relationship with a married neighbor. However, he is concerned what his teenage sons will say and do when they find out the truth about their parents. You are making good progress in helping Larry come to grips with his problem. Today, however, Larry tells you that he has lost his job and can no longer afford your fee. You are not yet sufficiently well established to carry free cases. There is no family service agency in the town that provides services free of charge. What should you do?

"Dumping the client" is one way that some practitioners have responded to clients who can no longer pay for services. There are various ways to dump a client. A worker may tell a client that his problem has been solved successfully (when it has not yet been solved) or that no more can be done for him (when, in fact, the worker could still be helpful). The worker may cancel appointments so frequently that the client loses interest, or the worker may refer a client who no longer can afford his services to a public or private not-for-profit agency. No matter what technique is used, the worker's objective is to get rid of the client who can no longer pay. Barker (1992) suggests that private practitioners "are far more likely to engage in the unethical behavior of premature or precipitous termination than are agency-based professionals" (p. 110). What can an ethical practitioner do when this situation arises? As insurance companies place limits on the number of sessions that they will cover, how should a social worker address problems that she feels will require more sessions than the insurance company will pay for? Should she do the best she can in the number of sessions allowed, work with the client to establish treatment goals that can be achieved in that time frame, or provide free or reduced cost services after the insurance coverage ends?

A national survey of experienced and well-established psychotherapists (psychologists) found that most continued care when insurance coverage ended. They chose the following options in descending order: (1) advocate for more benefits; (2) patient pays out of his or her own pocket; (3) reduce the fee for a patient who continues on a self-paying basis; (4) treat the person on a pro bono basis; (5) make a proper referral to an agency for continued treatment; (6) terminate treatment; and (7) alter the diagnosis so treatment would be covered (Murphy, DeBernardo, & Shoemaker, 1998). Another available option a social worker should consider is that the client will pay when his financial situation improves. None of these options is without problems. In the case of termination, much would depend on the state of the person, the nature of the problem, how close the client is to attainment of the goals of treatment, the number of persons being seen by the social worker, and other such variables.

MISREPRESENTATION

The NASW Code of Ethics specifically states: "Social workers should ensure that their representations to clients, agencies, and the public of professional qualification, credentials, education, competence, affiliations, services provided, or results to be achieved are accurate" (NASW, 1999, 4.06c). What seems like a simple ethical rule gives rise to a number of questions, including the following:

- Is it ethical for a social worker to identify herself as something other than a social worker (such as a marriage counselor or psychotherapist)?
- Is it ethical for a social worker to call herself "Doctor" when she has not earned a Ph.D., D.S.W., or other doctoral degree?
- Must a student social worker always identify herself as a student in field instruction placements, or can she present herself as "your social worker"?

Those who engage in these practices claim that they do so to give clients greater confidence in their worker and thus increase the chances for a successful outcome. Is this ethical? Finally, a social worker may claim or promise that she can help a client who comes to her seeking treatment. Can she ethically make such a promise?

PREPARATION AND READINESS FOR PRIVATE PRACTICE

Professional life in social agencies is influenced by rules, limitations on interventive modes that can be used, relatively low salaries, and—in general—the constraints of employment in complex organizations. In addition, many graduate social workers carry debt burdens from their educations. In a market economy, the establishment of private practices can be seductive because they potentially can provide the practitioner greater autonomy, freedom to select clients, and choice of treatment interventions.

Ethical social workers will assess their qualifications and readiness to establish private practices. Part of this assessment is objective. One either has a professional license or other credentials or not. Other criteria are more subjective, such as one's motivations and sense of discipline, skill levels, and the ability to deal with one's own difficulties and limitations. For example, private practice requires arrangements be made for office space, insurance, referrals, record keeping, management of crises, and supervision and consultation (Matorin, Rosenberg, Levitt, & Rosenblum, 1987); the social worker must assess her ability to successfully make these arrangements. What other resources need to be available to ensure ethical practice within a private practice setting? For example, do experienced social workers need to be available to provide supervision or consultation?

Ethical standards require that a social worker "provide services and represent themselves as competent within the boundaries of their education . . . or other relevant professional experience" (Code, 1.04a, b). How does one know prior to establishing a private practice that one is sufficiently prepared to engage in such an entrepreneurial effort? The "standard of care" and professional actions of social workers are judged against what a majority of practitioners in the profession would do with a particular type of client in a particular type of situation. As an ethical issue, how does one know with reasonable assurance what other private practitioners are doing with particular cases?

NEIGHBORHOODS, SOCIETY, AND MACRO PRACTICE

The Code of Ethics includes a number of standards that expect social workers to accept a responsibility to engage in efforts to improve their communities and society (6.01, 6.02, 6.03, and 6.04). Among these are to promote the general welfare of society, participate in the community to shape policies and institutions, provide services during emergencies, and engage in social and political action. Nevertheless, the Code makes no specific provisions for ethical dilemmas encountered in social work with groups and in community organizations.

COMMUNITY GROUPS

Although the Code refers to "clients" as individuals, families, groups, organizations, and communities (p. 1) and refers to social groups in passing (p. 6), the only direct attention to groups and families is in the context of confidentiality. Perhaps reflecting the Code's sparse attention, social work has paid rather scarce attention to ethical decisions in work with groups. Dolgoff and Skolnik (1992, 1996) studied the bases upon which social workers with groups make ethical decisions when faced with ethical dilemmas and what their decisions were regarding a series of dilemmas. The results overwhelmingly indicated that practice wisdom was the primary basis for ethical decision making by these social workers. Congress and Lynn (1997) examined a number of ethical dilemmas encountered in task groups in the community, including confidentiality, self-determination of the group and individual members, inclusion or exclusion of members, and conflicts of interest. Consider the following situations:

- You are a social worker employed by a city housing authority, and you are working with a group of mothers to improve a playground for their children. One resident brings a friend with her to the meeting. During the meeting, you discover the friend is living with the group member's family in the same apartment. This is unknown to both the housing authority and your employer, and it is against the law. What should you do?
- You are a social worker assigned to work with a community group concerned about trash pickup, speeding traffic that endangers neighborhood children, and public transportation accessibility. Your values and those of the group have been congruent regarding every concern so far. At this evening's meeting, a highly influential group member introduced the news that the state mental health department intends to establish a community residence in the neighborhood. When she took the leadership on this issue, the entire group agreed to make their opposition to the proposed residence their highest priority. You know there is a great need for such residences. If, however, you oppose their actions, you are concerned that it will undermine your effectiveness on all the other issues. How will you balance your values with those of the group? To whom do you owe loyalty: the group, yourself, the neighborhood, those who need such residences, or society in general?

Social workers with community groups may have somewhat different views about the implications of developing a friendship with a client or member, serving on community boards or committees with clients or members, or having another type of relationship with a client or member. For example, social workers who are community organizers or social planners may have no compunctions about going to a local diner or coffeehouse with a group of clients/members after a session whereas social workers who work with individuals may or may not draw a line on such behavior. Social work administrators often make their most important contacts with board members in social settings. Obviously, the definition of who is a client/member, the purpose of the professional relationship, and the context are factors that affect the ethical assessment of such dual-role relationships.

COMMUNITY AND SOCIETAL ISSUES

Standard 6.01 of the Code states "social workers should promote the general welfare of society . . . their communities, and their environments." Before leaving this section, we want to point out an example of ethical responsibility of social workers at a societal level. Blacks in the United States do not live as long as Whites. A Black male born in 1999 had a life expectancy of slightly more than 67 years. A White male born in that same year could expect to live until 74, an additional seven years of life. American Indians and Alaskan Native people born today will live five years fewer than people of any other American racial or ethnic group. When compared to Whites, Asian Americans, Blacks, and Hispanics are less likely to have a regular doctor. Poor people are more likely to go without needed medical care. Clearly, some groups in the United States are healthier in general than others and receive better health care (Center for Health Equity Research and Promotion, 2005).

For all social workers, the Code of Ethics sets forth several standards concerned with social workers' ethical responsibilities to the broader society. Among these responsibilities are the identification of disparities such as those cited above and working to address them. Doing so requires macro-level organizing and advocacy either in professional roles or as concerned citizens. For example, standard 6.04 (NASW Code, 1999) states: "Social workers should engage in social and political action that seeks to ensure that all people have equal access to the resources, employment, services, and opportunities they require to meet their basic human needs and to develop fully."

Community organizers, policy and social planning practitioners, advocates, and others involved with societal issues take as their focus issues at the community and societal levels. Are such matters the ethical concern only of social workers who are practicing macro methods? If not, what does this suggest are the ethical roles of direct service and clinical social workers in regard to these situations? Whatever the difficulties and dilemmas for social workers in macro practice, the Code of Ethics—for all social workers—explicitly requires engagement by social workers in social and political action "to prevent and eliminate domination of, exploitation of, and discrimination against any person, group, or class on the basis of race, ethnicity, national origin, color, sex, sexual orientation, age, marital status, political belief, religion, or mental or physical disability" (6.04d).

Some professional social workers hold stereotyped views of their colleagues who engage in macro practice. They believe that practitioners who engage in agency-wide change efforts, social planning, neighborhood and community organization and development, social action, and social policy efforts are operating in a highly politicized arena. They think that this practice area is grounded on techniques and methods based on pragmatism rather than on ethical considerations. This perception is fostered not only by the nature of the settings in which macro practitioners practice but also by the language they use, especially such terms as tactics, strategies, conflict, and advocacy. Indeed, with a few exceptions, references to ethics are only rarely found in macro practice textbooks.

Nevertheless, macro social workers do encounter many difficult ethical dilemmas in their daily practice. The Code of Ethics applies to all NASW members, including those in macro practice. The Code states that "Social workers' primary responsibility is to promote the well-being of clients" (1.01) and "Social workers should promote the general welfare of society, from local to global levels" (6.01). Further, "the social worker should engage in social and political action that seeks to ensure that all people have access to the resources, employment, services, and opportunities they require to meet their basic human needs and to develop fully" (6.04a).

When the social worker is attempting to comply with all of these standards, many dilemmas are encountered. These include determining who is the client to whom primary responsibility is owed and selecting the persons who have access to resources when not every needy person can be supplied because these resources are in short supply. Another type of dilemma occurs when there are several similarly disadvantaged groups. How does the worker choose the one group that will receive her priority attention? In the social planning situation in Exemplar 12.7, the social worker has to choose between many different groups. The choices to be made clearly deal with promoting the "general welfare of society." In this instance, who is society? Which group deserves priority consideration?

12.7 ESTABLISHING A CANCER TREATMENT UNIT

You are the director of social work in a large urban community hospital located in a low-income area serving people from various economic levels. You have been assigned to staff the planning committee charged with creating a plan for the future of the hospital. You grew up in the community and have family and long-standing friends who reside there. You also have relationships with many community human service administrators and staff members.

As the planning process proceeds, it becomes clear that most committee members favor the creation of a specialized cancer treatment unit, which will gain status and recognition for the hospital and also attract patients from throughout the state. Such a recommendation, however, will make it impossible to recommend improvements for emergency and ambulatory care that are desperately needed by the neighborhood. A recommendation for a cancer treatment unit will change the nature of the available health care, who will get the jobs, use of community space, kinds of housing that will be available, and so forth.

It becomes clear to you that the local community will gain very little and may lose much if a cancer treatment unit is installed. You are torn between loyalties to the hospital, to the community in general, to the social and human service agencies in the community, and to the community's population, including your friends and relatives who need a different type of service.

As a member of the planning group, you are faced with the dilemma of choosing between groups to determine who will benefit from the distribution of resources. What criteria will help you choose between the cancer patients who do not necessarily come from the immediate community and the health needs of the local community, including your family, friends, and neighbors? Choosing between two groups, both of which have real health needs, is a typical ethical dilemma faced by social workers who are social planners. Whose good is primary? As a social worker, you owe first priority to the potential recipients of health services, but which of the groups has a higher priority? In addition, is the hospital's long-term viability a consideration that should affect the ethical decision-making process?

A review of the ethical principles screen (EPS) in 4 can be helpful as you think about this dilemma. We would suggest that a consideration of Ethical Principles 1 and 2 is most compelling in the present case.

> Principle 1—Protection of life. All medical services ultimately deal with the protection of life. Cancer patients are at a great risk and inevitably face life-threatening situations that require early treatment—the earlier the better. On the other hand, the emergencies typically treated in a hospital ER range from routine treatments to life-threatening situations that require immediate treatment; for the latter, any delay may be a death sentence. Principle 1 does not provide unambiguous guidance, but it can be used to buttress either choice.

> Principle 2—Equality and inequality. Cancer is today a very high-profile disease. A cancer treatment unit will be established in at least one hospital in the state, no matter what the board of Neighborhood Hospital decides. For the neighborhood residents, however, Neighborhood Hospital is the only chance for receiving timely emergency services; transportation to the next nearest hospital would add 10 to 15 minutes' travel time—too much when every minute counts. Under this principle, neighborhood persons have the ethical right to expect preferred consideration. The social worker, therefore, can support a recommendation in favor of improving emergency services.

Social workers are expected to be open and honest. Among the standards in the Code of Ethics is the expectation that "social workers should not participate in, condone, or be associated with dishonesty, fraud, or deception" (NASW Code, 1999, 4.04). At every step in their education and later in agency practice, social workers are encouraged not to engage in secretive, hidden, or disguised actions or to be manipulative. Much attention has been paid in the literature to efforts to change social agencies, always with the justification that one's efforts are designed to improve services for clients or to attain some general good. In some cases, concealed and unacknowledged action may be thought necessary to gain a greater good for a community or for clients. In these cases, social workers have to weigh the ethical balance between a greater good and hidden actions. What is the best way for the worker to respond in the situation presented in Exemplar 12.8? How should Ed use the information he has? Should he be open and rebut the charges of the opponents? Should he retaliate and fight fire with fire behind the scenes? Should he use the facts he possesses with strategically located opinion molders to undermine the influence of the real estate group?

Hardina (2004) explored the ways in which community organizers encounter ethical dilemmas in practice. Concepts such as self-determination, informed consent, and

<table>
<tr><td>**12.8**</td><td>HOW TO FIGHT THE HALF-TRUTHS OF THE REAL ESTATE LOBBY</td></tr>
</table>

Ed Corey is a community organizer employed by a social agency to develop new housing in a neighborhood. Ed staffs a community coalition that is vigorously working on the new housing. The early activities of the coalition were very successful, but powerful real estate interests who wanted to block the development of the new housing began to spread rumors about Ed's personal history and life. They also used deceptive and distorted facts in advertisements to destroy the coalition's efforts and to undercut Ed's potential influence.

Ed, for his part, knows about the shady dealings of some members of the real estate group. He senses there will be no new housing unless aggressive action is taken, but he is unsure what he should do to combat the half-truths and lies of the opponents of the new housing. How should Ed use the information he has? Should he be open and rebut the charges of the opponents? Should he retaliate and fight fire with fire behind the scenes? Should he use the facts he possesses with strategically located opinion molders to undermine the influence of the real estate group?

protection of confidentiality are relevant to both micro and macro practice, but their application in community organization is different than in direct or clinical practice. She identifies the values inherent in community practice, describes ethical issues encountered, and examines available tools for resolving common ethical dilemmas.

Among the ethical dilemmas Hardina (2004) identifies for community organizers are conflicts of interest and choice of tactics. Many community organizers are members of the neighborhood or community they are trying to organize. The interventions involved in the organizing effort may force the organizer to choose between loyalty to the organizing effort and participants and friends, relatives, and other neighborhood residents. Patronizing some concerns so as to obtain information may create a conflict with other businesses in the area, influencing who can be involved in the organizing effort and how. Financial conflicts can also occur when an organizing group invests in some businesses in the community only to find that their organizing efforts will help or hinder their organization's own investments, creating conflicts of interest. Conflicts may also occur when organizers develop friendships, sexual relationships, or inappropriate personal boundaries with persons involved in the organizing efforts. Furthermore, the choice of tactics, including confrontational tactics, may present ethical dilemmas for organizers. Will the ends to be attained justify the tactics chosen to pursue the outcome?

Hardina introduces several tools for use by community organizers to deal with the ethical dilemmas they encounter, including the Code of Ethics, the ethical principles screen presented earlier in this book, and an ethical decision-making framework for organizers (Reisch & Lowe, 2000). Hardina then suggests the practitioner construct her own ethics model using the above mentioned tools, to which can be added other principles such as mutual learning and empowerment to develop a personal framework to be used in community practice. Efforts to develop ethical decision-making literature and exploration of issues in social work with community groups and in macro practice are in their initial stages, although both areas of practice deal continuously with ethical dilemmas.

EXERCISES

1. In a group, discuss how technologies present ethical dilemmas for your agencies and for social workers. Identify how these ethical dilemmas could be avoided and/or dealt with ethically.
2. You are serving on the committee in Exemplar 12.1, "What the Pine Tree Insurance Company Wants." Which of the options suggested by committee members would you choose? What standards in the Code of Ethics support your choice?
3. Have a class discussion or debate about whether evidence-based practice is ethically necessary.
4. If you are confronted by the ethical dilemma that faces the director of social work in Exemplar 12.7, "Establishing a Cancer Treatment Unit," what do you think your decision would be? What arguments support your decision? What arguments exist contrary to your point of view?

SUGGESTIONS FOR ADDITIONAL READINGS

Keefe, Hall, and Corvo (2002) examined a sample of clinical social workers, psychologists, and psychiatrists to determine what percentage of their caseloads consisted of persons who had been denied reimbursement by managed care organizations for ongoing therapy. Their findings have potential ethical and legal complications for private practitioners. Santhiveeran (2004) presents an historical overview of e-therapy and the current state of the art as it relates to social work. Available research is evaluated and ethical concerns based on the NASW Code of Ethics are considered. Marziali, Donahue, and Crossin (2005) report on Internet video conferencing supports for family caregivers of persons with neurodegenerative disease (dementia, stroke, and Parkinson's disease) and discuss the professional and ethical implications of providing clinical interventions using the Internet.

WEB SITES OF INTEREST

- The University of Maryland, Baltimore Health and Human Services Library provides links to a number of evidence-based practice resources: www.hshsl.umaryland.edu/resources/evidence.html
- Haworth Press publishes the *Journal of Evidence-Based Social Work:* www.haworthpress.com/store/product.asp?sku=J394
- The NASW and ASWB Standards for Technology and Social Work Practice are available at: www.socialworkers.org/practice/standards/NASWTechnologyStandards.pdf
- For a review of transcranial magnetic stimulation see Martin et al. [2002] in the Cochrane Library at: www.cochraneconsumer.com

CHAPTER 13

WHOSE RESPONSIBILITY ARE PROFESSIONAL ETHICS?

Ethical decision making is often presented in a way that suggests the social worker who must make a decision is completely alone and cut off from every support system that might give her guidance. Many have questioned this view. Philosopher W. D. Walsh (1969) wrote, "Morality is first and foremost a social institution, performing a social role, and only secondarily, if at all, a field for individual self-expression" (cited in Frankena, 1980, p. 33).

While every social worker is, of course, responsible for her ethical decisions, it must be recognized that she is a participant in a number of networks and social systems that support—or should support—her ethical decision making. One of the purposes of the Code is to help social workers "identify relevant considerations when professional obligations conflict or ethical uncertainties arise" (NASW Code, 1999, Purpose of the NASW Code of Ethics). Decision making, however, always occurs within a social setting that influences, rewards, or guides certain behaviors and limits, while it sanctions or disapproves others. The social agency employing the social worker is one such setting; the service delivery team, unit, or office is another; and the professional association is a third. Any discussion of steps designed to facilitate and strengthen ethical decision making is incomplete if it fails to take these systems into consideration. Professional ethical actions are not only a result of individual choices.

Organizations also must play a part in supporting correct ethical decision making by social workers. Essential to all techniques that agencies employ to establish ethical norms and enhance ethical conduct (e.g., staff education and training, accountability systems, etc.) is the establishment of an ethical climate in the agency that is visible, deemed important, and understood by all participants. The establishment of such a climate involves the use of the executive leadership influence and the participation of staff members and other parties at every level of the system to ensure high ethical standards throughout the work and life of the agency (Grundstein-Amado, 1999).

RESOURCES THAT SUPPORT ETHICAL DECISION MAKING

Whereas there will never be a time when clear guidelines will be available for every ethical decision that a social worker must make, various societal and institutional mechanisms have been developed to provide guidance and support. In this chapter we will discuss a number of mechanisms that may be particularly helpful for social workers.

CLIENTS' BILL OF RIGHTS

Many hospitals and other service organizations distribute a bill of rights to new clients and patients. These brief statements inform people of the type of information they are entitled to know about their situation. They are also told they can expect to be treated with dignity and respect, they will participate in decision making about their situation, they will be informed about available options, and they have a right to speak to an ombudsman or other person if they are dissatisfied with their treatment.

Social workers should consider the use of a clear and informative statement to inform new clients about what they can expect from the professional personnel they will encounter, the mechanisms for raising questions or seeking clarification where needed, and the procedures for registering grievances. While social workers can and should inform their clients about these things, transmitting such information verbally is *not* a bill of rights. That must be in writing and can be issued only by the agency, not by the individual social worker. The situation is different for those in private practice, who can and should issue such a written document to every new client. The document should include statements about what the client can and cannot expect to happen in the professional service.

AGENCY RISK AUDITS

Many types of audits are conducted in human service agencies—financial, safety, quality control, and utilization review. Agencies can also conduct an audit of professional knowledge of social work ethics that can include two major foci: (1) social workers' knowledge of identified ethics-related risks (such as complaints and lawsuits filed against social workers, ethics committees' past experience, and court cases not specific to social work but with implications for social workers and social agencies) in their field of service and practice settings; and (2) current agency procedures for handling ethical issues, dilemmas, and decisions. Among the ethical risks are client rights, confidentiality and privacy, informed consent, service delivery, boundary issues, conflicts of interest, documentation, defamation of character, client records, supervision, staff development and training, consultation, client referrals, fraud, termination of services and client abandonment, practitioner impairment, and evaluation and research. Agencies that periodically engage in social work ethics audits have the opportunity to strengthen their own ethical performance, but they also provide support and preparation for practitioners and supervisors, thus sharing as an organization the burden of ethical decision making by staff members (Reamer, 2001).

The importance of ethics risk management has begun to be recognized in social work and other human service professions. The social work ethics audit provides for systematic attention to steps that can minimize the likelihood of harm to clients and staff, prevent ethics complaints, and prevent lawsuits alleging some kind of ethics-related negligence. Kirkpatrick, Reamer, and Skyulski (2006) conducted and reported on an ethics audit in three health care settings that were part of a large hospital corporation affiliated with a medical school. The results for each of the sites differed, but the most significant risks were related to policies and procedures concerning informed consent (e.g., interpreter and translation for non–English speaking persons; and handling of confidential information, such as disclosure of a patient's substance abuse history or sensitive information to managed care organizations); maintenance of proper boundaries with patients (e.g., developing friendships with patients); supervision of staff (e.g., frequency, quality, and documentation of supervision); staff consultation (e.g., when and how to obtain consultation); and documenting ethical decisions The audit provided administrators and staff with opportunities to examine their policies and practices, identify risk areas, and develop strategies for improving their handling of ethical issues (Kirkpatrick, Reamer, & Skyulski, 2006).

In addition, a series of guidelines regarding documentation have been developed that can help ensure risk-management standards to enhance the delivery of services to clients and to protect practitioners who may be required to defend themselves against ethics complaints brought either to state licensing boards or to NASW. Reamer (2005) places these guidelines into four categories: (1) content of documentation, (2) language and terminology, (3) credibility, and (4) access to records and documents. Essentially, these guidelines suggest balancing detail against overly sparse recordkeeping, as well as careful uses of language. "Too much content, too little content, or the wrong content can harm clients and expose practitioners to considerable risk of liability" (Reamer, 2005, p. 328). Too little detail in some circumstances can compromise the quality of service so that an "on call" backup person only has vague or incomplete information for dealing with the situation, or the record of steps taken has insufficient detail in the event of a complaint or lawsuit. Be cautious with personal notes when documenting services to families and couples in a unified record, and be careful not to expose confidential information, as records and personal notes may be subpoenaed. Social workers should also avoid defamatory language, acknowledge errors, be familiar with relevant laws, and make certain records are secure.

PEER REVIEW AND COMMITTEES ON THE ETHICS OF SOCIAL WORK PRACTICE

Peer review permits a social worker to test her ethical decision making against that of her colleagues, either informally in groups that practitioners create for mutual aid or formally in agencies. In the past, social workers have used informal groupings to review their professional practice decisions. Such groupings can also be useful for reviewing ethical decisions. Peer review groups are particularly important for social workers in private practice because they are more isolated than workers in agency-based practice and because they have less opportunity for interaction with peers. Controls and accountability of private practice social workers depend almost entirely upon the sensitivity and knowledge of the individual practitioner. Peer pressures, which are so immediate in agency practice, are much less evident in private practice. Because of these considerations, social workers in private practice may want to organize peer review systems that are specifically geared to review their ethical decision making. In this way, they can be more certain that their decisions will be of the highest quality.

Each agency should establish a *Committee on the Ethics of Social Work Practice*, analogous to Human Research Protections Offices (HRPO) or Institutional Review Boards (IRB) that exist in every academic research organization. Practitioners who have an ethical question may consult with the committee about a problem. Such a committee is a forum where social workers can think through difficult ethical questions occurring in everyday practice. Most important, this committee can be the locus for the routine monitoring of ethical practice within the agency.

As a service to current members, the NASW Office of Ethics and Professional Review provides ethics consultations to those who are experiencing an ethical dilemma. These consultations guide people through the Code and point them toward the relevant standards related to their concerns. Dialogues may help members to make ethical decisions. Members may be referred to particular resources if the questions are not related to ethics but to legal issues or standards of social work practice.

Accountability Systems

Professional social workers working in agencies or in private practice will be held accountable for their professional activities. Courts, third-party payers, governmental regulators, and empowered clients and patients as citizens play roles in regard to accountability in our increasingly litigious society. Social agencies are accountable for what they do. Social agencies that want to implement this responsibility in a positive way must develop and operate accountability systems. These systems are characterized by the following features: information systems and monitoring; methods for sampling activities and decisions; clear indicators of the desired quality of performance; clear indicators or criteria of the desired quantity; and feedback systems that permit an early alert to problem situations.

Accountability systems relate primarily to practice performance, but there is no reason why such systems could not incorporate additional indicators that focus on the ethical aspects of practice. Just as agencies evaluate the effectiveness and efficiency of the services they deliver and the social work practices of their social work employees, agencies can also track and evaluate systematically the ethical decision making of social work practitioners.

Training and Consultation

Most agencies make a heavy investment in providing in-service training, continuing education opportunities, and consultation for their staff. Though the focus is often on more effective practice and more efficient administration, these sessions should also include a focus on the ethical implications of practice in order to strengthen the ethical level of practice. Social workers in private practice are expected to continue learning about ethical decision making and the further development of their ethical decision-making abilities. Many states now require ethics content as part of the continuing education requirements for relicensure, a factor which may help encourage social workers to remain current in their ethics knowledge.

AGENCY APPEALS PROCEDURES AND OMBUDSMEN

Many agencies have appeals procedures, but clients are often not aware of them. "Forgetting" to inform clients about them may simplify the life of the practitioners and administrators, but this does not make for a high level of ethical practice. The use of appeals procedures does more than correct mistakes made by social workers. One of their most valuable functions is to sensitize social workers to the ethical aspects of practice. An ombudsman or another type of appeals procedure should be readily available to clients, who should be able to use these procedures without any risk of stigma. Ethical social workers will welcome such strategies. Administrative review procedures also have a place in the support system, but they do not take the place of appeals procedures freely available to clients.

PROFESSIONAL ASSOCIATIONS

Professional associations, such as NASW, can play a key role in strengthening ethical practice. The promulgation and periodic revision of the Code needs to be strengthened through the inclusion of case references and interpretive guidelines because the standards of practice and the limits of ethical behavior are difficult to define. Jayaratne et al. (1997) found in a study of Michigan NASW members that there is much confusion and disagreement as to what constitutes appropriate ethical practice. Maidment (2006) argues that in the current context there is a need to explore client/worker relationship boundaries that fall both within and outside conventional ethical professional practice. She argues there are alternative interpretations that can be useful regarding relationship, reciprocity, love, touch, and spirituality, thus suggesting that the NASW and other professional associations of social workers must develop additional strategies if they want to encourage clarification and strengthening of ethical decision making within the profession. The following are some of the ways to do so:

- Continue to revise and refine the Code of Ethics. It may be helpful to add case precedents.
- Encourage the formation of formal and informal groups to study and review critical ethical decisions arising from actual practice experiences.
- Develop a data bank of precedents with ethical implications. Knowledge about ethical decisions is valuable, but identifying and learning about those actions found to be unethical can also have positive consequences, including being instructive and warning members of the profession.
- Continue to schedule activities that focus on the ethical aspects of practice, both at professional conferences and as part of continuing education programs.

- In addition to discussion of monthly dilemmas on NASW's Web site, publish an "Ethics Reporter" or a regular ethics column in *Social Work* or in the *NASW News* in order to make social workers more familiar with their Code of Ethics.
- Further develop NASW's ethics hotline so that practitioners, supervisors, and administrators can obtain advice on ethical issues that arise in their practice. Modern communication technologies, such as instant messaging and electronic mail, can provide instant communication over long distances. At the same time, these technologies give the consultant sufficient time to reflect on the question or to consult with others.
- The NASW should publish an annual report, as does the American Psychological Association, regarding the number and types of ethical complaints investigated and the disposition of those cases.
- State licensing boards can also play a part in reporting on their activities and in other ways educating practitioners, supervisors, and administrators in their respective states.

It is desirable that the professional organization and its local chapters, as well as individual social agencies, begin to collect data on ethical decision making. Such a data bank should not be limited to "success stories" but should also include errors, unanswerable questions, and embarrassing situations. Collection of this type of data will be helpful to practitioners as well as to students. This information will explicate the ethical quandaries experienced by social workers, the preferred solutions, and the results achieved. Such a data bank will also be helpful in the creation of case materials, which are so necessary for the systematic development of new social work knowledge. Just as lawyers can draw on case law for guidance in making the difficult decisions, so social workers should be able to receive guidance from the suggested data bank.

NASW PROFESSIONAL COMPLAINT PROCEDURES

Requests for professional review (RPRs) may be submitted in the event of an alleged violation of the NASW Code of Ethics by the following:

- An individual who has engaged in a professional social work relationship with an NASW member
- A group of individuals in an agency or organization who have direct knowledge of an NASW member's professional conduct within a professional social work relationship or setting
- An individual on behalf of another person as long as that person is either mentally or physically incapacitated, or is a minor child, and the person to bring such an action on behalf of the incapacitated adult or minor has proper standing
- An individual who has concerns that his or her actions in a situation may have violated the NASW Code of Ethics

The individual against whom the RPR is filed must have been a member of the NASW at the time of the alleged violation.

In addition to particular forms being completed and filed, as well as other procedural matters, a complainant must describe how the alleged misconduct violated the NASW Code of Ethics by citing specific standards from the Code. Whenever possible, hearings and mediation sessions will be conducted by members of the NASW chapter where the violations under review were alleged to have occurred. If a chapter fails to take timely action, the National Ethics Committee may assume jurisdiction. Certain alleged actions will be referred for adjudication, whereas others will be referred for mediation (NASW, 2005).

ETHICS ADVOCACY, HUMAN SERVICES AGENCIES, AND INTERDISCIPLINARY TEAMS

Social workers are employed at a great variety of human service and other sites where members of the staffs include social workers and other professionals, all of whom may have varying statuses and exert varying degrees of control. Participation in those interdisciplinary situations means working with other social workers, psychologists, nurses, physicians, correctional personnel, as well as representatives of other disciplines. Both in settings where the predominant profession is social work and in other settings where other professions play prominent roles, social workers loyal to the social work Code of Ethics may have to engage in effective ethical advocacy. Dodd and Jansson (2004) recommend that social workers attain knowledge and skills that will allow them to contribute effectively in ethical discussions involving social workers and clients or patients, as well as other professionals.

Among the strategies Dodd and Jansson (2004) propose to promote an organization's ability to deal with power and politics in relation to ethical decision making are: seeking written protocols that identify the need for and nature of social work participation in ethical decision making by the team; seeking multidisciplinary ethical training sessions; and educating the members of other professions about the potential role of social workers in ethical decision making. Prior to involvement with the ethical decision making of interdisciplinary groups, social workers must develop their own knowledge of the ethics of the social work profession and the group. They must also develop advocacy skills as well as feelings of self-efficacy that can make them effective advocates for clients and patients. Finally, they must find constructive ways of interacting with other professionals in the ethical decision-making processes.

In this final chapter, we have presented ideas that may help social workers in their search for more effective ethical practice. The values of the social work profession form the background for ethical decision making. In turn, ethical decision making is the cornerstone for ethical practice. Ethical decision making begins with familiarity with the Code of Ethics and the clarification of one's own values. Knowledge of what one really believes is an inescapable basic step for social workers seeking to strengthen their ethical practice. Beyond this, it becomes important for social workers to clarify the values of society and of the various groups with which they work. Clarification of these values permits social workers to become more sensitive to and more aware of the values of others and of possible conflicts between different value systems.

Individual practitioners sometimes feel they are alone when facing ethical dilemmas, but there are others who can share these ethical problems. Formal peer review, agency consultations, and the professional association must share the burden of thinking through these dilemmas. Some persons have suggested that ethics do not exist outside of community. To base ethical decisions strictly on one's individual conscience can lead a person into very difficult situations and into playing God. All ethics are integral to community. There are many reasons for a professional social worker to connect with the professional community. Fellow professionals can provide opportunities to think through ethical questions and dilemmas, to discuss one's ethical concerns with other social work professionals, and to gain colleague support in seeking the most ethical of ethical decisions.

RETURNING TO THE BEGINNING

Early in the first chapter of this book, we began our case exemplar of Basanti Madurai, whom our social worker Ellen Aston had just met. We've returned to Basanti and Ellen several times in this book, adding information each time, much like an actual case might slowly be unveiled. As we end this book, let us assume that it is now two years later, and we find:

> About a year ago, Basanti stopped attending the South Asian women's support group that Ellen ran. During the past year, Ellen has occasionally seen Basanti in the community; when they meet they always say hello and chat for a few minutes in a friendly manner. On their most recent meeting, Basanti mentioned that things are going very well for her, and that she would like to give something back to the group that helped her so much. She asked Ellen if they could schedule a time to meet as friends and to discuss ways that Basanti could help with the South Asian women's support group.

> How should Ellen respond to this request? What are the possible ethical dilemmas involved, and where could Ellen turn for help with reaching an ethical decision?

EXERCISES

1. Identify your strengths and limitations in regard to ethical decision making when you are engaged in social work practice. How can you better prepare yourself for being an ethical social worker?
2. Identify in your field instruction placement, your agency of employment, or other social agency what you consider to be the limitations of the ethical decision-making patterns used. If you could improve one thing about ethical decision making in this organization, what would you choose to alter and how could you go about trying to improve the situation?
3. Review the NASW Procedures for Professional Review (2005) to become familiar with the filing of a complaint with the professional association.

SUGGESTIONS FOR ADDITIONAL READINGS

Strom-Gottfried (2003) helps practitioners and others to increase their understanding of ad-judication as she reviews the origins, targets, and outcomes of ethics complaints. Kelly (2005) in "Beyond Problem-Solving: The Social Worker as Risk Manager and Educator in

Educational Host Settings" describes how social workers in educational host settings engage in risk management and ethics education to address ethical dilemmas encountered in school settings. Advocacy has been inherent in social work and a number of the standards in the Code suggest the importance of serving as advocates. Whistle-blowing is explored by Greene and Latting (2004) as a means to protect clients' rights and as an ethical means.

WEB SITES OF INTEREST

- You can find a copy of the NASW (2005) Procedures for Professional Review, Revised at: www.socialworkers.org/nasw/ethics/procedures.pdf
- The Ohio University Institute for Applied and Professional Ethics (see http://freud.citl. ohiou.edu/ethics/) has an "Ask the E-Team!" resource that allows you to e-mail them a question about applied or professional ethics: http://freud.citl.ohiou.edu/ethics/index. php?type=services&record=1

Additional Exemplars APPENDIX **A**

1. **Individual or Family Therapy?**
   The parents and adolescents in the Martin family have been having problems. There has been a series of incidents in which everyone involved has been shouting at each other, calling each other names, or not talking to each other for days. Christine Martin feels that she has failed as a mother. She asked Molly Aberdeen, a private practice social worker, to help her cope with her feelings. After talking with Christine, Molly felt that the problem went beyond Christine's feelings and that family therapy was indicated. Even though Molly is a competent social worker, she has had no training or experience in providing family therapy. However, there are no family therapists in this rural county. At first, Molly assessed the problem in such a way that individual intervention was appropriate. At least, this assessment makes it possible for her to help Christine. Hopefully, this will lead to changes in the family situation. Or, failing that, Christine will be able to cope more successfully. Is it ethical for Molly to prepare on her own to do family therapy and treat the family? Or to only offer individual therapy to Christine? What should she do?

2. **Praying with a Client**
   Madeleine Koenig, a social worker, has been seeing Sarah Lochdale weekly for more than a year. Things have not gone well for Sarah. She came to the agency shortly after she lost her job as an administrative assistant at a health services organization. Soon she found another job but that proved to be short-lived. She has struggled with depression for much of the time she has been seen in the agency. Her teenage children have also been encountering problems in high school, and they bring their concerns home to her, but she feels she can't really cope. Her savings held out for a while, but lately

227

she has been borrowing from her relatives, who have been kind but can't continue to support her family much longer. This morning in her weekly session, Sarah left the chair she was seated in and knelt on the floor, obviously intending to pray. Then she looked up at Madeleine with tears in her eyes and asked Madeleine to join her. Madeleine is an agnostic and the agency is nonsectarian. Does Madeleine have an ethical problem? If yes, what is it? What is the ethical thing to do?

3. **Report Drug Paraphernalia or Not?**
    Zacharia Jones is a social worker in a child development program run by a Beach County voluntary social agency for children. The program has a liaison relationship with the local child protective services but is not part of the Department of Social Services. This morning Zacharia was assigned to visit the home of Virginia Dabney to make an assessment of the situation: Virginia's daughter, Beatrice, has not attended the early childhood program for three days and phone calls made to the home were unanswered. This morning when he visited the home for discussions with Virginia, Zacharia observed what appeared to be illegal drug paraphernalia. Virginia showed no signs of being on drugs. It was unclear whether she uses drugs or not. It turned out that her daughter was sick with a virus and the doctor she consulted told her to keep her daughter home until the illness cleared up. Obviously, she was not neglecting her child. During his training period, Zacharia was told that if he is on a home visit and observes illegal drugs in the home, he is not to report the presence of the drugs to either legal authorities or child protective services because to do so would destroy any possible constructive relationship with the client and cost the agency reimbursement for its service. Furthermore, the word would go out in the neighborhood and interfere with serving other families. The training personnel and his supervisor suggest that the relationship with the client takes priority over all else because the relationship is necessary for the good of the child. The problem Zacharia perceives, however, is that he knows the law demands that he report the paraphernalia. What should he do? Follow the training guidelines he received that have been reinforced by his supervisor? Suggest to Virginia that if she is using the illegal drugs she could use the local substance abuse counseling services? Tell Virginia that he will report his observations to law enforcement? Forget what he saw? Who is he responsible to? The child? Virginia? The state and the law? His supervisor? The agency?

4. **Reimbursement? Discontinuing Treatment or What?**
    Teenagers sent to the Lasswell Residential treatment facility are hostile, sullen, and angry young people. Many of them have family health insurance, and the staff has to check with the insurance company to determine the length of acceptable treatment. Ordinarily, the insurance company believes that intensive therapy can be accomplished in 30 days. The young residents and the social workers have to form a trusting relationship for the work together to be done at all. Most of the residents take from 30 to 60 days before they are willing to let down their guard and reveal the issues personal

and otherwise that are bothering them, including issues related to their families' functioning. What should the social worker do when the insurance company informs the treatment center it will not pay for treatment beyond next week and the agency administrators say clearly that the treatment center cannot keep residents without payment? Discharge the resident? File a claim and appeal to the state insurance commission? Try to involve agencies in the local community where the resident lives that will also be interested in some kind of payment, if the agency is equipped to help the youth? If local services can be found, based on past experiences there are few chances the resident and family will follow through. It seems that either way, the young person and the family are set up for failure. What is the ethical thing to do?

5. **A Shortage of Beds**
While working on an inpatient oncology unit in an acute care hospital, Viveca Chin, a social worker, was told by the physician to discuss follow-up care with the family of a terminally ill patient, Sam Marino. The order also indicated the patient could be discharged today. The patient was too out of it to participate in any discussion, but his wife and family members were distraught. They didn't understand that Sam couldn't remain in the hospital today but had to choose either home or inpatient hospice care. At the same time, social workers were told to get as many patients out of the hospital today as possible because the hospital is short of beds. The patient's physician was unavailable and the resident physician was reluctant to meet with the family. Viveca thought about delaying discharge and a referral until the end of the day because doing so might keep Sam in the hospital for a day or two longer. What should she do? To whom does Viveca owe loyalty: Sam, his family, his physician, the hospital?

6. **A Little Extra Will Make Her Life More "Worth Living"**
Marie Cummings is in her early 70s, lives by herself, and ekes by financially. In previous years, she received Low Income Home Energy Assistance (LIHEAP). She just told you that she purposely stopped paying her heating bills—even though she can afford to do so—with the expectation that she will also receive help this year. This strategy has proven successful for several years and earns her some scarce evenings out at bingo. She feels doing so makes her life "worth living." It is your understanding that the funds available for this program are more limited this year. Marie's strategy is helpful for her, but you also know there are more applicants this year than last whose needs are as great as or even greater than Marie's. What ethical issues are involved here? What should you do?

7. **Who Decides?**
Rochelle Diego is 82 years old and has been disabled and living at home. Gradually her physical abilities have been eroding. In fact, her physical abilities have deteriorated much more and faster than her cognitive abilities. She has become more dependent physically but remains intellectually alert and active. It appears that her caretaker during the day has been neglecting

her. Although there is no hard evidence, there is a suspicion that her caretaker may also be abusing her. Rochelle, however, has been very protective of the caretaker and makes no suggestions of dissatisfaction. Sophia Breckenridge, her social worker, feels Rochelle needs to become a resident of a nursing home. Although no proof of neglect or abuse exists, she obviously needs more care than can be provided by a visiting home health care aide and a day worker. Whenever the topic is raised, Rochelle refuses to be moved. A close younger friend once offered to care for her if she were moved to the friend's spacious home. After Rochelle agreed to do so, several of Rochelle's adult children were furious with her and forced her to back out. But none of them offered to care for her in their homes. There was also an attempt to transfer her to a nursing home but other adult children objected. What should Sophia do? After all, Rochelle's thoughts are generally clear, but she does not recognize or accept her physical disabilities. Who should decide what to do, especially since Rochelle is growing more and more feeble?

8. **Tradition and Family? Or?**
   You have been seeing a quiet but very bright young high school student, an immigrant woman from Ethiopia. She has been offered a full scholarship and room and board at the prestigious Parkside Preparatory School. She says the offer creates a conflict with her traditional family. Her parents want her to marry and have children. Education is for men. She wants to go to school, but her family feels that if she does so, she will be betraying her family and culture. She is sad, torn, and confused. She asks you what she should do. Does it make a difference if you are an ardent feminist? What if you are also an Ethiopian immigrant?

9. **Mrs. Walker or Her Husband?**
   You are seeing Susan Walker for a first session at the base. You learn that her husband is a helicopter pilot and she tells you that she cannot stand his continual drinking. She has come to see you to get help living with the situation. Captain Walker regularly goes on beer-drinking binges, and although he has never been abusive to her or their children, he often passes out and collapses into bed. Susan asks for treatment for herself but strongly resists your reporting her husband's behavior. Furthermore, she says that if you report her husband she won't continue in treatment and will move out of the house. She says if you "tell," you will be responsible for anything that occurs in her family—after all, they are getting along now. What should you do? Does his behavior make it difficult for him to perform his duties safely? Is this a life-threatening situation? To whom do you owe loyalty? Susan? The military? Society? Should you reveal Susan's confidences or keep quiet and begin work with her, hoping you can do something later about her husband's flying and drinking? Can you find guidance in the Code as to what your correct actions should be?

10. **Should I Tell?**

Amanda Winterspoon is a licensed social worker employed by a general hospital in a small town. She has been active in general discharge planning and providing therapy for psychiatric patients after they are discharged from the psychiatry unit. Also, she has developed a small private practice outside the hospital. Over the years, Amanda has developed excellent work relationships with nurses and physicians. She is highly respected. Last week, she was in an automobile accident and was seriously injured so that she could not reach her patients, who did not know what happened to her or where she is. A long-standing social work colleague and friend—Sarita Bonhomme—called the social work department to inquire about Amanda's situation. The social worker who answered the call told her that because Amanda was an employee, no information about her could be given out, including whether she was a patient or not. Sarita explained that, as a social worker and old friend, she wanted to know how things were going for Amanda, but she also wanted to respond to several patients who anxiously inquired as to Amanda's whereabouts. Again, she was told that no information could be given to her. What is the ethical thing for the hospital social worker to do in this situation?

11. **Is an Indeterminate Agreement Binding?**

Ruth Martini, a single mother of two young children, had accomplished so much working at the Libertyville Mental Health Center. She was well respected by her colleagues and was promoted to supervisor by this mental health clinic, which was owned by two psychiatrists who—in addition to being owners—saw patients and consulted with the staff. The time was rapidly approaching when Ruth should move on. Not only was she sure she was ready to establish a private practice, but her family needed additional income and this was the only way she could earn more. As a result, she decided to keep her job but also see patients privately on a part-time basis. She decided that she could approach Julie Goodheart, a middle-aged and middle-class patient with whom she had been working successfully and helpfully for over a year. She would let her know she would be leaving the agency sometime in the near future. If Julie were interested, perhaps Ruth could see her privately. After all, Julie had dealt successfully with the problems she brought to the agency and was going to terminate treatment within the next couple of months. There was only one "fly" in the "ointment." When Ruth was hired by the center, she agreed verbally to a contract not to see agency clients privately, either while she was employed by the center or for an undefined period following her termination of employment. Does Julie's right to self-determination overrule any commitment to the agency? Would Ruth's patients have a right to follow her if she left the agency if she did not tell them she was doing so but they found that she was in private practice? Would agreeing to an indeterminate period forbidding a private practice impose an undue hardship on Ruth? She owes loyalty to the agency but also to herself and her family. What are her choices and what should she do?

12. **To Report or Not?**

A number of undocumented immigrants recently showed up at the Evergreen Family Social Service Resource Center. The majority of the agency's funds come from state revenues and taxpayers. The immigrants have serious financial, food, and housing needs and are typically under great stress. There are laws that demand that workers report undocumented immigrants to immigration authorities. The agency supervisors inform the workers that if one is working with an immigrant family and some members of the family do not have Social Security numbers, they should not be reported to the U.S. Bureau of Citizenship and Immigration Services as it would be detrimental to the helping relationship. Rosa Martinez is a legal resident, but her husband is an undocumented immigrant. Their three children are American citizens because they were born in the United States. Several workers in the agency disagree with the agency's policy to ignore the law. What should a social worker do? On the one hand, social workers are to obey the law. On the other hand, they want to be helpful to the immigrant families who have serious individual and family needs. To whom should the social workers be loyal? The law and citizen taxpayers? The entire family? The state and society?

13. **My Supervisor, My Colleague, or the Children?**

The Riverside Therapeutic Foster Care Agency requires social workers to see foster parents twice every month in their homes. As a social worker you are fulfilling this responsibility, but you have discovered accidentally that your colleague, Rene Flambeau, who joined the staff within the past six months, has not done so for several families. When he told you about this situation, he explained to you that these parents have jobs where they work odd and changing evening hours. He has found it almost impossible to visit them regularly. As a result, he lies to his supervisor, who is also your supervisor. You are now meeting with your supervisor, Clem LaPoint, with whom you have a long, friendly, and trusting relationship. Clem unexpectedly asks you about Rene's frequency of visits to foster homes. What should you do? Be loyal to the hardworking families? The children in foster care? Your colleague? Your friend and supervisor? The agency?

14. **My Patient or My Son?**

Fran Reilly is a social worker who has a well-deserved reputation in Pittsfield because of her outstanding work with adolescents. She has been working for approximately a year with Millicent Jasowitz, a shy, lonely young woman, who goes to school but has little other social life. This morning quite by accident Fran learned that her son, Wally, who is a loner and has been unpopular for some time both in middle school and in his new high school, has had a couple of "dates" with Millicent, her patient. What should Fran do? She has a very good relationship with Millicent, who is making good progress in treatment, and she also is hopeful that Wally has begun to make a relationship with another teenager. Is this a dual relationship by proxy? Should she discontinue treatment with Millicent? She cannot imagine asking her son to discontinue his relationship with Millicent. What should she do?

15. A Fellow Student May Be Impaired

Cynthia Messing is a graduate student in social work. She is a highly motivated student who enrolled in the school after several years practice in a drug and alcohol abuse program. She is friendly and forms good relationships with faculty members, field instructors, and her fellow students. Yesterday one of her fellow students, Claudia Arroz, told her confidentially that she thinks Erika Luft—another classmate—has a substance abuse problem. She said she was speaking to Cynthia because she knows she has work experience in substance abuse and because she didn't trust the faculty member who teaches this class. Cynthia asked her how she knew. Claudia said that she noticed Erika has missed several sessions and knows the faculty member has not discussed absences with Erika. Erika is forgetful, told Claudia she often doesn't feel well, did not pull her weight on a group assignment, misses meetings at their field placement, and is very "touchy." Despite the fact that Cynthia is a student and not yet a professional social worker, she understands that student social workers have a responsibility to live up to the standards of the NASW Code of Ethics. What is her responsibility in this situation to Claudia, Erika, the faculty member teaching the course, the school, profession, and herself? What should Cynthia Messing do?

16. Stabilized and Ready to Go Frees a Bed

Three weeks ago Joseph Clark was admitted involuntarily to Los Gatos Mental Hospital following a psychotic episode. He has been involved in a fracas at a local library and caused a disturbance on the street, which resulted in the police taking him to a hospital emergency room, which in turn led to his being admitted to Los Gatos. Jeremy Blake is a social worker who is assigned to the unit in which Joseph is housed and to Joseph's case. The unit has a long waiting list. Joseph is stabilized but resists taking his medications. Today Jeremy was asked by the unit's psychiatrist to somehow persuade Joseph to take his meds so he can be discharged, thus opening a bed for the unit. What ethical issues does this raise and what should Jeremy do?

17. St. Louis or Singapore?

Several relatives of Derrick Lin, a native of Singapore, crowded into a St. Louis hospital room to meet with a social worker, Linda Flowers, to hear the news that Derrick's kidney cancer is incurable. Derrick was in another room. As soon as his relatives heard the prognosis, they were immediately unanimous in their opinion and made it clear to Linda that they did not want him to know his prognosis. They told Linda that in Singapore the practice of informing a patient of his diagnosis is left to the family's discretion and it was extremely important to the family that their culture be respected. Linda wondered what she should do. Should she simply tell the oncologist the family demands Derrick not be told his prognosis and tell the physician of their reasons? However, American doctors take action only with the approval of their patients, and only after fully informing them of their prognoses. Should she advocate for the relatives' point of view? What role, if any, should Derrick play in any discussions? Who should decide?

18. **Testing and Treatment for All?**
A state department of social services (DSS) developed a new program to evaluate potential recipients for depression or substance abuse before they enter the public assistance system. The program has been a success and clients interviewed who are in the program felt it helped them to get back to work because they were treated for depression. You are employed by another state's DSS that has created a similar but different program. Only clients who are receiving cash assistance qualify for the testing. Those clients who already have a job do not get tested. Most of these persons had just taken the job to qualify for the program to begin with. Those clients who are depressed or have other psychological problems who are forced to work without proper treatment usually get fired or quit one job after another. They end up experiencing even more failure, which deepens their depression. A suggestion has been made that a psychiatric assessment should be required for every DSS client and those who are found to have emotional problems should be forced into treatment in order to receive payments or to have a job. What stance should you take?

19. **Both Keeping Quiet and Speaking Do Potential Harm**
Brian Philbrick was called by Irene Courtney asking for an appointment with her husband, Dennis, for marital counseling. They had attended four sessions when Dennis requested an individual session. Irene acknowledged the individual session was a good idea and agreed to it. During the individual session, Dennis indicated he was having an affair with a woman with whom he worked. But when it was suggested that he tell this information to Irene, he refused to do so. Brian maintained the confidentiality of this private information, but he was certain that the possibility of successful marital therapy was compromised and now not possible. Not sharing the information threatens the help he can provide and can undermine the communication of the couple and his reputation for competence. Sharing the information breaks the confidentiality of the individual session. Should Brian suggest the couple discontinue treatment with him? What should he do?

20. **To Lie or Just Not Tell Everything?**
A licensed clinical social worker employed in an agency and who has a small private practice receives treatment from a psychiatrist and takes medications prescribed for her depression. She is paying by cash and not through health insurance. She functions adequately at her job, and her evaluations have been at a sufficiently high level. She and her therapist agree that she is capable of serving her private clients effectively. She wants to apply to be

included in a panel of practitioners who will be referred cases and receive third-party payments. The application asks if she has ever had a diagnosis for mental illness. The extra money is important. She has family expenses, and she has to pay for her treatment and medication. What should she do?

21. **Who Has Veto Power?**
Joseph Gerden is a member of a therapy group for recently divorced persons. At the suggestion of his probation officer, he requests that group records be submitted to the court. He may be permitted to visit his 7-year-old son if the records show he has made progress in the group. Another member of the group will not agree under any circumstance to the release of the records. As the facilitator of this group, what should you do?

22. **A Late Night Phone Call**
Your supervisor—Stephanie Hamlet—just called you at 11:30 p.m. at home. She said the state legislature will vote this week to require parental notification of pregnant teenagers seeking abortions. She said, "I know you will want to sign our petition in the morning. Although we have never discussed this issue, I just feel you will agree and want to sign the petition since you have so much empathy for teenagers and their problems." You have no idea how to respond to the comments Stephanie made. Actually, you believe parents should be notified, but your relationship with Stephanie has been less than stellar and your six-month probation evaluation is due soon. Should you tell Stephanie that you don't want to sign the petition? Should you just agree and somehow fail to sign the petition? Should you tell her that you agree with the petition's ideas and will be glad to sign in the morning? What should you do?

autonomy self-determination, self-rule, being able to make free choices.

autonomous ethics ethical systems in which humans determine the moral rules.

beneficence to promote the client's good and take care to prevent, remove, or minimize harm.

client bill of rights a statement distributed to all clients/patients informing them of the information they are entitled to know about their situation, treatment expectations, and participation in decision making; that they will be informed about available options; and that they have a right to speak to an ombudsman or other person if dissatisfied with treatment.

code of ethics a collection of aspirations, regulations, and guidelines that represent the values of a group or profession to which it applies; a compilation of ethical standards.

competence the ability to give informed consent to some or all decisions; clients/patients are located along a range of capabilities, extending from completely competent to those who are somewhat competent to those who are not at all competent.

competing loyalties two or more loyalties that cannot be honored at the same time.

competing values two or more values that cannot be honored at the same time.

confidentiality a rule of duty requiring one entrusted with private or secret matters to refrain from divulging them; a contract not to reveal information about an individual except with his or her consent.

conflict of interest a situation in which a social worker in a position of trust that requires exercising judgment on behalf of clients, agencies, or others has competing professional or personal interests, which can make it difficult to fulfill impartially and objectively her professional duties and/or give the appearance of being unable to do so.

conflicting obligations two or more obligations that cannot be fulfilled at the same time.

deontology a philosophy of ethics holding that ethical rules for the right course of action are self-evident, can be formulated, and should hold under all circumstances.

direct liability supervisors may be charged with ethical breaches or negligence when harm is caused by the supervisor's acts of omission or commission.

dual-role relationship situation in which professionals fill more than one role at a time and should avoid conflicts of interest that interfere with the exercise of professional discretion and impartial judgment, especially to protect clients' interests and not to take unfair advantage of them.

duty to warn an obligation to use reasonable care to protect intended victims, also referred to as the *Tarasoff* principle.

effectiveness criterion the degree to which a desired outcome is achieved.

efficiency criterion relative cost of achieving a stated objective.

ethical absolutism any ethical theory that claims there are ethical rules that hold regardless of society, culture, or religion; correct standards applicable to everyone everywhere.

ethical decision making the process of analyzing and assessing the ethical dimensions of practice in order to develop ethically appropriate professional behavior.

ethical dilemmas choice by the social worker between two or more relevant but contradictory ethical directives; when every alternative results in an undesirable outcome for one or more persons.

ethical problem identifying the right thing to do in a given practice situation.

ethical priorities screen (EPS) a guide for rank-ordering ethical principles and priorities.

ethical relativism the belief that there is no absolute or universal moral standard and what is right or wrong is relative to an individual, group, or culture.

ethical rules screen (ERS) used as a step in ethical decision making by consulting the Code of Ethics for guidance.

ethics branch of philosophy that deals with the rightness or wrongness of human actions.

general ethics the obligations that are owed by one person to another.

group values values held by subgroups within a society.

heteronomous ethics ethical systems that derive moral rules from nonhuman sources.

informed consent the knowledgeable and voluntary agreement by a client/patient to undergo an intervention that is in accord with the patient's values and preferences.

least harm principle when harm will come to someone in the situation, it is the choice of the option that results in the least harm, the least permanent harm, or the most easily reversible harm.

malpractice professional negligence or misconduct; failure to exercise a degree of care that a similar professional of ordinary prudence would demonstrate under the same circumstances.

morality a concern with personally held ethical beliefs, theories of obligation, and the social elements that reinforce ethical decisions.

paternalism the act of overriding the autonomous decisions of a person or making decisions for the person with the intention of benefiting that person.

personal (individual) values the values held by one person but not necessarily by others.

prima facie **correct** apparently correct upon first viewing.

privacy a zone of individual autonomy in which people ought to be free to behave as they wish; the constitutional right protecting individuals from unwarranted governmental interference in intimate personal relations or activities.

privileged communication a legal concept protecting against forced disclosure in legal proceedings that would break a promise of privacy—based on ethical principles of confidentiality and privacy.

professional code of ethics a compilation of values, ethical principles, and ethical standards of a particular profession.

professional ethics codification of the special obligations that arise out of a person's voluntary choice to become a professional, such as a social worker.

professional social work ethics those ethical standards promulgated by the social work profession through its Code of Ethics and other publications.

professional values those values proclaimed by a professional group.

religious ethics ethics based upon a religion and its beliefs.

self-determination a person's right to make his or her own decisions.

situational ethics the position that all ethical decisions must be made in the light of individual circumstances and not according to moral rules or universal laws.

societal values values recognized by major portions of the entire social system or, at least, by the leading members or spokespersons of that system.

teleology philosophy of ethics that justifies ethical decisions on the basis of the context in which they are made or on the basis of the consequences they create.

unethical behavior violations of the profession's principles established by the profession's Code of Ethics.

utilitarianism a philosophy of ethics that defines right action as that which results in the greatest happiness for the greatest number of people.

value dilemmas two or more values that cannot be reconciled and simultaneously enacted.

values preferences that serve as guides or criteria for selecting good or desirable behaviors.

vicarious liability a supervisor is responsible for a supervisee's conduct during the course of employment or field instruction, including ethical lapses.

voluntariness acting on the basis of meaningful and free consent obtained without coercion.

BIBLIOGRAPHY

This bibliography lists the books and articles cited in this book, as well as additional literature on ethical problems in professional practice that may be of interest to the reader.

Abbott, A. A. (1999). Measuring social work values: A cross-cultural challenge for global practice. *International Social Work, 42*(4), 455–470.

Abbott, A. A. (2003). A confirmatory factor analysis of the Professional Opinion Scale: A values assessment instrument. *Research on Social Work Practice, 13*(5), 641–666.

Abney, P. C., & Maddux, C. D. (2004). Counseling and technology: Some thoughts about the controversy. *Journal of Technology in Human Services, 22*(3), 1–24.

Abramson, J. S. (1993). Orienting social work employees in interdisciplinary settings: Shaping professional and organizational perspectives. *Social Work, 38*(2), 152–157.

Abramson, M. (1984). Collective responsibility in interdisciplinary collaboration: An ethical perspective for social workers. *Social Work in Health Care, 10*(1), 35–43.

Abramson, M. (1985). The autonomy-paternalism dilemma in social work practice. *Social Casework, 66*, 387–393.

Abramson, M. (1989). Autonomy vs. paternalistic beneficence: Practice strategies. *Social Casework, 70*, 101–105.

Abramson, M. (1996). Toward a more holistic understanding of ethics in social work. *Social Work in Health Care, 23*(2), 1–14.

Acker, G. M. (1999). The impact of clients' illness on social workers' job satisfaction and burnout. *Health and Social Work, 24*(2), 112–119.

Adams, R. E., Boscarino, J. A., & Figley, C. R. (2006). Compassion fatigue and psychological distress among social workers: A validation study. *American Journal of Orthopsychiatry, 76*(1), 103–108.

Addams, J. (1902). *Democracy and social ethics.* New York: The Macmillan Co. Electronic version, no pagination. Chap. 7, Political reform. Retrieved October 4, 2006, from www.gutenberg.org/files/15487/15487-h/15487-h.htm

Adler, S. S. (1989). Truth telling to the terminal ill. *Social Work, 34*, 158–160.

Advocate Web (2002). Helping overcome professional exploitation. Sexual exploitation litigation issues. Retrieved July 18, 2002, from www.advocateweb.org/hope/litigation.asp

Agbayani-Siewert, P. (1994). Filipino American culture and family: Guidelines for practitioners. *Families in Society, 75*, 429–438.

Aguilar, G. D. (2004). A comparative study of practitioners' and students' understanding of sexual ethics. *Journal of Social Work Values and Ethics, 1*(1). Retrieved December 27, 2006, from www.socialworker.com/jswve/content/view/7/30

Aguilera, E. (2003, February 10). Cuba's low HIV rate belies the stigma, ignorance many face. *Denver Post.* Retrieved March 11, 2003, from www.denverpost.com/stories/O

Ajzen, I. (2005). *Attitudes, personality, and behavior* (2nd ed.). Maidenhead, U.K.: Open University Press.

Ajzen, I., & Madden, T. J. (1997). Prediction of goal-directed behavior: Attitudes, intentions, and perceived behavioral control. In M. Hewstone, & S. R. Manstead et al., *The Blackwell reader in social psychology* (pp. 245–267). Malden, MA: Blackwell Publishers.

Albert, R. (1986). *Law and social work practice*. New York: Springer Publishing.

Aldarondo, E., & Straus, M. A. (1994). Screening for physical violence in couple therapy: Methodological, practical, and ethical considerations. *Family Process, 33*, 425–439.

Algana, F. J., et al. (1979). Evaluating reaction to interpersonal touch in a counseling interview. *Journal of Counseling Psychology, 26*, 465–472.

Alle-Corliss, L., & Alle-Corliss, R. (1999). *Advanced practice in human services agencies: Issues, trends, and treatment perspectives*. Belmont, CA: Wadsworth Publishing Co.

Almason, A. L. (1997). Personal liability implications of the duty to warn are hard pills to swallow: From *Tarasoff* to *Hutchinson v. Patel* and beyond. *Journal of Contemporary Health, Law and Policy, 13*, 471–496.

Altman, L. K. (1999, August 31). Focusing on prevention in fight against AIDS. *New York Times*, p. F5.

Altman, L. K. (2002, July 3). U.N. forecasts big increase in AIDS death toll. *New York Times*, pp. A1, A6.

American Association of Social Work Boards. (2005). ACE, Approved Continuing Education, Provider News. Retrieved March 13, 2007, from www.aswb.org/0505acenews.pdf

American College of Physicians ACP Observer. (1997). Patients often forget physician's diagnosis. *News Briefs*. www.acponline.org/journals/news/feb97/brief297.htm

American Medical Association. (1997). Code of Ethics. www.ama-assn.org

American Medical Association. (2007). Health law. Retrieved January 30, 2007, from www.ama-assn.org/ama/pub/category/15549.html

American Psychiatric Association. (2000). *Diagnostic and statistical manual of mental disorders* (4th ed.).Washington, DC: Author.

Anderson, D. K., & Saunders, D. G. (2003). Leaving an abusive partner. *Trauma, Violence, & Abuse, 4*, 163–191.

Andrews, A. B., & Patterson, E. G. (1995). Searching for solutions to alcohol and other drug abuse during pregnancy: Ethics, values, and constitutional principles. *Social Work, 40*, 55–64.

Antle, B. J., & Regehr, C. (2003). Beyond individual rights and freedoms: Metaethics in social work research. *Social Work, 40*, 135–144.

Arendt, H. (1977). *Eichmann in Jerusalem: A report on the banality of evil*. New York: Penguin Books.

Ashton, V. (1999). Worker judgments of seriousness about and reporting of suspected child maltreatment. *Child Abuse and Neglect, 23*(6), 539–548.

Ashton, V. (2001). The relationship between attitudes toward corporal punishment and the perception and reporting of child abuse. *Child Abuse and Neglect, 25*(3), 389–400.

Athanassoulis, N. (2006). Virtue ethics. *The Internet encyclopedia of philosophy*. Retrieved September 9, 2006, from www.iep.utm.edu/v/virtue.htm

Austin, J. B., & Dankwort, J. (1999). Standards for batterer programs. *Journal of Interpersonal Violence, 14*, 152–168.

Baier, K. (1958). *The moral point of view: A rational basis of ethics*. New York: Random House.

Ballie, R. (2001). Medicare will now cover some telehealth psychotherapy services. *Monitor on Psychology, 32*(10). www.apa.org/monitor/nov01/telehealth.html

Barker, R. L. (1988a). "Client dumping": Some ethical considerations. *Journal of Independent Social Work, 2*, 1–5.

Barker, R. L. (1988b). Just whose code of ethics should the independent practitioner follow? *Journal of Independent Social Work, 2*(4), 1–5.

Barker, R. L. (1992). *Social work in private practice* (2nd ed.). Washington, DC: NASW Press.

Barksdale, C. (1989). Child abuse reporting: A clinical dilemma. *Smith College Studies in Social Work, 59*, 170–182.

Barnett-Queens, T. (1999). Sexual relationships with educators: A national survey of masters-level practitioners. *The Clinical Supervisor, 18*(1), 151–172.

Baretti, M. (2004). What do we know about the professional socialization of our students? *Journal of Social Work Education, 40*(2), 255–283.

Basham, K. K., Donner, S., Killough, R. M., & Rozas, L. W. (1997). Becoming an anti-racist institution. *Smith College Studies in Social Work, 67*, 564–585.

Bates, C. M., & Brodsky, A. M. (1989). *Sex in the therapy hour: A case of professional incest*. New York: Guilford.

Bauman, Z. (1996). Morality in the age of contingency. In P. Heclas, S. Lash, & P. Morris (Eds.), *Detraditionalization: Critical reflections on authority and identity* (pp. 49–58). Cambridge, MA: Blackwell Publishers.

Bayer, R. (1998). AIDS and the ethics of prevention, research, and care. In G. Wormser (Ed.), *AIDS and other manifestations of HIV infection* (3rd ed., pp. 799–807). Philadelphia: Lippincott-Raven Publishers.

Bayles, M. D. (1981). *Professional Ethics*. Belmont, CA.: Wadsworth Publishing.

Beck, J. C. (1998). Legal and ethical duties of the clinician treating a patient who is liable to be impulsively violent. *Behavioral Sciences and the Law, 16*, 375–389.

Beder, J. (1998). The home visit, revisited. *Families in Society, 79*, 514–522.

Behnke, S. (2006). Ethics and interrogations: Comparing and contrasting the American

Psychological, American Medical and American Psychiatric Association positions. *Monitor on Psychology, 37*(7).

Benotsch, E. G., Wright, V. J., Cassini, T. A. D., Pinkerton, S. D., Weinhardt, L., & Kelly, J. A. (2006). Use of the Internet for HIV prevention by AIDS service organizations in the United States. *Journal of Technology in Human Services, 24*(1), 19–35.

Bergeron, L. R., & Gray. B. (2003). Ethical dilemmas of reporting suspected elder abuse. *Social Work, 48,* 96–105.

Bergin, A. E. (1980). Psychotherapy and religious values. *Journal of Consulting and Clinical Psychology, 48*(1), 95–105.

Bergin, A. E. (1991). Values and religious issues in psychotherapy and mental health, *American Psychologist, 46*(4), 394–403.

Bergeron, M., & Hebert, M. (2006). Evaluation of a group interview using a feminist approach for victims of sexual abuse. *Child Abuse & Neglect, 30*(10), 1143–1159.

Berlin, S. (2005). The value of acceptance in social work direct practice: A historical and contemporary view. *Social Service Review, 79*(3), 482–510.

Berliner, A. K. (1989). Misconduct in social work practice. *Social Work, 34,* 69–72.

Bern, D. J. (1970). *Beliefs, attitudes and human affairs.* Pacific Grove, CA: Brooks/Cole Publishing.

Bernsen, A., Tabachnick, B. G., & Pope, K. S. (1994). National survey of social workers' sexual attraction to their clients: Results, implications, and comparison to psychologists. *Ethics & Behavior, 4*(4), 369–388.

Bernstein, S. (1960). Self-determination: "King or citizen in the realm of values." *Social Work, 5,* 3–8.

Bernstein, S. R. (1990). Contracted services: Issues for the nonprofit agency manager. In *Towards the 21st century: Challenges for the voluntary sector.* Proceedings of the 1990 Conference of the Association of Voluntary Action Scholars. London.

Besharov, D. J., & Besharov, S. H. (1987). Teaching about liability. *Social Work, 32,* 517–522.

Besharov, D. J., & Laumann, L. A. (1996). Child abuse reporting. *Society, 33*(4), 40–46.

Beyerstein, D. (1993). The functions and limitations of professional codes of ethics. In E. R. Winkler & J. R. Coombs (Eds.), *Applied ethics* (pp. 416–425). Cambridge, MA: Blackwell Publishers.

Bisman, C. (2004). Social work values: The moral core of the profession. *British Journal of Social Work, 34,* 109–123.

Black, D. (1972). The boundaries of legal sociology. *Yale Law Journal, 81,* 1086–1101.

Bloom, M. (1975). The paradox of helping: Introduction to the philosophy of scientific helping. New York: John Wiley & Sons.

Bogodanoff, M., & Elbaum, P. L. (1978). Touching: A legacy from the encounter movement to social work practice. *Social Work in Health Care, 4,* 209–219.

Boland-Prom, K., & Anderson, S. C. (2005). Teaching ethical decision making using dual relationship principles as a case example. *Journal of Social Work Education, 41*(3), 495–510.

Bonnie, R. J., & Wallace, R. B. (2003). *Elder mistreatment: Abuse, neglect, and exploitation in aging America.* Washington, DC: The National Academies Press.

Bonosky, N. (1995). Boundary violations in social work supervision: Clinical, educational, and legal implications. *The Clinical Supervisor, 13*(2), 79–95.

Borenzweig, H. (1983). Touching in clinical social work. *Social Casework, 64,* 238–242.

Borys, D. S., & Pope, K. S. (1989). Dual relationships between therapist and client: A national study of psychologists, psychiatrists, and social workers. *Professional Psychology: Research and Practice, 20,* 283–293.

Bowden, P. (1997). *Caring: Gender-sensitive ethics.* New York: Routledge.

Bowers v. Hardwick, 106 S. Ct. 2841 (1986).

Brabeck, M. M., & Ting, K. (2000). Feminist ethics: Lenses for examining ethical psychological practice. In M. M. Grabeck (Ed.), *Practicing feminist ethics in psychology.* Washington, DC: American Psychological Association.

Brager, G. A. (1968). Advocacy and political behavior. *Social Work, 13*(2), 5–15.

Brandeis, L. D., & Warren, S. D. (1890). The right to privacy. *Harvard Law Review, IV*(5), December 15.

Brill, C. K. (2001). Looking at the social work profession through the eye of the NASW Code of Ethics. *Research on Social Work Practice, 11*(2), 223–234.

Broadie, S. (1991). *Ethics with Aristotle.* New York: Oxford University Press.

Brown, H. J. (1970). Social work values in a developing country. *Social Work, 15*(1), 107–112.

Bufka, L. F., Crawford, J. I., & Levitt, J. T. (2002). Brief screening assessments for managed care and primary care. In M. M. Anthony & D. H. Barlow (Eds.), *Handbook of assessment and treatment planning for psychological disorders* (pp. 38–63). New York: The Guilford Press.

Butz, R. A. (1985). Reporting child abuse and confidentiality in counseling. *Social Casework, 66,* 83–90.

State of California, Department of Consumer Affairs (2004). Professional therapy never includes sex. Retrieved June 22, 2006, from www.psychboard.ca.gov/pubs/psychotherapy.pdf

Callahan, D. (1987, October/November). Terminating treatment: Age as a standard. *Hastings Center Reporter,* 21–25.

Callahan, J. (1988). *Ethical issues in professional life.* New York: Oxford University Press.

Callahan, J. (1994). The ethics of assisted suicide. *Health and Social Work, 19,* 237–244.

Canda, E. R. (1988). Spirituality, religious diversity, and social work practice. *Social Casework, 69,* 238–247.

Canda, E. R., Nakashima, M., & Furman, L. D. (2004). Ethical considerations about spirituality in social work: Insights from a national qualitative survey. *Families in* Society, *85*(1), 27–35.

Caputo, R. K. (1991). Managing information systems: An ethical framework and information needs matrix. *Administration in Social Work, 15*(4), 53–64.

Carey, B. (2006, October 10). An analyst questions the self-perpetuating side of therapy. *New York Times,* p. D2.

Carlson, S. (2002, November 15). Virtual counseling. *The Chronicle of Higher Education,* pp. A35–36.

Carpenter, M. C., & Platt, S. (1997). Professional identity for clinical social workers: Impact of changes in health care delivery systems. *Clinical Social Work Journal, 25,* 337–351.

Carter-Pokras, O., & Zambrana, R. E. (2001). Latin Health Status. In M. Aguirre-Molina, C. W. Molina, & R. E. Zambrana (Eds.), *Health Issues in the Latino Community* (pp. 23–54). San Francisco: Jossey-Bass.

Castillo, R. (2007). Glossary of key terms in culture and mental illness. Retrieved March 27, 2007, from www2.hawaii.edu/~rcastill/Culture_and_Mental_Illness/Glossary.html.

Cavaiola, A. A., & Colford, J. E. (2006). *A practical guide to crisis intervention.* Boston: Houghton Mifflin.

Cervera, N. J. (1993). Decision making for pregnant adolescents: Applying reasoned action theory to research and treatment. *Families in Society: The Journal of Contemporary Human Services, 74,* 355–365.

Chan, S. (2007, January 23). New York City puts millions into high-tech worker tracking. *New York Times,* p. C11.

Chow, J. (1999). Multiservice centers in Chinese American immigrant communities: Practice principles and challenges. *Social Work, 44,* 70–80.

Christensen, K. E. (1986). Ethics of information technology. G. R. Geiss & N. Viswanathan (Eds.), *The human edge* (pp. 72–91). Binghamton, NY: Haworth Press.

Citizen Link (2003). Dutch (Holland/Netherlands) euthanasia: The Dutch disaster. Retrieved January 8, 2003, from www.family.org/cforum/research/papers/a0001021.html.

Clark, C. (1998). Self-determination and paternalism in community care: Practice and prospects. *British Journal of Social Work, 28,* 387–402.

Clark, C. (1999). Observing the lighthouse: From theory to institutions in social work ethics. *European Journal of Social Work, 2*(3), 259–270.

Clark, C. (2006). Moral character in social work. *British Journal of Social Work, 36,* 75–89.

Clifford, D., & Burke, B. (2005). Developing anti-oppressive ethics in the new curriculum. *Social Work Education, 24*(6), 677–692.

Cohen, E. (2004). Advocacy and advocates: Definitions and ethical dimensions. *Generations, 28*(1), 9–16.

Cohen, J. (2003). Managed care and the evolving role of the clinical social worker in mental health. *Social Work, 48*(1), 34–43.

Cohen, R. (1980). The (revised) NASW Code of Ethics. *NASW News, 26* (April), 19.

Coleman, E., & Schaefer, S. (1986). Boundaries of sex and intimacy between client and counselor. *Journal of Counseling and Development, 64,* 341–344.

Congress, E. P., & Lynn, M. (1997). Group work practice in the community: Navigating the slippery slope of ethical dilemmas. *Social Work with Groups, 20*(3), 61–74.

Congress, E., & McAuliffe, D. (2006) Social work ethics: Professional codes in Australia and the United States. *International Social Work, 49,* 151–164.

Conte, H. R., Plutchik, R., Picard, S., & Karasu, T. B. (1989). Ethics in the practice of psychotherapy. *American Journal of Psychotherapy, 43,* 32–42.

Corey, G., Corey, M. S., & Callanan, P. (2003). *Issues and ethics in the helping professions* (6th ed.). Pacific Grove, CA: Brooks/Cole Thomson Learning Publishing Co.

Cottone, R. R., & Tarvydas, V. M. (2007). *Counseling ethics and decision making* (3rd ed.) Upper Saddle River, NJ: Pearson/Merrill Prentice Hall.

Council on Social Work Education. (2004). *Educational policy and accreditation standards.* Alexandria, VA: Author.

Courtney, M. E., Barth, R. P., Berrick, J. D., Brooks, E., Needell, B., & Park, L. (1996). Race and child welfare services: Past research and future directions. *Child Welfare, LXXV,* 99–137.

Csikai, E. L. (1999a). Euthanasia and assisted suicide: Issues for social work practice. *Journal of Gerontological Social Work, 31*(3/4), 49–63.

Csikai, E. L. (1999b). The role of values and experience in determining social workers' attitudes toward euthanasia and assisted suicide. *Social Work in Health Care, 30*(1), 75–95.

Csikai, E. L. (1999c). Hospital social workers' attitudes toward euthanasia and assisted suicide. *Social Work in Health Care, 30*(1), 51–73.

Csikai, E. L., & Sales, E. (1998). The emerging social work role on hospital ethics committees: A comparison of social worker and chair perspectives. *Social Work, 43*(3), 233–242.

Currie v. Doran, U. S. Court of Appeals, 10th Circuit. 2001.

Curtis, P. A., & Lutkus, A. M. (1985). Client confidentiality in police social work settings. *Social Work, 30*, 355–360.

Cwikel, J. G., & Cnaan, R. A. (1991). Ethical dilemmas in applying secondwave information technology to social work practice. *Social Work, 36*(2), 114–120.

Cyrns, A. G. (1977). Social work education and student ideology: A multivariate study of professional socialization. *Journal of Education for Social Work, 13*(1), 44–51.

Daley, M. R., & Doughty, M. O. (2006). Ethics complaints in social work practice: A rural-urban comparison. *Journal of Social Work Values and Ethics, 3*(1).

Darlington, Y., Feeney, J. A., & Rixon, K. (2005). Interagency collaboration between child protection and health services: Practice, attitudes, and barriers. *Child Abuse & Neglect, 29*, 1085–1098.

Daro, D. (1988). *Confronting child abuse: Research/or effective program design.* New York: Free Press.

Davis, K. (1997). Managed care, mental illness and African Americans: A prospective analysis of managed care policy in the United States. *Smith College Studies in Social Work, 67*, 623–641.

Dean, H. (1998). The primacy of the ethical aim in clinical social work: Its relationship to social justice and mental health. *Smith College Studies in Social Work, 69*, 9–24.

Dean, R. G., & Rhodes, M. L. (1992). Ethical-clinical tensions in clinical practice. *Social Work, 37*, 128–132.

Delaronde, S., King, G., Bendel, R., & Reece, R. (2000). Opinions among mandated reporters toward child maltreatment reporting policies. *Child Abuse and Neglect, 24*(7), 901–910.

Dent, S. (2000). Illiteracy: "Hidden disability" creates health care confusion. *FP Report, 6*(1). Retrieved October 16, 2002, from www.aafp.org/fpr/20000100/illiteracy.html

Department of Health & Human Services, Centers for Disease Control and Prevention. (2001). *HIV prevalence trends in selected populations in the United States: Results from national serosurveillance, 1993–1997.*

Department of Health and Human Services (2002). Modifications to the standards for privacy of individually identifiable health information—final rule. Retrieved November 25, 2002, from www.hhs.gov/news/press/ 2002pres/ 20020809.html

Desai, K. (2003). Ethical decision making within the bureaucratic context: A case study. *Child Management Journal, 4*(3), 122–128.

Deutscher, I., Pestello, F. P., & Pestello, H. F. G. (1993). *Sentiments and acts.* New York: Aldine de Gruyter.

DiMarco, M., & Zoline, S. S. (2004). Duty to warn in the context of HIV/AIDS-related psychotherapy: Decision making among psychologists. *Counseling and Clinical Psychology, 1*(2), 68–85.

Dobrin, A. (1989). Ethical judgments of male and female social workers. *Social Work, 34*, 451–455.

Dodd, S., & Jansson, B. (2004). Expanding the boundaries of ethics education: Preparing social workers for ethical advocacy in an organizational setting. *Journal of Social Work Education, 40*(3), 455–465.

Dolgoff, R. (2002). An exploration in social policy and ethics: Ethical judgment before or after the fact? *Social Work Forum, Wurzweiler School of Social Work, 35*(Winter/Spring, 2001–2002), 67–86.

Dolgoff, R., & Skolnik, L. (1992). Ethical decision making: The NASW code of ethics and group work practice: Beginning explorations. *Social Work with Groups, 15*(4), 99–112.

Dolgoff, R., & Skolnik, L. (1996). Ethical decision making in social work with groups: An empirical study. *Social Work with Groups, 19*(2), 49–65.

Dryden, W., & Ellis, A. (1988). Rational-emotive therapy. In *Handbook of Cognitive-Behavioral Therapies* (pp. 214–272). New York: The Guilford Press.

Dumont, M. P. (1996). Privatization and mental health in Massachusetts. *Smith College Studies in Social Work, 66*, 293–303.

Durana, C. (1998). The use of touch in psychotherapy: Ethical and clinical guidelines. *Psychotherapy: Theory, Research, Practice, Training, 35*(2), 269–280.

Dworkin, G. (1985). Behavioral control and design. *Social Research, 52*, 543–554.

Dwyer, S. (2005). Older people and permanent care: Whose decision? *British Journal of Social Work, 35*(7), 1081–1092.

Edward, J. (1999). Is managed mental health treatment psychotherapy? *Clinical Social Work Journal, 27*, 87–102.

Egan, M., & Kadushin, G. (2004). Job satisfaction of home health social workers in the environment of containment. *Health & Social Work, 29*(4), 287–296.

Egley, L. C. (1992). Defining the *Tarasoff* duty. *Journal of Psychiatry and Law, 19*, 93–133.

Ellis, A. (1973). *Humanistic psychotherapy: The rational-emotive approach.* New York: McGraw-Hill.

Eriksen, K., & Kress, V. E. (2005). *Beyond the DSM story: Ethical quandaries, challenges, and best practices.* Thousand Oaks, CA: Sage Publications.

Ewalt, P. L., & Mokuau, N. (1995). Self-determination from a Pacific perspective. *Social Work, 40*, 168–175.

Ewing, C. P. (2002). *Tarasoff* update: Psychotherapy threats alone provide no basis for criminal prosecution. *Monitor on Psychology, 33*(2),

1–3. Retrieved July 17, 2002, from www
.apa.org/monitor/feb02/jn.html.

Ewing, C. P. (2005). *Tarasoff* reconsidered: The-*Tarasoff* rule has been extended to include threats disclosed by family members. *Monitor on Psychology, 36*(7), 112.

Federal Globe–Federal Employee Benefits FAQ. (2007). What the gay, lesbian, or bisexual employee needs to know. Retrieved January 30, 2007, from www.fedglobe.org/issues/benefitsfaq5.htm

Federal Psychotherapist-Patient Privilege (*Jaffee v. Redmond,* 518 U.S. 1): History, documents, and opinions. Retrieved September 5, 2002, from http://psa-uny.org/jr/

Feldman, K. A., & Newcomb, T. M. (1994). *The impact of college on students.* New Brunswick, NJ: Transaction Publishers.

Fellin, P. (2000). Revisiting multiculturalism in social work. *Journal of Social Work Education, 36*(2), 261–278.

Felthous, A. R., & Kachigian, C. (2001). The fin de millénaire duty to warn or protect. *Journal of Forensic Science, 46*(5), 1103–1112.

Festinger, L. (1957). *A theory of cognitive dissonance.* New York: Harper & Row.

Figley, C. R. (1995). Compassion fatigue: Coping with secondary traumatic stress disorder in those who treat the traumatized. New York: Brunner/Mazel Publishers.

Figley, C. R. (1999). Compassion fatigue: Toward a new understanding of the costs of caring. In B. Hudnall Stamm (Ed.), *Secondary traumatic stress: Self-care issues for clinicians, researchers, and educators* (2nd ed., pp. 1–28). Baltimore: Sidran Press.

Finkelhor, D. (1990). Is child abuse over-reported? *Public Welfare, 48,* 22–29.

Finkelhor, D. (1998). Improving research, policy, and practice to understand child sexual abuse. *Journal of the American Medical Association, 280,* 1864–1865.

Finn, J. (1990). Security, privacy, and confidentiality in agency microcomputer use. *Families in Society: The Journal of Contemporary Human Services* (May), 283–290.

Finn, J., & Banach, M. (2002). Risk management in online human services practice. *Journal of Technology in Human Services, 20*(1/2), 133–153.

Fishkin, J. S. (1982). *The limits of obligation.* New Haven, CT: Yale University Press.

Flaherty, J. (2002, August 14). Girls link their use of family planning clinics to keeping parents in the dark. *New York Times,* p. A14.

Flanagan, E. H., & Blashfield, R. K. (2005). Gender acts as a context for interpreting diagnostic criteria. *Journal of Clinical Psychology, 61*(12), 1485–1498.

Fleck-Henderson, A. (1991). Moral reasoning in social work practice. *Social Service Review* (June), 185–202.

Flexner, A. (1915). Is social work a profession? *Proceedings of National Conference of Charities and Corrections* (pp. 576–590). Chicago: Hindman.

Fodor, J. L. (1999, February). Computer ethics in higher education. *Syllabus,* 12–15.

Frank, J. (1991). *Persuasion and healing* (Rev. ed.). New York: Schocken Books.

Frankel, A. J., & Gelman, S. R. (2004). *Case Management* (2nd ed.). Chicago: Lyceum Books.

Frankena, W. K. (1973). *Ethics* (2nd ed.). Englewood Cliffs, NJ: Prentice Hall.

Frankena, W. K. (1980). *Thinking about morality.* Ann Arbor: University of Michigan Press.

Frankl, V. (1968). *The doctor and the soul.* New York: Alfred A. Knopf.

Frans, D. J., & Moran, J. R. (1993). Social work education's impact on students' humanistic values and personal empowerment. *Arete, 18*(1), 1–11.

Freedman, T. G. (1998). Genetic susceptibility testing: Ethical and social quandaries. *Health & Social Work, 23,* 214–222.

Freeman, J. M., & Mc Donnell, K. (2001). *Tough decisions: Cases in medical ethics* (2nd ed.). New York: Oxford University Press.

Freud, S. (1999). The social construction of normality. *Families in Society, 80*(4), 333–339.

Freud, S., & Krug, S. (2002). Beyond the code of ethics, Part 1: Complexities of ethical decision making in social work practice. *Families in Society: The Journal of Contemporary Human Services, 83*(5/6), 474–482.

Frost, N., Robinson, M., & Anning, A. (2005). Social workers in multidisciplinary teams: Issues and dilemmas for professional practice. *Child and Family Social Work, 10*(187–196).

Fukuyama, M. A. (2001). Counseling in colleges and universities. In D. C. Locke, E. L. Herr, & J. E. Myers (Eds.), *The handbook of counseling* (pp. 319–341). Thousand Oaks, CA: Sage Publications.

Furman, R., Downey, E. P., & Jackson, R. L. (2004). Exploring the ethics of treatments for depression: The ethics of care perspective. *Smith College Studies in Social Work, 74*(3), 525–538.

Galambos, C. M. (1999). Resolving ethical conflicts in a managed health care environment. *Health & Social Work, 24*(3), 191–197.

Galambos, C. (2005). Rural social work practice: Maintaining confidentiality in the face of dual relationships, 2 (2). Retrieved July 19, 2006, from www.socialworker.com/jswve/content/view/23/37

Galinsky, M. J., Schopler, J. H., & Abell, M. D. (1997). Connecting group members through telephone and computer groups. *Health & Social Work, 22,* 181–188.

Gambrill, E., & Pruger, R. (Eds.) (1997). *Controversial issues in social work ethics, values, and obligations.* Boston: Allyn & Bacon.

Gambrill, E. D. (2003). From the editor: "Evidence-based practice": Sea change or the emperor's new clothes? *Journal of Social Work Education, 39*, 3–23.

Gambrill, E. (2006). Evidence-based practice and policy: Choices ahead. *Research on Social Work Practice, 16*(3), 338–357.

Garb, H. N. (1994). Cognitive heuristics and biases in personality assessment. In L. Heath(Ed.), *Applications of heuristics and biases to social issues* (pp. 73–90). New York: Plenum Press.

Gerhart, U. C., & Brooks, A. D. (1985). Social workers and malpractice: Law, attitudes, and knowledge. *Social Casework, 66*, 411–416.

Gewirth, A. (1978). *Reason and morality.* Chicago: University of Chicago Press.

Gibelman, M., & Schervish, P. H. (1997). *Who we are: A second look.* Washington, DC: NASW.

Gibelman, M., & Mason, S. E. (2002). Treatment choices in a managed care environment: A multi-disciplinary exploration. *Clinical Social Work, 30*(2), 199–214.

Gibelman, M. (2005). Social workers for rent: The contingency human services labor force. *Families in Society: The Journal of Contemporary Social Services, 86*(4), 457–469.

Givelber, D., Bowers, W., & Blitch, C. (1984). *Tarasoff:* Myth and reliability. *Wisconsin Law Review, 2*, 443–497.

Glaser, R. D., & Thorpe, J. S. (1986). Unethical intimacy: A survey of sexual contact and advances between psychology educators and female graduate students. *American Psychologist, 41*(1), 43–51.

Glassman, C. (1992). Feminist dilemmas in practice. *Affilia, 7*, 160–166.

Goffman, E. (1959). *The presentation of self in everyday life.* Garden City, NY: Doubleday.

Goldenberg, I., & Goldenberg, H. (2000). *Family therapy: An overview* (5th ed.). Belmont, CA: Brooks/Cole.

Goldstein, E. G. (1997). To tell or not to tell: The disclosure of events in the therapist's life to the patient. *Clinical Social Work Journal, 25*, 41–58.

Goldstein, H. (1973). *Social work: A unitary approach.* Columbia: University of South Carolina Press.

Goldstein, H. (1987). The neglected moral link in social work practice. *Social Work, 32*, 181–186.

Goldstein, H. (1998). Education for ethical dilemmas in social work practice. *Families in Society: The Journal of Contemporary Human Services, 79*, 241–253.

Goodban, N. (1985). The psychological impact of being on welfare. *Social Service Review, 59*, 403–422.

Goode, E. (2001, August 27). Disparities seen in mental care for minorities. *New York Times,* pp. 1, 12.

Gottleib, M. C., & Cooper, C. C. (1993). Some ethical issues for systems-oriented therapists in hospital settings. *Family Relations, 42*(2), 140–144.

Green, R. (2003). Social work in rural areas: A personal and professional challenge. *Australian Social Work, 56*, 209–219.

Green, A. D., & Kantambu, J. L. (2004). Whistle-blowing as a form of advocacy: Guidelines for the practitioner and organization. *Social Work, 49*(2), 219–230.

Greene, A. D., & Latting, J. K. (2004). Whistle-blowing as a form of advocacy: Guidelines for the practitioner and organization, *Social Work, 49*(2), 217–230.

Greenhouse, L. (1998, December 2). High court curbs claim on privacy in a house. *New York Times,* p. A11.

Greenhouse, L. (1999a, April 11). Check out your driver. *New York Times, Week in Review,* p. 2.

Greenhouse, L. (1999b, April 6). Supreme court roundup; police searching car may include passenger's things. *New York Times,* p. A19.

Greenwood, E. (1957). Attributes of a profession. *Social Work, 2*(3), 45–55.

Grinnell, R. M. Jr., & Unrau, Y. A. (2005). *Social work research and evaluation.* New York: Oxford University Press.

Grisso, T., & Appelbaum, P. S. (1998). *Assessing competence to consent to treatment: A guide for physicians and other health professionals.* New York: Oxford University Press.

Group for the Advancement of Psychiatry (1994). *Forced into treatment: The role of coercion in clinical practice.* Report No. 137. Washington, DC: American Psychiatric Press.

Grundstein-Amado, R. (1999). Bilateral transformational leadership: An approach for fostering ethical conduct in public service organizations, *Administration & Society, 31*(2), 247–260.

Gursansky, D., Harvey, J., & Kennedy R. (2003). *Case management: Policy, practice, and professional business.* New York: Columbia University Press.

Guttmann, D. (1996). *Logotherapy for the helping professional: Meaningful social work.* New York: Springer Publishing Co.

Hadjistavropoulos, T., & Malloy, D. C. (1999). Ethical principles of the American Psychological Association: An argument for philosophical and practical ranking. *Ethics & Behavior, 9*, 127–140.

Haley, J. (1976). *Problem-solving therapy.* New York: Harper & Row.

Hall, M. L., & Keefe, R. H. (2006). Interfacing with managed care organizations: A measure of self-perceived competence. *Best Practices in Mental Health, 2*(1), 31–41.

Halmos, P. (1965). *Faith of the counselor.* London: Constable.

Hamel, J. (2005). *Gender-inclusive treatment of intimate partner abuse.* NY: Springer Publishing.

Handler, J. E., & Hollingsworth, E. J. (1971). *The deserving poor.* Chicago: Markham.

Hankins, C. A., Stanecki, K. A., Ghys, P. D., & Marais, H. (2006). The evolving HIV pandemic. In E. J. Beck, N. Mays et al. (Eds.), *The HIV pandemic: Local and global implications* (pp. 21–35). New York: Oxford University Press.

Hardina, D. (2004). Guidelines for ethical practice in community organization. *Social Work, 49*(4), 595–604.

Harris, G. C. (1999). The dangerous patient exception to the psychotherapist-patient privilege: The *Tarasoff* duty and the *Jaffee* footnote. *Washington Law Review, 74*, 33–68.

Hartman, A. (1995). Family therapy. In R. L. Edward (Ed.), *Encyclopedia of social work* (19th ed., Vol. 2, pp. 983–991). Washington, DC: National Association of Social Workers.

Hartman, A. (1997). Power issues in social work practice. In A. J. Katz, A. Lurie, & C. M. Vidal (Eds.), *Critical social welfare issues* (pp. 215–226). New York: The Haworth Press, 1997.

Haslam, D. R., & Harris, S. M. (2004). Informed consent documents of marriage and family therapists in private practice: A qualitative analysis. *American Journal of Family Therapy, 32*, 359–374.

Hayes, D. D., & Varley, B. K. (1965). The impact of social work education on students' values. *Social Work, 10*(4), 40–46.

Healy, T. C. (1998). The complexity of everyday ethics in home health care: An analysis of social workers' decisions regarding frail elders' autonomy. *Social Work in Health Care, 27*(4), 19–37.

Healy, T. C. (2004). Levels of directiveness: A contextual analysis of social work in health care. *Social Work in Health Care, 40*(1), 71–91.

Held, V. (2006). *The ethics of care: Personal, political, and global.* New York: Oxford University Press.

Helton, D. (2003). Online therapeutic social service provision (Therap-pc): A state of the art review. *Journal of Technology in Human Services, 21*(4), 17–36.

Hetzel, L., & Smith, A. (2001). The 65 years and over population: 2000. *Census 2000 Brief.* Washington, D.C., U.S. Census Bureau. Retrieved October 9, 2003, from www .census.gov/prod/2001pubs/C2kbr01-10.pdf

Hines, D. A., & Malley-Morrison, K. (2005). *Family violence in the United States: Defining, understanding, and combating abuse.* Thousand Oaks: Sage Publications.

Hiratsuka, J. (1994). When it's a helper who needs help. *NASW News* (June), 3.

Hodge, D. R. (2002). Does social work oppress evangelical Christians? A "new class" analysis of society and social work. *Social Work, 47*(4), 401–414.

Hodge, D. R. (2004). Developing cultural competency with evangelical Christians. *Families in Society, 85*(2), 251–260.

Hodge, D. R. (2005a). Spiritual life maps: A client-centered pictorial instrument for spiritual assessment, planning, and intervention. *Social Work, 50*(1), 77–87.

Hodge, D. R. (2005b). Epistemological frameworks, homosexuality, and religion: How people of faith understand the intersection between homosexuality and religion. *Social Work, 50*(3), 207–218.

Hodge, D. R. (2006). A template for spiritual assessment: A review of the JCAHO requirements and guidelines for implementation. *Social Work, 51*(4), 317–326.

Hoefer, R. (2006). *Advocacy practice for social justice.* Chicago: Lyceum Books, Inc.

Hogue, C. J. R., & Hargraves, M. A. (2000). The commonwealth fund minority health survey of 1994: An overview. In C. J. R. Hogue, M. A. Hargraves, & K. S. Collins (Eds.), *Minority Health in America* (pp. 1–18). Baltimore: Johns Hopkins University Press.

Hokenstad, M. C. (1987). Preparation for practice: The ethical dimension. *Social Work Education Reporter, 25*, 1–4.

Holland, L. M. *The HIV Pandemic: Locals and Global Implications.* NY: Oxford University Press, 21–35.

Hollingsworth, L. D. (2005). Ethical considerations in prenatal sex selection. *Health & Social Work, 30*(2), 126–134.

Holmes, S. A. (1998, December 6). Right to abortion quietly advances in state courts. *New York Times,* Section 1, p. 1.

Holroyd, J., & Brodsky, A. (1977). Psychologists' attitudes and practices regarding erotic and nonerotic physical contact with patients. *American Psychologist, 32*, 843–849.

HomeCare & Hospice, National Association for Home Care & Hospice (2006). The Medicare home health benefit: Utilization and outlays have dropped dramatically. Retrieved July 11, 2006, from www.congressweb.com/nahc/positionpapers.htm

Horner, W. C., & Whitbeck, L. B. (1991). Personal versus professional values in social work: A methodological note. *Journal of Social Service Research, 14*(1/2), 21–43.

Houston-Vega, M. K., Nuehring, E. M., & Daguio, E. R. (1997). *Prudent practice.* Washington, DC: NASW Press.

Howard, M. O., & Jenson, J. M. (1999). Clinical practice guidelines: Should social work develop them? *Research on Social Work Practice, 9*, 283–301.

Howard, M. O., McMillen, C. J., & Pollio, D. E. (2003). Teaching evidence-based practice: Toward a new paradigm for social work education. *Research on Social Work Practice, 13*, 234–259.

Howe, E. (1980). Public professions and the private model of professionalism. *Social Work, 25*, 179–191.

Hughes, R. C. (1993a). Child welfare services for the catastrophically ill newborn: Part I—A confusion of responsibility. *Child Welfare, 72,* 32–40.

Hughes, R. C. (1993b). Child welfare services for the catastrophically ill newborn: Part II—A guiding ethical paradigm. *Child Welfare, 72,* 423–437.

Human Rights Campaign (2003). Medicaid expansion. Retrieved January 27, 2003, from www.hrc.org/issues/hiv_aids/background/medicaid.asp

Illich, I. (2006). Deschooling society. Retrieved October 30, 2006, from http://reactor-core.org/deschooling.html

Imbert, R. C. (2006). Personal letter (November 20). NASW Insurance Trust and the American Professional Agency.

Imre, R. E. (1989). Moral theory for social work. *Social Thought, 15*(1), 18–27.

Iserson, K. V. (1986). An approach to ethical problems in emergency medicine. In K. V. Iserson et al. (Eds.), *Ethics in emergency medicine* (pp. 35–41). Baltimore: Williams & Wilkins.

Iversen, R., Gergen, K. J., & Fairbanks, R. P. II, (2005). Assessment and social construction: Conflict or co-creation? *British Journal of Social Work, 35*(5), 689–708.

Jackson, J. (2000). Duties and conscience in professional practices. In Q. de Stexhe & J. Verstraeten (Eds.), *Matter of breath: Foundations for professional ethics* (pp. 239–258). Leuven, Belgium: Peeters.

Jackson, J. S., & Sellers, S. L. (2001). Health and the elderly. In R. L. Braithwaite & S. E. Taylor (Eds.), *Health issues in the black community* (pp. 81–96). San Francisco: Jossey-Bass Publishers.

Jaques, L. H., & Folen, R. A. (1998). Confidentiality and the military. In R. M. Anderson Jr., T. L. Nardello, & H. V. Hall (Eds.), *Avoiding ethical misconduct in psychology specialty areas.* Springfield, IL: Charles C. Thomas Publishers.

Jayaratne, S., Croxton, T., & Mattison, D. (1997). Social work professional standards: An exploratory study. *Social Work, 42,* 187–199.

Jiminez, J. (2006). Epistemological frameworks, homosexuality, and religion: A response to Hodge. *Social Work, 51*(2), 185–187.

Johner, R. (2006). Dual relationship legitimization and client-self-determination. *Journal of Social Work Values and Ethics, 3*(1). Retrieved July 19, 2006, from www.socialworker.com/jswve/content/view/30/44.

Jones, W. T., Sontag, F., Beckner, M. O., & Fogelin, R. J. (1977). *Approaches to ethics.* New York: McGraw-Hill.

Jory, B., Anderson, D., & Greer, C. (1997). Intimate justice: Confronting issues of accountability, respect, and freedom in treatment for abuse and violence. *Journal of Marital and Family Therapy,* 399–419.

Joseph, M. V. (1983). The ethics of organization. *Administration in Social Work, 7,* 47–57.

Joseph, M. V. (1985). A model for ethical decision-making in clinical practice. In C. B. Germain (Ed.), *Advances in clinical social work practice* (pp. 207–217). Silver Spring, MD: NASW.

Judah, E. H. (1979). Values: The uncertain component of social work. *Journal of Education for Social Work, 15*(2), 79–86.

Kalichman, S. C. (1999). *Mandated reporting of suspected child abuse: Ethics, law, and policy.* Washington, DC: American Psychological Association.

Kaslow, F. (1998). Ethical problems in mental health practice. *Journal of Family Psychotherapy, 9*(2), 41–54.

Keefe, R. H., Hall, M. L., & Corvo, K. N. (2002). Providing therapy when managed care organizations deny reimbursement: Are private practitioners and their clients taking the fall? *Social Work in Health Care, 36*(2), 49–64.

Keith-Lucas, A. (1977). Ethics in social work. *Encyclopedia of social work* (pp. 350–355). Washington, DC: National Association of Social Workers.

Kelly, D. C. (2005). Beyond problem solving: The social worker as risk manager and educator in educational host settings. *School Social Work Journal, 29*(2), 40–52.

Kelly, T. B. (1994). Paternalism and the marginally competent: An ethical dilemma, no easy answers. *Journal of Gerontological Social Work, 23*(1/2), 67–84.

Kirk, S. A., & Kutchins, H. (1988). Deliberate misdiagnosis in mental health practice. *Social Service Review, 62,* 225–237.

Kirk, S., & Kutchins, H. (1992). Diagnosis and uncertainty in mental health organizations. In Y. Hasenfeld (Ed.), *Human services as complex organizations* (pp. 163–183). London: Sage.

Kirkpatrick, W. J., Reamer, F. G., & Sykulski, M. (2006). Social work ethics audits in health care setting: A case study. *Health & Social Work, 31*(3), 225–228.

Kiselica, M. S., & Ramsey, M. L. (2001). Multicultural counselor education. In D. C. Locke, J. E. Myers, & E. L. Herr (Eds.), *The handbook of counseling* (pp. 433–451). Thousand Oaks, CA: Sage Publications.

Kitchner, K. S. (1984). Intuition, critical evaluation and ethical principles: The foundation of ethical decisions in counseling psychology. *Counseling Psychology, 12,* 43–55.

Klosterman, E. M., & Stratton, D. C. (2006). Speaking truth to power: Jane Addams's values base for peacemaking. *Affilia, 21*(2), 158–168.

Kluckhohn, C. (1951). Values and value-orientations in the theory of action: An exploration in definition and clarification. In T. Parsons &

E. A. Shils (Eds.), *Toward a general theory of action* (pp. 388–433). Cambridge, MA: Harvard University Press.

Koenig, T. L., & Spano, R. N. (2003). Sex, supervision, and boundary violations: Pressing challenges and possible solutions. *The Clinical Supervisor, 22*(1), 3–19.

Kohlberg, L. (1984). *The psychology of moral development.* New York: Harper & Row.

Kopels, S., & Kagle, J. D. (1993). Do social workers have a duty to warn? *Social Service Review, 67,* 101–126.

Kroll, B. (2004). Living with an elephant: Growing up with parental substance misuse. *Child and Family Social Work, 9,* 129–140.

Kuhse, H., & Singer, P. (1985). Ethics and the handicapped newborn infant. *Social Research, 52,* 505–542.

Kupperman, J. J. (1999). *Value . . . and what follows.* New York: Oxford University Press.

Kurri, K. (2005). Placement of responsibility and moral reasoning in couple therapy. *Journal of Family Therapy, 27*(4), 352–369.

Kurzman, P. A. (1995). Professional liability and malpractice (pp. 1921–1927). *Encyclopedia of social work* (19th ed.). Washington, DC: NASW Press.

Kutchins, H. (1991). The fiduciary relationship: The legal basis for social workers' responsibilities to clients. *Social Work, 36,* 106–113.

Kutchins, H., & Kirk, S. A. (1987). DSM-III and social work malpractice. *Social Work, 32,* 205–211.

Kutchins, H., & Kirk, S. A. (1988). The business of diagnosis: DSM-III and clinical social work. *Social Work, 33,* 215–220.

Kutchins, H., & Kirk, S. A. (1995). Review of diagnostic and statistical manual of mental disorders (4th ed.). *Social Work, 40,* 286–287.

Kutchins, H., & Kirk, S. A. (1997). *Making us crazy.* New York: The Free Press.

Kwak, J., & Haley, W. E. (2005). Current research findings on end-of-life decision making among racially or ethnically diverse groups. *The Gerontologist, 45*(5), 634–641.

Landau, R. (1996). Preparing for sudden death or organ donation: An ethical dilemma in social work. *International Social Work, 39,* 431–441.

Landau, R. (1998a). Secrecy, anonymity, and deception in donor insemination: A genetic, psychosocial, and ethical critique. *Social Work in Health Care, 28*(1), 75–89.

Landau, R. (1998b). The management of genetic origins: Secrecy and openness in donor assisted conception in Israel and elsewhere. *Human Reproduction, 13*(11), 3268–3273.

Landau, R., & Osmo, R. (2003). Professional and personal hierarchies of ethical principles. *International Journal of Social Welfare, 12,* 42–49.

Lange, J. M. (2006). Antiretroviral treatment and care of HIV. In E. J. Beck, N. Mays et al. (Eds.), *The HIV pandemic: Local and global implications* (pp. 86–104). New York: Oxford University Press.

Leach, M. M. & Sullivan, A. (2001) The intersection of race, class, and gender on diagnosis. In D. B. Pope-Davis, & H. L. K. Coleman, (Eds.), *The Intersection of Race, Class, and Gender in Multicultural Counseling* (pp. 353–383). Thousand Oaks, CA: Sage Publications, Inc.

Lens, V. (2000). Protecting the confidentiality of the therapeutic relationship:*Jaffee v. Redmond. Social Work, 45*(3), 273–276.

Lens, V. (2006). Work sanctions under welfare reform: Are they helping women achieve self-sufficiency? *Duke Journal of Gender Law and Social Policy, 13*(1), 255–280.

Lewis, N. A. (2005, July 6). Psychologists warned on role in detentions. *New York Times,* A14.

Loewenberg, F., & Dolgoff, R. (1988). *Ethical Decisions for Social Work Practice* (3rd ed.). Itasca, Illinois: F. E. Peacock Publishers, Inc.

Loewenberg, F. M., & Dolgoff, R. (1992). *Ethical Decisions for Social Work Practice* (4th ed.). Itasca, Illinois: F. E. Peacock Publishers, Inc.

Levy, C. (1976a). Personal versus professional values: The practitioner's dilemma. *Clinical Social Work Journal, 4,* 110–120.

Levy, C. (1976b). The value base of social work. *Journal of Education in Social Work, 9,* 34–42.

Lewis, H. (1984). Ethical assessment. *Social Casework, 65,* 203–211.

Lewis, H. (1989). Ethics and the private non-profit human service organization. *Administration in Social Work, 13*(2), 1–14.

Lilienfeld, S. O., Fowler, K. A., Lohr, J. M., & Lynn, S. J. (2005). Pseudoscience, nonscience, and nonsense in clinical psychology: Dangers and remedies. In R. H. Wright & N. A. Cummings (Eds.), *Destructive trends in mental health: The well-intentioned path to harm* (pp. 187–218). New York: Routledge.

Lipsyte, R. (2002, November 17). Johnson and Augusta mask bigger issues. *New York Times, Sports Sunday,* p. 5.

Lloyd, C., King, R., & Chenoweth, L. (2002). Social work, stress, and burnout: A review. *Journal of Mental Health, II*(3), 255–265.

Lo, B., Dornbrand, L., Wolf, L. E., & Groman, M. (2002). The Wendland case—Withdrawing life support from incompetent patients who are not terminally ill. *The New England Journal of Medicine, 346,* 1489–1493.

Lorenz, K. (2006). Is your boss spying on you? Retrieved February 8, 2007, from http://edition.cnn.com/2006/US/Careers/03/24/cb.boss.spying/

Lott, B., & Bullock, H. E. (2001). Who are the poor? *Journal of Social Issues, 57*(2), 189–206.

Luftman, V. H., Veltkamp, L. J., Clark, J. J., Lannacone, S., & Snooks, H. (2005). Practice guidelines in child custody evaluations for licensed clinical social workers. *Clinical Social Work Journal, 33,* 327–357.

Lum, D. (2000). Social work practice and people of color (4th ed.). Belmont, CA: Brooks/Cole.

Lundahl, B. W., Nimer, J., & Parsons, B. (2006). Preventing child abuse. A meta-analysis of parent training programs. *Research on Social Work Practice, 16*(3), 251–262.

Lystad, M., Rice, M., & Kaplan, S. J. (1996). Family violence. In S. J. Kaplan (Ed.), *Domestic violence* (pp. 139–180). Washington, DC: American Psychiatric Press.

MacIver, R. (1922). The social significance of professional ethics. *Annals, 101,* 5–11.

Mackelprang, R. W., & Mackelprang, R. D. (2005). Historical and contemporary issues in end-of-life decisions: Implications for social work. *Social Work, 50*(4), 315–324.

MacMurray, J. (1961). *Persons in relation.* Atlantic Highlands, NJ: Humanities Press.

Maesen, W. A. (1991). Fraud in mental health practice: A risk management perspective. *Administration and Policy in Mental Health, 18,* 431–432.

Maher, V. F., & Ford, J. (2002). The heartbreak of parens patriae. *Jona's Healthcare, Law, Ethics, and Regulation, 4,* 18–22.

Mahony, R. (2006, March 22). Called by God to help. *New York Times,* Op. Ed., Section A, p. 25.

Maidment, J. (2006). The quiet remedy: A dialogue on reshaping professional relationships. *Families in Society: The Journal of Contemporary Social Services, 87*(1), 115–121.

Manetta, A. A., & Wells, J. G. (2001). Ethical issues in the social worker's role in physician-assisted suicide. *Health and Social Work, 26*(3), 160–166.

Manning, R. C. (1992). *Speaking from the heart: A feminist perspective on ethics.* Lanham, MD: Rowman & Littlefield Publishers.

Manning, S. S. (1997). The social worker as moral citizen: Ethics in action. *Social Work, 42,* 223–230.

Manning, S. S., & Gaul, C. E. (1997). The ethics of informed consent: A critical variable in the self-determination of health and mental health clients. *Social Work in Health Care, 25*(3), 103–117.

Manstead, A. S. R. (1996). Attitudes and behavior. In G. R. Semin & K. Fiedler (Eds.), *Applied social psychology.* Thousand Oaks, CA: Sage Publications.

Marcuse, P. (1976). Professional ethics and beyond: Values in planning. *Journal of the American Institute of Planners, 42,* 264–274.

Maritain, J. (1934). *Introduction to philosophy.* London: Sheed & Ward.

Marson, S. (1993). Social work discussion list. Retrieved October 18, 1993. socwork@umab .bit-net

Marshall, T., & Solomon, P. (2004). Confidentiality intervention: Effects on provider-consumer-

family collaboration. *Research on Social Work Practice, 14*(1), 3–13.

Martin, J. L. R., Barbanoj, M. J., Schlaepfer, T. E., Perez, V., Kulisevsky, J., & Gironell, A. (2002). Transcranial magnetic stimulation for treating depression (Cohrane review). In *The Cochrane Library,* 2, Oxford, U.K.: Update Software.

Marziali, E., Donahue, P., & Crossin, G. (2005). Caring for others: Internet health care support interventions for family caregivers of persons with dementia, stroke, or Parkinson's disease. *Families in Society, 86*(3), 375–383.

Maslow, A. H. (1962). *The farther reaches of human nature.* New York: Penguin Books.

Maslow, A. H. (1969). Toward a humanistic biology. *American Psychologist, 24,* 724–735.

Mason, R. O. (1994). Morality and models. In W. A. Wallace (Ed.), *Ethics in modeling* (pp. 183–194). Tarrytown, NY: Pergamon.

Matorin, S., Rosenberg, B., Levitt, M., & Rosenbaum, S. (1987). Private practice in social work: Readiness and opportunity. *Social Casework, 68*(1), 31–37.

Mattison, D., Jayaratne, S., & Croxton (2002). Client or former client? Implications of ex-client definition on social work practice. *Social Work, 47*(1), 55–64.

Mayer, L. M. (2005). Professional Boundaries in Dual Relationships: A Social Work Dilemma. *Journal of Social Work Values and Ethics,* 2(2). Retrieved July 19, 2006, from www. socialworker.com/jswve/content/view/25/37/

Mayo Clinic. Transcranial magnetic stimulation: An experimental depression treatment. Retrieved April 24, 2007, from www .mayoclinic.com/health/transcranial-magnetic stimulation/MH00115

McCann, C. W. (1977). The codes of ethics of the NASW: An inquiry into its problems and perspectives. In B. E. Olvett (Ed.), *Values in Social Work Education* (pp. 10–19). Salt Lake City: University of Utah Graduate School of Social Work.

McCarty, D., & Clancy, C. (2002). Telehealth: Implications for social work practice. *Social Work, 47*(2), 153–161.

McGowen, B. G. (1995). Values and ethics. In C. H. Meyer & M. A. Mattaini (Eds.), *The foundations of social work practice* (pp. 28–41). Washington, DC: NASW Press.

McMahon, A., & Allen-Meares, P. (1992). Is social work racist? A content analysis of recent literature. *Social Work, 37,* 533–539.

Melton, G. B. (1988). Ethical and legal issues in ATOS-related practice. *American Psychologist, 43,* 941–947.

Meyer, C. H. (1985). Different voices: Comparable worth. *Social Work, 30,* 99.

Meyers, C. J. (1997). Expanding *Tarasoff:* Protecting patients and the public by keeping subsequent caregivers informed. *The Journal of Psychiatry & Law,* Fall, 365–375.

Mickelson, J. S. (1995). Advocacy. In R. L. Edwards (Ed.), *Encyclopedia of social work.* (Vol. 1, 19th ed., pp. 95–100). Washington, DC: National Association of Social Workers.

Miller, D. J., & Thelen, M. H. (1986). Knowledge and beliefs about confidentiality in psychotherapy. *Professional Psychology: Research and Practice, 17,* 15–19.

Miller, H. (1968). Value dilemmas in social casework. *Social Casework, 13,* 27–33.

Millstein, K. (2000). Confidentiality in direct social work practice: Inevitable challenges and ethical dilemmas. *Families in Society, 81*(3), 270–282.

Mishna, F., Antle, B. J., & Regehr, C. (2002). Social work with clients contemplating suicide: Complexity and ambiguity in the clinical, ethical, and legal considerations. *Clinical Social Work Journal, 30*(3), 265–280.

Mitchell, C. G. (1999). Treating anxiety in a managed care setting: A controlled comparison of medication alone versus medication plus cognitive-behavioral group therapy. *Research on Social Work Practice, 9,* 188–200.

Mittendorf, S. H., & Schroeder, J. (2004). Boundaries in social work: The ethical dilemma of worker-client sexual relationships. *Journal of Social Work Values and Ethics, 1*(1). Retrieved July 19, 2006, from www.socialworker.com/jswve/content/view/11/30

Moberg, D. O. (2005). Research in spirituality, religion, and aging. *Journal of Gerontological Social Work, 45*(1/2), 11–40.

Moody, H. R. (2004). Hospital discharge planning: Carrying out orders? *Journal of Gerontological Social Work, 43*(1), 107–118.

Moran, J. R. (1989). Social work education and students' humanistic attitudes. *Journal of Education for Social Work, 25*(1), 13–19.

Moreno, J. D., Caplan, A. L., & Wolpe, P. R. (1998). Informed consent. *Encyclopedia of Applied Ethics* (Vol. 2). New York: Academic Press, 687–697.

Morgan, D., & Levi, J. (2006). The HIV epidemic section of chapter, The United States of America, by B. Fetter, D. Morgan, & J. Levi. In E. J. Beck, N. Mays, A. W. Whiteside et al. (Eds.), *The HIV pandemic: Local and global implications* (pp. 581–587). New York: Oxford University Press.

Morin, D., Tourigny, A., Pelletier, D., Robichaud, L., Mathieu, L., Vezina, A., Bonin, L., & Buteau, M. (2005). Seniors' views on the use of electronic health records. *Informatics in Primary Care, 13,* 125–134.

Morris, E. K., Laney, C., Bernstein, D. M., & Loftus, E. F. (2006). Susceptibility to memory distortion: How do we decide it has occurred? *American Journal of Psychology, 119*(2), 255–274.

Moser, C. (1980). Letter. *NASW News, 25*(9), 6.

Moser, D. J., Schultz, S. K., Arndt, S., Benjamin, M. L., Fleming, F. W., Brems, C. S., Paulsen, J. S., Appelbaum, P. S., & Andreasen, N. C. (2002). Capacity to provide informed consent for participation in schizophrenia and HIV research. *American Journal of Psychiatry, 159,* 1201–1207.

Mullen, E. J., & Streiner, D. L. (2004). The evidence for and against evidence based practice. *Brief Treatment and Crisis Intervention, 4*(2), 111–121.

Munson, C. E. (2005). Personal communication, October 14, 2005.

Murdock, V. (2005). Guided by ethics: Religion and spirituality. *Journal of Gerontological Social Work, 45*(1/2), 131–154.

Murphy, M. J., DeBernardo, C., & Shoemaker, E. (1998). Impact of managed care on independent practice and professional ethics: A survey of independent practitioners. *Professional Psychology: Research and Practice, 29,* 43–51.

Myers, L. L., & Thyer, B. A. (1997). Should social work clients have the right to effective treatment? *Social Work, 42,* 288–298.

NASW Ad Hoc Committee on Advocacy. (1969). The social worker advocate: Champion of social victims. *Social Work, 14*(2), 16–23.

National Association of Scholars (2006). National association of scholars urges U. S. Dept. of Health and Human Services to drop CSWE requirement for social workers. Retrieved January 30, 2007, from www.nas.org/print/pressreleases/hqnas/releas_25oct06.htm

National Association of Social Workers. (1987). *AIDS: A social work response.* Washington, DC: National Association of Social Workers.

National Association of Social Workers. (1990a). People in the news. *NASW News, 35*(5), 17.

National Association of Social Workers. (1990b). *Standards for social work personnel practices.* Washington, DC: National Association of Social Workers.

National Association of Social Workers. (1992). *NASW standards for social work case management.* Retrieved January 22, 2007, from www.socialworkers.org/practice/standards/sw_case_mgmt.asp

National Association of Social Workers. (1993). A study of trends in adjudication of complaints concerning violations of NASW's Code of ethics—Overview of results. Washington, DC: Author.

National Association of Social Workers. (1994). Client self-determination in end-of-life decisions. In *Social work speaks* (pp. 58–61). Washington, DC: Author.

National Association of Social Workers. (1995a). Lawsuits: No more immunity. *NASW News, 40*(1), 7.

National Association of Social Workers. (1995b). A study cites most reported ethics breaches. *NASW News, 40*(4), 4.

National Association of Social Workers. (1999a, October). Assembly lowers BSW's dues, alters ethics code, eyes itself. *NASW News, 44*(9), 1, 10.

National Association of Social Workers. (1999b). *Code of Ethics*. Washington, DC: Author.

National Association of Social Workers. (2000). Agency restricts Internet counseling. *NASW News, 45*(8), 12.

National Association of Social Workers. (2001a). Caution urged before web counseling. *NASW News, 46*(January), 5.

National Association of Social Workers. (2005). *NASW procedures for professional review*. Rev. (4th ed.). Washington, DC: Author.

National Association of Social Workers. (2002). HIPAA alert! Retrieved October 1, 2002, from www.socialworkers.org/practice/hipaa/default.asp

National Association of Social Workers. (2003). Practice Research Network. Survey 2002. Private practice. Retrieved February 2007.

National Association of Social Workers & Association of Social Work Boards. (2005). Standards for technology and social work practice. Retrieved August 9, 2006, from www.aswb.org/Technology SWPractice.pdf

National Association of Social Workers. (2001). *NASW standards for cultural competence in social work practice*. Washington, DC: Author.

National Association of Social Workers (2006a). Executive Director's Office and NASW Insurance Trust. Personal communication. Types of claims.

National Association of Social Workers (2006b). Social work speaks abstracts, professional impairment. Retrieved August 7, 2006, from www.socialworkers.org/resources/abstracts/abstracts/profimpairment.asp

National Research Council. (1993). *Child abuse and neglect*. Washington, DC: National Academy Press, Author.

Negretti, M. A., & Weiling, E. (2001). The use of communication technology in private practice: Ethical implications and boundary dilemmas in therapy. *Contemporary Family Therapy, 23*(3), 275–293.

Netting, F. E. (1987). Ethical issues in volunteer management and accountability. *Social Work, 32*, 250–252.

Netting, F. E., Kettner, P. M., & McMurtry, S. L. (1998). *Social work macro practice* (2nd ed.). White Plains, NY: Longman Publishing Group.

Whistle-blowers being punished, a survey shows. (2002, September 3). *New York Times*, A14.

North, R. L., & Rothenberg, K. (1993). Partner notification and the threat of domestic violence against women with HIV infection. *New England Journal of Medicine, 329*, 1194–1196.

Northen, H. (1998). Ethical dilemmas in social work with groups. *Social Work with Groups, 21*(1/2), 5–17.

Nugent, W. R. (2004). The role of prevalence rates, sensitivity, and specificity in assessment accuracy: Rolling the dice in social work process. *Journal of Social Service Research, 31*(2), 51–75.

Nyberg, D. (1996). Deception and moral decency. In R. A. French, T. E. Vehling Jr., & H. K. Wettstein (Eds.), *Midwest studies in philosophy Vol. XX, Moral concepts*. Notre Dame, IN: University of Notre Dame Press.

Odell, M., & Stewart, S. P. (1993). Ethical issues associated with client values conversion and therapist value agendas in family therapy. *Family Relations, 42*(2), 128–133.

O'Neill, J. V. (2001). Webcams may transform online therapy. *NASW News, 46*(7), 4.

O'Neill, J. V. (2002). Internet-based therapy draws criticism. *NASW News, 47*(4), 12.

Oppenheim, S., Hay, J. B., Frederich, M. E., & von Gunten, C. F. (2002). Palliative care in human immunodeficiency virus: Acquired immunodeficiency syndrome. In A. M. Berger, R. K. Portenoy, & D. E. Weissman (Eds.), *Principles and practice of palliative care and supportive oncology* (pp. 1071–1085). New York: Lippincott Williams and Wilkins.

Oregon Health Services Commission (2006). Oregon health plan. Retrieved November 8, 2006, from http://egov.oregon.gov/DAS/OHPPR/HSC/

Orovwuje, P. R. (2001). The business model and social work: A conundrum for social work practice. *Social Work in Health Care, 34*(1/2), 59–70.

Padilla, Y. C. (1997). Immigrant policy: Issues for social work practice. *Social Work, 42*, 595–606.

Palmer, N., & Kaufman, M. (2003). The ethics of informed consent: Implications for multicultural practice. *Journal of Ethnic & Cultural Diversity in Social Work, 12*(1), 1–26.

Panchanadeswaran, S., & Koverola, C. (2003). The voices of battered women in India. *Violence against Women, 11*, 736–758.

Parker, L. (2003). A social justice model for clinical social work, *Affilia, 18*(3), 272–288.

Parker-Oliver, D., & Demiris, G. (2006). Social work informatics: A new specialty. *Social Work, 51*, 127–134.

Pear, R. (2006, June 28). New rules force states to limit welfare rolls. *New York Times*, pp. 1, 17.

Peckover, S. (2002). Supporting and policing mothers: An analysis of the disciplinary practices of health visiting. *Journal of Advanced Nursing, 38*, 369–377.

Pellegrino, E. D. (1991). Trust and distrust in professional ethics. In E. D. Pellegrino, R. M. Veatch, & J. P. Langan (Eds.), *Ethics, trust, and the professions* (pp. 69–85). Washington, DC: Georgetown University Press.

Pemberton, J. D. (1965). Is there a moral right to violate the law? *Social Welfare Forum, 1965* (pp. 183–196). New York: Columbia University Press.

Perlman, H. H. (1965). Self-determination: Reality or illusion? *Social Service Review, 39,* 410–422.

Perry, C., & Kuruk, J. W. (1993). Psychotherapists' sexual relationships with their patients. *Annals of Health Law, 2,* 35–54.

Pike, C. K. (1996). Development and initial validation of the social work values inventory. *Research in Social Work Practice, 6,* 337–352.

Planned Parenthood of Southeastern Pa. v. Casey, 505 U.S. 833 (1992).

Pollack, D. (2004). Getting informed consent: More than just a signature. *Policy & Practice of Public Services, 62*(2), 28.

Pollack, D., & Marsh, J. (2004). Social work misconduct may lead to liability. *Social Work, 49*(4), 609–612.

Pope, K. S. (2000). Therapists' sexual feelings and behaviors: Research, trends, and quandaries. In L. T. Szuchman & F. Muscarella (Eds.), *Psychological perspectives on human sexuality* (pp. 603–658). New York: John Wiley & Sons.

Pope, K. S., & Bouthoutsos, J. C. (1986). *Sexual intimacy between therapist and patient.* New York: Praeger Publishers.

Pope, K. S., & Feldman-Summers, S. (1992). National survey of psychologists' sexual and physical abuse history and their evaluation of training and competence in these areas. *Professional Psychology: Research and Practice, 23*(1), 353–361.

Pope, K. S., Levenson, H., & Schover, L. R. (1979). *American Psychologist, 34*(8) (August), 682–689.

Pope, K. S., Tabachnick, B. G., & Keith-Spiegel, P. (1987). Ethics of practice: The beliefs and behaviors of psychologists and therapists. *American Psychologist, 42,* 993–1006.

Pope, K. S., & Vasquez, M. J. T. (1998). *Ethics in psychotherapy and counseling* (2nd ed.). San Francisco: Jossey-Bass.

Powderly, K. (2001). Ethical and legal issues in perinatal HIV. *Clinical Obstetrics and Gynecology, 44,* 300–311.

Powell, W. E. (1994). The relationship between feelings of alienation and burnout in social work. *Families in Society, 75,* 229–235.

Pumphrey, M. W. (1959). The teaching of values and ethics in social work education. New York: CSWE.

Rabkin, J. G., & Struening, E. L. (1976). *Ethnicity, social class and mental illness.* New York: Institute on Pluralism & Group Identity.

Rawls, J. (1971). *A theory of justice.* Cambridge, MA: Harvard University Press.

Reamer, F. G. (1983). Ethical dilemmas in social work practice. *Social Work, 28,* 31–35.

Reamer, F. G. (1993). *The philosophical foundations of social work.* New York: Columbia University Press.

Reamer, F. G. (1998). The evolution of social work ethics. *Social Work, 43,* 488–500.

Reamer, F. G. (1999). *Social work values and ethics* (2nd ed.). New York: Columbia University Press.

Reamer, F. G. (2001). *The social work ethics audit: A risk management tool.* Washington, DC: NASW Press.

Reamer, F. G. (2003). Boundary issues in social work: Managing dual relationships. *Social Work, 48*(1), 121–133.

Reamer, F. G. (2004). Ethical decisions and risk management. In M. Austin & K. M. Hopkins (Eds.), *Supervision as collaboration in the human services: Building a learning culture* (pp. 97–109). Thousand Oaks, CA: Sage Publications.

Reamer, F. G. (2005). Documentation in social work: Evolving ethical and risk-management standards. *Social Work, 50*(4), 325–334.

Reamer, F. G. (2005). Update on confidentiality issues in practice with children: Ethics risk management. *Children & Schools, 27,* 117–120.

Regehr, C. & Antle, B. (1997). Coercive influences: Informed consent in court-mandated social work. *Social Work, 42,* 300–306.

Reid, W. J. (1997). Research on task-centered practice. *Social Work Research, 21,* 132–137.

Reid, W. J., Kenaley, B. D., & Colvin, J. (2004). Do some interventions work better than others? A review of comparative social work experiments. *Social Work Research, 20*(2), 71–81.

Reiser, S. J., Burstajn, H. J., Applebaum, P. S., & Gutheil, T. G. (1987). *Divided staffs, divided selves: A case approach to mental health ethics.* England: Cambridge University Press.

Reisch, M., & Lowe, J. I. (2000). "Of means and ends" revisited: Teaching ethical community organizing in an unethical society. *Journal of Community Practice, 7*(1), 19–38.

Reybould, C. & Adler, G. (2006). Applying NASW standards to end of life care for a culturally diverse aging population. *Journal of Social Work Values and Ethics, 3*(2). Retrieved October 19, 2006, from http://www.socialworker.com/jswve/content/view/38/46/

Riccucci, N., Meyers, M. K., et al. (2004) Implementation of welfare reform policy: The role of public managers in front-line practices. *Public Administration Review, 64*(4), 438–448.

Rice, D. S. (1994). Professional values and moral development: The social work student. Unpublished dissertation. University of South Carolina.

Rizzo, V. M., & Rowe, J. M. (2006). Studies of the cost-effectiveness of social work services in aging: A review of the literature. *Research on Social Work Practice, 16*(1), 67–73.

Roberts, C. S. (1989). Conflicting professional values in social work and medicine. *Health and Social Work, 14,* 211–218.

Roberts, S. (2006, October 15). It's official: To be married means to be outnumbered. *New York Times,* p.14.

Rock, B. (2001). Social work under managed care: Will we survive, or can we prevail? In R. Perez-Koenig & B. Rock (Eds.), *Social work in the era of devolution: Toward a just practice* (pp. 69–85). New York: Fordham University Press.

Rodenborg, N. A. (2004). Services to African American children in poverty: Institutional discrimination in child welfare. *Journal of Poverty, 8*(3), 109–130.

Rooney, R. H. (1992). *Strategies for work with involuntary clients.* New York: Columbia University Press.

Rosa, L., Rosa, E., Samer, L., & Barrett, S. (1998). A close look at therapeutic touch. *Journal of the American Medical Association, 279,* 1005–1010.

Roseborough, D. J. (2006). Psychodynamic psychotherapy: an effectiveness study. *Research on Social Work Practice, 16*(2), 166–175.

Rosen, A., and Proctor, E. K. (Eds.) (2003). *Developing practice guidelines for social work intervention: Issues, methods, and research agenda.* New York: Columbia University Press.

Rosenthal, R. N. (2004). Overview of evidence-based practice. In A. R. Roberts & K. Yeager (Eds.), *Evidence-based practice manual: Research and outcome measures in health and human services.* New York: Oxford University Press.

Ross, J. W. (1992). Editorial: Are social work ethics compromised? *Health and Social Work, 17,* 163–164.

Rothman, J. (1989). Client self-determination: Untangling the knot. *Social Service Review, 63,* 598–612.

Rothman, J., Smith, W., Nakashima, J., Paterson, M. A., & Mustin, J. (1996). Client self-determination and professional intervention: Striking a balance. *Social Work, 41,* 396–405.

Rothstein, E. (2002, July 13). Moral relativity is a hot topic? True. Absolutely. *New York Times,* pp. A13, A15.

Roy v. Hartogs. 366 N. YS. 2d297 (1975).

Rubin, A., Cardenas, J., Warren, K., Pike, C. K., & Wambach, K. (1998). Outdated practitioner views about family culpability and severe mental disorders. *Social Work, 43*(5), 412–422.

Rubin, A., & Parrish, D. (2007). Views of evidence-based practice among faculty in master of social work programs: A national survey. *Research on Social Work Practice, 17*(1), 110–122.

Rust v. Sullivan, 500 U.S. Supreme Court, 173 (1991).

Ryder, R., & Hepworth, J. (1990). AAMFT ethical code: "Dual relationships." *Journal of Marital and Family Therapy, 16*(2), 127–132.

Ryan, S. D., Pearlmutter, S., & Groza, V. (2004). Coming out of the closet: Opening agencies to gay and lesbian adoptive parents. *Social Work, 49*(1), 85–95.

Sackett, D. L., Straus, S. E., Richardson, W. S., Rosenberg, W., & Haynes, R. B. (2000). *Evidence-based medicine: How to practice and teach EBP* (2nd ed.). New York: Churchill-Livingstone.

Saenz v. Roe, U.S. Supreme Court, 1518, 1999.

Sammons, C. C. (1978). Ethical issues in genetic intervention. *Social Work, 23,* 237–242.

Santhiveeran, J. (2004). E-therapy: Scope, concerns, ethical standards, and feasibility. *Journal of Family Social Work, 8*(3), 37–54.

Sasson, S. (2000). Beneficence versus respect for autonomy: An ethical dilemma in social work practice. *Journal of Gerontological Social Work, 33*(1), 5–16.

Schamess, G. (1996). Who profits and who benefits from managed mental health care? *Smith College Studies in Social Work, 60,* 209–220.

Schild, S., & Black, R. B. (1984). *Social work and genetic counseling: A guide to practice.* Binghamton, NY: Haworth Press.

Schlossberger, E., & Hecker, L. (1996). HIV and family therapists' duty to warn: A legal and ethical analysis. *Journal of Marital and Family Therapy, 22,* 27–40.

Schoener, G. R. (1995). Assessment of professionals who have engaged in boundary violations. *Psychiatric Annals, 25*(2), 95–99.

Schopler, J. H., Abell, M. D., & Galinsky, M. J. (1998). Technology-based groups: A review and conceptual framework for practice. *Social Work, 43,* 254–267.

Sedlak, A. J., & Broadhurst, D. D. (1996). *Third national incidence study of child abuse and neglect: Final report.* Washington, DC: U.S. Department of Health and Human Services.

Selznick, P. (1961). Sociology and natural law. *Natural Law Forum, 6,* 84–108.

Sharma, S., & Patenaude, A. (2003). HIV/AIDS. Retrieved January 24, 2003, from www .emedicine.com/aaem/topic252.htm

Sharwell, G. R. (1974). Can values be taught? *Journal of Education for Social Work, 10,* 99–105.

Shavit, N., & Bucky, S. (2004). Sexual contact between psychologists and their former therapy patients: Psychoanalytic perspectives and professional implications. *American Journal of Psychoanalysis, 64*(3), 229–248.

Shaw, G. B. (1932). *The doctor's dilemma.* London: Constable.

Shea, S. C. (1999). *The practical art of suicide assessment.* New York: John Wiley & Sons.

Sherer, R. A. (2004). The debate over physician-assisted suicide continues. *Psychiatric Times, 21*(1). Retrieved March 21, 2007, from http://www.psychiatrictimes.com/p040101b.html

Sherwood, D. A. (1997). The relationship between beliefs and values in social work practice: Worldviews make a difference. *Social Work and Christianity, 24*(2), 115–135.

Shillington, A. M., Dotson, W. L., & Faulkner, A. O. (1994). Should only African-American community organizers work in African-American neighborhoods? In M. J. Austin & J. I. Lowe (Eds.), *Controversial issues in communities and organizations* (pp. 128–111). Boston: Allyn & Bacon.

Siebert, D. C. (2004). Depression in North Carolina social workers: Implications for practice and research. *Social Work Research, 28*(1), 30–40.

Siebert, D. C. (2005). Help seeking for AOD misuse among social workers: Patterns, barriers, and implications. *Social Work, 50*(1), 65–75.

Simon, R. I., & Gutheil, T. G. (1997). Ethical and clinical risk management principles in recovered memory cases: Maintaining therapist neutrality. In P. S. Appelbaum, L. A. Uyehara, & M. R. Elin (Eds.), *Trauma and memory* (pp. 477–495). New York: Oxford University Press.

Siporin, M. (1982). Moral philosophy in social work today. *Social Service Review, 56*, 516–538.

Siporin, M. (1983). Morality and immorality in working with clients. *Social Thought, 9*(Fall), 10–28.

Siporin, M. (1985a). Current social work perspectives for clinical practice. *Clinical Social Work Journal, 13*, 198–217.

Siporin, M. (1985b). Deviance, morality, and social work therapy. *Social Thought, 11*(4), 11–24.

Skolnik, L., & Attinson, L. (1978). Confidentiality in group work practice. *Social Work with Groups, 1*(2), 165–174.

Slaughter, S., Cole, D., Jennings, E., & Reimer, M. A. (2007). Consent and assent to participate in research from people with dementia. *Nursing Ethics, 14*(1), 27–40.

Smith, C. (2004). Trust and confidence: Making the moral case for social work. *Social Work & Social Sciences Review, 11*(3), 5–15.

Smith, C. J., & Devore, W. (2004). African American children in the child welfare and kinship system: From exclusion to over-inclusion. *Children and Youth Services Review, 26*(5), 427–446.

Smith, S. (2006). Mandatory reporting of child abuse and neglect. Retrieved September 26, 2006, from www.smith-lawfirm.com/mandatory_reporting.htm.

Social Work (1991) 36(2), 106–144. This issue contains a series of articles on the theme "Ethics and Professional Relationships."

Soderfeldt, M., Soderfeldt, B., & Warg, L. E. (1995). Burnout in social work. *Social Work, 40*, 638–646.

Sokolowski, R. (1991). The fiduciary relationship and the nature of professions. In E. D. Pellegrino, R. M. Veatch, & J. P. Langan (Eds.), *Ethics, trust, and the professions* (pp. 23–39). Washington, DC: Georgetown University Press.

Solomon, A. (1992). Clinical diagnosis among diverse populations: A multicultural perspective. *Families in Society, 73*(6), 371–377.

Soss, J., Schram, S. F. et al. (2004). Welfare policy choices in the states: Does the hard line follow the color line? *Focus, 23*(1), University of Wisconsin–Madison, Institute for Research on Poverty, 9–15.

Soyer, D. (1963). The right to fail. *Social Work, 8*(3) (July), 72–78.

Spelman, E. V. (2004). The household as repair shop. In C. Calhoun (Ed.), *Setting the moral compass: Essays by women philosophers*. New York: Oxford University Press.

Spero, M. H. (1990). Identification between the religious patient and therapist in social work and psychoanalytic psychotherapy. *Journal of Social Work and Policy in Israel, 3*, 83–98.

Steinberg, K. L., Levine, M., & Doueck, H. (1997). Effects of legally mandated child-abuse reports on the therapeutic relationships: A survey of psychotherapists. *American Journal of Orthopsychiatry, 67*, 112–122.

Stevens, J. W. (1998). A question of values in social work practice: Working with the strengths of black adolescent females. *Families in Society, 79*, 288–296.

Stoesen, L. (2002). Recovering social workers offer support. *NASW News*, www.socialworkers.org/pubs/news/2002/07/recovering.asp?back=yes

Stout, C. E., & Grand, L. C. (2005). *Getting started in private practice*. Hoboken, NJ: John Wiley & Sons.

Strean, H. S. (1997). Comment on James C. Raines, Self-disclosure in clinical social work, *Clinical Social Work Journal, 25*, 365–366.

Strom, K. (1992). Reimbursement demands and treatment decisions: A growing dilemma for social workers. *Social Work, 37*, 398–403.

Strom, K. (1994). Social workers in private practice: An update. *Clinical Social Work Journal, 22*, 73–89.

Strom-Gottfried, K. (1998a). Informed consent meets managed care. *Health and Social Work, 23*, 25–33.

Strom-Gottfried, K. (1998b). Is "ethical managed care" an oxymoron? *Families in Society: The Journal of Contemporary Human Services, 79*, 297–307.

Strom-Gottfried, K. (1999). When colleague accuses colleague: Adjudicating personnel matters through the filing of ethics complaints. *Administration in Social Work, 23*(2), 1–16.

Strom-Gottfried, K. (2000). Ensuring ethical practice: An examination of NASW code violations, 1986–97. *Social Work, 45*(3), 251–261.

Strom-Gottfried, K. (2003). Understanding adjudication: Origins, targets, and outcomes of ethics complaints. *Social Work, 48*(1), 85–94.

Strom-Gottfried, K., & Mowbray, N. D. (2006). Who heals the healer? Facilitating the social worker's grief. *Families in Society, 87*(1), 9–15.

Strozier, M., Brown, R., Fennell, M., Hardee, J., & Vogel, R. et al. (2005). Experiences of mandated reporting among family therapists. *Contemporary Family Therapy, 27*(2), 175–189.

Strozier, A. L., Kmzek, C., & Sale, K. (2003). Touch: Its use in psychotherapy. *Journal of Social Work Practice, 17*(1), 49–62.

Strug, D. L., Grube, B. A., & Beckerman, N. (2002). Challenges and changing roles in HIV–AIDS social work: Implications for training and education. *Social Work in Health Care, 35*(4), 1–19.

Sunley, R. (1997). Advocacy in the new world of managed care. *Families in Society, 78,* 84–94.

Sutherland, P. K. (2002). Sexual abuse by therapists, physicians, attorneys, and other professionals. *Worldwide Legal Information Association.* Retrieved July 17, 2002, from http://www.wwlia.org

Szasz, T. S. (1994). *Cruel compassion: Psychiatric control of society's unwanted.* New York: John Wiley & Sons.

Tarasoff v. Regents of the University of California. S. Ct. of CA (1976).

Taylor, L., & Adelman, H. S. (1989). Reframing the confidentiality dilemma to work in children's best interest. *Professional Psychology: Research and Practice, 20,* 79–83.

Taylor, M. F. (2006). Is self-determination still important? What experienced mental health social workers are saying. *Journal of Social Work Values and Ethics, 3*(1), 1–12. Retrieved October 12, 2006, from www.socialworker.com/jswve/content/view/29/44/.

Taylor-Brown, S., & Garcia, A. (1995). Social workers and HIV-affected families: Is the profession prepared? *Social Work, 40,* 14–15.

Thyer, B. A. (2004). What is evidence-based practice. *Brief Treatment and Crisis Intervention, 4*(2), 167–176.

Timms, N. (1983). *Social work values: An enquiry.* London: Routledge & Kegan Paul.

Tong, R. (1998). Feminist ethics. In *Encyclopedia of applied ethics.* (Vol. 2, pp. 261–268). New York: Academic Press.

Tong, R. (2006). Feminist ethics. *Stanford encyclopedia of philosophy.* Retrieved September 5, 2006, from http://plato.stanford.edu/entries/feminism-ethics

Toporek, R. L., & Liu, W. M. (2002). Advocacy in counseling: Addressing race, class, and gender oppression. In D. B. Pope-Davis & H. L. K. Coleman (Eds.), *The intersection of race, class, and gender in multicultural counseling* (pp. 385–413). Thousand Oaks, CA: Sage Publications.

Torczyner, J. (1991). Discretion, judgment, and informed consent: Ethical and practice issues in social action. *Social Work, 36,* 122–128.

Tower, K. D. (1994). Consumer-centered social work practice: Restoring client self-determination. *Social Work, 39*(2), 191–196.

Towle, C. (1987). *Common human needs.* Silver Spring, MD: National Association of Social Workers.

Trolander, J. A. (1997). Fighting racism and sexism: The CSWE. *Social Service Review, 71,* 110–134.

Tropman, J. E., Erlich, J. L., & Rothman, J. (2001). *Tactics and techniques of community intervention* (4th ed.). Itasca, IL: F. E. Peacock Publishers.

Tully, C. T., Craig, T., & Nugent, G. (1994). Should only gay and lesbian community organizers operate in gay and lesbian communities? In M. J. Austin & J. I. Lowe (Eds.), *Controversial issues in communities and organizations* (pp. 86–96). Boston: Allyn & Bacon.

Turner, F. J. (2002). *Diagnosis in social work: New imperatives.* New York: Haworth Social Work Practice Press.

Ulrich, B., & Beck-Gemsheim, E. (1996). Individualization and "precarious freedoms." In P. Heclas, S. Lash, & P. Morris (Eds.), *Detraditionalization: Critical reflections on authority and identity* (pp. 23–48). Cambridge, MA: Blackwell Publishers.

U.S. Census Bureau; Hobbs, F. B. (2003). The elderly population. Retrieved January 30, 2003, from www.census.gov/population/www/pop-profile/elderpop.html

U.S. Department of Health and Human Services, Administration on Children, Youth, and Families (2006). *Child maltreatment 2004.* Washington, DC: U.S. Government Printing Office.

Vanderwoerd, J. R. (2005). Ethical conflicts between religion and sexual orientation in North American social work education. Retrieved January 26, 2007, from www.aspecten.org/teksten/IS2005/Vander Woerd_Panel.pdf

Van Hoose, W. H., & Kottler, J. A. (1985). *Ethical and legal issues in counseling and psychotherapy* (2nd ed.). San Francisco: Jossey-Bass.

Varley, B. K. (1963). Socialization in social work education. *Social Work, 8*(4), 102–105.

Varley, B. K. (1968). Social work values: Changes in value commitment of students from admission to MSW graduation. *Journal of Education for Social Work, 4,* 67–76.

VandeCreek, L., Knapp, S., & Herzog, C. (1988). Privileged communications for social workers. *Social Casework, 69,* 28–34.

Vernberg, D., & Schuh, M. J. (2002). Internet bibliotherapy: A narrative analysis of a reading simulated support group. *Journal of Social Work in Disability and Rehabilitation, 1*(1), 81–97.

Verschelden, C. (1993). Social work values and pacifism: Opposition to war as a professional responsibility. *Social Work, 38,* 765–769.

Vigilante, J. L. (1974). Between values and science: "Education for the profession during a moral crisis or is proof truth?" *Journal of Education for Social Work, 10,* 107–115.

Vigilante, J. L. (1983). Professional values. In A. Rosenblatt & D. Waldfogel (Eds.), *Handbook of clinical social work* (pp. 58–69). San Francisco: Jossey-Bass.

Wagner, L., Davis, S., & Handelsman, M. M. (1998). In search of the abominable consent form: The impact of readability and personalization. *Journal of Clinical Psychology, 54,* 115–120.

Walcott, D. M., Cerundolo, P., & Beck, J. C. (2001). Current analysis of the *Tarasoff* duty: An evolution towards the limitation of the duty to protect. *Behavioral Sciences and the Law, 19,* 325–343.

Walker, R., & Clark, J. J. (1999). Heading off boundary problems: Clinical supervision as risk management. *Psychiatric Services, 50*(11), 1435–1439.

Walker, R., & Staton, M. (2000). Multiculturalism in social work ethics. *Journal of Social Work Education, 36*(3), 449–462.

Walrond-Skinner, S., & Watson, D. (1987). *Ethical issues in family therapy.* London: Routledge & Kegan Paul.

Walsh, W. D. (1969). *Hegelian ethics.* New York: St. Martin's Press, pp. 16–17.

Ward, J. W., & Drotman, D. P. (1998). Epidemiology of HIV and AIDS. In G. P. Wormser (Ed.), *AIDS and other manifestations of HIV infection* (3rd ed., pp. 1–17). Philadelphia: Lippincott-Raven.

Weick, A. (1999). Guilty knowledge. *Families in Society, 80*(4), 327–332.

Weinberg, J. K. (1998). Balancing autonomy and resources in health care for elders, *Generations, 22*(3), 92–96.

Weinstein, B., Levine, M., Kogan, N., et al. (2000). Mental health professionals' experiences reporting suspected child abuse and maltreatment. *Child Abuse & Neglect, 24*(10), 1317–1328.

Weiss, I., Gal, J., & Cnaan, R. A. (2004). Social work education as professional socialization: A study of the impact of social work education upon students' professional preferences. *Journal of Social Work Research, 31*(1) 13–31.

Werth, J. L. & Rogers, J. R. (2005). Assessing for impaired judgment as a means of meeting the "duty to protect" when a client is a potential harm-to-self: Implications for clients making end-of-life decisions. *Mortality, 10*(1), 7–21.

Wheeler, D. L. (1993). Physician-anthropologist examines what ails America's medical system: Instead of treating patients, Melvin Konner probes health care in general. *Chronicle of Higher Education,* June 2, A6–A7.

WhistleblowerLaws.com (2006). The law: An overview: False Claims Act whistleblower employee protections. Retrieved November 7, 2006, from http://whistleblowerlaws.com/protection.htm.

Wikipedia Encyclopedia. (2004). Categorical imperative. Retrieved September 13, 2004, from http://en.wikipedia.org/wiki/Categorical_Imperative.

Williams, R. M., Jr. (1967). Individual and group values. *Annals, 371,* 20–37.

Wilson, C. A., Alexander, J. R., & Turner, C. W. (1996). Family therapy process and outcome research: Relationship to treatment ethics. *Ethics & Behavior, 6,* 345–352.

Wineburgh, M. (1998). Ethics, managed care, and outpatient psychotherapy. *Clinical Social Work Journal. 26,* 433–443.

Witkin, S. L. (1998). The right to effective treatment and the effective treatment of rights: Rhetorical empiricism and the politics of research. *Social Work, 43,* 75–80.

Wodarski, J. S., Pippin, J. A., & Daniels, M. (1988). The effects of graduate social work education on personality, values and interpersonal skills. *Journal of Social Work Education, 24,* 266–277.

Woldeguiorguis, I. S. (2003). Racism and sexism in child welfare: Effects on women of color as mothers and practitioners. *Child Welfare, 82*(2), 273–288.

Wolf, L. E., Lo, B., Beckerman, K. P., Dorenbaum, A., Kilpatrick, S. J., & Weintraub, P. S. (2001). When parents reject interventions to reduce postnatal human immunodeficiency virus transmission. *Archives of Pediatrics & Adolescent Medicine, 155,* 927–933.

Wolfson, E. R. (1999). The fee in social work: Ethical dilemmas for practitioners. *Social Work, 44*(3), 269–273.

Woodside, M. (2003). *Generalist case management.* Pacific Grove, CA: Brooks/Cole, Thomson Publishing.

Worrell, J., & Remer, P. (2003). *Feminist perspectives in therapy: Empowering diverse women* (2nd ed.). New York: John Wiley & Sons.

Worthington, R. L., Tan, J. A., & Poulin, K. (2002). Ethically questionable behaviors among supervisees: An exploratory investigation. *Ethics & Behavior, 12*(4), 1–22.

Wyatt, T., Daniels, M. H., & White, L. J. (2000). Noncompetition agreements and the counseling profession: An unrecognized reality for private practitioners. *Journal of Counseling & Development, 78*(1), 14–20.

Yang, J. A., & Kombarakaran, F. A. (2006). A practitioner's response to the new health privacy regulations. *Health & Social Work, 31,* 129–136.

Yip, K-S. (2005). Taoistic concepts of mental health: Implications for social work practice with Chinese communities, *Families in Society: The Journal of Contemporary Social Service, 86*(1), 35–45.

Yu, M., & O'Neal, B. (1992). Issues of confidentiality when working with persons with AIDS. *Clinical Social Work Journal, 20,* 421–430.

Yurkow, J. (1991). Abuse and neglect of the frail elderly. *Pride Institute Journal of Long Term Home Health Care, 10*(1), 36–39.

Zayas, L. H., Cabassa, L. J., & Perez, M. C. (2005). Capacity-to-consent in psychiatric research: Development and preliminary testing of a screening tool. *Research on Social Work Practice, 15,* 545–556.

Zellman, G. L., & Fair, C. C. (2002). Preventing and reporting abuse. In J. E. B. Myers, L. Berliner et al. (Eds.), *The ASPSAC Handbook on Child Maltreatment* (2nd ed.). Thousand Oaks, CA: Sage Publications.

Zetlin, A. G., Weinberg, L. A., & Shea, N. M. (2006). Seeing the whole picture: Views from diverse participants on barriers to educating foster youths. *Children & Schools, 28,* 165–173.

Zur, O., & Lazarus, A. A. (2002). Six arguments against dual relationships and their rebuttals. In A. A. Lazarus & O. Zur (Eds.), *Dual Relationships and Psychotherapy* (pp. 3–24). New York: Spring Publishing Co.

Zygmond, M. J., & Boorhem, H. (1989). Ethical decision-making in family therapy. *Family Process, 28,* 269–280.

Index